Business Practices in Higher Education

The new edition of *Business Practices in Higher Education* offers aspiring higher education and student affairs professionals an understanding of the fundamental business practices of colleges and universities. The authors apply business concepts and models and explain how they can be leveraged to improve the overall efficiency and effectiveness of higher education institutions. Useful examples from a wide range of institutions—including small private colleges, large public universities, and community colleges—address macro-level higher education and student population issues, while also addressing micro-level issues for individual institutions or students. Business practices are critical to the academic, student affairs, and administrative sides of higher education. This book helps readers understand the true nature of higher education and appreciate how the academy effectively incorporates business practices into everyday work lives.

New in this edition:

- Updated coverage of current practice and research
- New chapters on accounting, strategic planning, and fundraising
- End-of-chapter questions for discussion

Mark A. Kretovics is Associate Professor of Higher Education Administration and Student Affairs at Kent State University, USA.

Erica Eckert is Assistant Dean for Assessment and Accreditation and Assistant Professor in the School of Foundations, Leadership, and Administration at Kent State University, USA.

Business Practices in Higher Education

A Guide for Today's Administrators

Second Edition

Mark A. Kretovics
Erica Eckert

Routledge
Taylor & Francis Group
NEW YORK AND LONDON

Second edition published 2020
by Routledge
52 Vanderbilt Avenue, New York, NY 10017

and by Routledge
2 Park Square, Milton Park, Abingdon, Oxon, OX14 4RN

Routledge is an imprint of the Taylor & Francis Group, an informa business

[First edition published by Routledge 2011]

Library of Congress Cataloging-in-Publication Data
Names: Kretovics, Mark author. | Eckert, Erica (Erica L.), author.
Title: Business practices in higher education : a guide for today's administrators / by Mark A. Kretovics and Erica Eckert.
Description: Second Edition. | New York : Routledge, 2019. | "First edition published by Routledge 2011"—T.p. verso.
Identifiers: LCCN 2019013993| ISBN 9781138365315 (Handcover) | ISBN 9781138365384 (Paperback) | ISBN 9780429430770 (eBook)
Subjects: LCSH: Universities and colleges—United States—Business management—Handbooks, manuals, etc.
Classification: LCC LB2341.93.U6 K74 2019 | DDC 378.1/060973—dc23
LC record available at https://lccn.loc.gov/2019013993

ISBN: 978-1-138-36531-5 (hbk)
ISBN: 978-1-138-36538-4 (pbk)
ISBN: 978-0-429-43077-0 (ebk)

Typeset in Bembo and Helvetica Neue
by Swales & Willis Ltd, Exeter, Devon, UK

Contents

Preface vii
Acknowledgments xi

PART 1
Environment and Structure 1

1 Today's Environment 3

2 Organizational and Administrative Structures 19

PART 2
Finance and Funding 37

3 Economic Principles 39

4 Finance 59

5 Accounting 79

6 Budgeting Basics 95

PART 3
People and Processes 123

7 Management Principles 125

8 Strategic Planning 153

9 Managing Human Resources: Recruitment, Selection, and Retention of Competent Staff 177

10 Marketing Basics 203

PART 4
Perspectives on the Future 227

11 Fundraising 229

12 Where Do We Go from Here? What Is Next? 249

References 263
Index 279

Preface

The world of higher education may appear to be operating as it was the 1960s. We still have large public universities, small private liberal arts colleges, community colleges, technical schools, residential environments, and commuter institutions. However, most people do not see are the inner workings of these institutions. The operation of colleges and universities has changed dramatically over the years in how they are funded, managed, and structured. These changes did not take place overnight but rather evolved over several decades. Some critics refer to this as the "corporatization" of higher education while others who support these changes believe higher education is more efficient and possibly more effective. It seems there is always a crisis in higher education, whether it is an enrollment crisis, a leadership crisis, a dropout crisis, a funding crisis, a cost crisis—the list continues. The reality is that while the sky is not falling, there are and most likely always will be some problems within higher education in the United States and throughout the world. These "manufactured crises" (Berliner & Biddle, 1995) are not the downfall of higher education as we know it. Higher education has evolved over time to become what it is today, and it will continue to evolve as it adapts to the changing world around it. Higher education does not exist in a vacuum, or alone in an ivory tower, but rather is an integral part of a vibrant world economy—perhaps the engine of progress.

The outlook for higher education in the world continues to be positive. As the world becomes more technology-driven there is greater demand for individuals with more than a secondary education. This demand is being met by the numerous systems of education that provide postsecondary opportunities for tens of millions of individuals around the globe each year. As the industrialized world expands and developing countries strive to improve their economies, most of them turn to education to fuel that growth. There is no one model of education that works for every country and it is this increasing diversity of postsecondary educational opportunities that has placed higher education institutions in the center of the world economy.

PURPOSE OF THE BOOK

This book is designed to provide the reader with a general understanding of the business nature of institutions of higher education. On the one hand, critics within the academy believe that the movement toward business practices is the downfall of higher education. On the other hand, critics from outside of higher education lament—if only higher education would *act more like a business* they could solve *all* of their problems. On which side of this discussion you fall is actually quite irrelevant. It is our contention that higher education *is* an industry, and individual institutions do operate like a business enterprise whether the faculty and staff think they do or not. Ever since the first employee was retained and compensated, higher education institutions have operated like a business. The core business of higher education is **educating students**. While we do have other functions (research, service, entertainment, etc.), the education of students is our primary reason to exist.

It is not the intention of this book to promote a specific administrative or leadership style nor to try to convince you that there is a better way to do what it is you do. It is hoped that after you finish this book you will have a greater understanding of and appreciation for the nature of higher education and the ways in which we incorporate *business practices* into our everyday work lives. Whether you are on the academic, student affairs, or administrative affairs side of your institution, you will see that business practices pervade. As a supervisor, you hire and terminate employees, develop and manage budgets, revise or create policies, and interact with stakeholders on a regular basis, among other functions.

We are not advocating that colleges and universities should or should not operate like a business, but rather hope to show you the ways in which they do operate like a business. Each institution is unique in its offerings and its structure. To assume that there is a "one size fits all" solution to the complex problems that currently exist within higher education is a bit naïve. This text will discuss the practical application of business models and how those applications contribute to the efficiency and effectiveness of our institutions of higher education. Our discussion will address macro-level higher education and student population issues, while also addressing micro-level issues for individual institutions or students. Because of the significant diversity of institutions and institutional offerings, some of the examples provided within these pages may not seem relevant to your specific circumstances, but we encourage you to explore how each may fit within your institution.

ORGANIZATION OF THIS BOOK

Geared toward the college or university administrator, this book is segmented into four parts, and within each part the functional areas that are relevant are discussed. There are chapters on each of the major business functional areas that show and explain business principles and provide examples of current higher education practices. The examples provided are not intended to be exemplary, but simply examples that indicate the wide use of these business principles.

What is different in the second edition? You will notice that the chapter on politics and power has been eliminated (it is now its own book) and three chapters—Chapter 5, Accounting; Chapter 8, Strategic Planning; and Chapter 11, Fundraising—have been added. Additionally, content in the other chapters has been updated to reflect the changes over the past eight years.

Part 1: Environment and Structure

Chapter 1 provides a brief overview of the current context of higher education and slight prognostication as to what may lie ahead for the future administrators. Some of the topics introduced include: accountability, assessment, funding and demographic shifts, and the movement toward privatization. Whether you are stepping into your first academic administrative position, studying to be a student affairs administrator, or have been recently hired to aid students in their transition through your institution, an understanding of today's context is important.

Chapter 2 sets the stage with an examination of the organizational structures within higher educational institutions. This edition includes updated organizational charts and more information about institutional hierarchy. Regardless of the type of institution, state in which you reside, or the tax status of your institution, you should be able to recognize your institution among the several basic organizational structures presented. This chapter will provide a map through the organizational maze and describes many of the typical administrative positions represented throughout higher education. You will leave with a better understanding of the hierarchical and bureaucratic nature of higher education organizations.

Part 2: Finance and Funding

Chapter 3 is an introduction to common economic concepts that impact higher education, and briefly defines some of these economic principles and discusses how they impact higher education. This second edition has an expanded discussion of supply and demand, and discusses other concepts, such as utility, marginality, economies of scale, and elasticity. This edition places more emphasis on the impact economics has on administrative decision-making. If understood and used appropriately, these principles may be able to help administrators become more efficient in their everyday operations and perhaps give them a better insight into the institution's short- and long-term planning.

Chapter 4 discusses the financing of higher education. This is not an in-depth discussion of all of the nuances of state and federal support of higher education, but rather an overview of how institutions are funded. This edition includes a discussion of how funding and revenue patterns have changed over time. Whether you work in a public or private institution, and regardless of your institution's tax status, you will have at least one source of revenue (money) coming into the institution.

Chapter 5 introduces the reader to the fundamentals of accounting and its associated vocabulary needed to understand the budget basics provided in Chapter 6. Understanding the terminology used can be helpful in budget meetings with the institution's central staff.

Chapter 6 helps you spend the money you just acquired in Chapter 4. This chapter introduces the reader to some basic principles of budgeting within higher education. The emphasis here is on understanding how to read, manage, and manipulate your budget. This is not meant to train someone to be a senior budget officer, but rather to be a "good fiscal steward" over the funds that have been allocated to your unit. We will take a closer look at two specific models: incremental (the most popular) and responsibility-centered or decentralized budgeting.

Part 3: People and Processes

Chapter 7 provides the reader with an introduction to the managerial functions of an administrator. It is important to understand the leadership role you have, the responsibilities that are incumbent in your position, and how you are expected to interact within the organization as well as with your institution's external stakeholders. There will also be a discussion of the accreditation process and the role you may be expected to play.

Chapter 8 is an introduction to the strategic planning process necessary to keep any organization on track and remaining true to its mission and values. Understanding the planning process is useful when working with accrediting bodies and when there are changes in senior administrative positions.

Chapter 9 is a look into the processes of recruiting and retaining employees. Regardless of your functional reporting line, if you serve as a hiring manager the recruiting and retaining of quality employees will consume an inordinate amount of your time. Additionally, other human resource (HR) functions of administrators and the relationship between the HR office and the individual units will be discussed. We also take a closer look at the use of executive search firms and their roles in the hiring process.

Chapter 10 examines the marketing functions employed throughout higher education. Marketing is not simply the advertising that we see on billboards or the advertisements that are in newspapers or on the television. Typically, there are several units within most institutions that collaborate on the marketing efforts of the institution. Rarely is there one unit that assumes the responsibility for all of the institution's marketing efforts. This edition emphasizes the importance of a services marketing approach for higher education and helps readers understand the connection with strategic planning.

Part 4: Perspectives on the Future

Chapter 11 discusses fundraising in higher education and is a new addition to the text. Readers are given an overview of the fundraising world and its importance to all aspects of higher education institutions.

Chapter 12 concludes this text by tying together the business concepts discussed in the first eleven chapters with current issues throughout higher education.

Acknowledgments

This edition would not have been possible without the efforts of my co-author, Dr. Erica Eckert. Her unique insights and scholarly contributions significantly strengthened this edition of the book. It is also important for me to recognize the loving support from my spouse, Deb Saito, who also served as an initial reader/editor and supplied the index.

I am grateful for the unwavering encouragement of my family: Tricia and Dave Eckert, Sarah Eckert, and Dodie Ottman. My work would not have been what it is without my partner Dr. David Taylor, who exercised superhero-level patience in reviewing drafts, providing timely feedback, and serving as the best sounding board anyone could ever hope for. Brittney Braydich provided critical insight (and a strong dose of reality) for the Fundraising chapter, and our discussion of Lean was enhanced by the extensive experience and wisdom of Jane DeLue and Holly Slocum. Finally, many thanks to Dr. Mark Kretovics for inviting me to join him on this edition—this book was a joy (really!) to work on.

PART 1

Environment and Structure

CHAPTER 1

Today's Environment

Higher education in the United States continues to be attacked for a perceived inability to keep pace with societal and corporate demands, and it is constantly being asked to defend itself as to its effectiveness and its quality. These attacks have been challenging institutions of higher education for quite some time. Altbach (2001) notes "hardly a day goes by without an attack on academic institutions for inefficiency, irresponsibility, and ungovernability" (p. 3). Politicians continue to focus their attention on higher education, and if we are not careful they will wrestle away institutional control and impose state or national policies that will shape our future.

Unfortunately, as long as institutions of higher education rely on the student financial aid dollars and research grant monies from the federal government, they will continue to be required to implement unfunded mandates imposed by politicians at the national level. Many of these mandates, while seemingly well intended, have had significant impacts on the organizational structure and academic offerings at many institutions. Entirely new positions, and in some instances new departments, have had to be created within institutions specifically to address a government policy or to comply with restrictions placed on government monies.

It is assumed that the vast majority of today's high school students will continue their education in some form or another, as it is seen as a key to a middle- or upper-class lifestyle. Whether they attend a community college, university, or career or technical institute is not the point. They will be continuing their education. In 2016, nearly 70 percent of high school completers enrolled in a postsecondary education institution as compared to less than 50 percent in 1980. As we look toward the future, we must consider several issues being discussed at the local, state, regional, national, and international levels that impact higher education. Below, you are provided with a glimpse of several of these issues and how they are impacting the world of higher education.

THE FIVE A'S OF HIGHER EDUCATION

Within higher education, there are many important issues and depending on the writer's and/or the reader's perspective, one issue will tend to be considered more important than the others. From our perspective, we believe no issue to be more important in today's economy than what we like to call the five A's of higher education: *accountability*, *accreditation*, *assessment*, *access*, and *affordability*. Since the 1970s much has changed within higher education, but few things have had the level of impact of the five A's. We prefer to merge these topics together because of the influence they have had on one another and higher education as a whole. The accountability movement of the 1970s and 1980s put pressure on individual institutions to rethink their respective missions, and put pressure on the accreditation associations to rethink how institutional evaluations are conducted. This combination of pressures resulted in the assessment movement of the 1980s and 1990s. Each of these will be described briefly below as there is a plethora of information on each in the higher education literature if the reader desires more details.

Accountability

The accountability movement has taken hold in higher education and comes at us from a variety of angles depending on the institution's mission and vision. For institutions receiving federal monies (financial aid, research grants, etc.), the government is pushing for more information as to how this taxpayer money is being spent. There have been numerous instances of misuse of federal government money that have resulted in institutional fines and administrative turnover. Institutions of higher education must be the example of transparent, trustworthy, and accountable organizations.

What does *accountability* mean? And to whom are we accountable? These are very important questions that may not have easy answers. According to Burke (2005a) "accountability is the most advocated and least analyzed word in higher education" (p. 1). It seems that individual legislators, bureaucrats, students, and citizens have their personal definition as to what it means to be accountable. Burke goes on to put forth six demands that are placed on colleges and universities: they must demonstrate they have used their powers appropriately; show that they are working toward their mission; report on their performance; demonstrate they are effective and efficient; ensure quality in services provided; and show they serve the public interest (p. 2). It is not uncommon for institutions to require additional staff to collect and collate data to satisfy government demand for information. Yet, institutions have no choice but to play along, especially where funding is contingent upon a satisfactory fulfillment of accountability requirements. In addition, government control almost always results in greater stifling of creativity on the part of higher education institutions. Nevertheless, the handwriting on the wall clearly spells more control and accountability in virtually every country, both developed and developing (Michael, 2005).

The demands of accountability imply that higher education is accountable to both internal and external stakeholders. The external stakeholders include our government officials (state and federal), the business community, and the taxpayer base, while the internal stakeholders include the students, faculty, staff, and administrators of the respective institutions. It is easy to understand now why trying to meet the needs and wants of these varied stakeholders has resulted in so many institutional missions to declare, albeit unofficially, "we are all things to all people." Such broad missions in turn make it difficult if not impossible to ensure any such accountability.

At the macro level, higher education in general is primarily accountable to the public at large (even most private institutions receive a substantial amount of public funding support through research grants, financial aid, vouchers, etc.). Accountability does not ensure either efficiency or effectiveness in higher education institutions. In fact, it is important to point out that many of the governmental and accrediting body accountability measures require institutions to put structures or processes in place that ultimately reduce the efficiency and the effectiveness of the institution. Many of these unfunded mandates in turn divert revenues from the core mission of the institution (teaching and research) to the accountability initiatives (Michael, 2005).

Accreditation

According to the Council for Higher Education Accreditation (2019), "'Accreditation' is review of the quality of higher education institutions and programs. In the United States, accreditation is a major way that students, families, government officials, and the press know that an institution or program provides a quality education." In general, accreditation is a combination of a self-study and a peer review process in which an institution is formally reviewed (curriculum, financial, staffing, resources, among others) to determine whether it meets the specified criteria. The peer review portion of this process is conducted by representatives from other accredited institutions within that particular region. Institutions that meet the criteria are accredited or re-accredited and may continue to award federal financial aid to eligible students. The ability to award degrees is not necessarily the purview of accrediting bodies but rather falls under the jurisdiction of the states. Institutions that are accredited must seek permission from their respective accrediting body when making changes to their degree offerings, but they are also bound to the requirements set forth in their institutional charter. Wolff (2005) refers to this as the accreditation triad:

> Accreditation operates within what is called the triad of overlapping state, federal, and accreditation interests. Under the triad, states have the responsibility to license institutions using minimum standards to protect against consumer fraud, the federal government to recognize accrediting agencies and ensure compliance with title IV on financial aid, and accrediting agencies to ensure quality and effectiveness.
>
> (p. 83)

There are several types of accreditation that play a role in higher education. The most important aspect is that the accrediting body needs to be recognized by the Department of Education (DOE) in order for the institutions accredited to be eligible for federal funding such as financial aid. The DOE does not accredit institutions or academic programs. There are regional accrediting bodies, national accrediting bodies, and programmatic or professional accrediting bodies. Visit the Council for Higher Education Accreditation's web site (www.chea.org/) for a current listing of all DOE-approved accrediting agencies.

As of January 2019, there were 62 organizations that accredit institutions or programs, and if your institution participates in the federal financial aid programs it must be accredited by one of the seven regional or six national accrediting bodies.

Regional Accreditation

At present there are six regional accrediting agencies/bodies recognized by CHEA (1–6) and one additional agency recognized by the DOE (7):

1. Accrediting Commission for Community and Junior Colleges Western Association of Schools and Colleges
2. Higher Learning Commission
3. Middle States Association of Colleges and Schools
4. New England of Schools and Colleges Commission on Institutions of Higher Education
5. Southern Association of Colleges and Schools Commission on Colleges
6. WASC Senior College and University Commission
7. Northwest Commission on Colleges and Universities

These groups accredit at the institutional level and are responsible for accrediting the vast majority of higher education institutions in the United States. Accrediting the entire institution implies the accreditation of each degree granted or certificate program offered at the institution.

National Accreditation

In 2018–2019, there were six national accrediting bodies recognized by CHEA, four that focused on faith-related institutions and two that focused on career-related institutions. Like the regional associations, these accrediting bodies accredit the entire institution, and therefore, by definition, accredit the degree or certificate programs offered within those institutions.

Programmatic or Professional Accreditation

There are 49 professional accrediting bodies recognized by CHEA (2018–2019). This group includes agencies such as AACSB International (business schools), the Accrediting Board for Engineering and Technology, and the Council for Accreditation of Educator Preparation. These organizations accredit specific academic programs and/or professional schools (business, education, engineering, etc.). While the overall health of the institution is considered by these accrediting bodies, the reviewers focus on the specific programs and do not concern themselves with institutional matters unless they impact the disciplines being reviewed.

Accreditation by these groups is not required for an institution to obtain federal funding. While there may be significant benefits obtained by a blessing from one of these organizations, it is hardly a requisite for programmatic survival, unless accreditation is mandated by the state (i.e., for the issuance of licenses).

Assessment

While we wish it could be said that higher education has been proactive in assessing student learning, that is unfortunately not the case. It has become quite common for accreditors to levy assessment-related sanctions such as reports or focused visits on institutions. Higher education has been reacting to governmental and accreditation pressures. It is safe to say that higher education would like to avoid the governmental intrusion that has plagued the K-12 educational environment. Having witnessed the debacle created in primary and secondary education by the "No Child Left Behind" legislation, higher education decided to react a little quicker to the calls for accountability and subsequently began to assess the learning outcomes of students. There is still no consensus as to how to report the results, but progress is being made.

It is important to differentiate between the assessment of learning and the assessment of student satisfaction or needs (wants). During the 1960s and 1970s, higher education was focused on assessing whether or not students were satisfied with their experiences, classes, and instructors. Additionally, there were massive attempts to gauge the needs (read *wants*) of the students. Institutions were interested in learning from students what courses needed improvement and what activities should be discontinued. It was not until the late 1980s and early 1990s that higher education began to take seriously the need to assess student learning. We still have a long way to go before we can claim to have been broadly successful in this area. While most people will agree that critical thinking skills are important, it is also well understood that all critical thinking does not look the same, and that presents a measurement challenge few institutions have truly risen to meet.

When considering an assessment strategy for your institution, keeping it simple makes the most sense. Perhaps the most important piece to the assessment issue is being intentional. This is where Deming (1986) would say that you need to begin with the end in mind. Before we can assess our educational activities or programs, we need to concentrate on the intended outcome(s). If we are intentional with our programs, be they curricular or extracurricular, then we should have a good idea as to what outcomes we hope to see at the end. There will be more discussion on assessment in Chapter 7.

Access and Affordability

Presently, there are over 4,000 postsecondary institutions in the United States, and every state has at least one major state-supported institution thereby, placing a postsecondary institution within reach of every resident of this nation. For those unable to travel the distance necessary to physically attend the nearest institution, there is a growing number of postsecondary opportunities offered via distance education so students do not have to leave the comfort of their homes (or other physical location). So, from a simple geographic perspective, postsecondary education is quite accessible. However, for many *accessibility* also implies *affordability*. If one cannot afford the tuition, proximity becomes irrelevant, thereby rendering higher education inaccessible, and with no end in sight to the increasing cost of attendance, affordability and access have become industry concerns. Once we connect access to higher education with affordability, the conversation shifts from geography to finances. If higher education is not affordable, then how can it be accessible?

The 2006 Spellings' Commission report, *A Test of Leadership*, states:

> access to American higher education is unduly limited by the complex interplay of inadequate preparation, lack of information about college opportunities, and persistent financial barriers. Substandard high school preparation is compounded by poor alignment between high schools and colleges, which often creates an 'expectations gap' between what colleges require and what high schools produce.
> (U.S. DOE, 2006)

There is no doubt that the current financial state of affairs has placed a greater burden on the student and the institution. This is not simply a trend in the United States but world-wide. As states reduce their financial support for higher education so do most countries around the world. Many more countries have recently adopted the "tuition model" in use in the United States.

In the United States, the availability of financial support through federal grants for the most needy, and federal loans for the rest, as well as private sources of funding, has made college affordable for academically qualified students. By 2018, eleven states had implemented some type of "free college" program and another ten had pending legislation (Campaign for Free College Tuition, n.d.). Additionally, some of the more financially well-off institutions (most notably Harvard) are re-defining affordability by offering *free* tuition to admissible students with incomes below a specified amount.

Postsecondary education is not mandatory and therefore has not been designed for everyone, although the need for a college-educated workforce continues to increase. While universal access may be an ideal to strive toward, it still remains a significant challenge within our current economic system (see Chapter 3 for more information on the impact of economics). In Chapter 4, we will take a closer look at the financing of higher education and some basic financial aid practices which can (and in our opinion do) make higher education affordable to even the lowest of income levels. Additionally, in Chapter 10 we will discuss the "expectations gap" mentioned in the Spellings Commission report, *A Test of Leadership*.

RANKINGS

To some of you this may seem out of place. Why would rankings be addressed here? It is our belief that the numerous national and international rankings which are now engrained in the higher education landscape have contributed to the increasing costs of higher education. While most administrators publicly dismiss the rankings as having little to no merit, they still participate, thereby perpetuating the system. Whether it is *U.S. News*, *BusinessWeek*, *Princeton Review*, the *Financial Times*, or any of the other rankings too numerous to name, it is difficult if not impossible to find one that is truly objective and that has a sound enough methodology to warrant the headlines they draw. Zemsky (2005) comments that the data *U.S. News* so arduously collects tell us nothing about what actually happens on campus or in the classroom. These rankings continue to be fed by this country's obsession with reducing complex phenomena into simplistic lists or categories. There must be one best, regardless of the circumstances. We have national and world championships (even if the only teams are in the United States), we rank our high school graduates, and essentially we turn everything into a competition to crown the best. Additionally, as higher education moves more and more to a market system, the tendency toward institutional rankings continues to grow (Michael, 2005, p. 23) as institutions look for more ways to differentiate themselves from their competitors.

This quest to be the best is very expensive, as the price of prestige continues to escalate. Priest and Boon (2006) noted that "the drive to improve in the rankings has an effect of forcing costs up" (p. 175). In order to move up in the rankings institutions are concentrating on selectivity of admissions, reputation among peer institutions, and endowments, as these are the main criteria in many of the rankings. Institutions try to increase their applicant pools, so they can in turn reject more applicants, thereby becoming more selective. They send out institutional or departmental reports to peers to establish name recognition and increase the likelihood of being selected by their peers on their respective rankings' ballots. These rankings also "reward colleges that use financial aid to buy talented students and penalizes those who admit students from low-income, at-risk, and underserved populations requiring high aid" (Volkwein & Grunig, 2005, p. 258). Likewise, institutions hire more fundraising experts to increase donations to their endowments, so they can brag about all of the money they have (but do not spend), which in turn helps them move up in the rankings, which contributes to the rich getting significantly richer, complaining all the while about how unfair the rankings systems are.

These media-generated rankings "reflect prestige, a concept sufficiently amorphous as to lose most of its meaning when one tries to describe the difference between two institutions with similar profiles but ranked twenty places apart" (Zemsky, 2005, p. 284). There is one simple solution to this "arms race" for prestige. If all of the *elite institutions* refused to participate in the rankings game and refused to make note of their rank on any of their promotional materials, the rankings would disappear rather quickly. If the presidents really believe the rankings are not legitimate, then they have the power to stop them. No one in their right mind would ever believe that XYZ state institution is really the best of the best.

Another alternative to the rankings game is for institutions of higher education to become more transparent with their institutional data. Making data easily available on an institution's web site would aid potential students in their selection processes and could also result in making the ranking systems irrelevant. The more open institutions are about whom they serve and how well they serve, the better off higher education will be as an industry.

DEMOGRAPHIC SHIFTS

The U.S. DOE's National Center for Education Statistics (NCES) reports that postsecondary enrollment peaked at 21 million students in 2010 and had declined slightly to 19.7 million by 2017. According to the NCES enrollment is expected to experience a slight increase to 20.3 million between 2016 and 2027. Those increases will be concentrated in specific regions of the country, leaving other regions still in decline. Since 1978 the United States has witnessed a remarkable shift in the demographic profile of its student body (see Figure 1.1). In 1978, female enrollment surpassed male enrollment for the first time, and female students have maintained that majority ever since. Additionally, increases in minorities, first-generation students, and students of lower socioeconomic status have truly changed the face of education. Minority enrollment nearly tripled as a percentage of all college enrollments between 1976 and 2017 (Figure 1.2). In 1981, 50.3 percent of bachelor's degree recipients were female, marking the first time the majority of graduates were not male (based on Table 318.10 in the NCES 2018 Digest). In 2017, that percentage rose to 57.3 percent, and the NCES projects that to increase to 57.4 percent by 2027 (based on Table 318.10). As you can see, not only are more women and minorities entering postsecondary education in the United States, but they are also graduating at a higher rate than their male and White counterparts.

Most institutions of higher education must be prepared for stable or reduced enrollment over the next decade (see Chapter 3). With these demographic shifts we will probably see continued closings of smaller, less fiscally stable institutions in the Midwest and Northeast while institutions in the Southwest and Southeast will experience some growth along with a continuing shift in the racial and ethnic mix of their student bodies.

FUNDING SHIFT

Over the past few decades, we have witnessed a significant shift in how institutions are being funded. States, according to Zusman (2005), "have become minority partners in

Figure 1.1 Enrollment Sex

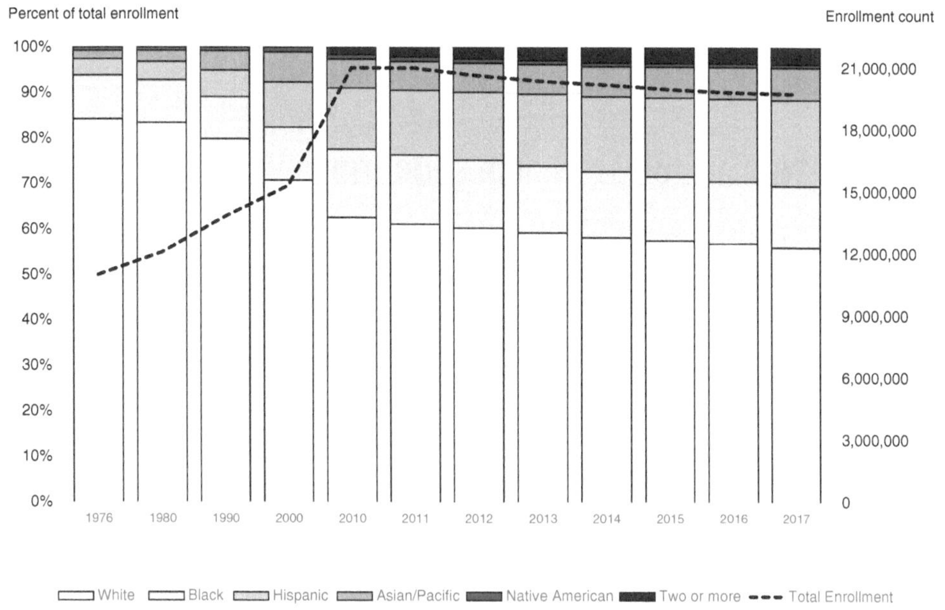

Figure 1.2 Enrollment by Race

the colleges and universities that bear their names" (p. 116). It is also noteworthy that the private institutions have not remained unscathed by this funding shift.

There has been a great deal of criticism leveled at higher education for the significant increases in tuition over the past several decades. According to the NCES (2018, Table 330.10), during 2017–2018, private not-for-profit four-year institutions reported average tuition and required fees for full-time undergraduates of $33,755, up from $15,811 in 2000–2001, while public four-year institutions reported charging in-state undergraduates an average of $9,037, up from $3,501 in 2000–2001. These substantial increases in tuition have not occurred simply because of inflationary pressure. There is more on this in Chapter 4.

While there continues to be federal financial aid available to assist students in funding their education, an increasing percentage of this aid is in the form of loans (subsidized and un-subsidized), which means that greater numbers of students are leaving our institutions with sizable debt burdens. The increased debt has a negative impact on the economy because that leaves less discretionary money for new graduates to spend on goods and services in their local communities.

This shift in institutional funding has generated a great deal of interest in the fundraising community as some of the shortfall needs to be made up through contributions from other stakeholders. According to the *Chronicle of Higher Education*, as of fall 2018 there were just over 100 institutions boasting over $1 billion in institutional endowments, with Harvard leading the way, topping the $38 billion mark. In their quest for external support and in some respect an increase in financial independence, institutions continue to hire development officers, investment consultants, and fund managers. Institutions with larger endowments have garnered the attention of state and national legislators who show an increased interest in the idea of taxing endowments over a specified amount.

PRIVATIZATION OF PUBLIC HIGHER EDUCATION

The funding shift mentioned above has in many respects started higher education down the path of privatization, and according to St. John and Priest (2006), that privatization of public universities is well underway and shows no sign of slowing down. While several states have implemented "free college" programs, these programs have not provided significant increases in funding to individual institutions; rather, the money has been given to the students to cover their costs. As stated earlier, state support for public institutions has, with rare exceptions, decreased steadily over the past few decades. Institutions made up for lost state revenue by increasing tuition, seen as the easiest solution at the time. This tuition increase, combined with reduced state funding, prompts public colleges and universities to act more like private institutions.

Additionally, more institutions are turning to outsourcing of specific services as a way to theoretically reduce their operating costs. The concept here is that the private sector can provide the same services less expensively because that is what they are in business to do. For example, institutions of higher education are not in business to sell textbooks or fast food to their students; even though both of these examples may be student needs, there may be other external or independent organizations that can provide the same (or perhaps higher) quality of service in a less expensive way. Hence the institution contracts with a local fast food vendor to operate a venue in the student center, and may also contract with a national bookseller to operate its bookstore in the hopes of reducing costs to students and possibly increasing revenue to the institution. This topic will be addressed further in Chapter 4.

Lastly, we believe this movement toward privatization has helped the for-profit sector of higher education. As tuition in the public sector continues to rise it makes the for-profit sector seem reasonably priced. As you can see in Table 1.1 below, the

Table 1.1 Fall enrollment, 2016

Sector	*Total*	*Undergraduate*	*Post-baccalaureate*
Total students	19,841,014	16,869,212	2,971,802
Public four-year	8,741,896	7,300,010	1,441,886
Public two-year	5,841,076	5,841,076	0
Private not-for-profit four-year	4,027,240	2,762,212	1,265,028
Private not-for-profit two-year	50,557	50,557	0
Private for-profit four-year	981,633	716,745	264,888
Private for-profit two-year	198,612	198,612	0

Source: NCES (2017), Table 311.15.

private for-profit sector continues to enroll a significant number of students within the higher education market place.

GLOBALIZATION OF HIGHER EDUCATION

Globalization can refer to the increase in international students attending colleges and universities, as well as the breakdown or perhaps disintegration of geo-political borders throughout the world when it comes to education. The European Union through the Bologna Process has made it easier for students to cross borders and enroll in a university in any of the participating countries. Additionally, as technology improves, it is becoming easier and easier for individuals to take courses and earn degrees from foreign institutions without leaving the comfort of one's own home or office. This has dramatically changed the nature of competition and will continue to alter the landscape of higher education well into the future. While many institutions within the United States have a regional or local market, this will begin to change, and an institution's competition may no longer be across the state or across the country but rather could be on a different continent. It is no longer strictly a brick and mortar, stationary, unmoving building.

If institutions of higher education do not keep current with stakeholder needs (i.e., students and corporations, among others) and continuously improve their programs, pedagogy, and performance, they run the risk of becoming irrelevant in today's global environment. Citizens have access to a plethora of educational opportunities from across the globe. Conversely, academic programs at the local institution may not necessarily be catering to the local constituents but rather to a global community.

THE NATURE OF STUDENTS

Much is written each year regarding the type of student attending our colleges and universities. The purpose of this section is not to reiterate what others tell us about this particular generation of students or the next, but rather to discuss ways in which we, as higher education administrators, can frame our views of the students on our respective campuses. Whether our students are residents or commuters, traditional or non-traditional, we tend to treat them based on a set of assumptions about the role of education. There are several metaphors that have been used over the years to describe or define our students. Three of the more popular are the student as a product, a customer/client, or a co-producer. Others in the academy suggest that students are students, no more, no less. While accurate, this does not provide one with a framework for defining the interaction between the student and the institution, whereas the *customer*, *product*, and *co-producer* metaphors imply such a relationship (Hoffman & Kretovics, 2003).

With the diverse nature of higher education in general it seems logical to believe that multiple metaphors can be used simultaneously to describe students within any particular institution depending on one's specific job responsibilities. Individuals will choose the metaphor that most closely relates to the functions performed or services provided. For example, the housing staff may view the student as a customer whereas the alumni or advancement staff may choose to view the student as a product.

The Metaphor of Student as Customer

The metaphor of *student as customer* comes from the belief that students are customers who enter higher education with a specific set of "wants" needing to be met if the relationship with the admitting institution is to be successful (Ivancevich & Ivancevich, 1992; Measelle & Egol, 1992). Potential students search for a college or university from among the alternatives, narrowing their search based on a set of variables that may include price (tuition and fees), location, degrees offered, majors offered, and reputation, among others. This behavior gives the students and their parents the perception they are indeed customers. And of course, at many institutions, prior to admission and enrollment students (and their parents) are more often than not treated as customers by the admissions personnel. Colleges and universities market themselves much like other industries market their respective products. However, once the student enrolls in an institution the customer metaphor begins to lose its appeal, especially among the faculty.

Once enrolled, students pay tuition, select specific degree programs, register for classes, and participate in extracurricular activities. However, it is important to point out that while these appear to be *customer-like* activities, there is no guarantee the students get what they want. They may not qualify for the degree program desired, the intended course may be filled, and the student may not be selected to participate in the select club or activity. Similarly, being admitted to an institution does not guarantee a student a degree. Students must successfully complete the requirements set forth by the institution, not by the students themselves, to earn their respective degrees. Enrolling in an institution of higher education gives students permission to pursue a degree, not a right to receive a degree. While the customer metaphor may be more acceptable in auxiliary services such as Housing and Food Service or the bookstore, it does not usually work in the Academic or Student Affairs divisions.

The Metaphor of Student as Product

With its roots in the manufacturing sector, the metaphor of *student as product* has been applied to higher education. This metaphor assumes that a student enters a college or university as a moldable entity and through a standard process is transformed into a finished good; i.e., a graduate. In this scenario, the implication is students are products, graduating with "job-ready" skills, and the employers of the corporate world are the customers. Additionally, this metaphor is also subtly reinforced by regional and professional accrediting bodies as well as other external stakeholders when they ask for assessment data on learning outcomes which can easily be equated with adding value to students (Kretovics, 1999). This assessment movement in education is an example of higher education's adaptation of quality principles.

While this may be appealing to some of our stakeholders, this metaphor has significant limitations—the product is a human being capable of critical thinking and individual decision-making. An employer cannot "purchase" (hire) a student without his or her consent. Students have an active involvement in their education and how that education is used in their future. This view runs contrary to the view that educators are responsible for fostering independent learning while actively engaging students in the classroom (Measelle & Egol, 1992). This *students as products* perspective fails to acknowledge the student's role as payer whereby students are consumers and academic degree programs are the product (Conway, Mackay, & Yorke, 1994).

The Metaphor of Student as a Co-producer

In higher education it is not possible to separate the educational process into distinct parts such as those found in other transactional encounters. Education is a service encounter (Hoffman & Kretovics, 2003), whereby in the classroom experience the faculty member is physically connected to the course material being delivered; the student is directly involved in the educational process; and other students share the educational experience. The students' direct involvement in the educational experience makes them an active participant in their learning, leading us to refer to them as co-producers, not customers or products.

A student's role in higher education is complex and not adequately described by the singular terms of "customer" or "product." The *student as co-producer* perspective overlaps, and thereby ties together, the more traditional perspectives of students as customers and products. As co-producers, students enhance their traditional customer role by performing tasks that facilitate the co-production of the educational process. These tasks include students choosing majors, registering for classes, participating in activities, and joining organizations.

The co-producer metaphor works well with the experiential education movement within higher education and complements the continuing shift from teaching-centered classrooms to ones focused on the learners and the learning process. Adopting the *students as co-producers* perspective involves viewing the educational process as a collaborative environment in which educators are transformed from lecturers to coaches and facilitators, which can ultimately help transition higher education into a more engaging experience for today's students.

The higher education literature is replete with examples of how students are taking more responsibility for their educational progress by becoming actively involved in the educational process. Here are a few of those examples about the student–institution relationship:

- Students must be active participants in their learning (Astin, 1985; Hu & Kuh, 2003; Kolb, 1984; Kuh, 1996); therefore, it is inherent within higher education that students assist in educating themselves. For example, students must complete homework, read assignments, take tests, write papers, and participate in class discussions, to name a few activities. If students fail to actively participate, they will ultimately fail in the educational process. This does not mean that students cannot earn degrees, but that the degrees earned do not necessarily certify student achievement. They are an acknowledgement of the students' academic preparation.

- As institutions move more and more services online, the staff members who previously performed those duties now perform different tasks while students perform many of the more routine duties or services themselves, such as registering for classes.
- When choosing a major or career path most students are actively involved in the decision. Choosing a direction that is of interest to oneself and matches one's skills, interests, and abilities is an important part of the educational process. Students are not required to choose a major that the "state" needs; rather, this is the free choice of the student.
- Student government, clubs, and organizations are dependent upon student involvement to be successful (Zuckerman & Kretovics, 2003). Students must co-produce their experience within these organizations.

Which metaphor you believe is most relevant will be determined by your institutional culture and the culture of the institutions in which you co-produced your education. These metaphors are the most common in use today and influence how you will perceive your role within your institution and how you will perceive your institution's role within the larger context of the higher education market.

THE CONSTANT CRISIS

During the last half of the twentieth century and through the first two decades of the twenty-first century, one will be hard pressed to find a month in which higher education has not been declared to be in a state of crisis. Crisis and change have been the rule not the exception (Zusman, 2005). According to Birnbaum and Shushok, Jr. (2001), there are four types of crises that can be found within the higher education literature: pandemic, chronic, sporadic, and idiosyncratic. These crises can be initiated from either an internal or external perspective.

Pandemic Crisis

A *pandemic crisis* is one that is claimed continually. One of the best examples of a pandemic crisis is "finance," or the funding of higher education. Whether it is a lack of state funding or federal financial aid, institutions are constantly describing their financial peril. Yet somehow over the past several decades, higher education has expanded tremendously. While it is true that numerous institutions have closed their doors over the last half century, it is also true that a greater number of new institutions have opened. There are more institutions and more students attending those institutions than ever before.

Chronic Crisis

The *chronic crisis* appears less often but still frequently and is exemplified by access and accountability, or perhaps Title IX in higher education. Politicians and pundits seem to spew a never-ending stream of criticisms toward higher education for not being affordable, not providing access, or not being accountable. Additionally, the sexual assaults and sexual harassment incidents on campuses across the country show no signs of letting up. Colleges and universities are under fire for ignoring or covering up these incidents. These criticisms will most likely continue into the foreseeable future, until higher education begins to proactively address the concerns.

Sporadic Crisis

A *sporadic crisis* is usually in response to a current or passing social condition such as literacy or morals. In 1987, Bloom's *The Closing of the American Mind* and E. D. Hirsch's *Cultural Literacy* declared that higher education was in crisis because of its failure to educate its students in an appropriate fashion. While garnering a great deal of attention, neither was impactful with regard to educational reform.

Idiosyncratic Crisis

Finally, an *idiosyncratic crisis* is one that represents a special interest group but is not seen by others to be that important. There are numerous watchdog groups that hope to impose their respective agendas on campuses across the country or try to prevent other points of view from being discussed. These come from both liberal and conservative political viewpoints.

Regardless of your position on the "crisis *du jour*," administrators within higher education are expected to respond to whoever has proclaimed it as such. Keep in mind that not every crisis has to impact campuses in a negative fashion. There are times when these problems can be turned into solutions by showing the powers-that-be that an institution can respond quickly to the needs of its stakeholders. Administrators must also keep focused on the road ahead rather than dwelling on the problems of the past. We in higher education must recognize that just because someone external declares it a crisis does not make it so.

CONCLUDING COMMENTS

While there are many pressing issues for higher education today, those listed above show no signs of being resolved anytime soon and are crucial in determining the future environment of administration and teaching within higher education. Throughout this book we will refer to these and other issues as we highlight the business practices employed in our institutions of higher education. These practices may not be the answer to all of these issues, but their implementation is definitely a step in the appropriate direction to help resolve many of them. How you view these issues depends on where you sit—whether within higher education or from the outside. What may appear to be a critical issue for the insiders may not even be on the radar screens of those outside the academy. Likewise, what seems to be important to corporate executives, politicians, or the general public may appear to be simply afterthoughts to those sitting within the hallowed walls of higher education.

Higher education in most states is generally one of the top five budget items, which also include Medicaid (health care), transportation (including roads), prisons, and Pre-K through 12 education. Each of these line items is considered by many as required, while higher education, as important as it is, is not required. You will see headlines in local newspapers as well as in our trade papers and journals decrying the sad state of affairs in higher education while calling for greater accountability. Personally, we hesitate to refer to this as a public outcry because we do not see compelling evidence of the general public being overly concerned about the status of higher education. Rather, it seems as though it is simply a convenient political topic or an occasional story for the media.

As the cries for accountability in higher education continue, they place higher education funding in the position of being a state budget item that seems ripe for sacrifice, especially during tough economic times. We in higher education, public and private institutions alike, must do a better job of showing just how important this industry is to our state and local communities as well as to the national and world economies. Connecting higher education to economic gains both in the public and private sector is critical for our future success. We believe that everyone employed within higher education has an obligation to promote the industry and their respective institutions. We must do a better job of detailing the importance of higher education to this country and its politicians.

REFLECTIVE QUESTIONS

1. In what types of accreditation does your campus participate?
2. Why is accreditation important for institutions and why is accreditation important for specific academic programs?
3. How does your institution's most recent self-study compare to your experiences with and beliefs about the institution?
4. Why is it important to understand demographic trends? What is the current and potential impact on your institution?
5. Identify an example of the four types of crises discussed in the chapter.

CHAPTER 2

Organizational and Administrative Structures

There are over 4,500 postsecondary degree-granting institutions in the United States. As an administrator or potential administrator within the higher education sector, it is important to understand what this industry looks like and how its operations differ by institutional type. This chapter discusses the current organizational structures within higher education in the United States, segmenting the institutions into distinct categories. According to this scheme there are public and private institutions, not-for-profit and for-profit, and two- and four-year institutions. These three segmentations are distinct enough to give the reader an understanding of some of the differences and similarities between higher education institutions in the United States.

According to the National Center for Educational Statistics (NCES), in 2016 there were over 19.8 million students enrolled in colleges and universities throughout the United States (see Table 1.1). This is up considerably from the 15.3 million enrolled in 2000. In 2016, just under 70 percent of high school graduates attended a postsecondary institution immediately after graduation. While these data are not earth-shattering in and of themselves, they do document a trend of increasing postsecondary participation in the United States. As a larger proportion of high school seniors decide to undertake postsecondary education, there is greater pressure placed on the existing infrastructure.

This increase in demand for postsecondary education has been met by an increase in the number of spaces (virtual and physical seats) available at existing institutions, and in addition, growth in the overall number of institutions offering postsecondary opportunities. The NCES reports that in the 2015–2016 academic year there were 4,583 Title IV degree-granting institutions in the United States. This is up from 4,084 during the 1999–2000 academic year but down from a peak of 4,726 institutions in 2012–2013. However, what is most interesting about this overall increase is that the for-profit sector has accounted for the majority of the growth, increasing from 718 institutions in 1999–2000 to a peak of 1,451 in 2012–2013, and then declining to 1,262 institutions in 2015–2016.

THE NON-SYSTEM OF HIGHER EDUCATION

Unlike most of the developed world, the United States has no single system of higher education controlled at the national level. Constitutionally, the education of its citizens has been decentralized and is a state's right, not the responsibility of the federal government. Every state in the country has developed its own way of providing higher education for its residents. This autonomy has proven to be one of the greatest strengths of higher education in the United States and is what permits and perhaps even fosters the development of such a diverse offering of postsecondary opportunities. It is precisely this diverse set of institutional offerings that became the envy of the world in the early twentieth century.

Ironically, this diverse set of institutional offerings and accompanying autonomy has also become one of the most contentious points about higher education in the United States. Many critics believe that this multi-layered, inconsistent, and varied state-to-state structure has led to significant duplication of effort and an incredible amount of redundancy in individual states and within the overall context of higher education in the United States. On the one hand, this redundancy is considered a waste of resources and one of the most inefficient aspects of higher education within the United States, while on the other hand it is considered a point of competitiveness which has fueled innovation and creativity.

Within each state one will find a variety of individually chartered postsecondary options, be it public or private, two- or four-year institutions, and for-profit or not-for-profit types of institutions. Essentially, each state delegates an authorization function to a coordinating board, which determines the institutions that can operate within its borders and what degrees those institutions can offer (Birnbaum, 1988; Zusman, 2005).

INSTITUTIONAL STRUCTURE

The governance and coordination of higher education will differ whether it is under public or private control (Zusman, 2005); however, there is not as much of a difference in the actual institutional structure as one might think. The general organizational structure of individual institutions of higher education is bureaucratic in nature and typically has a well-established hierarchy. According to Balderston (1995), "large organizations—including universities—tend to obey laws of bureaucratic accretion, under which functions are added and the hierarchy grows as units proliferate" (p. 327). This concept holds true for public and private, not-for-profit and for-profit, as well as for liberal arts colleges and community colleges. Regardless of the ownership structure, there are several common elements across these institutions. Most all institutions of higher education in the United States have some sort of governing board (trustees, regents, directors), a chief operating officer (chancellor or president), a chief academic officer (CAO; a provost or dean), and a layer of vice-presidents or directors. Figures 2.1 through 2.4 provide a sample of what these organizational structures may look like.

According to Bush (2003), sociologist and economist Max Weber suggests that bureaucratic organizations have the following characteristics:

- There is a hierarchical authority – as seen in the organizational charts below there are direct lines of reporting creating a supervisory–subordinate relationship.

- Institutions are goal-oriented – higher education institutions must have goals and objectives in place to aid in accomplishing their respective missions.
- Division of labor exists and there is staff specialization – within colleges and universities there are multiple divisions: Academic Affairs, Student Affairs, Administrative Affairs, etc. These divisions of labor require staff specialization. It would be unrealistic to expect a chemistry professor to teach an English literature class or to have a psychology instructor double as a mathematics faculty member. Administrators, too, must be specially trained to manage people and budgets.
- Decisions and behaviors are governed by rules and regulations – higher education institutions are replete with rules and regulations. There are student handbooks, faculty handbooks, procurement guidelines, and hiring procedures, among a plethora of others.
- Decisions are made through a rational process – it would be difficult to find an organization that had more committees, task forces, or commissions than in higher education. Theoretically, this structure of shared governance within institutions ensures a rational, albeit lengthy, decision-making process.
- Leaders are accountable to external bodies – all not-for-profit and the vast majority of the for-profit institutions have governing boards composed of members external to the institution. These governing boards retain the legal authority for decisions made at the institution. Therefore, by their very nature, institutions of higher education are bureaucracies.

As mentioned earlier there are two sectors of the higher education market in the United States: the not-for-profit sector and the for-profit sector. Both sectors have two- and four-year institutions and the primary differences between these sectors are their tax status and their academic missions. While all institutions of higher education attempt to generate excess revenue (i.e., make a profit), it is what is done with the revenue that determines in which sector they fall. In the not-for-profit sector, which consists of public and private institutions, each college or university must re-invest its excess revenues (profits) in the institution. In the for-profit sector, each institution distributes its profits to its owner(s), which could be an individual or a group of stockholders.

Regarding the difference in academic mission, the vast majority of for-profit institutions are focused on training their students for immediate employment in today's workforce. Typically, their programs are vocationally oriented, and they offer few if any courses in the traditional liberal arts fields. In the not-for-profit sector the institutions profess to be educating their students and preparing for career opportunities in the global economy. While this may appear to be semantics to some readers, it is an important differentiation for many others.

The next few sections will describe several organizational structures that are found within the not-for-profit and for-profit educational sectors. The first will focus on the structures of the not-for-profit sector and will also describe many of the positions found within those institutions. This is followed by a look at the for-profit sector and how those institutions may be structured.

THE NOT-FOR-PROFIT SECTOR

Each institution of higher education has some type of governing board to which the president or chancellor reports. Although the legal status of these boards has not changed, there are differences as to how much power these boards hold within their respective states (Birnbaum, 1988, p. 5). In reviewing the organizational charts provided, the reader must also take into consideration that there may also be a state-wide or system super-structure that encompasses the individual institutions.

First let us take a closer look at the four-year institution category. Currently within the United States there are several sub-categories of these institutions. There are a number of ways to classify four-year institutions, such as: liberal arts colleges, comprehensive colleges, master's-level colleges, doctoral-granting universities, and research universities. However, due to mission creep more and more colleges and universities are trying to transform themselves into research-oriented universities. With this trend and the space limitations of this text, the two most common will be discussed: research universities and liberal arts colleges.

Research Universities

Research-oriented universities can be public or private and are typically the largest universities within each state. While there may be some large, non-research institutions present, their institutional structures tend to closely approximate those of the research institutions. As shown in Figure 2.1, research-oriented institutions are hierarchical with several layers of administrative positions. This figure has only the top of the organizational chart represented. Some larger research-oriented universities may have ten to fifteen vice-presidential-level positions.

Additionally, for each vice-president there is a support staff and numerous associate and assistant vice-presidents and directors and department heads. Later in this chapter these vice-presidential units or functional areas will be described in more detail.

Liberal Arts/Four-Year Colleges

The four-year liberal arts colleges differ slightly from the larger research universities. The primary difference is the size of the bureaucracy. These institutions will have fewer vice-presidents and oftentimes fewer layers within the organizational structure. There are still a few institutions that choose not to use the vice-presidential title at all but rather refer to their senior management positions as deans (Figure 2.2).

There are many four-year institutions that call themselves liberal arts colleges when in fact they look and operate more like comprehensive institutions offering professional and graduate degree programs. This mission creep has and will continue to reduce the number of true liberal arts institutions.

Two-Year/Community Colleges

There are several types of two-year colleges whose educational offerings and functions differ based on their respective mission. There are junior colleges, technical and

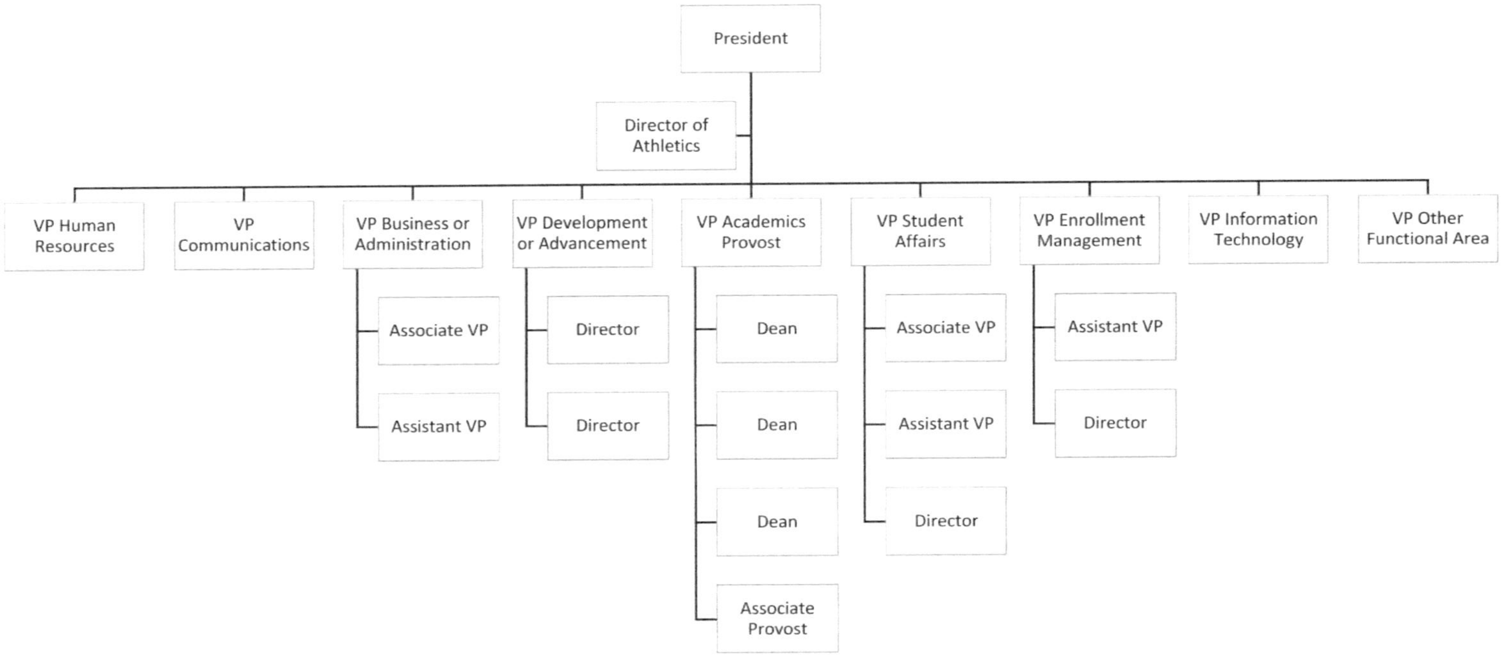

Figure 2.1 Large Research-Oriented University Model

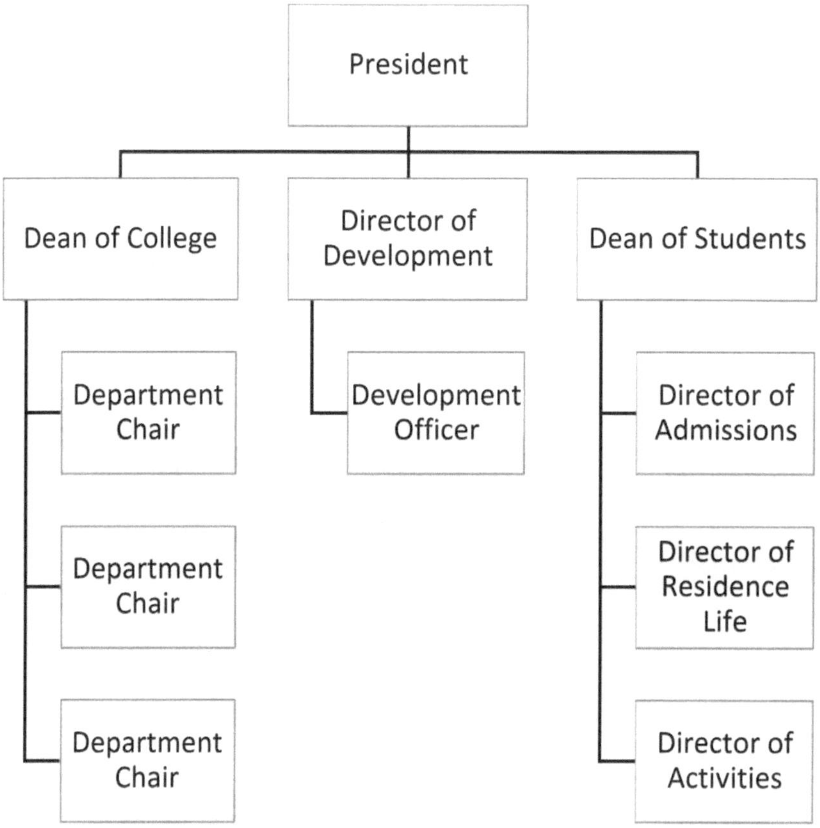

Figure 2.2 Liberal Arts College Model

vocational colleges, city colleges, and community colleges. According to Cohen and Brawer (2008) the term "junior college" was applied to the private two-year colleges while "community college" was used to describe the publicly supported colleges. Additionally, the for-profit schools have typically been called vocational or technical colleges. Today all of these institutions are commonly grouped together and referred to as community colleges.

Two-year colleges may take on one of many organizational structures. Perhaps one of the more common (Figure 2.3) is quite similar to that of its four-year counterparts. As these institutions continue to grow in size and complexity their organizational structures begin to resemble those of large research universities. Cohen and Brawer (2008) point out, "all colleges must have administration, although the way this function is organized and staffed differs from one college to another" (p. 141).

The most important difference between two- and four-year colleges is the degree offerings. Historically, two-year colleges offered associate degrees and certificates. However, recently several states have granted these institutions the authority to offer baccalaureate degrees.

The three models discussed are examples of the three most popular institutional models within U.S. postsecondary education. These are meant to provide a context

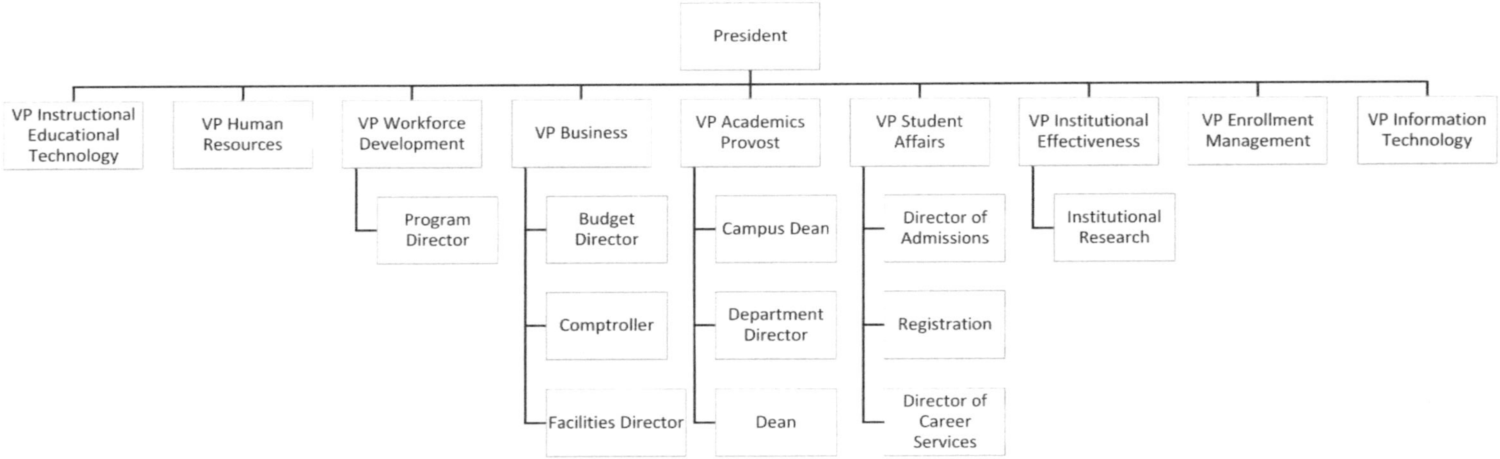

Figure 2.3 Community College Model

as to the similarities between the higher education industry and that of the corporate world. The next several sections of this chapter provide examples of some of the more common divisions or departments within our institutions.

Institutions of higher education appear to be structured hierarchies with a position for every task. However, Cohen and March (1974) place these institutions in "a class of organizations that can be called organized anarchies" (p. 2). They go on to describe them as "characterized by problematic goals, unclear technology (it does not understand its own processes), and fluid participation [participants vary in the amount of time and effort they devote to the organization]" (p. 3). This class of organizations may help explain why there is such an assortment of organizational missions and structures within higher education.

Executive Vice-President

In recent years several intuitions, regardless of type, have adopted a slightly different model by inserting a senior or executive vice-president into the hierarchical structure (Figure 2.4). In this model the executive vice-president typically has expanded powers and quite often supervises one or more of the other vice-presidents. In most cases this executive vice-president also serves either as the provost or the vice-president for business and administration.

The executive vice-president is typically involved in the day-to-day decision-making and is often viewed as the internal president, thus freeing up the president to focus more on fundraising and lobbying activities.

SENIOR ADMINISTRATIVE POSITIONS/FUNCTIONAL AREAS

Within higher education institutions there are some titles which are often used interchangeably but may have slightly different functions depending on the state or campus structure. For example, the terms "chancellor" and "president" can refer to either

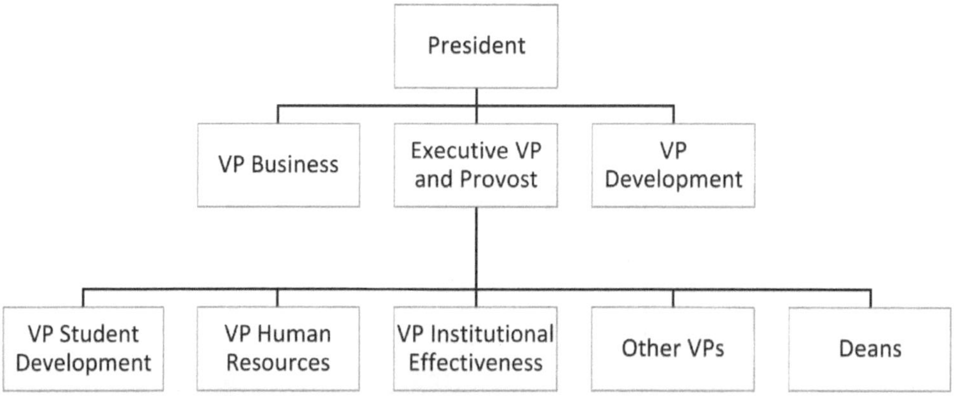

Figure 2.4 Executive Vice-President Model

the chief executive officer (CEO) of a system or individual institution. The systems of the University of California and the University of Wisconsin refer to their system CEOs as presidents and individual campus CEOs as chancellors. The Colorado State University and the University of Texas systems refer to their system CEOs as chancellors and their individual campus CEOs as presidents. To date, there is not a common lexicon for titles within educational institutions, so when examining the figures presented in this chapter remember that titles will vary depending on the individual campus' preference.

President/Chancellor

Cohen and March (1974, p. 2) succinctly wrote, "the presidency is important to the president." The president is also important to others inside and outside of the institution and is often viewed as the public face of the institution. Reporting to the governing board, it is the president's job to "persuade themselves and others that things are going well in their particular organization" (p. 26). Moreover, in recent years the president has been labeled as the academic leader, chief fundraiser, and institutional lobbyist. The role of the president is not standard across institutions but rather remains open to interpretation by the governing board and the individual hired to assume the role at the respective institution. Accordingly, one goal of just about all institutional CEOs is that they want their respective institutions to prosper. Additionally, they want to leave their mark on the institution, and they prefer to be associated with important changes during their tenure. College and university presidents are no different (Cohen and March, 1974).

Academic Affairs

The CAO will typically have one of three position titles—vice-president, provost, or dean—and is responsible for the backbone of the institution: the curriculum and the faculty. The size and complexity of the institution will dictate the size and structure of this area. Larger institutions with multiple colleges will have several subordinate staff, such as associate or vice-provosts, within the central office (see Figure 2.5). These subordinate staff do not have direct authority over faculty but rather oversee support functions such as curricular processes, collective bargaining, or assessment and accreditation. At some colleges and universities the registrar will report to the CAO, while at other institutions this position may report to the vice-president of Enrollment Management or Student Affairs.

Administrative Affairs/Business and Finance

This division of the institution is generally headed by a vice-president (chief financial officer) and supervises non-academic units such as Campus Operations (maintenance, building and grounds, custodial services, and utilities), Parking Services, the Bursar (student billing), Payroll, the University Budget Office, Procurement, Institutional Investments, and Campus Safety. At many institutions this division will have the

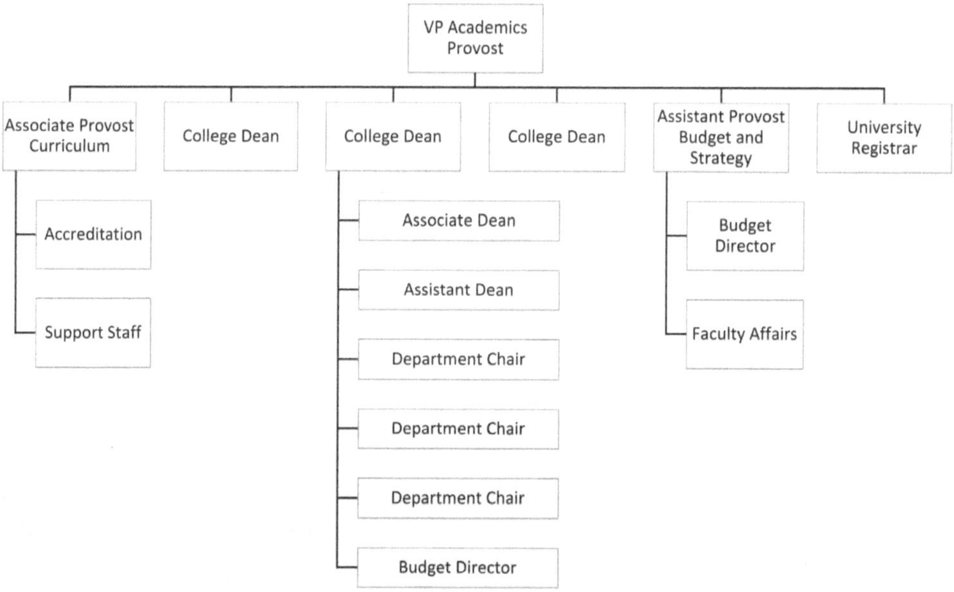

Figure 2.5 Academic Affairs Model

largest staff but not necessarily the largest budget. It is of utmost importance to note here that while this vice-president supervises the administration of the college or university budget, this office is not responsible for determining that budget. Every institution has its own budgeting process that solicits input from a wide variety of institutional stakeholders, including faculty, staff, and in some instances students.

Human Resources

At many institutions this unit may be housed within the Administrative Affairs division, but at larger institutions it will have its own vice-president and supporting staff. Usually one will find subordinated within this unit the institution's compensation and benefits, training and development, affirmative action, staffing (typically, all but faculty), employee orientation, and employee assistance program. See Chapter 9 for a more detailed description of this area and its functions within an institution.

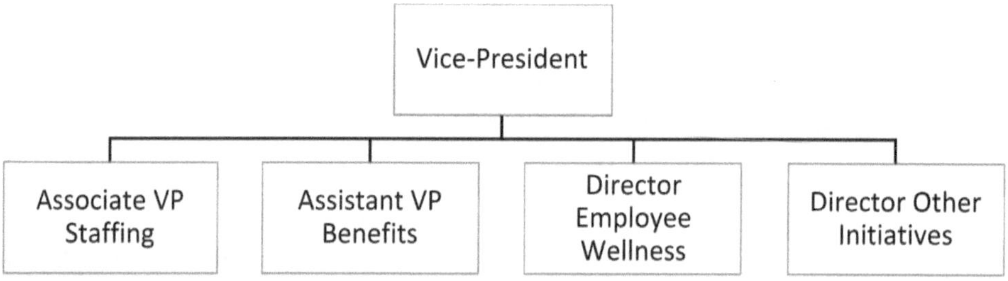

Figure 2.6 Human Resources Model

Institutional Research (IR)

This is the unit on campus that is responsible for providing data about the institution and its students, faculty, and staff to its internal and external stakeholders. While other units may collect data for their specific needs, the IR office is responsible for reporting institutional data to governmental agencies (the Department of Education, state finance office) and regional and professional accrediting bodies. IR is also responsible for answering the surveys sent out by rankings organizations/publications. In larger institutions this may be a stand-alone unit, while in smaller and mid-sized institutions this unit may be housed in Academic Affairs or within the Administrative Services area. This is a very important unit on the campus and its importance will only increase as accountability becomes ever more present.

Advancement/Development

This is the fundraising arm of the institution and in today's world an institution without a fundraising arm is destined for very difficult financial times, if not outright financial failure. This area may include annual giving, major gifts, planned gifts, and corporate and foundation relations. In larger institutions, each functional unit within the advancement arm of the institution will be overseen by associate or assistant vice-presidents, or directors. The funds raised through these offices help institutions award scholarships, renovate or build new facilities, supplement faculty salaries (endowed chairs), provide travel funding, and supplement operational expenditures.

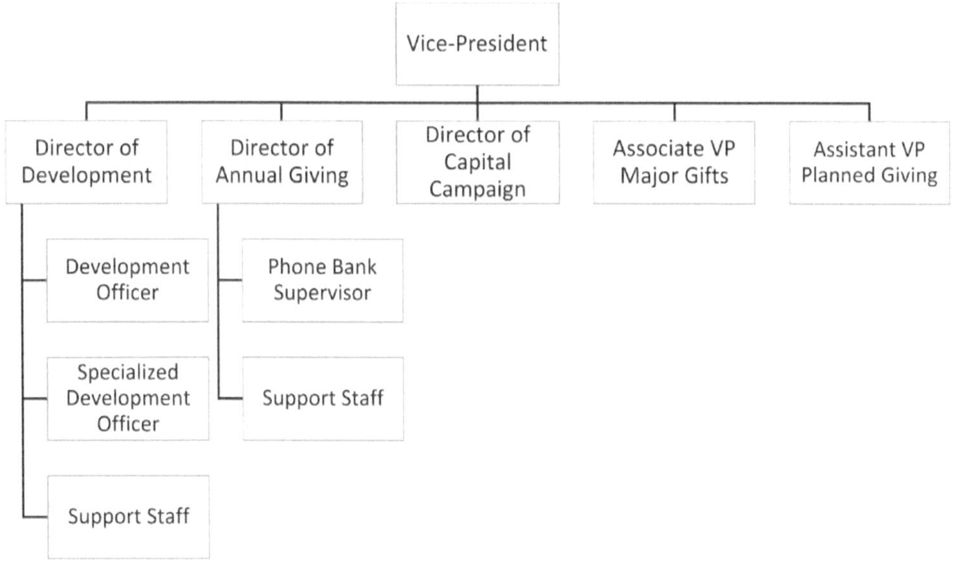

Figure 2.7 Advancement or Development Model

Communications and Marketing

Institutions of higher education have realized that a coordinated marketing effort is needed to establish "brand awareness" (see Chapter 10 for more details). This is the unit responsible for developing the institution's tag line, such as "Excellence in Action" or "Preparing Tomorrow's Leaders Today." It also promotes the institution through local and national press releases.

Enrollment Management

The division of Enrollment Management is relatively new, arriving on campuses beginning in earnest during the 1980s. Figure 2.8 shows a structure that includes admissions, financial aid, and the registrar. Prior to this time these functions were typically housed within the Student Affairs division. Most institutions have realized the importance of coordinating admissions and financial aid decisions to maximize the yield rate of each incoming class. Within some organizational structures the registrar's office may be housed within Enrollment Management as opposed to Academic Affairs.

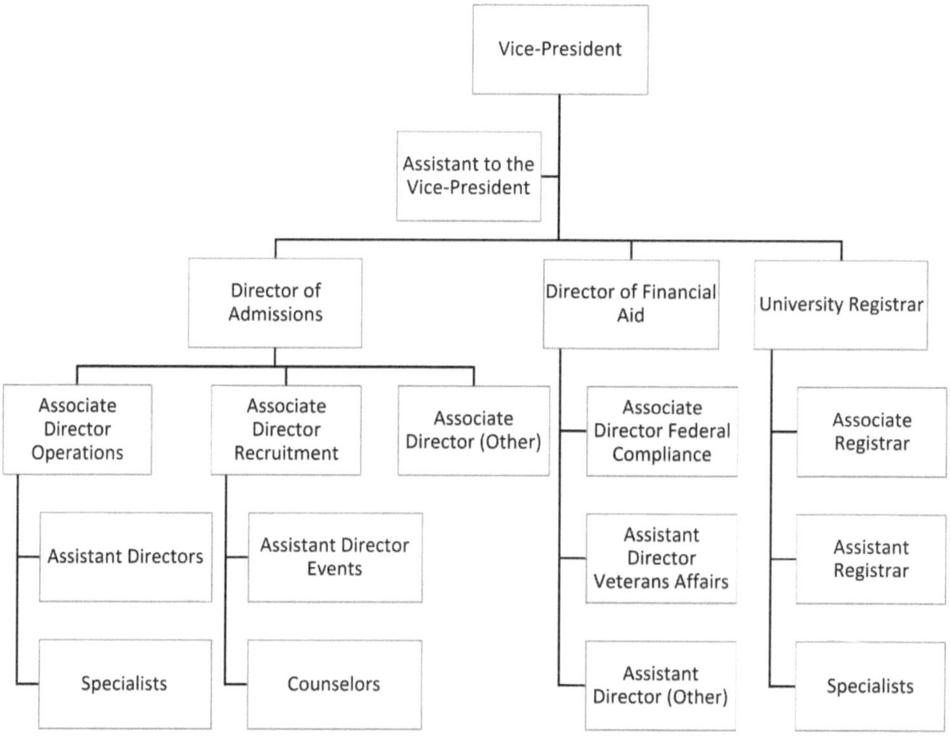

Figure 2.8 Enrollment Management Model

Student Affairs

This is the division that works directly with students once they arrive on campus. Student Affairs exists primarily to ensure the out-of-class experiences complement students' academic pursuits. As shown in Figure 2.9, the more common functional areas in the division include student activities and organizations, residence life, recreational services (including intramurals), Greek life (social fraternities and sororities), student orientation, career services, non-traditional student services, student senate, judicial affairs, and counseling and health services.

Many of the services provided within this division are supported through student fees collected simultaneously with each student's tuition. However, some of the

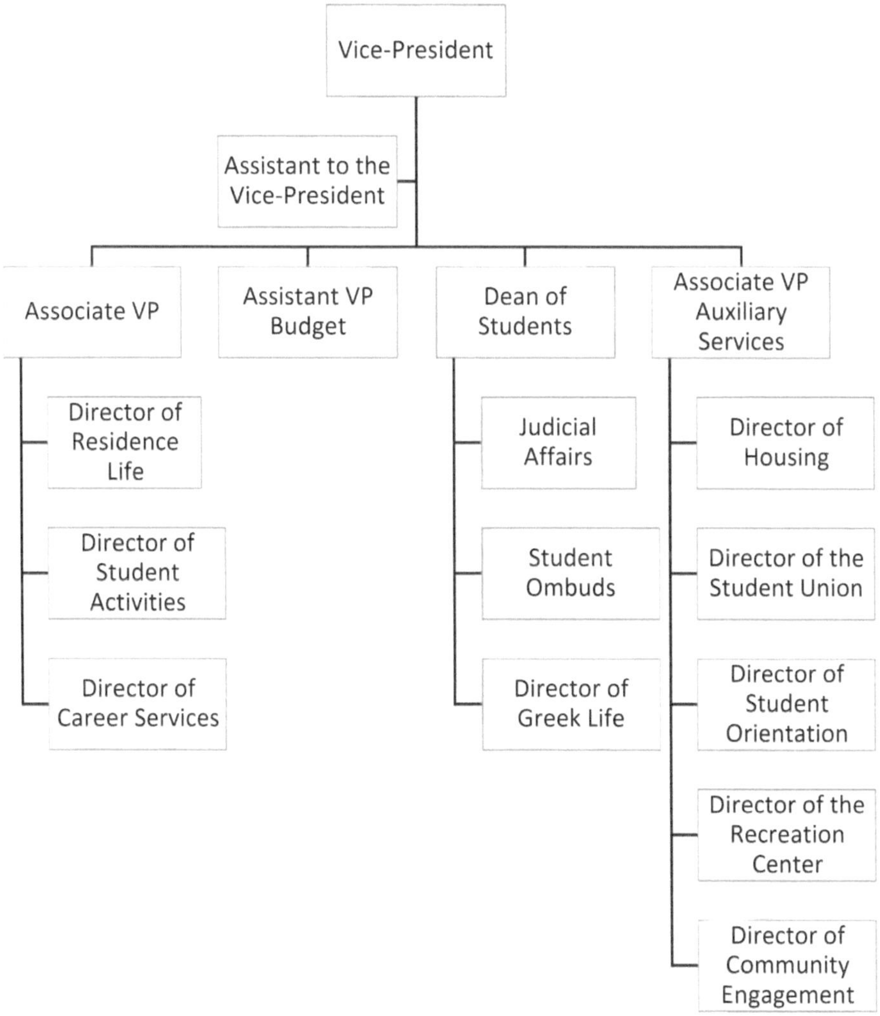

Figure 2.9 Student Affairs Model

functional areas within this division will also attach a user fee that is collected at the time the service is provided (e.g., admission to events, such as concerts). Typically, the fees collected are not intended to cover the entire cost of the activity or event but rather serve as a partial user fee which helps the unit defray the costs of the production.

Auxiliary Services

An auxiliary service is a unit on campus that is supposed to be self-sufficient, i.e., it must generate enough revenue through fees to cover its expenses. The most common auxiliary units on a campus are Student Housing, the Student Center (union), Recreational Services, and Parking Services. These auxiliary services do not have a separate vice-president but rather are generally found within the divisions of Student Affairs or Administrative Affairs, depending on the university's mission or operating philosophy. These units generate their revenues through user fees which are often built in to the student fee structure that all students pay. For example, many institutions charge students a fee for the recreation center whether the student uses that facility or not.

THE FOR-PROFIT SECTOR

For-profit or proprietary colleges and universities represent the fastest-growing sector within the postsecondary education industry. According to the NCES, in 2009 there were over 2,800 for-profit institutions with Title IV eligibility. This represents slightly more than 42 percent of all Title-IV-eligible institutions. Of these institutions, 1,043 were degree-granting colleges and universities.

These proprietary institutions are typically privately owned by an individual or family, or they are owned by a corporation which may be publicly traded. Two of the most well-known proprietary institutions, the University of Phoenix and DeVry University, are wholly owned subsidiaries of publicly traded companies. The University of Phoenix is owned by the Apollo Group, which also owns the College for Financial Planning, Insight Schools, the Institute for Professional Development, and Western International University. Similarly, DeVry University is owned by DeVry, Inc., which also owns Advanced Academics, Apollo College, Becker Professional Education, Chamberlain College of Nursing, Ross University, and Western Career College.

The organizational structures can vary widely depending on the ownership type. Many of the positions commonly found within the not-for-profit institutions are not necessarily present within the for-profit sector. However, many of the functions, such as marketing, recruitment and admissions, financial aid, and academic affairs are present. Two structures are shown below. Figure 2.10 represents a structure for the larger national (perhaps international) universities owned by corporations. Figure 2.11 represents a structure for a privately owned (individual or family) institution.

One of the primary reasons that for-profit institutions can actually generate a profit is that they are adept at keeping their costs down. Their tuition rates are actually at or

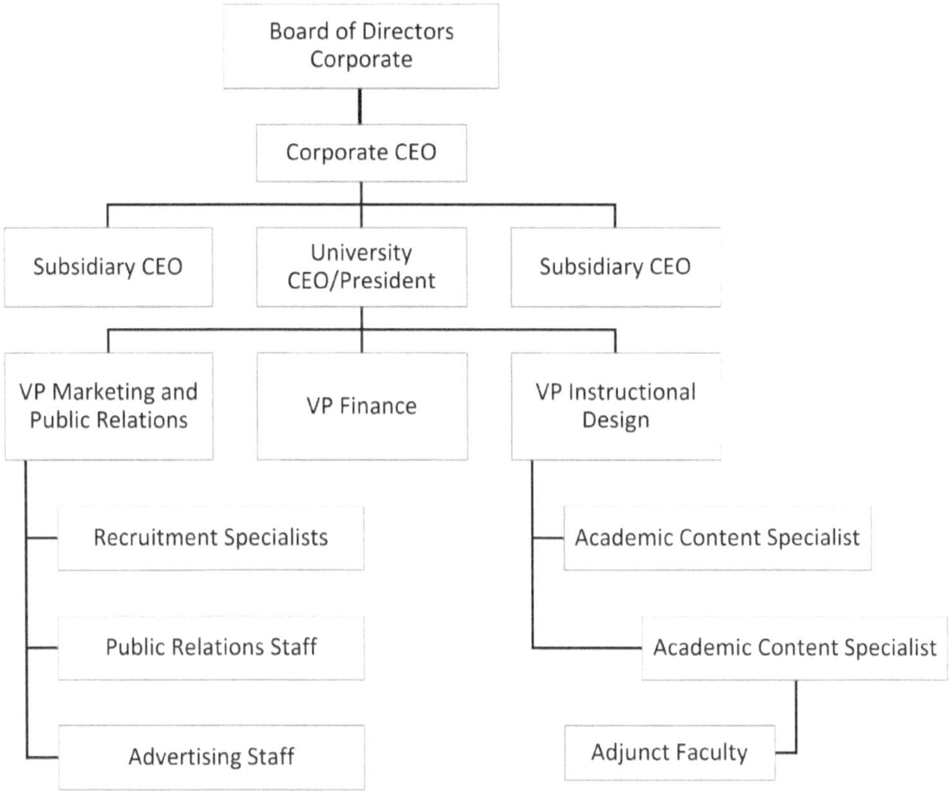

Figure 2.10 Corporate University Model

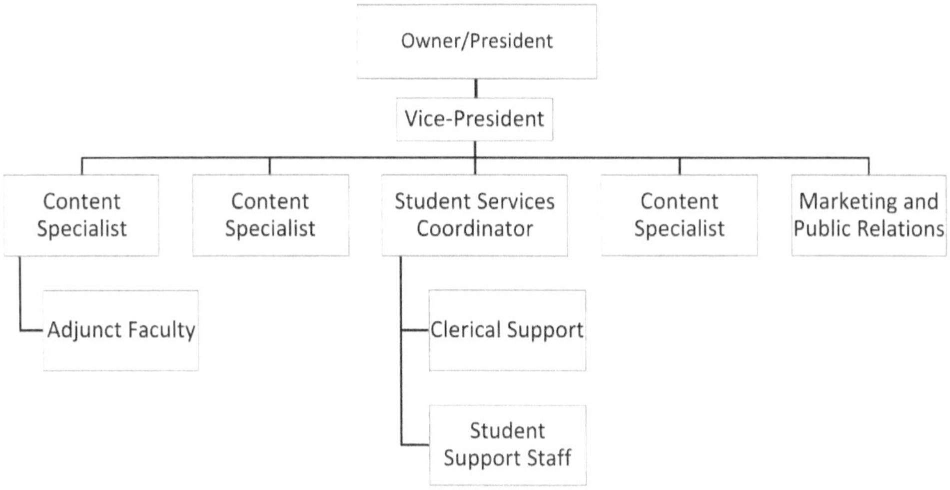

Figure 2.11 Privately Owned Institution Model

above the tuition charged at most state-supported institutions in the country, typically ranging from $300 to $500 per credit hour for undergraduate instruction. By charging a similar tuition but generating lower expenses they are able to earn a profit. They are able to keep their costs low because they minimize their course offerings by focusing on vocational or workforce skills; not providing amenities for their students such as extracurricular activities, housing, and recreation facilities; and generally not hiring full-time faculty.

CONCLUDING COMMENTS

This chapter described the structure of higher education in the United States—a decidedly non-system of "mass higher education" (Zusman, 2005, p. 128). Common elements of organizational hierarchy were also presented from both the not-for-profit sector and the for-profit sector. These hierarchies are influenced by their mission, funding, and intended audiences—with research universities having the largest organizational hierarchies, and small private liberal arts colleges having the smallest. The unique nature of for-profit education clearly impacts their organization.

However, no discussion of higher education institutions would be complete without addressing Robert Birnbaum's (1988) alternative way of looking at these institutions. He believed that framing the institution in light of its governance and communication model, or models of organizational functioning rather than the actual organizational structure, would give the viewer a more realistic perspective as to how the institution(s) actually works.

Birnbaum (1988) described four models he believed best depict how colleges and university function. He then added a fifth model which was put forth as an integrated way for institutions to operate. A collegial model places emphasis on shared governance, consensus, and shared values—and de-emphasizes hierarchy. To some readers, this may resemble a small private liberal arts college. A bureaucratic model has more structure and a greater sense of a "pecking order," and emphasizes rules, policies, procedures, and roles—and relationships are defined and experienced more formally. Community colleges often emulate some of these characteristics. A political model is more fractured, with groups operating in competition within the existing hierarchy; in this model relationships are interdependent but competitive and the president has a great deal of power. The reader may notice some similarities between this model and the operations of public non-flagship colleges and universities. An anarchical model is more decentralized, with units operating autonomously from one another, held together by status and symbols. Anarchical institutions pursue numerous, possibly conflicting goals, and as a consequence decisions or changes in one area may negatively impact another. Finally, a cybernetic model emphasizes integration across the institution, with a balance of hierarchy and collegiality, autonomy with cross-unit feedback and collaboration, and institutional goals being largely defined by the subunits' goals. In these organizations, change is slow, but change does occur.

Birnbaum did qualify his descriptions by stating that "no model illuminates all aspects of any institution all of the time, and every model illuminates some aspect of every institution some of the time" (p. 84). This basic understanding of one's institution will assist new administrators in navigating the complexities of their institutions by providing a starting point from which the administrator can develop collaborative relationships. No two institutions are alike, and therefore no two institutions will function in the same manner. The remainder of this book will discuss different business concepts, which are better understood when considered alongside the organization itself. Organizational structures have implications for accounting, budgeting, and human resource functions, and are a critical tool for managers as they plan, organize, lead, and control operations.

REFLECTIVE QUESTIONS

1. Which organizational model(s) best describes your institution?
2. Where do you sit within the institutional hierarchy and how does this seat impact your ability to communicate effectively with your colleagues?
3. Describe the functioning of the state-wide governing board(s) in your state. How effective is this body?
4. How does the organizational structure impact the functioning of individual institutions? Does tax status matter (profit/not-for-profit)?

PART 2

Finance and Funding

CHAPTER 3

Economic Principles

Economics is the study of choice-making and is based on the assumption that "individuals act to make themselves as well off as possible" (Wheelan, 2010, p. 6). Human beings have been making decisions like this since the dawn of time. Choice-making is part of our DNA—and the individuals who made the smartest choices are the ones who have descendants alive today (Guyenet, 2017). The most important of decisions for our earliest ancestors revolved around food—which serves as a great, straightforward example in this case. The foods that *best* served our ancestors were high-calorie foods that could be obtained with minimal effort and time expended. In economics jargon, this is called *maximizing utility*.

Another way to describe the practice of choice-making is *optimization*—individuals attempt to maximize the value obtained in relation to the resources expended. Institutions do the same, attempting to allocate financial and other resources to maximize institutional benefit. Institutions, like individuals, have different preferences and therefore attempt to maximize utility differently. In making these decisions, individuals and institutions accept that decisions involve trade-offs (Wheelan, 2010). For example, one can get a cheeseburger at a local fast-food restaurant for five dollars, or at a local gastropub (free-range, organic grass-fed beef with bacon marmalade, arugula greens, artisan cheese, and a fried egg on a pretzel bun) for fifteen dollars. One person may opt for the fast-food variety while another opts for the gastropub version. Both individuals will likely believe they maximized their utility due to individual preferences.

Optimization and maximization are important economic concepts in the study of higher education, as they serve as a lens through which to consider policies and student enrollment choices. These can be considered from a focused perspective (micro level) or a wide perspective (macro level). Examples of micro-level issues are: an individual student's decision if *and where* to attend college, an institution's decision on how many students to admit (and in time, enroll) at a given tuition rate, and a state or grant-providing agency's decision on which institution will receive funding, and how much. Examples of macro-level economic issues include: the decisions of groups of students to enroll (or not); the aggregate interplay of tuition levels and enrollment; institutional competition for students, faculty, and resources; and state- and federal-level policies to increase or decrease support to institutions or incentives for students to enroll.

From a higher education perspective, we are also involved in a world economy. While not as volatile as the world oil or financial markets, it is no less of a world market. Students have the opportunity to study in almost every country in the world (provided they have the means). The European Union has made it easier for residents of participating nations to cross borders for academic preparation. Australia and New Zealand have joined the competition for international students and China and India are beginning to promote academic opportunities in their countries as well. This world economy is impacted daily by basic economic principles that many of us may never have considered.

Many within the academy have the impression that higher education is immune to the economic principles of the world. They could not be further from the truth. Basic economic principles impact not only individual institutions but higher education as a whole on both a daily basis and a long-term basis. Archibald and Feldman (2011) explain, "a driving engine of rising cost in higher education is economic growth itself" (p. 49). In the pages that follow, some of the basic economic principles will be described and their impact on higher education will be discussed. Concepts such as optimization, markets, supply and demand, marginality, economies of scale and scope, and elasticity impact everyday decision-making. If understood and used appropriately these principles may be utilized by individual institutions or higher education systems to increase efficiency in everyday operations and provide insight into their short- and long-term planning strategies.

A FEW DEFINITIONS

The following definitions can be found in most economics textbooks and many have become part of our everyday language; in this case, they are largely drawn from Locke Anderson, Putaliaz, and Shepherd (1983) and Toutkoushian and Paulsen (2016) unless otherwise specified.

It is important to understand that *economics* is a social science focused on production, exchange, and consumption in a system in which resources are limited and the consumer has choices. Simply stated, it is about comparing alternatives and choosing among them. When considering higher education, students have numerous choices: institutional location, institutional type, and what academic discipline to study. This multitude of alternatives helps frame higher education as an economic system.

Economists also study the relative value of *incentives* in affecting the behavior of decision-makers. Incentives are changes to policies to provide a special benefit to change behaviors. Federal, state, and local government appropriations (an incentive) come with compliance requirements, and are a critical component of public institution budgets, comprising 44 percent of two-year colleges' and 20 percent of four-year colleges' revenues in 2012–2013 (Johnson, 2016). Policy changes in higher education (such as late registration fines) are attempts by institutions to encourage more positively-viewed behaviors (such as registering early). Another often-used incentive by states is grant programs for institutions or high-performing students to make up for scarce resources (Johnson, 2016).

Scarcity is the fundamental economic condition. The resources available to produce goods and services are limited, so most goods themselves are scarce (Locke Anderson et al., 1983). Most individuals have a variety of wants or desires—but usually also have limited resources. The scarcer a good or service, the greater the perceived value in the market (Pfeffer, 1992) and the greater the price a consumer will be willing to pay (e.g., precious metals, luxury goods). In higher education we see this in our "highly selective" institutions.

Optimization behavior, or *self-interest*, is considered by economists to be the primary motive of households and firms. This means that individuals and corporations attempt to maximize their satisfaction within the limits of their income. *Satisfaction* is also referred to as *utility*.

Rational behavior is assumed by economists; this means that decision-makers are acting in accordance to their self-interests and making rational decisions as they work to deploy their scarce resources—though it is known that what is rational to one person is not rational to another (Wheelan, 2010).

An *economy* is a system in which the production and distribution of goods and services are organized around people's needs and wants. *Markets* are defined as niches within an industry; higher education is an industry containing several markets. Higher education markets can be defined a variety of ways; usually the institutions within a market are seen by consumers as substitutes for one another. That is, the institutions are different, but the experience is similar in a meaningful way (institutional prestige, degrees offered, programs of study available, campus setting) (Becker & Toutkoushian, 2015). Economists use specific markets as the foundation for evaluating supply and demand.

Demand is the relationship between the price that is charged and the quantity of the product or service provided. When demand is analyzed it is from the consumer or buyer's side of the market for the service or product in question. "The general conclusion from the literature is that the demand for postsecondary education is relatively unaffected by price changes" (Toutkoushian & Paulsen, 2016, p. 152). While overall demand may be unaffected by price, different higher education markets have different price sensitivity (or elasticity).

Supply is the total quantity of a good or service that is available for purchase at a given price, and when analyzed it is from the producer or seller's side of the market. The quantity of services can be conceptualized as the number of seats, credit hours, or some other indicator of volume.

Elasticity refers to consumers' and producers' willingness to consume or produce (respectively) additional units of a product or service as the price changes. Consumption or production of items said to be *inelastic* are not sensitive to price, while items with *elasticity* are sensitive to price. Another way to think of elasticity is how flexible demand or supply is in relation to price changes. The more elastic demand is for an item, the more the quantity demanded will change (downward or upward) in response to price changes (increases or decreases). The more elastic supply is for an item, the more producers will adjust (downward or upward) in response to price changes (decreases or increases).

Marginal revenue is the change in revenue resulting from the sale of one more unit of output. For example, this could refer to the additional revenue generated when one more student enrolls in your institution.

Marginal cost is the change in cost resulting from the production of one more unit of output. For example, this could refer to the additional costs generated when one more student enrolls in your institution.

Marginal utility is the amount of utility obtained by the addition of one more unit of the good or service desired; this decreases as the number of units obtained increases.

Opportunity cost is a term used to describe what value must be exchanged (money, time) in order to obtain something of value. It is called an *opportunity* cost, because when you select one option, you choose to forego other potential opportunities.

While there are many other terms that will be used and discussed, the terminology above includes some of the most common terms used by higher education stakeholders.

MARKETS

The word "market" can be used to describe a specific niche of higher education or a broader one. The higher education industry differs widely by country (due to options, focus, level of control) and across the states within (Archibald & Feldman, 2011; Becker & Toutkoushian, 2015). Therefore, it is possible to describe higher education markets in a variety of ways: local, regional, national, and international. Understanding the market your institution inhabits is important for considering your competition. The market under consideration defines the competitors and the attributes on which one can compete (Becker & Toutkoushian, 2015; Clotfelter & Rothschild, 1993), although the notion of having to compete makes some people uncomfortable. Competition is a given in higher education; institutions engage in competitive practices in recruiting students, hiring faculty and administrators, fundraising, applying for grants, and obtaining state funding.

A market for a given product or service is strongly affected by the number of competitors and how easy (or difficult) it is to gain entry to the market (Toutkoushian & Paulsen, 2016). Markets with few competitors are described as *monopolies*, where a producer holds most of the power over price and barriers to entry are therefore high; in *oligopolies* a small number of producers are available, and their decisions affect each other (such as pricing, mix of products and services); and in *monopolistic competition* many producers exist, it is simpler to gain entry, and the actions of one producer may not have a direct consequence or effect on another.

Becker and Toutkoushian (2015) note that while institutions of higher education share many characteristics, there are many different product markets based on degree and areas of study. Institutions differ by mission as related to teaching, research, and service, and this further separates institutions into distinct markets. Despite institutional uniqueness, there is still sufficient institutional homogeneity in institutional focus and policy to allow some institutions to considered substitutes for one another within markets. Becker and Toutkoushian (2015) classify markets by the highest degree offered, but identify other characteristics that can be used to understand higher education markets. These characteristics include: number of competitors, number of degrees awarded, institutional control (public or private), tax status (for-profit or not-for-profit), prestige level (high prestige, low prestige, or seeking prestige), and where their students come from. These characteristics may impact tuition, the practice of tuition discounting, the information provided to consumers, and the degree to which certain services are offered (i.e., instruction, academic support, student services, extra-curricular activities, and the student experience on campus and nearby).

SUPPLY AND DEMAND

Within higher education individual institutions are both producers and consumers, so in the discussion that follows we clarify which side of the market is being discussed. As defined earlier, *demand* is the relationship between the price that is charged and the quantity of the product or service that will be purchased at that price and *supply* is the quantity of a good or service made available for purchase. Both are illustrated graphically as lines on a graph where price is the vertical axis and quantity is the horizontal axis.

The demand curve is a downward sloping line where the *quantity demanded* refers to a particular point on the curve, while *demand* refers to the entire curve. Figure 3.1 represents a single student's point of view, evaluating the quantity of credits they will register for based on tuition price—but institutions can use this to forecast the total credit registration at varying tuition thresholds if they understand the slope of their demand curve. *A change in quantity demanded* refers to movement along the curve; in the example above a change in price would either reduce the number of credit hours selected or increase it. Movement along the demand curve is caused by a change in price (Locke Anderson et al., 1983). A change in the *market conditions* (total demand) could cause a shift of the entire demand curve to the right if it is an increase (if the population desiring the good or service increases) or to the left if it is a decrease in demand (if the population desiring the good or service decreases).

The supply curve is an upward sloping line where the *quantity supplied* refers to a particular point on the curve, while *supply* refers to the entire curve. Figure 3.2

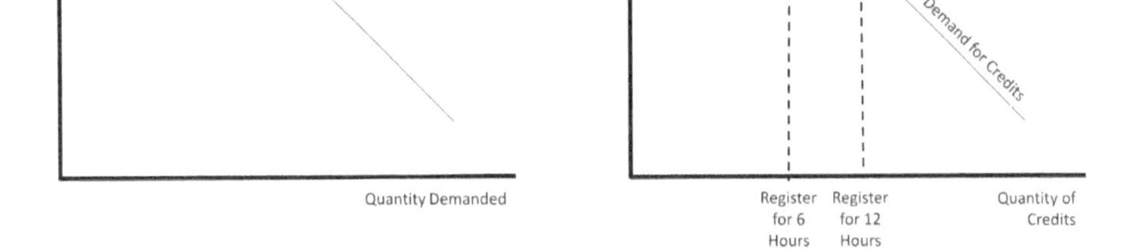

Figure 3.1 Demand

represents the institution's point of view—the total number of credit hours supplied at different price points. *A change in quantity supplied* refers to movement along the curve; in the example below a change in supply would either reduce the number of credit hours or increase it, depending on the direction in supply change. Theoretically, movement along the supply curve can *only* be caused by a change in price (Locke Anderson et al., 1983). A change in the *market conditions* (total supply) could cause a shift of the entire supply curve downward and to the right to reflect an increase (new suppliers enter the market or a change in capacity of existing suppliers) or left and upward to represent a decrease (a reduction of suppliers in the market or a change in capacity of existing suppliers).

These curves represent a specific relationship between the price and the quantity of the good or service: as the price increases, the quantity of an item demanded will decrease while the quantity supplied will tend to increase. Where the two curves

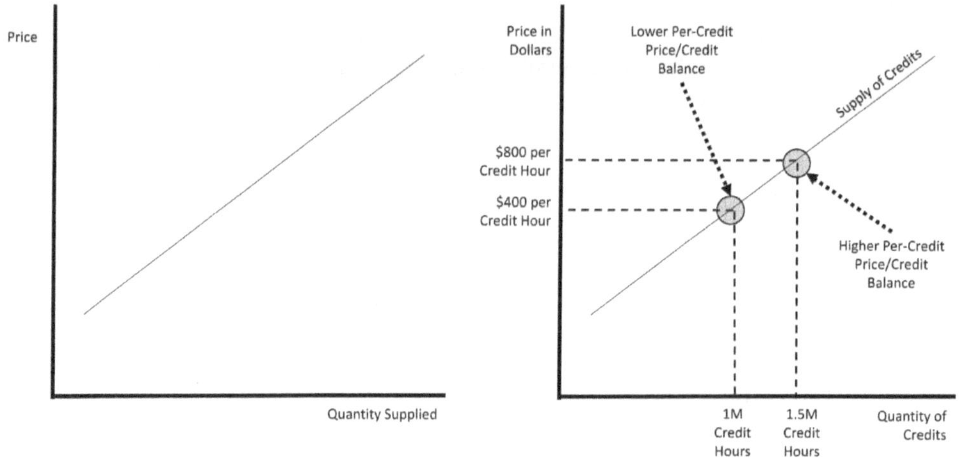

Figure 3.2 Supply

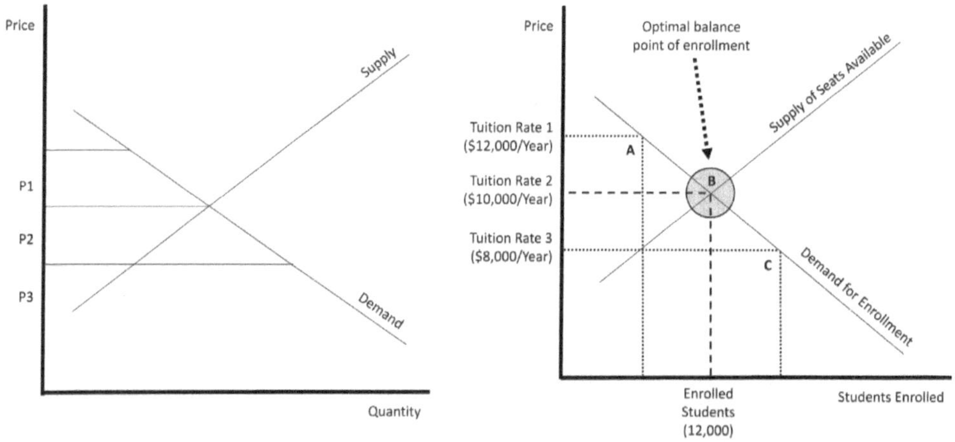

Figure 3.3 Demand and Supply

intersect (see Figure 3.3) is the equilibrium point which represents the price where the consumers are willing to purchase the same quantity that the producers are willing to supply. The more a consumer is willing to pay, the greater likelihood that the supplier is willing to offer more for sale. Similarly, the greater the price the greater the likelihood that the consumer will purchase less.

In Figure 3.3, three pricing scenarios are presented—only tuition rate 2 (P2 in the conceptual example), where supply and demand intersect, is efficient for an institution. When supply is presented in excess of demand, seats go unfilled. When an institution fails to meet demand, it does not enroll enough students. If the institution sets tuition above the equilibrium price (B), demand will fall short of supply—not enough students will be willing to pay the higher tuition rate (as shown in point A). If an institution sets tuition below the optimal rate (as shown in point C), its demand will be in excess of its supply. This means not enough seats will be available.

Shifts in Demand

In higher education, for the demand curve to shift there must be a change in the population, which includes the market being served. Over the years there have been several shifts in demand for higher education; for example, after World War II, the GI Bill provided economic incentives for returning military personnel to enroll in postsecondary education. This represented an increase in demand, shifting the demand curve outward. Similarly, we saw another outward shift in the demand curve when the children of the baby boom generation came of age in the 1960s and 1970s. We also witnessed a downward shift in demand during the late 1970s and 1980s when the baby boomers were through the system and the next generation was significantly smaller. Figure 3.4 represents a demand curve at a period of high demand (D1) and then a retraction of the market, or, a reduction in demand (D2). In the example, one curve depicts the demand when baby boomers entered college and the line labeled "1970/80s Demand" depicts the decrease in demand after the boomers left college.

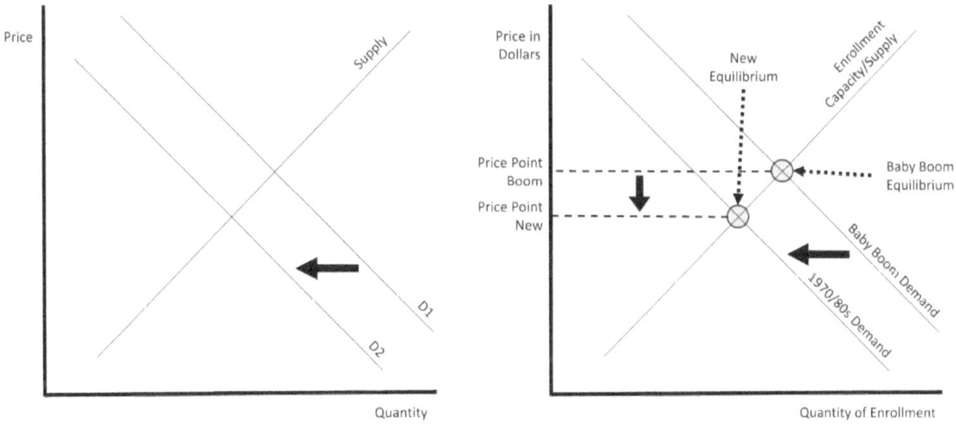

Figure 3.4 Demand Shift

Another way for the population to "change" is for there to be a change in viable substitutes, thereby increasing or decreasing the available population. For example, when the economy is booming there may be ample employment opportunities for individuals without a postsecondary education. In this scenario, many high school graduates may choose to enter the workforce rather than attend college, thereby decreasing the population available to attend college. Likewise, there are other substitutes, such as the military or short-term certificate or training programs. As these options appear more attractive, fewer individuals may choose to participate in higher education.

Toutkoushian and Paulsen (2016) also suggest demand can shift due to changes in "incomes of students and their families, the prices of competing institutions, the consumptive benefits of college, and the number of students in the market" (p. 166). At an institutional level, perhaps your basketball team makes it to the Final Four as a Cinderella story and you have a great mascot. These *positive* changes could lead to increased demand in the form of more students wishing to enroll at your institution, as shown by applications for admission. Demand can shift upward when the population increases, the economy slows (removing substitutes), more financial aid becomes available, and so on. Conversely, a demand curve can shift downward (to the left) if demand drops—a new competitor, a competitor that lowers tuition, or a major public relations scandal, such as losing accreditation. These would cause shifts in the demand curve for an institution, just like the reduction in college-age students in the 1970s and 1980s affected total demand for higher education.

Theoretically, these shifts in demand should make the price go up or down respectively, changing the equilibrium point, assuming there is not a simultaneous shift in the supply curve. In Figure 3.4, D1 represents the original demand curve, and D2 represents a decrease in demand. As you can see in the accompanying example, the price point is higher with the boom in demand, and lower in the post-boom era, demonstrating that if there is no change in supply, as demand increases the price will increase, and if the demand decreases the price should decrease. Between 2026 and 2031, graduation rates are expected to decrease 9 percent nationally, which will have a large but uneven impact on demand for higher education (Selingo, 2018). If the proportion of graduating high school students attending colleges increases, the effects may be less palpable—but that is not a given, according to Grawe (2018).

Shifts in Supply

An increase or decrease in quantity produced is merely movement along the existing supply curve. In order for the supply curve to shift there must be a change in the number of suppliers in the market. The quantity of services can be conceptualized as the number of seats or credit hours, or some other indicator of volume (Toutkoushian & Paulsen, 2016). The angle of a supply curve for a specific institution would vary depending on whether it was open-enrollment (open-access) or using a selective admission process—but in the aggregate higher education markets demonstrate a sloping line. The curve is influenced by appropriations from state (or local) governments, internal costs for faculty and staff, and technology.

The best way to conceptualize this in higher education is more institutions entering the market. In the 1880s, with the passing of the Morrill Acts, agricultural and mechanical arts colleges were created, which caused a shift in the overall higher education supply curve. Then in the early 1900s we saw the development of the "Normal Schools" to train teachers, and again in the 1960s there was an explosion of growth in the community college sector. All of these resulted in shifts (to the right) of the supply curve. Most recently we have seen several new institutions being built in California, Florida, and several other southern states, once again shifting the supply curve. All of these increases in supply would result in a shift of the supply curve to the right and downward. If, in the unlikely event that the United States were to experience a number of institutional closures (with no additions), we would witness a decrease in supply shifting the curve, as if going back toward S1, or the pre-Morrill Acts position, in Figure 3.5.

Figure 3.5 shows the original supply curve (S1) with two other curves representing the explosive growth of providers (S2, S3). As you can see, if there is not a corresponding shift in the demand curve an increase in supply will cause a reduction in price, while a reduction in supply will cause an increase in price. As the price moves so does the quantity demanded.

Figures 3.4 and 3.5 are focused on the national and regional (macro) level and have not considered individual institutions. At the local or institutional (micro) level, supply and demand are also important concepts. The implications can be far reaching, beginning with the admissions or enrollment management process, impacting the scheduling of classes and the assignment of residence hall rooms, among other aspects. If fewer students are graduating from feeder high schools, then one should expect less demand for the education being provided. Likewise, if there is an increase in graduating seniors one should similarly expect an increase in demand. Significant swings in student enrollment impact many other operations within the institution, especially if the institution is tuition-driven.

Applying Supply and Demand Theory

Seismic shifts are on the horizon in higher education due to demographic changes, according to Grawe (2018). Using advanced economic analysis outside the scope of

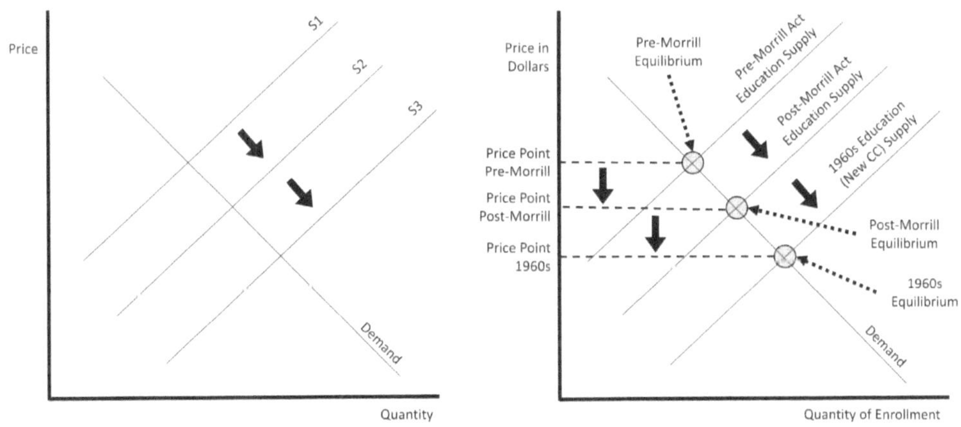

Figure 3.5 Supply Shift

this particular book, Grawe crafted the Higher Education Demand Index, which uses as inputs a variety of demographic factors. He notes the recent economic challenges, decline in birthrates, demographic shifts, migration patterns within the United States, and other critical factors that will reduce the demand for higher education in future. Not only are the actual numbers of graduating high school students predicted to vary by region, but within each region, graduating students have different likelihoods of pursuing higher education which are influenced by family income, parental education, race, and ethnicity. He cautions that institutions will need to make changes to serve their students properly.

But how does one do that with the limited population? A good example is to look back at what happened in the 1970s with regard to attracting non-traditional students to campuses and the increased effort put into recruiting international students. So today, one solution may be to aggressively recruit students from the regions of the country that have excess demand. This may work in the short term but is not necessarily a good long-term strategy for the average institution. Students typically prefer to stay within 200 miles or so of their family residence, which means that as soon as the local supply is increased they will most likely return to the local institutions. Another option is to emulate the elite colleges. Grawe (2018) estimates that highly selective institutions will not feel the same loss in demand—but will likely not increase their class sizes, so institutions who can successfully emulate the elite brands may attract students aiming for this type of experience. Regardless of the exact institutional prestige position or region, colleges will need to make changes.

On the academic side (and on the micro level) one can see how demand and supply play out with regard to course scheduling and staffing. When there are more students interested in a particular course than seats available, there is excess demand based on the current supply. In order to meet that demand we would need to increase the supply by offering additional sections of the class, shifting the supply curve to the right. Adding course sections (and hiring adjunct instructors to cover them) has budget implications. If additional course sections are not possible you may be able to find a larger classroom, creating more seats within the existing section. This is also movement along the supply curve. Another alternative could be to offer a substitute for this particular course. Perhaps you have a few low-enrollment classes (an over-supply or excess capacity) that you can encourage students to take by letting them substitute one of those sections for the oversubscribed course. Another option could be to encourage students to take the same or a similar class at a nearby institution and transfer the credits back to your institution if doing so would save your institution money in the long run.

At the macro level one could argue that there is an over-supply of educational opportunities available to individuals seeking a postsecondary education. This argument looks at the percentage of high school graduates who attend postsecondary institutions. Census data indicates that in 2017, 67 percent of recent high school completers had enrolled in some form of higher education; 44 percent enrolled at four-year institutions and 23 percent at two-year institutions (NCES, 2018, Table 302.10). The excess supply (having more spots in classrooms than there are interested students) has unintentionally placed individual institutions in the position of reducing their admissions requirements in an effort to fill classroom seats. This lowering of standards has created a bifurcated system that has a large number of institutions with selective admissions and an increasing number of seemingly open-admission institutions.

On the surface, supply and demand appear logical and help to explain some of what happens with college enrollments. However, when economists look at these models they more often than not invoke the term "*ceteris paribus*", which translates into "everything else staying constant". In other words, if an institution raises its price (tuition) the demand for the institution should decrease, assuming that there are no other environmental changes that might influence consumer demand. To the non-economist this does not sound reasonable. After all, when does everything else stay constant?

Demand and supply do not tell the whole story, or else tuition increases would reduce enrollment. Data comparing tuition rates and enrollment paint a clear picture of this counterintuitive reality. Although between 1970 and 2015 net tuition and fees increased (in constant dollars) 288 percent at four-year public institutions, and 221 percent at private institutions (NCES, 2018, Table 330.10 – 2016), enrollment has increased 133 percent in the same period, as shown in Figure 1.1. For higher education, there is more to the demand for these services than price alone. Historically, higher education has acted counter-cyclically to the economy. As the economy goes down, enrollments go up more quickly; as the economy improves, the rate of growth for higher education slows. Hence, if potential students can find a well-paying job without a college degree they are often very likely to take the position and forego their education; if there are not many good opportunities some individuals will choose to attend college in the hopes of positioning themselves better for the opportunities that do exist. There is also a societal component—the post-World War II generations viewed higher education as the fast track to a life in the middle or upper-middle class.

Price Elasticity of Demand

As discussed previously, when the price of an item changes the quantity of demand for that item also changes. The rate of that change is called the price elasticity of demand (commonly known as price elasticity). Understanding the price elasticity of an item can be very helpful in predicting how large an impact price changes will have on the quantity demanded. For example, if the price of coffee suddenly increased by 50 percent would consumers purchase 50 percent less? Or would their purchases be reduced by a greater or smaller percentage? This is what elasticity helps us estimate.

The higher the price elasticity, the more sensitive consumers are to price changes. An elasticity that is very high indicates that when the price increases, typical consumers will purchase much less of it, and when the price decreases, they will

$$\text{Price Elasticity of Demand} = \frac{\text{\% Change in Quantity Demanded}}{\text{\% Change in Price}}$$

purchase more. A low price elasticity (price *inelastic*) implies that changes in price have little influence on demand. If the price elasticity of demand is:

- Greater than "1", then demand is *price elastic* (demand is sensitive to price changes)
- Equal to "1", then demand is *unit elastic* (a 1 percent increase in price = a 1 percent decrease in demand)
- Less than "1", then demand is *price inelastic* (demand is not sensitive to price changes)
- Equal to "0", then demand is *perfectly inelastic* (demand does not respond to changes in price)

There are several factors that influence elasticity of demand of specific goods and services. First among these is the level of essentiality of the item. If the item in question is a necessity it becomes very difficult to eliminate from one's life, thereby making it relatively inelastic and mostly unresponsive to changes in price. If the item becomes extremely expensive consumers will attempt to reduce their consumption, but in all likelihood they will not be able to eliminate their need. For example, the fluctuations in gasoline prices may be quite irritating to many consumers but if they believe they still need to drive to and from work there is not much they can do in the short run. Thus, the price elasticity of demand for gasoline is relatively inelastic. In the long run they can purchase more fuel-efficient vehicles, reduce their consumption, and adjust their reliance on gasoline.

A second factor to consider is the availability of substitutes for the item in question. The more substitutes available, the more elastic the demand for a specific item or service provider. In the gasoline price example, the frustrated consumer could consider riding a bike to work, carpooling, or perhaps even switching to public transportation instead of driving themselves to work in a car alone. For higher education there are not a great many substitutes available to the general public that can help improve one's potential for economic gain at a micro level. The most popular substitutes are joining the military service or the workforce.

Third, elasticity also can be influenced by how substantial the item is in relation to the household budget; items that do not constitute a large percentage of an overall budget are generally price inelastic (they will still be purchased if prices increase), but expensive items are a different case (Toutkoushian & Paulsen, 2016). In higher education, price elasticity of demand varies by institution type and by the affluence of students they enroll. An institution that enrolls low-income students will have higher price elasticity (price increases reduce demand) unless the tuition is sufficiently low enough to comprise only a small proportion of the household budget.

How do these three factors of price elasticity influence higher education? First, is higher education a necessity? On the one hand most in academe would agree that higher education is not a necessity; therefore, it should tend toward being somewhat elastic. While it is very desirable it is not necessary. On the other hand, most Americans would argue that a college education is the fastest and most dependable way to assure oneself a middle- or upper-middle-class lifestyle. So while it may not be a necessity in the truest sense it is treated as such by many, especially those in the middle and upper brackets of socioeconomic status. These individuals want to maintain or improve their status and see higher education as the best way to accomplish that. Therefore, higher education will tend toward acting in an inelastic way, meaning that demand for education will not change much based on price.

As for the second factor, availability of substitutes, if an individual needs or desires a bachelor's degree in a specific discipline there really is not a good substitute. However, if we look at the macro picture, there are a few substitutes for a four-year degree—one could obtain a two-year degree, join the armed services, go directly into the workforce, or perhaps begin an apprenticeship. With few substitutes currently available, higher education will tend toward acting in an inelastic way once again, meaning that demand for education will not change much based on price. This could change, of course: if employers become more open to alternative credentials and employer-hosted workforce education, the higher education market could have even more substitutes (Society for College and University Planning, 2018).

The third factor, the percentage of household income being spent on higher education, can be viewed as simultaneously elastic and inelastic depending on one's current socioeconomic status. Tuition has, in recent years, represented a higher proportion of median family income (Zumeta, Breneman, Callan, & Finney, 2012). Those who are in the middle and upper brackets of socioeconomic status will tend to view higher education as relatively inelastic while those in the lower and lower-middle classes may generally treat higher education as quite elastic. Therefore, significant price changes in higher education will disproportionately impact lower-income households. While estimates of impact vary, researchers have found reductions in federal aid grant programs correspond with slower enrollment growth for low-income students. As federal aid programs decline due to a reduction in support, so does access to higher education for low-income families (Carlson, 2016; Protopsaltis & Parrott, 2017). Reductions in grant programs are also associated with lower persistence to graduation in low-income students, although the connections are complex.

On the macro level higher education as a whole appears to have a relatively inelastic demand curve in that changes in price do not have a significant impact on demand for higher education. As we have seen over the past several decades, the price of higher education has outpaced the rate of inflation, yet the demand for higher education continued to increase. However, on the micro level price elasticity of demand varies at an institution depending on the type of institution and its unique institutional characteristics. As presented in Figure 3.6, institutions that serve lower socioeconomic regions are more likely to see demand respond sensitively to changes in price (elastic). As price increases, demand for enrollment decreases. The price elasticity for elite, highly selective institutions is very different; as price increases, demand decreases only slightly, if at all (inelastic).

Price Elasticity of Supply

The price elasticity of supply measures the relationship between a change in price and the change in quantity supplied. This is viewed from the producer's perspective—in our case, the institution. How much am I willing to produce or how many students am I willing to admit at any given price? How many credits can be offered based on

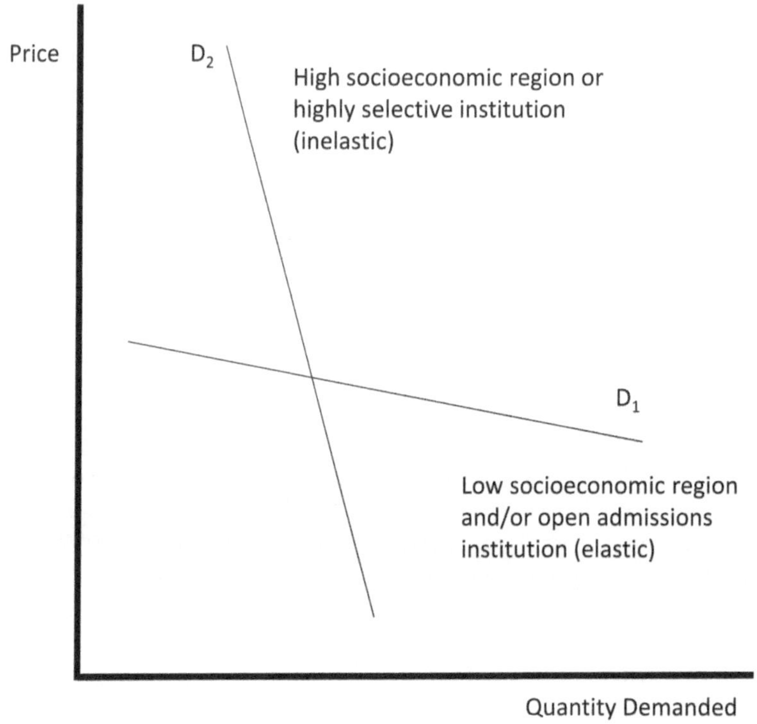

Figure 3.6 Demand Elasticity

$$\text{Price Elasticity of Supply} = \frac{\text{\% Change in Quantity Supplied}}{\text{\% Change in Price}}$$

the going rate for credits? Institutions that are more responsive to adjustments in the pricing are viewed as more competitive.

The higher the price elasticity, the more responsive institutions are to changes in price. An elasticity that is very high indicates that when the price *increases*, typical suppliers will produce *more* of it, and when the price *decreases*, they will produce *less*. A lower price elasticity implies that changes in price have little influence on supply. If the price elasticity of supply is:

- Greater than "1", then supply is *price elastic* (supply is responsive to price changes)
- Equal to "1", then supply is *unit elastic* (a 1 percent change in price = a 1 percent change in supply)
- Less than "1", then supply is *price inelastic* (supply is not responsive to price changes)
- Equal to "0", then supply is *perfectly inelastic* (does not respond to changes in price; e.g., highly selective institutions limit enrollment while at the same time increasing tuition)

Higher education as an industry (macro level) is somewhat elastic in supply, in that it can increase the supply relatively quickly because many institutions have excess capacity. They can admit more students, offer more class sections, and so on. If the demand for education increases and the potential students are mobile, an institution with excess capacity can be found to admit them. However, the reality is that not all students are mobile, which then creates more of a regional or local market. Therefore, on the micro level we will see slightly different rates of elasticity depending on the individual institutional characteristics (see Figure 3.7).

For example, highly selective institutions (Stanford, Yale, etc.) and those that cap enrollments at a set number are said to be perfectly inelastic with regard to the price elasticity of supply. No matter how much people are willing to pay, institutions like these will not change the supply (admit more students/raise the cap). On the other side we have open-enrollment institutions that, while not perfectly elastic, will continue to admit as many students as possible at the current price. At many institutions (especially public), when we have large increases in enrollments you will read about students living in residence hall lounges as well as classrooms that are bursting, sometimes with students sitting in the aisles.

It is important to point out here that in this section references to demand are not referring to applications to institutions but rather to the students who actually attend. On the micro level, institutions will typically admit far more students than they expect to attend because they understand that students apply to multiple institutions.

Figure 3.7 Supply Elasticity

The trick here is for the enrollment management staff to determine how many of the students admitted will actually enroll in the fall. The percentage of admitted students actually attending is called the "yield rate" and is a very important figure when trying to predict enrollments in future years.

COSTS IN HIGHER EDUCATION

Determining all of the costs associated with educating an individual student can be a challenge. The issues involve micro-level questions that need to be addressed at the individual institutional or departmental level. Tuition and fees do not represent the total cost of educating a student, as much of higher education is subsidized to some degree. The "sticker price" is only somewhat reflective of the cost of higher education; the balance of the cost must be met through subsidy and tuition discounts. As we look deeper into an institution's cost structure, we notice that there are several different types of costs and several ways to represent these costs. In this section several costs will be described, and they will be connected to the institutional level and in some cases to the program and perhaps even the student level.

When we consider the cost of educating a student, the simplest method of calculating/estimating that cost is to take the total cost of operating the institution and divide it by the number of students enrolled (TC/S); this will give you *a cost per student*. This treats all students the same regardless of their major, level of engagement, or special needs, or other extraneous costs. Even though it may not be the best method of determining the actual cost to educate a student, we still need to understand the concept of total cost and its basic sub-units by defining these costs and looking at them through an economic lens.

Total cost is what it costs to operate an institution at a particular level of enrollment. Simply stated, total cost is the sum of all the costs associated with operating the institution. If the institution is not experiencing fluctuations in enrollment (increases or decreases) then the total cost to operate will be equal to the institution's operating budget. Total cost can be divided into two portions: fixed costs and variable costs.

Fixed costs are financial obligations that must be met in the short run regardless of whether enrollments or other revenues increase or decrease. These are often referred to as overhead costs and include items such as: debt service or rent on buildings, interest on loans, tenured faculty and staff salaries, and utilities. The key here is that these costs do not change based on the volume of business or, in our case, the number of students enrolled *except in drastic cases.*

Variable costs are the part of the total cost that changes based on the institution's level of student enrollment. For example, if you add more students to housing there may be no cost increase for the bed space, provided you have a vacancy, but there will be a cost associated with the individual's meal plan, maintenance, and housekeeping, among other costs. On the academic side it may seem that the student can easily be absorbed into the system with no added costs, but when you look deeper the student will take advantage of resources that are available, such as advising, meeting with faculty members, and registering for classes, all of which have costs associated.

As a new administrator it is important for you to understand which costs you have some control over and which costs you will incur regardless of your budgeting expertise. Take a look at your current department or institution and determine which costs are fixed and which are variable.

Marginal cost (MC) in higher education is viewed as the cost to add one more student to the institution, department, class, residence hall, etc. In some cases the cost of adding one more student may be negligible, while in other situations the cost may be extraordinary. Perhaps there are open residence hall spaces or open seats in classes which need no additional costs to provide the service. Alternately, the institution may need to rent space in a local hotel to accommodate the new residential student or hire an additional instructor and open another section of the class to accommodate the additional student(s), thereby increasing costs.

Determining the actual costs associated with each decision is challenging and in many situations you will need to estimate or make your best guess. The use of economic theory and understanding these concepts allows you as the administrator to make a more informed decision. You must understand that it will be rare, if ever, that you will have complete information in a decision-making process. An essential piece of your role as a supervisor/administrator is to make an informed decision.

ECONOMIES OF SCALE AND SCOPE

In times of fiscal constraint, administrators are expected to help reduce the costs of educating students, and there are two economic concepts that can help reduce costs by increasing efficiency: economies of scale and economies of scope.

Economies of scale increase the scale of the production or service output without proportionately increasing costs (Lewis & Dundar, 2001), thereby causing the per-unit costs to decrease. In education the most visible example of this is when an institution puts several hundred students in a large lecture hall with one instructor. Typically, instructors do not get paid more for 200 students than for twenty students; therefore, the institution reduces its cost per student. This begs the question: What is the most economical way to deliver the course without compromising the academic integrity of the course and program or compromising the students' ability to actively engage in the material so they can co-produce a favorable learning outcome? If there are pedagogical reasons for limiting the class size then one must do so (e.g., few college faculty would want to teach a college writing class with fifty students). However, if the instructor lectures to students and gives multiple-guess tests, does it matter whether there are twenty-five or 250 students?

Examples of economy of scale outside the lecture hall can be found across institutions. An institution may decide to implement group-based academic advising for juniors and seniors, or housing may choose to increase the number of beds in their individual residence hall rooms. Look around your campus to see if you can find additional examples of economies of scale.

An *economy of scope* occurs when one uses the same resources of production to produce two or more different (usually complementary) products (Toutkoushian & Paulsen, 2016). In higher education this is also quite visible on the academic side when we see courses cross-listed or courses that fulfill the requirements for multiple majors. A campus can use this as an excellent way to reduce the redundancy in its curriculum. Typically, on larger campuses there are numerous examples of two or three different departments offering very similar courses within their respective majors. If these courses were to be combined and cross-listed the institution could eliminate the need for multiple sections of courses with much the same content. Likewise, this could be a way to avoid canceling similar classes in different departments that may be under-enrolled.

In student services, economies of scope may take the form of inviting the general public to participate in on-campus events (for a fee), thereby increasing their reach. Student unions are well-versed in economies of scope, often renting their facilities on evenings/weekends—but this practice can be extended to many campus facilities. Residence life units can utilize their living spaces to host off-campus conference and camp events, generating revenue at a time where fewer students are on campus.

It is prudent at this point to also mention that while economies of scale exist on our campuses and can help the institution become more efficient, there is also the possibility of creating a *diseconomy of scale*. This occurs when an increase in production causes per-unit costs to increase. You may have a new president who wants to increase enrollment and in doing so inadvertently increases per-student costs because you are now admitting more under-prepared students, which drives up instructional costs and adds supplemental education or tutoring costs as well. Or perhaps the administration decides to increase enrollment in your more selective majors, which drives up per-student costs because of the additional resources needed to provide the education. Therefore, prior to growing enrollments, there needs to be a discussion among faculty and administrators as to the type of student you will be targeting and what majors the institution is hoping to expand.

TUITION DISCOUNTING

The practice of offering discounted tuition or *institutional grants* is not new to higher education, although it is relatively new to public higher education. In the business sector this is commonly called price discrimination—charging different prices for the same item or service to different market segments. The most common application in the business world is the airline industry, where it is common to find two passengers sitting next to each other on a flight each having paid a different price for their seat depending on when or how the seats were purchased. While institutions do not advertise tuition discounts for different market segments, they do charge different tuitions based on internally defined characteristics. In higher education we are far more subtle in how we discriminate. Discounts can be given for a variety of reasons—athletic, academic, or other skills. The discount essentially functions as a coupon to the student, provided by the institution. The student receives a discount, and the institution pays the difference. Tuition discounting is used to shape incoming classes and ensure the institution has enough students to cover operations. At least, that is how it goes when it works as intended.

During the 2017–2018 academic year colleges and universities provided $60 billion in institutional grant aid for undergraduate and graduate students (Baum, Ma,

Pender, & Libassi, 2018, p. 3). In order to financially afford tuition discounting, the institution must set its tuition price higher than would be necessary if no discounts were offered. The actual discount comes in the form of an internal or institutionally funded grant to the student. This institutional funding comes from the monies generated by the students who pay full tuition, essentially subsidizing the non-full-paying students. For example, an institution may be trying to recruit more high-achieving students from rural high schools or more National Merit Finalists. In an effort to attract these students the institution will offer them an internally funded grant which effectively reduces their tuition/cost of attendance.

What makes this particularly challenging is the projected declining enrollments for the next decade. That means institutions are mortgaging their future to shape their incoming classes and meet their enrollment goals (Seltzer, 2017). The demographic shifts combined with spiraling "sticker prices" have led to a general discussion of whether the practice of offering tuition discounts is sustainable (Seltzer, 2016), although concerns with the practice have been raised for quite some time (Redd, 2000).

CONCLUDING COMMENTS

An understanding of these economic principles will not solve all of your institutional problems, but it should give you a better idea as to how significant an impact some decisions can have at your institution. Higher education is increasingly expensive, and to stay competitive institutions must be cognizant of the world in which they operate—and that world continues to evolve. The world economy influences the availability of government resources (Goldstein, 2012), and changes in the labor market and technology marketplace directly affect how colleges and universities operate (Selingo, 2016). While this is occurring, institutions will still compete with one another to attract, enroll, and retain students and faculty. Additionally, as you look at and gain a better understanding of the demographic shifts and changes occurring within the United States it becomes apparent that the demand for higher education may change, influencing the planning processes and recruitment strategies of numerous institutions.

It is crucial that leaders leverage knowledge of economic principles to think strategically about facing current and future challenges. The importance of understanding supply and demand is obvious, especially in light of demographic changes. Perhaps less obvious is the importance of the concepts of marginal costs and marginal revenues. Many of today's institutional leaders were hired on promises of enrollment growth, facilities development, and perhaps new academic programs—but consideration of marginal cost and marginal revenue, or MC and MR, is critical when considering enrollment, new programs, and their impact on the budget. Economies of scope and scale can be leveraged for both savings and generation of new revenue when institutions understand the MC and marginal revenue of programs and services. An increase in students on campus does not always translate into more money at the departmental levels. In today's economy, increasing quality by doing less with less (but doing it better) may be a better approach than doing more with less.

REFLECTIVE QUESTIONS

1. What markets does your institution currently operate within? What does that mean for your institution?
2. To whom does price of tuition matter? Why?
3. When you selected your undergraduate college, what factors were most important in maximizing your utility?
4. At your current institution (considering its selectivity, population served, and market conditions), how impactful would an increase in tuition price be on number of credit hours enrolled? Why?
5. What factors need to be included in a decision to build a new residence hall (for a campus with and for a campus without halls currently)?
6. How does an institution know if/when it is a good idea to enroll more students?

CHAPTER 4

Finance

Throughout the world, the percentage of the population participating in postsecondary education has risen rapidly over the past few decades. In the United States, the college-going rate of recent high school graduates has increased from 45.1 percent in 1960 to 69.2 percent in 2015 (NCES, 2018, Table 302.10 – 2016). This increase in demand is influencing the financing of education.

Government funding support for higher education is often seen as the centerpiece of a country's ability to participate in the twenty-first-century economy. Around the world, in countries that once provided free access to higher education, tuition is now being charged to make up for revenue shortfalls caused by reduced government support and increasing costs for technology, healthcare, and other important expenses (Michael, 2005). Table 4.1 illustrates the growing revenues of colleges and universities in the last three decades in the United States. The total revenue of postsecondary institutions in the United States approached $600 billion during the 2014–2015 academic year, making higher education one of the largest industries in the country.

Higher education is one of the few industries in which organizations are asked (sometimes required) to publicly justify their existence, or at least their funding. Elected officials throughout the country are asking tough questions of higher education institutions, and paramount on their minds is whether or not the public is getting an adequate return on its investment in education (McGee, 2015). The vast majority of colleges and universities in the United States receive some kind of local, state, or federal support. The largest form of government support comes through student

Table 4.1 Revenue

Year	*Public*	*Private Not-for-Profit*	*Private For-Profit*	*Total Revenue*
1994–1995*	119,312,493,039	69,808,077,432**		189,120,570,471
2004–2005	234,841,504,801	140,150,716,944	10,979,154,823	385,971,376,568
2014–2015	347,073,663,797	200,473,205,243	19,665,740,064	567,212,609,104

*Data from 1994–1995 have slight differences in labeling.

**Prior to the 2000s, data for private institutions were not broken out by profit status.

Sources: Data from NCES 2018 Digest of Education Statistics (tables listed). Public: 328 (1997) and 333.10 (2008, 2016). Private Not-for-Profit: 328 (1997) and 333.40 (2008, 2016). Private For-Profit: 328 (1997) and 333.55 (2008, 2016).

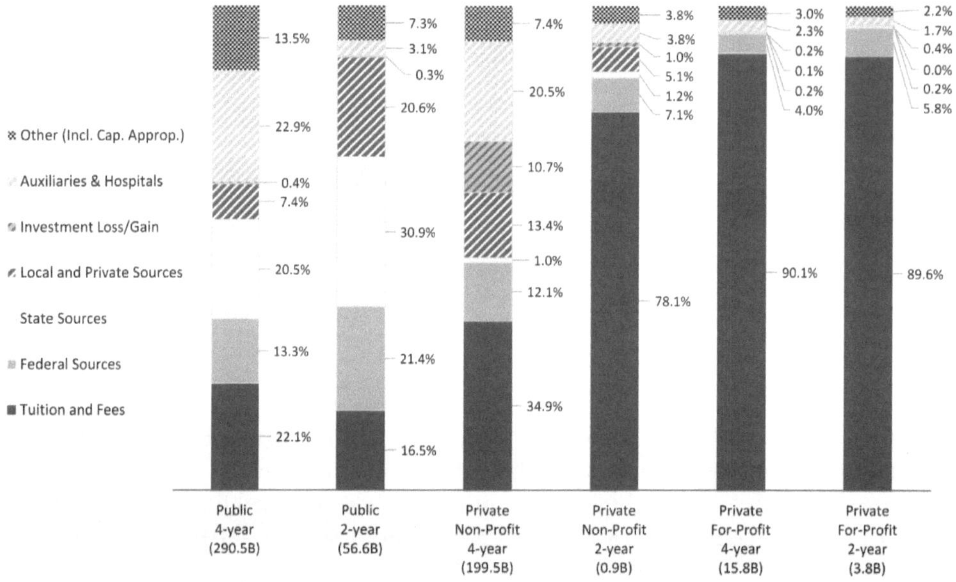

Figure 4.1 Revenue by Source, 2014–2015
Source: NCES, 2018, Tables 333.10, 333.40, 333.55.

financial aid (Title IV funding). Because of this funding, politicians have a vested interest in the success and overall well-being of postsecondary institutions, especially those in their legislative districts.

For the past several decades, much has been written about the need for a workforce that has been educated beyond the secondary level. Simultaneously, higher education has been criticized for being unresponsive to change, overloaded with duplicative programs and personnel, and careless with tuition (Dickeson, 2010). Although many of these critiques fall prey to a lack of understanding about the complexities and nature of higher education, we cannot ignore them (Archibald & Feldman, 2011). As the calls for accountability continue and continue, it becomes prudent for policy makers and institutional administrators to re-examine institutions and their finances. This is of particular importance as the federal government and state governments re-evaluate how to best allocate scarce resources. Higher education is a unique industry, and to serve as good fiscal stewards, administrators must understand its financial underpinnings.

REVENUES

Higher education institutions rely on multiple sources of revenue to fund their respective missions. For most institutions, the primary revenue sources are tuition and fees, federal appropriations, state appropriations, sales and services, private gifts and grants, and endowment income. As each of these sources of revenue (Figure 4.1) are described one must keep in mind that this is only part of the picture. "Revenue can also be analyzed according to whether it is largely trend related (enrollment) or episodic (gifts)" (Balderston, 1995, p. 179). Balderston also points out the importance to institutions of having multiple sources of revenue so that institutional leaders can "reduce the risk of subordination to any one funding source" (p. 178). Put simply, deriving some or all revenue from a single source puts the institution at risk.

Tuition and Fees

The most visible aspect of the price of a college education is an institution's tuition and fees, with annual tuition exceeding the $50,000 mark and the total cost of attendance approaching $70,000 per year at some of the most selective institutions (*Chronicle of Higher Education Almanac*, 2018). Tuition and fee data also reflect monies paid by students for services such as recreational activities, intercollegiate athletics, and student support. Public institutions enrolled nearly 74 percent of all college-going students in the United States in 2017 and have seen their dependence on tuition and fees increase steadily, albeit modestly, throughout the past few decades (NCES, 2018, Table 303.10). Figure 4.2 demonstrates changes in the both the amount and percentage of current fund revenue accounted for by tuition and fees between 1980–1981 and 2014–2015. Tuition and fees at public institutions as a proportion of total revenues slowly climbed during the period, but at nowhere near the pace of total revenues in the sector.

Both public and private not-for-profit (two- and four-year) institution revenues have increased a great deal since 1980. During that same period, enrollment increased

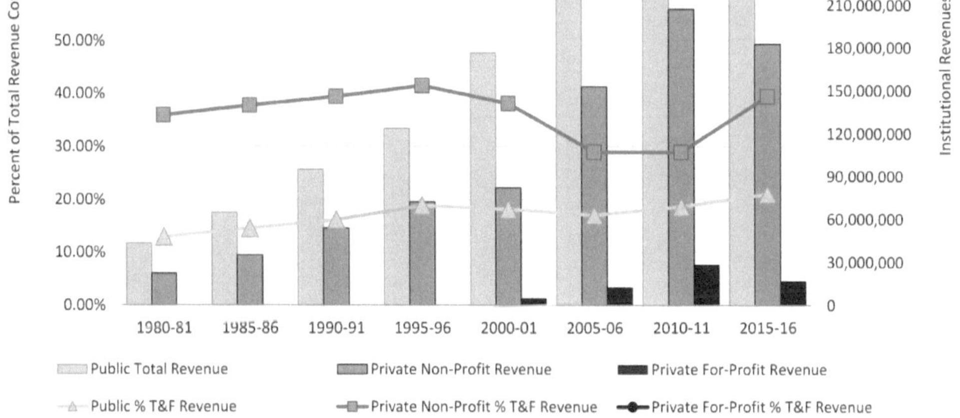

Figure 4.2 Tuition and Fees and Percentage of Revenue

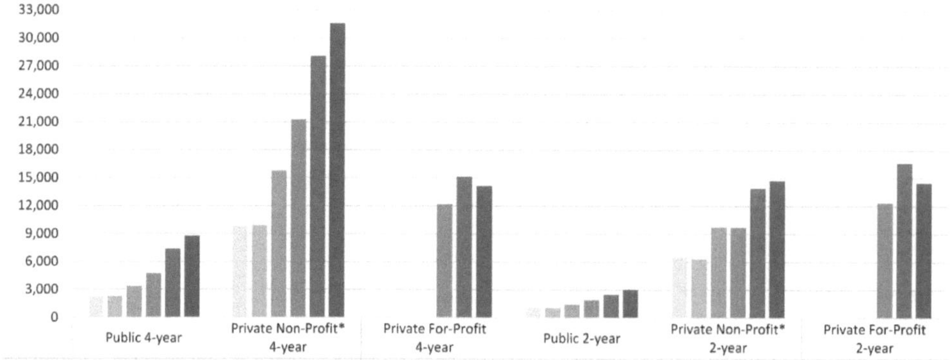

	Public 4-year	Private Non-Profit* 4-year	Private For-Profit 4-year	Public 2-year	Private Non-Profit* 2-year	Private For-Profit 2-year
1969-70	2,260	9,852		1,123	6,522	
1979-80	2,264	9,898		1,089	6,328	
1989-90	3,340	15,756		1,419	9,751	
1999-2000	4,713	21,297	12,190	1,897	9,701	12,338
2009-10	7,384	28,073	15,138	2,510	13,892	16,635
2015-16	8,778	31,580	14,154	3,038	14,724	14,472

1969-70 1979-80 1989-90 1999-2000 2009-10 2015-16

Figure 4.3 Tuition and Fees

from 12.1 million to nearly 20 million. Figure 4.3 presents average undergraduate tuition and fees in inflation-adjusted constant dollars between 1969 and 2016. In current dollars, undergraduate tuition was twenty-five times as expensive in 2015 as it was in 1969: $348 versus $8,778 (NCES, 2018, Table 330.10 – 2016).

Although tuition (in both constant and current dollars) has increased over time, the most dramatic increases occurred after 1990. Due to changes to federal financial aid programs and a per-student reduction in state appropriations during the past four decades, students at public colleges and universities have been asked to pick up a gradually increasing proportion of the cost of their education while the overall tuition bill increased (Kelchen, 2018; McGee, 2015; Michael, 2005; Zumeta, Breneman, Callan, & Finney, 2012). Average tuition data by sector is presented in Table 4.2.

Table 4.2 Tuition and fees

Type	*Total*	*Tuition and Required Fees*	*Housing*	*Board*	*Tuition %*	*Housing %*	*Board %*
Public four-year	19,189	8,778	5,850	4,561	45.7	30.5	23.8
Private not-for-profit four-year	43,191	31,580	6,495	5,116	73.1	15.0	11.8
Private for-profit four-year	23,722	14,154	5,842	3,726	59.7	24.6	15.7
Public two-year	9,939	3,038	3,772	3,128	30.6	38.0	31.5
Private not-for-profit two-year	24,344	14,724	5,379	4,240	60.5	22.1	17.4
Private for-profit two-year	24,305	14,472	5,928	3,905	59.5	24.4	16.1

Source: NCES, 2018, Table 330.10 – 2016.

Differential Tuition Structures

Many institutions have a different or broader focus than educating undergraduate students for associate and baccalaureate degrees. For decades, U.S. colleges and universities have charged differential tuition rates to their students. In the public systems there are in-state, out-of-state, and international student tuitions; in universities there are differences between graduate and undergraduate tuition, and in some instances between specific majors/programs; and within community colleges, there are differences between technical and transfer courses. This practice has accelerated since the 1990s (Hearn, 2006) and while most institutions have had specific course or lab fees in place for years, differential tuition is taking the pricing strategy to a different level. The logic is simple. The increased tuition accommodates the additional cost associated with delivering courses and programs.

Tuition Discounting

A tuition discount is financial aid that comes from institutionally generated monies often called an *institutional grant*. The use of tuition discounting throughout higher education enables institutions to reduce the out-of-pocket price to students—not the actual cost. According to Wu (2017), tuition discounting started as a noble idea to allow access and has been corrupted into a bidding-war tool for academically talented students. According to the *Chronicle of Higher Education Almanac* (2018), an estimated 49.9 percent of first-time, full-time freshmen and 44.8 percent of all undergraduate students received tuition discounts at private, not-for-profit colleges during the 2017–2018 academic year (p. 61). These discounts averaged nearly half of tuition and fees for undergraduates (Table 4.3).

The basic cost formula is: Cost = Price + Subsidy, where *price* is the sticker price charged to students, and *subsidy* is a reduction of the price from revenue generated from other sources. For example, an institution's published sticker price may be $20,000 per year, but for a student with exceptional ACT scores or demonstrated financial need, it may provide a subsidy of $12,000 per year. Therefore, the cost to the student for the year is $8,000. The subsidy provided ($12,000) may contain a mix of federal grants, federal loans, state grants, and tuition discounts.

Although they may be called scholarships, tuition discounts are simply a subsidy paid for by the *full-paying* students. While this strategy has many student-recruitment-related benefits, Hossler (2006) notes, "it is important to acknowledge that increasing

Table 4.3 Percentage of first-time full-time students receiving aid

Type	*2004–2005*	*2009–2010*	*2014–2015*
Private not-for-profit doctoral	67%	72%	73%
Private not-for-profit master's	80%	85%	92%
Private non-for-profit bachelor's	74%	78%	84%
Public doctoral	36%	46%	53%
Public master's	27%	31%	45%
Public bachelor's	23%	27%	38%

enrollments just to attract more revenue is not always a wise method to generate more campus revenue . . . this movement can often be counterproductive" (p. 117). Breneman, Doti, and Lapovsky (2001) found a relationship between increases in institutional grants and increases in both tuition and enrollment which may actually reduce tuition revenue, creating severe long-term consequences. As discussed in Chapter 3, the number of traditional-age college students declines in the mid-2020s, there will be a smaller pool of potential students from which to draw.

Tuition discounting must be viewed as *one of many tools* to make tuition more affordable, rather than the only tool to attract a good mixture of students. There is no doubt that for the foreseeable future, tuition revenue will continue to play an important role in the funding of postsecondary institutions: institutions are relying on it more and more as less per-student aid is available at federal and state levels (Baum, Ma, Pender, & Libassi, 2018). Colleges and universities must also rely on other sources of income to help stabilize the volatile swings in their institutions' student enrollments. Institutions experiencing financial difficulties are not going to be able to grow themselves out of their troubles. Administrators must be cognizant of the economic forces that influence participation rates, and prepare their institutions for the rocky road ahead.

Government Funding

Higher education institutions receive government funding in two distinct methods: direct funding or indirect funding. Direct funding occurs in a variety of forms, such as grants, research awards, or stimulus funding, and goes straight to the institution. The primary source of indirect funding, financial aid is awarded to the student and can be used at any Title IV institution—a designation that indicates the institution is accredited by a U.S. Department of Education-recognized regional accreditor.

Michael, Holdaway, and Small (1993) suggest that government contributions to higher education are a function of three factors: the state of the economy, the relative cost and priority of competing needs, and the demand for higher education. Reflective of these factors, federal and state governments, through their funding appropriations, indicate to what extent higher education is valued and to what extent they believe higher education is a public good. For example, the greater the funding level, the greater the perceived value and the more they believe in the public benefits of higher education. Currently, while funding in the aggregate is increasing in dollar value, it is declining as a proportion of the overall budget in most states (State Higher Education Executive Officers Association (SHEEO), 2018), and federal financial aid is increasingly in the form of loans, rather than grants to students (Zumeta et al., 2012), which communicates Congress' intentions loud and clear.

Federal Government

The federal government has a unique role in higher education and it is the largest provider of financial assistance for education in the United States. As noted earlier, there is no national system of higher education in the United States, but that does not mean that the government has no control or influence over higher education institutions.

Perhaps the most visible involvement of government is through the federal financial aid programs which are mostly governed by the Higher Education Act (HEA). The HEA was signed into law in 1965 and goes through periodic re-authorization by Congress. It is through this Act that government influences policies and practices on campuses throughout the country. Colleges and universities that receive federal financial aid dollars (Title IV institutions) must abide by certain federal rules and regulations in order to remain eligible to receive these funds. In other words, if an institution wants the money, it must play by the government's rules.

Initially, government support for education was provided to veterans through the Servicemen's Readjustment Act of 1944 (commonly known as the GI Bill). This was followed by the HEA, intended to reduce poverty by widening access to higher education through provision of grants to students—and higher education enrollment exploded. Aided by federal research grants (direct funds), some universities also increased their research activities in the 1960s. Then in the 1970s, the precursor to the Stafford Loan (loans with federally-subsidized interest) was introduced and as shown in Figure 4.4, the proportion of federal funds devoted to grants has dropped in relation to loan support (Heller, 2015).

Taking a cue from the federal government, state-supported financial aid morphed from need-based to merit-based simultaneously with two phenomena: increasing tuition and decreasing money-saving behaviors (McGee, 2015). Thus, the 1990s were characterized by offering benefits (aid, loans, tax credits) to students and families who would have gone to college regardless, instead of helping students from low-income families pursue higher education (Heller, 2015; Zumeta et al., 2012). Perna (2015) found "that changes in tuition and financial aid have a larger effect on college enrollments from lower-income families than higher-income families and for African Americans and Hispanics than for Whites" (p. 381), leading to a widening gap in enrollment between high school graduates in the lowest family income quintile and those in the highest income quintile.

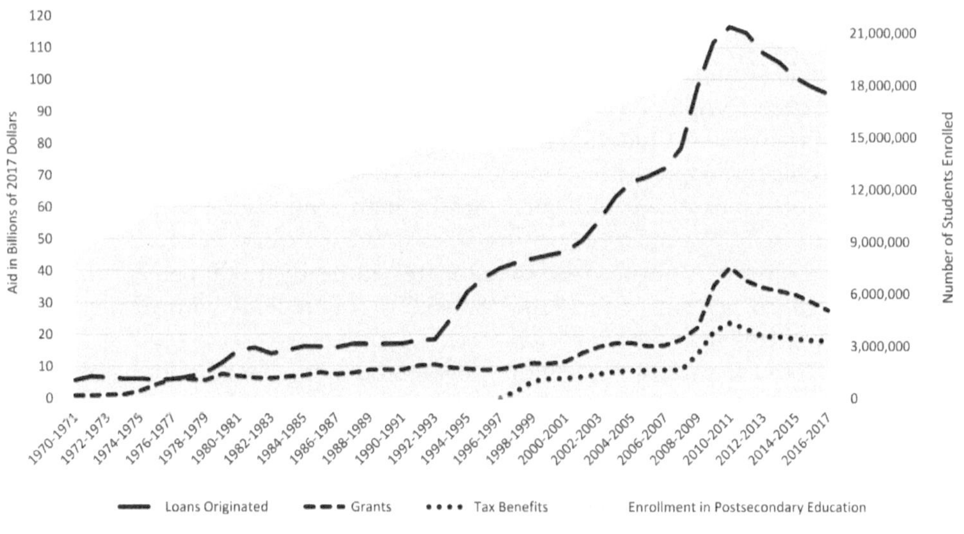

Figure 4.4 Aid Over Time and Enrollment

The most recent re-authorization of the HEA was passed in 2008 and is called the Higher Education Opportunity Act – 2008 (HEOA). A few of the new provisions require Title IV institutions to report graduation rates, retention rates, and most common majors to the U.S. Department of Education. Some of this information is now made available to students who complete the Free Application for Federal Student Aid (FAFSA). For example, students will receive the graduation rate and first- to second-year retention rates for each institution to which they have their FAFSA report sent. The intent is to provide students and their families with more information about institutions so they can make a more informed decision.

Additionally, these Title IV institutions must also present a "net price calculator" on their website. The calculator must allow prospective students to enter financial and personal data to approximate their Expected Family Contribution and use that to provide estimates on the following variables: total cost of attendance, including tuition and fees, room and board, books and supplies, assorted other expenses, and potential grant aid. This enables students to establish an estimated net price of attendance (Net Price Calculator Information Center, 2018). Failing to comply with the regulations set forth in the HEOA places the institutions in jeopardy of losing financial aid dollars. For many institutions, especially for-profit schools, loss of federal financial aid revenues would mean certain closure, as for-profit schools typically rely heavily on student financial aid revenue: of 1,838 institutions reporting in 2014–2015, 550 (30 percent) received 80 percent or more of their total tuition and fee revenue through federal financial aid dollars (Kelchen, 2018, p. 62).

State and Local Appropriations

State governments served a significant role in creating educational opportunities through their support of colleges and universities taking an active role in promoting higher education through governance or coordinating boards. Appropriations were provided for both the creation of new facilities and new academic programs—and funding was also provided directly to students in the form of grants (Heller, 2015; Zumeta et al., 2012). Initially, these grants were based on financial need. For example, between 1970 and 1990, states awarded between 89 percent and 98 percent of aid based on need (NASSGAP, 2016). This changed during the 1990s when Georgia introduced the Helping Outstanding Pupils Educationally Program (Heller, 2015). Other states quickly adopted similar models, with scholarships based on merit awarded on the basis of standardized test scores and/or high school grades. Data from the 1990s indicate state expenditures on need-based aid increased nearly 200 percent, while expenditures on non-need-based aid increased nearly 1,000 percent. In 2016, states allocated 76 percent of the $10,738,345,301 for students with financial need (NASSGAP, 2016).

Palmer (2009) warns that "one of the salient trends in higher education since 1980 has been the shrinking proportion of total revenues accounted for by state appropriations" (p. 2). States have other problems to contend with, such as an aging population, rising healthcare costs, and economic issues. As has been noted by numerous authors, state appropriations are accounting for a significantly smaller percentage of public institutions' operating budgets (Michael, 2005). According to SHEEO, colleges and universities received $83.9 billion from state appropriations as well as $10.6 billion in local appropriations in 2017. Due to previous reductions and budgetary shortcuts, states have many other backlogged issues to deal with before they can provide more support to colleges and universities. Generally speaking, state finances have recovered, but state and local support for higher education has decreased *as a proportion of revenues*. In 2005, higher education received 6.5 percent of the revenues gained through taxes and lottery receipts, and in 2015 it received only 5.7 percent of those revenues. Even with post-recession increases in tax-related income, "in 2017 states appropriated almost $2,000 less per student than they did in 2001, and $1,000 less than before the Great Recession" (SHEEO, 2018, p. 19).

Performance Funding

Historically, many states have used an incremental approach for determining appropriations: starting with last year's budget and adjusting upward or downward based on inflation, cost of living, and demonstrated improvements in performance. The remainder use a formula based on enrollment or physical facilities' square footage (Dougherty & Natow, 2015). Facing resource limitations, some states have adjusted their support of higher education to encourage accountability in achieving state goals by turning to performance funding, which "is based on outcomes such as retention, course and degree completion, and job placement, not on inputs such as enrollments" (Dougherty, Natow, Bork, Jones, & Vega, 2015, p. 66). However, some states are focusing on "intermediate student outcomes, such as course completion, developmental education passing certain gateway courses (e.g., college math or English), and reaching specified credit thresholds (e.g., 15, 30, or 45 credits)" (Dougherty & Natow, 2015, p. 17). In most states the performance component of funding is a small percentage of the total appropriation. As of September 2014, thirty states were operating some form of performance funding (Dougherty & Natow, 2015). In a 2017 survey by SHEEO, twenty out of twenty-eight responding states indicated using an outcomes-based funding model; in most cases, the model was only recently implemented. In the two-year sector, most of the states using performance funding indicated the model accounted for less than 10 percent of the total funding given to these institutions. In the four-year sector more than half of the responding institutions indicated 10 percent or more of the funding was awarded through the model (SHEEO, 2018).

Performance funding is intended to encourage institutions to contribute to common goals but often relies on imperfect measures (Burke, 2002). However, "critics charge that indicators often used for performance reporting owe more to the availability of data and ease of measurement than to their importance as policy concerns" (Burke, p. 44). Zumeta et al. (2012) worry this metrics-focused approach could sacrifice the success of marginalized student populations, and create uneven institutional benefits. Unfortunately, there is little research that links performance funding to improvement or deterioration in student outcomes. While Dougherty and Natow (2015) could not be certain that performance funding would continue to be adopted in the future, they did note that nearly twenty European countries have adopted performance funding models, most of which have fewer indicators than the models used in the United States. Kelchen (2018) recommends selecting metrics that promote deep, positive changes, rather than change for the sake of change. When attempting to satisfy accountability or performance metrics institutions may be tempted to engage in tactics that do not serve students well—namely serving the sub-groups they feel will get the institution the biggest performance bonuses. It is important for accountability measures to connect with institutional missions, measuring what is relevant to the institutions and to the state rather than what is easy to measure. Additionally, states and institutions need to incorporate safeguards that prevent institutions from gaming the system.

FUNDRAISING

Most colleges and universities employ individuals specifically tasked with working with alumni, friends (non-alumni supporters), corporations, foundations, current students, faculty, and staff to foster relationships that could result in donations being made to the institution (Council for Advancement and Support of Education, 2018). Individuals with strong ties to an organization are more likely to engage in philanthropy (the donation of time, talent, and treasure), which is why alumni giving is an important component of fundraising (Dodge, 2016; Drezner, 2011; Starsoneck, 2017). As enrollment challenges grow and state and federal funding is spread thinner and thinner, philanthropic contributions have become more and more important, becoming a substantial source of revenue for higher education; the Council for Aid to Education (CAE; 2018) reported colleges and universities raised $43.6 *billion* in 2017. These gifts funded an estimated 10.5 percent of institutional expenditures—though that varies by type of institution (CAE, 2018).

Institutions engaged in fundraising typically do so through a campaign designed to solicit gifts of all types; however, most campaigns emphasize major gifts (typically more than $100,000). Other types of gifts solicited include annual or current gifts (to be used in ongoing operations), planned gifts (provided as part of an estate), and grants (typically through corporations or foundations). Gifts differ in both their amounts and in their intentions: some are flexible and can be used as the institution sees fit (unrestricted) while others are provided for specific purposes (restricted). Chapter 11 will outline how giving has increased over time while the relative makeup of total donations has been fairly consistent. Alumni, non-alumni individuals, and foundations provide the majority of donations, although the balance has changed with foundation support exceeding alumni giving.

Successful fundraisers, assisted by institutional leaders, engage in a process of research, donor cultivation, solicitation, and stewardship. Individual, foundation, and corporate donors see themselves as change agents and supporters of progress, and are far more likely to engage with an organization that adopts an agenda that aligns with their own. The importance of an all-in approach of senior leaders cannot be understated. Fundraising is about connecting with important stakeholders and influencers, and asking them to support something that they are already likely to support. The majority of donors with whom an institution engages anticipate being asked to contribute, or they would not have engaged in the first place.

OTHER FUNDING SOURCES

Colleges and universities seek revenue from a diverse array of potential streams, although the reliance on any particular source varies by institutional type and mission (Weisbrod, Ballou, & Asch, 2008). McGee (2015), Carlson (2018), and others believe that the changing demographics and economy will force institutions to differentiate and become more entrepreneurial in order to survive. This section will briefly address some of the more traditional ways institutions raise money.

Sales and Services, Special Programs

Institutions are able to leverage their on-site facilities and expertise to provide services to individuals and partnering organizations. Typically, income earned this way is referred to as *sales and services*. Goldstein (2012) lists several examples: "demonstration schools, dairy creameries, hotels, theaters, and numerous other academic activities that, through instruction, create goods or services for sale" (p. 48). Other common examples include golf or recreation center membership sales, or agreeing to let a major conference football team win against your mediocre football program (on their turf) for a substantial fee (Weisbrod et al., 2008). Institutions can also offer on-site conferences or *special programs* (academic or non-academic), which can encompass a variety of offerings, resulting in revenue coming back to the institution.

Auxiliary Enterprises

Auxiliary units on campuses are expected to be self-sufficient and contribute a specified dollar amount or percentage of revenue back to the institution's general revenue fund. This overhead fee is charged to cover expenses generated by the institution in support of these units. For example, many institutions have a centralized marketing division that develops promotional materials for housing and dining, or it may be that the maintenance or custodial services are provided through the institution's centralized unit. These expenses are directly attributable to the auxiliary unit and need to be paid by said unit. Auxiliary units are also expected to maintain reserve accounts, enabling them to cover large anticipated (technology upgrades) or unanticipated (flood-damage repair) expenses. Much like endowments (see Chapter 11), these funds are designated for specific purposes and are not meant to fund other institutional priorities.

Contracts, Licensing, and Partnerships

Colleges and universities are increasingly involved in contracts with third parties for specific services; examples include soda contracts, branded clothing, naming rights (scoreboards), third-party-operated grocery stores, and telecommunication providers. Although this is a bit more controversial, some campuses have adopted preferred cell phone providers, banks, credit card companies, and study-abroad planning firms—most of which provide faculty, staff, and students with reduced prices or specialized services (and possibly a kickback to the institution) (Alstete, 2014; Weisbrod et al., 2008).

Campuses also can contract with private citizens or companies to use their campus property or infrastructure. Many institutions have engaged in public–private partnerships (P3) in which the institution contracts with a private developer to build a facility on the institution's property, then commits to a long-term lease from the developer. These arrangements appear to be a good short-term strategy but there are potential long-term costs associated. At least one campus has allowed a company to drill oil on its grounds, while others loan equipment or facilities (such as lab space), or allow for rental of land for private use (Alstete, 2014). Colleges have also engaged in licensing of "symbols, logos, and mascots to manufacturers of everything from clothing to caskets" (Weisbrod et al., 2008, p. 6). Researchers can also engage in contracted research with private companies to run clinical trials and test products, and institutions can enter into contracts with corporations to provide specialized programs and services focused on employee training and development.

Many institutions partner with state and local governments or private corporations to offer workforce development, focused on retraining workers or education for the community (Weisbrod et al., 2008). With private corporations there is often an agreement to provide education at a reduced tuition rate to employees of the partnering company in exchange for the company's willingness to indicate the college or university as its preferred partner (Alstete, 2014). Further, these partnerships can be international, providing education abroad. Partnerships with corporations for educational delivery can bring substantial revenues to an institution.

Colleges can also partner with each other to launch new academic programs and study-abroad experiences (Alstete, 2014; Brown & Gamber, 2002). This strategy could, of course, be used for both revenue generation and cost reduction. Joint educational ventures have the potential of generating new enrollment for an institution while also spreading the risk and costs across both institutions. In the case of a two-year/four-year partnership, the use of articulation agreements can encourage students from a two-year institution to transfer to a specific four-year institution, which may prompt higher enrollment in both institutions and lower total costs for both the student and the institutions involved.

Sponsored Research Grants, Patents, and Royalties for Discoveries

For some institutions (about 25 percent; Weisbrod et al., 2008) pursuing federal grants for research is considered important. In 2017, colleges spent $71.6 billion on research and development, much of it funded by federal grants (*Chronicle of Higher Education Almanac*, 2018). Corporations and foundations also provide grant funding, although their support may come with an agenda (Weisbrod et al., 2008). At the state level, appropriations are the primary funding resource, but institutions can also vie for "capital funds, grants, and contracts" from the state (Dougherty & Natow, 2015, p. 14). Grant monies must be used specifically for the purposes intended, although a specific amount can be used to cover indirect costs to the institution (such as utilities, payroll, and other services provided broadly by the institution) (Goldstein, 2012).

Institutions that secure grants (particularly federal ones) are able to engage in focused research and development activities that could result in an important discovery that can be patented. If the discovery is commercially viable—that is, if it is something a company wants to produce—the institution could experience a huge windfall through the licensing of the patent (Weisbrod et al., 2008). Examples of this include Gatorade (University of Florida) and Ziagen, a drug used to treat AIDS (University of Minnesota). When a patent is licensed (sold to a company for production), the ongoing income generated is referred to as royalties. To capitalize on this, many institutions have created Technology Transfer offices, who work to help connect faculty with opportunities, support ongoing research, and handle the patenting and licensing processes so royalties can be earned (Alstete, 2014).

NEW SOURCES OF REVENUE, REDUCING COSTS

It has become obvious that if educational opportunities are going to continue to expand, new sources of revenue must be developed. Tuition increases, government support, and private donations can take higher education only so far. Colleges and universities will need to become more entrepreneurial in their administrative approach. Institutions can grow tuition revenue (and reduce costs) through individual actions and through collaboration with partners. While the ideas presented in Figure 4.5 are organized by revenue-generation and cost-reduction strategies, the distinctions are not always clear—for example, institutions can find ways to save money by delivering study-abroad programs more efficiently, which may also result in revenue being generated by more students wishing to engage in study abroad.

Generating Revenue

Colleges and universities are already adept at developing new programs to attract students—this can be seen throughout higher education history. Many institutions have studied their current offerings, identified gaps that could be addressed using existing faculty and resources, and added new degree programs (Alstete, 2014). Most institutions will not be able to recruit their way out of the demographic changes on the horizon, but many would be well served by exploring new pipelines for students

Doing More (Generating Revenue)	Doing Less (Reducing Costs)
Individual Solutions *New programs* *New pipelines or services* Partnership Solutions *Research collaboration, program collaboration, licensing, sales, space rental* *Lobbying*	Individual Solutions *Program reviews, restructuring and cuts* *Facilities sustainability* Partnership Solutions *Collaboration for cost-sharing, efficiency* *Outsourcing and Auxiliaries*

Figure 4.5 Strategies

(such as postsecondary enrollment in high school, adult students, and under-served populations). Previously, institutions have created degree-completion programs crafted to allow adult students to combine transfer credits with life experiences and package them into a degree with limited additional coursework. Some institutions, most notably Western Governor's University and Southern New Hampshire University, offer competency-based education programs which are likely to be adopted by more institutions (Zumeta et al., 2012).

Another option is to change the mode of delivery of education (from in-person to online, or a hybrid format that incorporates both), which would give students more flexibility, although this often requires a substantial amount of time and money to do well. Other options include adopting shorter semesters (twelve weeks or fewer), providing credit for life experience, providing specialized advising and counseling services and special institutional aid (Alstete, 2014), and operating extension campuses across the United States or even abroad (Weisbrod et al., 2008). Further, institutions must focus on better supporting current students so they are retained to graduation—and this is of special importance for under-represented student populations, whose graduation rates typically trail that of middle- to upper-class Caucasian students (Carlson, 2018).

However, a word of caution: implementing new academic programs does not guarantee new revenues. Hearn (2006) identifies the pitfalls possible when seeking new revenues: program cannibalization, failure to identify wants and needs of customers, failure to establish guidelines for program development, remaining committed to old-style pedagogy and curricular organization, and assuming that simply providing the program will be enough, absent efforts to market it (p. 98).

Whether in the academic or non-academic units, institutions must gather the data necessary to inform their decision-making processes (Alstete, 2014; Dickeson, 2010). In short, it is fairly easy to tell colleges and universities to find new sources of revenue to maintain their long-term interests . . . it is harder to actually accomplish this.

Reducing Costs

As revenue streams tighten and basic costs such as those associated with personnel (healthcare, salaries), campus infrastructure (technology, physical plant, safety, accessibility), and attracting students (student services, tuition discounting) increase, it becomes more expensive for institutions to *conduct business* (Archibald & Feldman, 2011; Brown & Gamber, 2002). And because higher education institutions tend to spend as much money as they bring in (Zumeta et al., 2012), institutions have had little incentive to reduce costs. However, the time has arrived where institutions must focus on reducing expenses to improve their financial well-being, as new sources of revenue are unlikely to match escalating costs (McGee, 2015).

In reaction to economic turmoil, colleges tend to make short-term cuts that, without the real and necessary long-term strategies for cost-containment, can be more expensive in the long term (Zumeta et al., 2012). Typically, institutions tend to make simplistic cuts, such as leaving vacant positions open, across-the-board cuts, or identifying inconsequential expenses for reduction, which are some of the worst solutions for the long-term health of the institution. These actions have short-term impact and simply put off long-term issues. Institutions should instead focus on truly understanding their costs (and the revenues they generate) so they can take a hard look and make strategic decisions to remain viable (Dickeson, 2010). While it may be more politically acceptable to make across-the-board cuts, it is the least effective way to deal with financial constraints. Cost reduction must be strategic and carried out with surgical precision. Simply stated, colleges and universities must begin to consider *doing less with less*, but doing it better, which means reducing offerings, reducing services, and focusing on the institutional mission and needs to support what the institution does best.

Noting that most colleges and universities have more academic programs than they can reasonably support, Dickeson (2010) argues for careful prioritization and re-allocation of resources. To do this with the appropriate level of care, it is recommended that all programs and departments engage in a *comprehensive review* process (program review) that is data-driven and outcome-focused. In this process, each program submits a *self-study* for review by teams of internal and, perhaps, external colleagues. To engage in program review, leadership, ground rules, and transparency are exceptionally important.

These processes and conversations will be, without exception, awkward and stressful. Promoting change is hard and requires courage—according to Dickeson, "Higher education has produced some spectacular examples of institutional cowardice in the fulfillment of necessary but unpopular reform" (p. 31). Conversely, Carlson (2018) notes some institutions have been very successful in engaging in academic program reviews and realignments, the use of lean principles (Chapter 7) to reduce or eliminate inefficient practices, and restructuring an institution's academic colleges using a "blow the place up" mentality (pp. 58–59).

Sometimes an institution can find efficiencies through *restructuring* or *right-sizing* itself—for example, the merger of academic programs (or colleges, in a university), as well as the realignment of administrative divisions and services. Restructuring is an approach that reflects a desire to become more efficient. However, higher education with tenure and shared governance is more complex than many corporations—so efforts to restructure are often long and very difficult. They may even be criticized as simply moving game pieces around a board with no positive outcomes. To engage in successful restructuring, an institution must go back to its mission and vision and take a hard look at how to make itself more effective.

As a result of tough economic conditions, colleges may choose to *cut* or reduce programs and services in order to meet their bottom line. Examples of cuts include: eliminating remedial education courses (or partnering with another institution for delivery) and implementing efficiency programs focused on energy, human resources, information technology, insurance, and procurement (Brown & Gamber, 2002). Determining which programs or services to cut can be determined by program review or some other mechanism, but the task is a complex one (Brown & Gamber, 2002; Dickeson, 2010). Some authors suggest cost-cutting decisions involve the sacrifice of educational quality (Archibald & Feldman, 2011; Brown & Gamber, 2002). We completely disagree and submit that cost reductions can in fact *increase academic quality* by focusing institutional resources toward academic strengths. In today's competitive marketplace, reductions to educational quality will most likely reduce institutional revenues as much as they will reduce expenses.

Another problem plaguing higher education is *deferred maintenance*. Carlson (2018) notes, "Roughly two-thirds of the lifetime cost of a new building accrues after it opens, in the form of operations, maintenance, utilities, and finally, demolition" (p. 25). At many colleges, preventative maintenance is not a priority, as institutions wait until these buildings need extensive repairs or need to be replaced entirely—requiring more resources in total than if they had been maintained properly all along (Brown & Gamber, 2002; Carlson, 2018). It seems as though administrators place more importance on building new facilities than maintaining the existing physical plant. To avoid ending up with an inadequate pool of resources to support the maintenance of newly-constructed facilities, many institutions are including *maintenance endowments* as part of their fundraising efforts for new facilities (Brown & Gamber, 2002). Additionally, institutions are also taking energy-sustainability practices more seriously.

Institutions have the opportunity to reduce costs through collaborations such as shared services, or consortia. These collaborations reduce costs through economies of scale and scope; examples include two-year institutions offering developmental courses on a four-year campus, institutions sharing payroll or human resource services, or a library consortium.

The implementation of a shared services facilities model such as that found at the College of Saint Benedict and Saint John's University in Minnesota is a prime example of a shared services collaboration (Carlson, 2018). These institutions share a library, courses, and key administrative personnel in order to reduce the costs that each institution would pay individually. Finance experts believe college–college collaborations are not yet as popular as they should be, indicating a host of potential opportunities.

States can also assist institutions through their appropriations to pursue goals such as strengthening links between the P-12 system and higher education (through college enrollment during secondary school, aligning curriculum, and connecting data systems). They can also foster increased collaboration between two- and four-year institutions, increase access to distance education, and provide information systems support for student tracking (Zumeta et al., 2012). The state of Georgia has taken it further than requesting shared services: the coordinating board for the Georgia state higher education system recently called for the consolidation of eighteen state institutions down to nine (Carlson, 2018), requiring multiple mergers. Similarly, the University of Wisconsin system recently required several two-year institutions to merge with nearby four-year universities.

Scholars note several trends making it harder for institutions to change for the sake of viability: competition and marketing for students (amenities, services, and proliferation of academic programs), increasing specialization within academic disciplines (more electives, less generalists), internal competition and redundancy between programs and services, state factors (policies, pet projects, temptation of mission creep, funding instability), fundraising's influence on the institution's direction, ineffective planning for the future, the shared governance model, and data collection constraints that make analysis of program viability difficult (Carlson, 2018; Dickeson, 2010;

McGee, 2015). Carlson also notes "many of higher education's problems come from an unwillingness to see institutions as businesses—a cultural intransigence rooted in nostalgia for what the system represented through much of the 20th century" (p. 11). While costs continue to increase, the above factors contribute to a lack of understanding of costs, making it difficult to control them.

CONCLUDING COMMENTS

The financing of higher education continues to evolve, and so must the way higher education leaders approach their decision-making relative to their respective institution's financial security. Enrollments have grown, revenues have grown, physical plants have grown, and so have the operational costs. External support declines as colleges and universities struggle to maintain infrastructure while simultaneously adding more amenities and services to compete with one another. Questions about the government's and the student's return on investment continue as the accountability movement shows no sign of slowing (nor should it). Not only has tuition continued increasing, but federal aid as a proportion of total tuition and fees continues to decline. The United States is not alone in this trend. Throughout the world, college and university students are being required to contribute more of their own resources toward their education (Michael, 2005).

Higher education has no shortage of capacity limitations that affect the extent of our financial future: escalating physical and technological needs, funding and revenue-generation problems (state, federal, tuition as a percent of family income), plus motivational and political structures and constraints that slow institutions' ability to change (Zumeta et al., 2012). Further, the demographic changes we are experiencing are altering the relationship between institutions and students and families. As institutions become more market-driven, competent administrators will need to fully understand the complexities of market forces. Colleges and universities have many "values, mores, practices, and traditions" which have a strong "anchoring power" on the institution, but may also put higher education completely out of touch with the market's expectations (McGee, 2015, p. 108). Too many administrators fail to recognize these changes and struggle to envision a reality different to the one currently being experienced, which unfortunately will lead to more institutional closures and more administrative failures.

What colleges and universities must understand is this: the world of higher education is in a constant state of change and policymakers are not going to become any less skeptical of higher education; they are asking tougher questions and demanding documented outcomes. States will likely continue to reduce the proportion of their budgets devoted to supporting the higher education sector, and smaller private institutions with sparse endowments will struggle with ever more aggressive tuition discounting practices. Additionally, there is no indication that costs will decline anytime in the foreseeable future.

While many commentators bemoan the cost of education, Archibald and Feldman (2011) note that for the *average* family in the United States, tuition is actually more affordable than it has been in the past. Specifically, they state,

> Over long stretches of time, college costs have been rising at a faster pace than income per worker, yet the average worker's actual dollar income has gone up by more than the costs, leaving more resources on the family table to spend on other things.
>
> (p. 190)

However, they note that during this time of tuition increase, income inequality has increased. There are fewer "average" families than there were in previous decades, and incomes of families in the lowest quintiles have not increased like those in the upper quintiles. If institutions were to instead take a stand and specify who they serve, to what ends, and how, better outcomes would follow. Michael and Kretovics (2005) state, "As institutions carve out their niches and refuse to become all things to all people, institutional cooperation and collaboration, which will reduce costs while enhancing mutual benefits, will become a strategic option for progressive higher education leaders" (p. 67). Institutions that fail to identify an appropriate focus and work to raise revenues and reduce costs specifically in relation to their niche will struggle as demographic changes fundamentally alter the higher education market (Grawe, 2018; McGee, 2015).

Many reports have suggested that one of the most intimidating barriers to enrollment and completion of a degree is of a financial nature (Hearn, 2006), particularly in minority populations (Perna, 2015). This is why the increased use of loans and decreased use of grants at the federal level is so concerning for the future. Further, if institutions had more discretionary monies for support of economically disadvantaged students, this could potentially increase access to higher education. Unrestricted or unencumbered endowments and private gifts can be effective tools to increase access to and the affordability of higher education. However, pursuit of these gifts does not absolve colleges and universities from their responsibility to find appropriate methods to reduce their costs. McGee (2015) states,

> All decision-makers continuously are faced with their own version of a gambler's dilemma. Even when we acknowledge imperfect information and incomplete knowledge, we still judge reward on the basis of what we might gain by virtue of taking a risk. At the same time, though, we must be cognizant of what we cannot afford to lose when the winds of fortune shift or do not blow kindly in our direction.
>
> (p. 19)

We will never have perfect information, but it is possible to act responsibly if consequences and worst-case scenarios are incorporated when planning occurs.

Questions about the value of college related to return on investment will continue to be asked as federal financial aid programs, increasingly reliant on loans, do not match needs of students seeking a college education. Families will continue to be concerned about the price of a college education, particularly in relation to their income, and will expect more outcomes and more accountability (McGee, 2015; Zumeta et al., 2012). Taxpayers have a right to know how their money is being spent, and the general public also has an obligation to understand the benefits of an educated populace. It is incumbent upon administrators to understand and control, generate revenues, and become more transparent with regard to the focus, value, and outcomes of public and private higher education. Administrators can no longer assume that the citizenry and politicians recognize the contribution of higher education to society: "On the contrary, higher education leaders must accept the responsibility of becoming public educators, individuals whose role includes sensitizing society toward responsible funding" (Michael & Kretovics, 2005, p. 66).

REFLECTIVE QUESTIONS

1. How do public and private institutions generate revenue?
2. How has tuition discounting changed over time and why?
3. What cost factors are contributing to increasing tuition?
4. How is state and federal support for higher education changing?
5. What are some benefits and concerns associated with performance funding?
6. What factors need to be considered in your institution's pursuit of a more secure financial future?

CHAPTER 5

Accounting

As an administrator within higher education, you have (or will have) the responsibility of managing a budget. Regardless of what type of institution you work in, it is imperative to be a *good fiscal steward* when you are responsible for any aspect of financial management. Understanding financial record-keeping and budgetary practices in college and university settings is a prerequisite for serving as a good fiscal steward. To do this, it is important to understand basic principles and practices of accounting, as they set the stage for the budget process.

Disclosure requirements for not-for-profit and for-profit organizations dictate data be shared on how well the organization is performing, and a growing variety of stakeholders have an interest in the efficiency with which resources are used. Institutions struggle to calculate the cost of services, which makes the requisite self-examination more difficult. This chapter provides an overview of accounting as an information system through which resource inflows and outflows are documented for two related but distinct purposes: reporting for external stakeholders, and internal organization, control, and planning. Accounting data are critical for budget-making processes and evaluation (Goldstein, 2005). In most college or university business offices, the personnel managing accounting and budgeting have credentials similar to members of the for-profit corporate world (MBA, CMA, and CPA, among others).

THE ROLE OF ACCOUNTING

Accounting principles and techniques create the basis of financial record-keeping and disclosure, and improve internal budgeting processes. This chapter provides an introduction to accounting for non-accountants. In short, "Accounting is an information system for measuring, processing, and communicating information that is useful in making economic decisions" (Needles & Powers, 1998, p. 1). *Accounting* can be used to refer to a task or to a whole set of tasks organized into a system for informing decision-makers through measuring activities and sharing data (Needles & Powers, 1998). Accountants work to enhance an organization's ability to efficiently develop and deliver quality services (and products) (Atkinson, Kaplan, Matsumura, & Young, 2007).

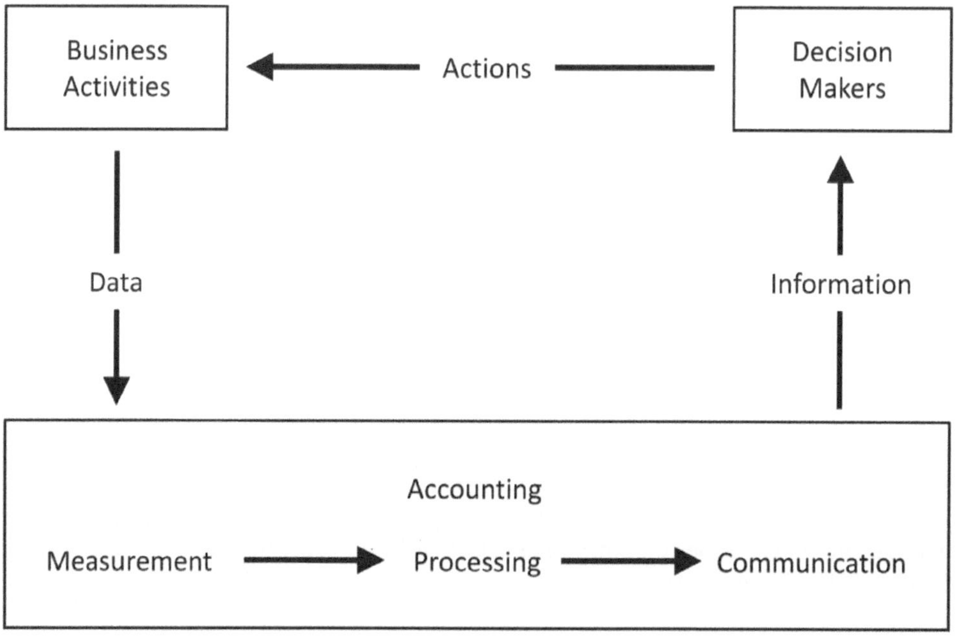

Figure 5.1 Accounting System (adapted from Needles & Powers, 2007)

Within the sphere of accounting, activities are usually divided into one of two functions: financial accounting and managerial accounting. Financial accounting tends to focus on external reporting and compliance activities for an organization, while managerial accounting, by contrast, focuses inward and is critical for continuous improvement efforts. Its primary function is internal analysis and planning to improve outcomes and decision-making (Needles & Powers, 2007).

PLANNING FOR EXTERNAL CONCERNS: FINANCIAL ACCOUNTING

Administrators who monitor transactions need to understand several accounting concepts: the accounting equation, assets and liabilities, and revenues and expenses. Administrators must also realize that a majority of the business activities that involve the exchange of value will, at some point, need to be listed in some type of financial report, regardless of for-profit or not-for-profit status (Needles & Powers, 2007). Accounting is both an activity and a system for organizing data—in many ways, it is a language with its own rules. When compiling financial data for release to stakeholders, institutions are subject to rules from a specific standard-setting body and practices called *generally accepted accounting principles* (GAAP) (Anthony & Young, 1999). Needles and Powers (2007) further explain GAAP as a set of guidelines or standard practices and procedures that are used for the compilation of data and financial statements. These practices evolve over time and are influenced by several bodies, including the Securities and Exchange Commission, the Financial Accounting Standards Board (FASB) and its counterpart, the

Governmental Accounting Standards Board (GASB), as well as the American Institute of Certified Public Accounting. Public institutions are subject to GASB rules, while private institutions are subject to FASB rules.

Financial reporting is not simply an exercise done for posterity: institutions are evaluated for their financial solvency and bond ratings by external organizations, such as Moody's and Standard & Poor's (S&P). These agencies incorporate financial, state (if applicable), and organizational factors when rating the financial quality of organizations, and their ratings are utilized by investors and other parties to evaluate their financial position. In 2018, both S&P and Moody's projected continued struggles in higher education. Moody's Investor Service downgraded the higher education sector's rating, noting "demographic challenges, weak revenue growth, and rising labor costs will bedevil colleges in the near term" (Carlson, 2018, para. 3). Moody's warned in a 2017 press release that revenues were not projected to keep pace with expenses in the upcoming year: "At least 15% of universities will be forced to cut costs in response to stagnant or weak revenue growth" (Moody's, 2017, para. 3). Similarly, S&P recently expressed concerns with the higher education sector, citing a variety of factors including recent tax law changes and higher education's reputation as being slow to make meaningful changes in operations (Harris, 2018).

Constituents and stakeholders within and outside an institution are watching to see how resources are used, and making judgments based on their perceptions (Lenington, 1996). Accreditors, as well as the U.S. Department of Education, also evaluate the financial position of institutions, and the results of this analysis can lead to sanctions. One recent notable example is ITT Tech, which operated 130 campuses and enrolled 45,000 students in 38 states and online. It was ordered to stop enrolling new students by the U.S. Department of Education in August 2016 due to financial viability concerns, among other issues (U.S. Department of Education, 2016). The department found that the institution did not have sufficient funds to cover its Title IV aid disbursements, and expressed concern about its ability to remain solvent. In that same month the Accrediting Council for Independent Colleges and Schools, ITT Tech's accreditor at the time, also cited concerns with its ability to meet the council's standard on financial stability and resource sufficiency. This ruling ultimately contributed to the institution's spectacular demise (Blumenstyk, 2016).

Further, institutions are subject to periodic audits to ensure record-keeping matches reality and safeguards against financial misdeeds are in place. Larger institutions may have their own internal audit team to monitor ongoing activities in-between external audits. The field of financial accounting is interested in the quality of record-keeping as well as procedures, with the goal of ensuring an organization is able to be evaluated using understandable, useful, and reliable data. "Whether an enterprise intends to earn money for owners or stockholders or is a not-for-profit organization, the goal is the same: creating value" (Atkinson et al., 2007, p. xvii).

Accounting Terminology

Below, common accounting terms and principles one might see in financial statements are defined. These standard definitions are paraphrased from Needles & Powers (2007) unless otherwise noted. Guidance from GAAP is used to create common definitions for types of assets (e.g., current assets, fixed assets, and intangible assets), liability, and elements of equity in order to ensure every organization's financial statements can be generally understood by an outsider.

Assets are items of value an organization holds, including cash, tangible items (buildings, equipment, supplies), non-tangible items (such as copyrights), and monies owed to the organization ("receivables"). There are three broad categories of assets that institutions will account for on their financial statements. *Current assets* can or will be converted to cash within the year (liquid assets). *Fixed assets* are long-term holdings such as land, buildings, and physical plant. *Intangible assets* are non-physical long-term assets such as patents, trademarks, copyrights, and goodwill.

Liabilities refers to debts owed by the organization: money owed to creditors, wages yet to be paid, services yet to be performed. These obligations will be retired by using the institution's economic resources, such as cash, to pay suppliers or creditors.

Net assets are the difference between liabilities and assets—and may also be referred to as equity, particularly in for-profit enterprises (Anthony & Young, 1999). In a not-for-profit organization net assets are saved to be used for enhancement of the organization, instead of being paid out to shareholders or owners.

Revenues and *expenses* (discussed in Chapter 4) refer to inflows and outflows of cash. Revenue and expenses can *lead* to assets, liabilities, and ultimately equity, but are not the same in an accounting sense. Revenues and expenses in a given period determine net income, which can also be called *retained earnings*—how much money an organization "makes" in a given period after accounting for what they spent to make it.

Assets, liabilities, and equity are tracked through the transactions that affect their value. To ensure this occurs in an organized and consistent way, accountants use a variety of tracking tools to perform their work. *Accounts* are named categories in which transactions for specific assets, liabilities, and equity are cataloged. One example common in higher education is "Office Supplies." Office supplies are a sub-category of the institution's assets, as they represent items of value held by the organization. Institutions also maintain liability accounts. Two common examples of liabilities are accounts payable (what the institution owes within the year) and notes payable (longer-term debt, such as loans). Accounts can appear as categories on a budget, which can be organized by line items and broader categories (Figure 5.2).

The *accounting equation* is the basis for the institutional balance sheet; it can indicate the fiscal health of the institution at a specific point in time by presenting the balance between assets, liabilities, and equity (referred to as net assets by most not-for-profit organizations, because net assets are retained for future use). In short, if an organization owes (liabilities) more than it is worth (assets), there is a problem.

Assets = Liabilities + Net Assets . . . or, if you prefer,
Net Assets = Assets – Liabilities

Department Budget for XYZ at Dagny College Index (Department) Number : 101123			
Category of Expense	*Account Number*	*Description*	*Amount Allocated*
Personnel	0001	Administrative Staff	1,205,478
	0002	Other Professional	0
	0003	Faculty	0
	0004	Student Hourly	372,681
Total Personnel			**1,578,159**
Benefits	0015	Benefits Pool	0
	0016	Tuition Waivers	150,000
	0017	GA Insurance Pool	0
Total Benefits			**150,000**
Operating Expenses	2001	Office Supplies	26,472
	2002	Telecommunications	18,500
	2003	Printing	36,200
	2004	Mailing	12,000
	2005	Travel	12,547
Total Operating Expenses			**105,710**

Figure 5.2 Budget Indexes

Financial Statements and Conventions

Financial statements are the accountant's best attempt to provide a stable, accurate snapshot of organizational performance at a set point in time so that it can be compared over time and across organizations (Needles & Powers, 2007). FASB and GASB promulgate rules related to the presentation of information on financial statements, and these are shared with governing boards and other stakeholders, depending on institutional control. Financial statements are completed at the conclusion of the accounting period—referred to as a fiscal year. A *fiscal year* is a twelve-month period that may or may not coincide with the start of a calendar year. Public institutions' fiscal year start date may be mandated by the state (Balderston, 1995).

The *balance sheet* is a fairly standard report in which the organization's financial position is documented in terms of currency across asset, liability, and equity categories as of a specific date. The categories on the sheet will be in balance; in a practical sense, this means the net asset total will equal the values in the assets once liabilities are subtracted. In not-for-profit organizations, this may be referred to as the *statement of net position*, which reflects use of the term "net assets" (or in this case, "net position") in place of "equity".

Dagny College—Statement of Net Position		June 30, 2018		June 30, 2017
Assets				
Cash and Cash Equivalents	$	616,452,252	$	574,897,168
Accounts Receivable	$	99,966,923	$	95,712,151
Capital Lease Receivable	$	298,289	$	209,502
Inventories	$	15,755,130	$	14,658,130
Prepaid Expenses	$	10,871,601	$	10,426,398
Total Current Assets	*$*	*743,344,195*	*$*	*695,903,348*
Endowment Investments	$	167,303,117	$	145,414,423
Student Loans Receivable	$	61,636,222	$	58,435,351
Capital Lease Receivable	$	106,742	$	383,138
Land	$	58,081,638	$	54,714,520
Other Improvements	$	75,531,160	$	67,795,005
Construction in Progress	$	85,485,926	$	77,662,656
Buildings	$	1,485,396,614	$	1,402,124,211
Equipment	$	523,264,150	$	497,071,885
Total Non-Current Assets	*$*	*2,456,805,569*	*$*	*2,303,601,189*
Total Assets	**$**	**3,200,149,764**	**$**	**2,999,504,537**
Deferred Outflows	$	301,562,720	$	413,519,929
Total Assets and Deferred Outflows	**$**	**3,501,712,484**	**$**	**3,413,024,465**
Liabilities				
Accounts Payable and Accrued Expenses	$	75,584,883	$	99,670,012
Notes and Bonds Payable	$	34,850,812	$	31,266,282
Capital Lease Obligations	$	751,275	$	1,410,345
Unearned Revenue	$	63,123,066	$	62,436,928
Compensated Absences	$	25,812,626	$	23,559,993
Total Current Liabilities	*$*	*200,122,662*	*$*	*218,343,559*
Notes and Bonds Payable	$	556,190,266	$	522,016,724
Capital Lease Obligations	$	10,703,371	$	10,538,214
Compensated Absences	$	26,046,034	$	23,207,604
Other Post-Employment Benefits	$	107,167,677	$	93,753,284
Net Pension Liability	$	41,698,504	$	77,160,894
Total Non-Current Liabilities	*$*	*741,805,851*	*$*	*726,676,720*
Total Liabilities	**$**	**941,928,513**	**$**	**945,020,280**
Deferred Inflows	$	133,155,318	$	165,403,658
Total Liabilities and Deferred Inflows	**$**	**1,075,083,831**	**$**	**1,110,423,938**
Net Position				
Net Investment in Capital Assets	$	1,625,263,764	$	1,534,136,712
Restricted: Nonexpendable	$	73,369,309	$	63,589,828
Restricted: Expendable	$	119,653,942	$	119,242,192
Student Loans	$	87,043,161	$	82,513,369
Other	$	180,638,329	$	158,689,977
Unrestricted	$	340,660,147	$	344,428,450
Total Net Position	**$**	**2,426,628,653**	**$**	**2,302,600,528**
Total Liabiltiies, Deferred Inflows, and Net Position	**$**	**3,501,712,484**	**$**	**3,413,024,465**

Figure 5.3 Statement of Net Position

Figure 5.4 reduces the information presented above and pulls a simplified view of the 2018 data into broad categories matching the accounting equation. This statement of net position balances by demonstrating that the institution's assets match what it has held as net assets along with its liabilities. (Recall that the accounting equation is Assets = Liabilities + Net Assets.) Dagny College system holds nearly $2.4 billion in net assets (capital assets, restricted funds, and unrestricted funds), nearly $1.1 billion in liabilities (accounts payable, bonds (short- and long-term), leases, benefits, pensions), which taken together equal the assets of the organization, listed at $3.5 billion (cash, accounts receivable, inventory, land, buildings). Considered another way (reversing the math), the university system has $3.5 billion in assets and $1.1 in claims against those assets (liabilities), meaning the resulting net assets equal approximately $2.4 billion. The result is the same, but the equation is reordered as Net Assets = Assets – Liabilities.

While the balance sheet (or statement of net position) is not the only financial statement issued by an organization, it is a good example of the information presented to stakeholders, and provides a good case study in studying the balance of assets to liabilities and net assets. Another statement, commonly known as the income statement (also referred to as the statement of revenues, expenses, and changes in net position) focuses on the revenues and expenses incurred throughout the fiscal year. These statements enable the reader to evaluate how an organization uses (and gains) resources.

Five conventions (Figure 5.5) guide accountants when making decisions on how, what, and when to report financial transactions and other data. These conventions, when well-applied, make financial statements easier to read by external and internal stakeholders (Needles & Powers, 2007). While they are often cited in accounting

Assets = Liabilities + Net Assets

Current Assets	743,344,195
Noncurrent Assets	2,456,805,569
Total Assets	3,200,149,764
Deferred Outflows	301,562,720
"Assets" for equation	**3,501,712,484**
Current Liabilities	200,122,662
Noncurrent Liabilities	741,805,851
Total Liabilities	941,928,513
Deferred Inflows	133,155,318
"Liabilities" for equation	**1,075,083,831**
Net Position	2,426,628,653
"Net Assets" for equation	**2,426,628,653**

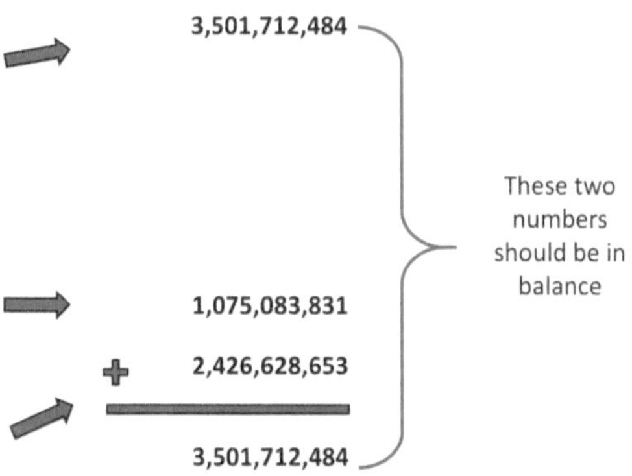

Figure 5.4 Net Position Simplified

literature, they are really just good practices for a variety of data collection and reporting processes, from accounting to assessment:

- *Comparability* promotes using GAAP to classify assets and liabilities, so that one organization's financial statement categories resemble another. *Consistency* focuses on reporting categories being used the same way over time, so that they are consistent. It is entirely acceptable for an organization to change its practices—those changes simply need to be noted.
- *Conservatism* refers to providing cautious estimates, forecasts, and analysis of consequences. It is critical to not be overly optimistic when forecasting enrollment, sources of revenue, or the consequences of challenging situations, economic and otherwise.
- *Materiality* refers to recording things of importance but also not going overboard—not every paperclip needs to be tracked.
- *Full disclosure* requires the reporting of all important data, *good and bad*, along with explanatory notes so that it can be understood in context.
- *Cost-benefit* suggests the cost of record-keeping should not outweigh its benefits. A simple way to remember this is the adage "Don't chase pennies with dollars."

Finally, it is important to be tracking and presenting the data *well*. The provision of "good" accounting data is not dissimilar to concepts of research design and measurement quality in educational settings. Needles and Powers (2007) recommend presenting data that are both *understandable* and *useful*, with the five conventions serving as the foundation of understandability. The five conventions help ensure users

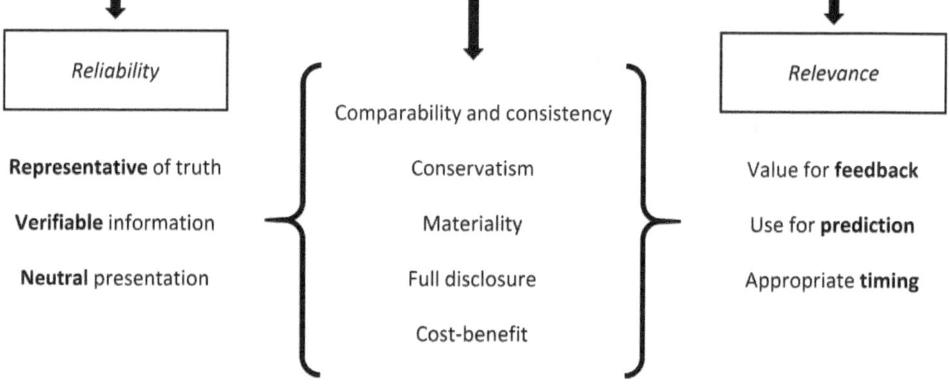

Figure 5.5 Qualities of Information (adapted from Needles & Powers, 2007)

of information will be able to interpret it as intended. The five conventions *support* the usefulness of data, but do not accomplish usefulness alone. Usefulness, a separate quality, requires the information provided by accountants to be *reliable* and *relevant* for decision-makers. For information to be reliable, it must be representative of the truth, obtained from a verifiable source, and neutral in nature. For information to be *relevant*, it must have value for feedback, assist in creating projections, and be provided at the right time.

Internal Control

Internal control is an important component in financial accounting and refers to separating authorization of expenditures, the documentation of expenditures (bookkeeping), and the actual custodianship of cash (Needles & Powers, 2007). In a practical sense, it is a series of activities designed to limit the occurrence of unforeseen losses or misdeeds and their impact on an organization's financial future.

Serna and Weiler (2016) emphasize the importance of control activities in higher education institutions. Strong internal controls can discourage embezzlement, which was termed an "epidemic" in a 2011 article documenting $16.5 million in recent fraud cases (Marquet, 2011). The following control procedures are recommended to minimize the probability of accidental losses (Needles and Powers, 2007, p. 302):

1. Authorization – limiting who can authorize purchases or transfers of resources over a certain value or dollar amount. For example, director-level approval may be required for all purchases in excess of $5,000, and then authorization at a senior administrative level may be required for anything beyond $10,000. State institutions also have the added complexity of procurement rules, requiring purchases above a certain value be sent out for bid with outside vendors before a contract for purchase can be generated.
2. Recording transactions – ensuring all transactions or exchanges of value are entered into the accounting information system. This should be simple, especially in an age of enterprise resource planning (ERP) systems being the conduit for the generation of payment for goods and services. Distributed purchasing responsibilities and decentralized decision-making and purchasing roles can complicate this control procedure.
3. Documents and records – collecting information in a decipherable and accurate way, and protecting the information within. The records have to be legible to other viewers, factually accurate, and appropriately preserved.
4. Physical controls – physical access to records related to transactions should be limited. This control is strengthened by keeping an audit trail, which tracks who has accessed records or made modifications. Records must be protected against unauthorized access and changes—paper and digital.
5. Periodic independent verification – verifying balances, inventorying supplies, pulling transaction records to look for missing or incorrect information. To accomplish this someone in the unit is responsible for verifying the accuracy and legitimacy of expenses based on the receipts and rationales provided. One common example

of this is the submission of travel expense reimbursement requests along with the receipts for purchases—food and gas purchases, along with statements from rental car agencies, airlines for tickets and baggage, and so on.

6. Separation of duties – ensuring a single individual's responsibilities are not so broad that they can hide financial misdeeds; in essence, ensuring the previous five functions are not performed by the same person. This is a critical component of control that will be illustrated in the later cases—in short, the person documenting purchases should not also be entrusted with the cash.
7. Sound personnel practices – employing background checks, hiring with care, supervising staff closely, and ensuring staff take vacations. Yes, that is right: providing paid time off is not just the right thing to do to ensure your workforce does not burn out—it is a control procedure! An organization can only do so much on the hiring side. Background checks and careful hiring are a good first step, and actively supervising staff to ensure procedures are followed is a good second step. In many cases, fraud is discovered while the offender is on vacation—when the wayward practice is revealed by its absence or the sharing of responsibilities with a colleague who is usually not involved.

There are numerous examples of where control procedures broke down; one simply has to read the *Chronicle of Higher Education* or visit Inside Higher Ed to find recent examples. Below is a sampling of what one can find:

- University of Kentucky – an unhappy staff member purchased more than $100,000 in excess equipment for the astronomy lab, took personal possession of the equipment, and sold the materials on eBay, pocketing the monies (Kocher, 2017).
- University of Oklahoma – a police officer stole money from evidence envelopes in the police station, netting just under $2,000 (McGuire, 2017).
- Emory University – an administrative assistant pocketed $317,000 in tuition payments in approximately 18 months by advising students to send their payments to a PayPal account mimicking Emory University (Boynton, 2015).
- University of Missouri – a volunteer treasurer for Sigma Alpha Epsilon (SAE) wrote himself a series of checks totaling more than $380,000. The perpetrator claimed to simply be careless in his record-keeping. SAE was not affiliated with the university at the time of the fraud (McLean, 2017).
- University of North Carolina (UNC) – the director of finance and administration for the Newman Catholic Center at UNC used parish credit cards for more than $125,000 in personal expenses. In addition, he wrote approximately $8,000 in checks to himself using the parish account by forging the signature of a Catholic priest (Grubb, 2017).
- University at Buffalo – a vice-president for University Life and Services resigned suddenly after being employed for nearly 40 years at the institution (Rey, 2016). It was found he spent $320,000 on personal expenses (including baseball, concert, and theater tickets, and his son's wedding) and was also prosecuted for filing false personal tax returns once his transgressions came to light (Tokasz & Besecker, 2017).

Students, administrators, and faculty have all been the perpetrators of schemes to unfairly benefit due to their access to resources. Most of the cases above occurred due to simple blending of roles or a lack of oversight and review of spending, and were discovered through audits, or a new reviewer of records being put in place. Use of the aforementioned control procedures greatly enhances institutions' chances of preventing unnecessary losses.

PLANNING FOR INTERNAL CONCERNS: MANAGERIAL ACCOUNTING

Managerial accounting looks inward and the managerial accountant (who may be referred to as a controller) is an internal staff member (or team) focused on costs and quality. The accuracy of the information managerial accountants use relies on careful financial accounting practices (use of the conventions) and their work to ensure there is a strong internal data system to collect these data (Goldstein, 2012). Managerial accountants support an organization's budgeting process through maintaining accurate records and useful data. They also forecast the effects of decisions, utilizing measures of costs and organizational controls. Service organizations are more challenging for management accountants due to the *intangibility* of services (see Chapter 9); timeliness and quality are critical (Atkinson et al., 2007; Braun & Tietz, 2013). When services rendered are intangible, institutions often use indicators of activity (rather than quality), such as number of credit hours, full-time-equivalent students, and dollars expended and generated. Each of the three basic overlapping and mutually reinforcing functions of a managerial accountant (controller) will be discussed, as they relate closely with the preparation of the operating budget of an institution.

Functions of the Management Accountant

The roles of the *controller* or internal financial unit are important: planning, organizing, and controlling operations through measuring and understanding costs at a unit and person level (Atkinson et al., 2007). The controller (or team) works to measure and manage activities related to improving efficiency (Atkinson, Banker, Kaplan, & Young, 1995). They use a variety of practices—with greater creativity and latitude than their financial-accounting-focused peers—to accomplish these functions.

Planning

Planning refers to the important decision-making an organization must do related to products, volume, and strategy. These decisions are informed by forecasts, expectations, and the internal and external environment—this involves analysis and prediction (Atkinson et al., 2007). Planning takes on particular importance in "high-skill" service organizations such as colleges and universities to avoid wasting valuable resources (Atkinson et al., 2007, p. 483). The budget planning process requires careful planning and forecasting of business activities, costs (expenses), and income (revenue).

Management accountants plan for a variety of elements that impact organizational performance and budgeting through the generation of revenue and expenses (income and costs). They base their plans on enrollment forecasts and market conditions (i.e., state subsidy, the effect of regulations), and create projections that become essential to organizational planning and budgeting processes (Atkinson et al., 2007; Braun & Tietz, 2013).

When evaluating potential costs, management accountants consider the different types of costs and revenues and how they work. For example, costs can be classified as either *direct* or *indirect* related to an activity, and exhibit certain *behaviors*—in proportion to activity, immutable to activity, or some variation therein (Table 5.1).

It is understanding these complex costs and the income that can be generated from them that allows management accountants to do the difficult work of forecasting the future operational and financial environment for an institution. As should be evident from the examples, a majority of the cost categories associated with instruction are indirect. Cost behaviors are a mix of variable, fixed, and mixed (or step-variable). In higher education, the addition of each student drives costs (expenses)—but also income (revenues) from tuition and state subsidy, if applicable. Understanding the expense and revenue balance for different programs and students is key to planning for budgeting. But it is important to also understand that budgets are not exclusively compiled at the organizational level—they are made up of smaller budgets at lower organizational levels contributing to the whole.

Organization

Organization refers to ensuring a *system* is in place to develop and deliver services efficiently and with sufficient quality (Atkinson et al., 2007). Management accountants work to operationalize the mission. The notion of a system can have multiple meanings: it may mean an information system or database, and in many cases it does. But a system goes beyond technology: it also means being organized into units capable of undertaking the functions and activities critical to operations. It can also refer to the process of organizing and compiling a budget, but budgeting transcends all three functions (planning, organizing, and controlling).

The management accountant structures the organization into units through which costs and income can be documented, analyzed, and evaluated (Braun & Tietz, 2013). In decentralized budget models (Chapter 6) these often take the form of what are called *responsibility centers*—which are "like a small business, and its manager is asked to run that small business to achieve the objectives of the larger organization" (Atkinson et al., 2007, p. 581). The use of responsibility centers can encourage innovation and lead to greater agility (Barr & McClellan, 2011), and allow for the tracking of costs, revenues, profits, and investments specific to the operations within them. Use of responsibility centers is further discussed in Chapter 6.

No system is perfect, but leadership must identify ways to operate an organization through a reasonable series of units and use tools to understand cost behaviors and cost types. Colleges and universities are struggling to maintain their ever-more complex organizations; understanding operations at a unit level is a critical component to controlling costs as tuition increases continue to outpace inflation (Dickeson, 2010).

Table 5.1 Cost Class and Behavior

Tool	*Explanation*	*Example*
Cost classifications	Costs that can be traced specifically to an activity are referred to as *direct*.	Within instruction, this would be an instructor's salary for teaching a specific course, as calculated as a proportion of his or her total job responsibilities. In a dining hall, this includes the cost of the food produced and salary of the person making it for the amount of time it required.
	Costs that cannot be traced directly to an activity are referred to as *indirect*.	Utilities costs, information technology costs for maintaining classroom technology, physical plant costs for maintaining the room and equipment used for the class (if face-to-face), advising and registration service costs to maintain the schedule, advise, and register students, and so on.
Cost behaviors	*Fixed* costs occur regardless of how much activity takes place.	A building on a brick-and-mortar campus requires maintenance, electricity, and heating (or cooling) regardless of how many classes are held within it. If enrollment or course offerings drop dramatically a building could be closed—but in general, facilities costs are fixed.
	Variable costs, by contrast, change in total with activities.	Supplies are a good example of variable costs. As more students enroll in a specific art course, the total cost of art supplies increases because more are being used with the addition of every student. Generally, the term "variable" is used to describe a proportional relationship where the cost increase per unit increase is uniform.
	Mixed costs are any costs that exhibit behaviors consistent with variable and fixed costs, together.	Utilities and operations exemplify mixed costs. While some utility costs will be incurred regardless of the number of occupied rooms within a residence hall (common areas, dining facilities), the total cost will decrease as occupancy decreases, as unoccupied rooms are not utilizing as much electricity or heating and cooling. Mixed costs are common in higher education, and are difficult to calculate because the pattern of adjustment will not always be clear.
	A sub-group of mixed costs, *step-variable* costs have fixed and variable elements that behave predictably based on activity.	If you have ever planned a banquet, you will be familiar with these costs—there is often a base charge tor service, and then a per-head cost for every individual that attends. What makes step-variable costs unique is their predictability—the variable cost component increases linearly with increased activities.

Control

In managerial accounting literature, *control* traditionally refers to performance measurement, evaluation, and monitoring (Atkinson et al., 2007). One might consider this the summative function of the management accountant, but it is a process that occurs continuously. The controlling function requires a properly organized organization, valid measures, and reliable data.

The notion of centralization or decentralization is important to management accountants. While typically determined by executive leadership, the degree of centralization within an institution has real consequences for the organization. Although most literature regarding centralization of control has focused on for-profit organizations, the concepts are essentially the same in not-for-profit organizations—they are just applied differently (Anthony & Young, 1999). Highly centralized organizations retain decision-making within the higher levels of the organization (Atkinson et al., 2007). Communication can be a challenge in centralized environments, and gathering high-quality information is more difficult, since the individuals closest to activities are not the decision-makers. By contrast, decentralization is the pushing of decision-making down to lower levels in the hierarchy—which can be very good for organizations in which a small group of core people at the top of the hierarchy cannot reasonably monitor every element of operations (Atkinson et al., 2007).

Decentralized organizations need strong technology for communication and data sharing, rules, and firmly established practices and training. Decentralized decision-making can be implemented in a variety of ways. The benefits of decentralization are many: it can lead to greater agility and better information being used for decision-making. One way to accomplish decentralization is to use responsibility-centered management budgeting, which relies on the responsibility centers described in the Organizing section.

Management accountants use an array of tools often cited in management (balanced scorecards, Total Quality Management (TQM), Lean thinking, strategic planning, and budgeting) to plan, organize, and control (evaluate, monitor, and manage) the organization's financial and operational well-being. Some of these tools will be discussed Chapter 7. Management accountants especially rely on strong data systems for performance monitoring (Atkinson et al., 2007; Braun & Tietz, 2013). Atkinson et al. (2007) and Barr and McClellan (2011) also note the use of the budget process itself as a management strategy. It can be created through an approach that is centralized and authoritative, decentralized and participative, or something in-between. Finally, management accountants rely on the budget. It serves as a plan of how things will be done (based on internal planning and organizing processes) and a device for organizational control and accountability (Goldstein, 2005).

CONCLUDING COMMENTS

Good administrators understand the principles and practices of financial accounting as they relate to organizing, reporting, and safeguarding resources and data. Institutions maintain a variety of assets and liabilities, and maintain net assets to the extent their assets outweigh their liabilities, which is reflected in the accounting equation. To ensure institutions understand their financial position, accuracy is of paramount importance, because the overall accuracy of financial statements is predicated upon the care that is taken from the bottom to the top of the organization.

The five conventions (comparability and consistency, conservatism, materiality, full disclosure, and cost-benefit) help accountants make decisions on how to compile information. Adherence to institutional definitions and conventions (informed by GAAP) for assets, liabilities, and net assets ensures financial statements are comparable and consistent with other organizations'. Financial accounting provides the numbers used for the preparation of financial statements and annual tax documents, and serves as the public face of an institution's financial position. Financial statements have consequence: they are used by external stakeholders and internal constituents to evaluate the financial position of an institution. Those stakeholders include accreditors and governmental agencies interested in the effectiveness with which institutions operate, and their evaluations have real consequence. They serve as a window into "how things are going" at an institution.

The practices and information generated through financial accounting practices are used for internal processes, as well—most notably in the budget planning process and evaluation of operational effectiveness. Managerial accounting (typically the responsibility of a controller or controller team) is focused inwardly on the organization. These functions rely in part on the data generated through the financial accounting system and have a profound impact on the budget model and process of an institution. As should be evident from Chapter 4, administrators have a duty to work to control costs through understanding cost behaviors and implementing internal and managerial controls. As colleges and universities are increasingly scrutinized for efficiency and effectiveness, the importance of sound internal practices will only grow larger over time. It is critical to carefully maintain records of how money is spent, who is spending it, and how it is being handled. Organizations that do this well set themselves up for successful budget creation, implementation, and execution, which will be discussed in the next chapter.

REFLECTIVE QUESTIONS

1. Why is it important that administrators understand accounting terminology and practices?
2. What are some examples of assets and liabilities?
3. What are examples of revenues and expenses?
4. What is the relationship between assets, liabilities, and equity?
5. How have individuals engaged in embezzlement and how can your institution mitigate its occurrence?
6. How do accounting conventions and practices impact the budget?

CHAPTER 6

Budgeting Basics

Few readers of this book will be responsible for the overall institutional budget, but most of you will be responsible for a piece of that budget at some point in your career. Many professionals working within higher education are substantially under-prepared to work with a budget (Serna & Weiler, 2016). To be a responsible *fiscal steward*, simply looking at the bottom line of the budget is not enough. Administrators must be able to thoughtfully review the budget to determine exactly where the potential problems are with regard to over- or under-estimation of revenues and expenses.

The ways through which institutions accumulate revenue and incur expenses were described in Chapter 4. The goal of Chapter 5 was to familiarize the reader with the language of accounting. Accounting is generally split into two camps. Financial accounting focuses on external reporting (including tax filings), conventions of record-keeping, and internal control of resources and records. Managerial accounting is focused inward, at how the organization is structured and positioned to incur and manage costs. In this chapter we connect the two, taking the revenues and expenses and pairing them with the governing structure in which they are outlined for an institution.

Public institutions continue to struggle with decreasing or stagnant state appropriations, oftentimes resulting in a net increase in student tuition. This trend is likely to continue as states balance their appropriations among sectors. For private institutions, declining enrollment and tuition discounting has created financial stress not unlike that experienced by public institutions (Barnshaw & Dunietz, 2015). At the same time, both public and private colleges and universities are facing increases in a variety of costs—notably health care, technology, physical plant enhancements, and maintenance. Many colleges and universities are exhibiting signs of present or future financial distress (Selingo, 2016).

Financial resources are critical to all aspects of higher education, and resource availability sets limits on the services that can be provided (Serna & Weiler, 2016). The overarching purpose of a budget is to provide administrators with a tool to monitor and control the assets and resources of an institution. The stage for strong performance and efficient use of resources is set through a thoughtfully designed and *realistic* budget relying on relevant, reliable, and understandable data—derived from solid accounting practices. The budgeting process is an opportunity to re-evaluate operations and change the status quo but is not often used in that manner

(Lenington, 1996). Through the budget process, an institution, department, or program operationalizes its plan and publicly expresses its priorities.

An institution's budget is used internally for planning, but also serves as an important communication device to external stakeholders. A budget can signal an institution's overall health and serves as a financial representation of the institution's values and priorities. Simply put, *if it is important it will get funded*. For example, when a colleague tells you that "We don't have the money for that project" or "It isn't in the budget," what is really being communicated is that it is not a priority, at least not at this time. As Shattock (2003) points out, "no university can become successful without concentrating and prioritizing its resources" (p. 32). While your institution may differ slightly from the approaches discussed, the information can be taken back to assist your unit in the decision-making process. Additionally, we provide an introduction to budgeting vocabulary that will help when communicating with institutional business office staff and senior leaders.

WHAT IS A BUDGET?

A budget, in a practical sense, is a living artifact of a control and planning system, built on organizational structures. Braun and Tietz (2013) note, "Budgeting is perhaps the most widely used management accounting tool employed by companies, organizations, and governments throughout the world" (p. 515). A budget serves many purposes, including the allocation of resources, providing incentives, communicating priorities, and controlling resources. Atkinson, Banker, Kaplan, and Young (1995) describe budgets as "summaries of the expected consequences of the organization's short-term activities" (p. 193). A budget *should* be strongly connected to the university's strategic plan or priorities. Serna and Weiler (2016) say, "the planning process provides a guide for reaching institutional goals; the budget provides a means of reaching them. Not linking the two is folly at best, and a failure of leadership at worst" (p. 139).

Budgets are compiled at many levels, feeding into a "master budget" (Braun & Tietz, 2013) and they present anticipated revenues and expenses by category (or function) with anticipated targets, to operationalize the strategic plan (Anthony & Young, 1999). Budgets allow for communication and alignment of spending to organizational priorities or plans in an uncertain world, and must be flexible enough that administrators can move money from one line item or unit to another to address institutional priorities. Hence, the administrator responsible must be willing to make adjustments, no matter how difficult, when necessary.

Within most institutions of higher education, two major types of budgets exist: operating and capital. While these will be discussed in greater detail later, the operating budget is the core budget of the institution and accounts for all revenue generated, including restricted funds as well as projected expenditures for the fiscal year (Barr, 2002; Goldstein, 2012). On the expense side of the operating budget the institution accounts for its educational and general expenses, which make up the vast majority of the overall budget. Capital budgets are typically used for new construction, long-term repair, and renovation programs. These projects must be linked to a comprehensive financial plan—new facilities create an ongoing financial commitment (Barr, 2002). In many public institutions, the money for capital improvements may be a direct allocation from the state coffers.

Individuals from all levels of the organization are involved, to different degrees, in the budget creation and implementation process. At the institution level, the chief financial officer (CFO) has ultimate responsibility for the budget process and accounting practices. To administer this role, the CFO usually employs a controller (the head internal accountant, who may also be referred to as a comptroller) and a budget officer (the person charged with keeping and maintaining the budget). Many people throughout the organization will share in this budget role—each college, division, school, and department (depending on organization) will likely have a "budget person" who holds responsibility for maintaining smaller, distributed budgets and reporting up the chain. This may be their sole responsibility, or fall within one function of their position.

This chapter is written with the assumption that the majority of readers of this chapter will be from public or private not-for-profit institutions, as they make up 77 percent of colleges and universities in the United States (NCES, 2018, Table 317.20) and account for more than 94 percent of students enrolled in two- or four-year (or above) institutions (NCES, 2018, Table 303.10). Not-for-profit organizations are distinct from for-profit organizations because they work to balance revenues with expenses, rather than attempting to earn a profit (Atkinson, Kaplan, Matsumura, & Young, 2007). "What defines an organization as a non-profit is regulation—commonly referred to as the 'nondistribution constraint'—that prevents it from distributing profit to board members, the chief executive officer, the executive director, or other stakeholders of the organization" (Lindahl, 2010). Not-for-profit organizations are exempt from taxes on profit, property, and sales for services directly related to their mission (Anthony & Young, 1999).

In record-keeping and budgeting, not-for-profit organizations operate very similarly to for-profit organizations. Strategic plans are followed by budgets, and then the organization's actual performance is analyzed for reporting (Anthony & Young, 1999). Atkinson et al. (2007) note, "Budgeting serves a slightly different but equally relevant role in . . . [not-for-profit] organizations such as charitable organizations and government agencies" (p. 483). Efficiency is an increasing concern in not-for-profit organizations. In that sense, colleges and universities are very much like for-profit organizations, hard as some try to deny this fact.

Colleges and universities are also complex due to their service orientation. Because services are rendered via interactions, not transactions, quality and timeliness are paramount considerations. Service organizations are less well-practiced at establishing measures that can be used to evaluate themselves (Atkinson et al., 2007). They are focused on delivering as much service as possible (however defined) at the highest quality possible (Anthony & Young, 1999). Service organizations make up the largest sector of the U.S. economy (Braun & Tietz, 2013), and salaries and benefits constitute a majority of the operating budgets within these organizations. Scholars estimate between 50 percent and 70 percent of an operating budget in a college or university will be composed of salaries and benefits, in large part due to health insurance (Goldstein, 2012; Lenington, 1996).

Goldstein (2005) notes that colleges and universities are also more complex than most other not-for-profit organizations because of their compliance requirements and diversity in revenue sources, and the restrictions on many of their revenue sources. This makes budget development more of a challenge but even more critical. Organizations operating in a highly regulated (or non-competitive) environment have historically been less focused on efficiency and productivity (Atkinson et al., 2007), and public institutions of higher education fit this description. Dickeson (2010) further notes myriad panels, inquiries, and commissions in the past thirty years exploring the inefficiencies and ineffectiveness of U.S. higher education by the U.S. Department of Education (the Spellings Commission), the National Governors' Association, the State Higher Education Executive Officers Association, and think-tanks. These inefficiencies have many origins, but Dickeson points to a culture problem: an unwillingness by institutions to slow growth and refocus themselves in the name of satisfying all possible constituents. In order to stay relevant and maintain the trust of an increasingly skeptical audience, higher education must work to understand its own costs, report on its effectiveness, and reassure the public of its financial stewardship.

BUDGETING: TYPES, MODELS, AND PROCESS

A budget is a financial representation of the institution's values and priorities and serves as a guide for an organization, identifying how funds will be used. Anticipated revenues and expenditures are divided into categories with numerical targets reflecting the anticipated dollars received and expended (Atkinson et al., 2007). Budgets establish and communicate the financial plan for the organization; when done properly, they align spending to priorities and are informed by the strategic plan (Braun & Tietz, 2013). Further, a budget can be used to create early drafts of financial statements (Goldstein, 2005).

Although many colleges and universities are not-for-profit organizations, and many individuals within scoff at the notion of them operating like businesses, we must adopt strong budgeting procedures. Anthony and Young (1999) note, "Budgeting . . . is even more important in a non-profit organization than in a for-profit company . . . for two reasons—cost structure and spending flexibility" (p. 445). In short, because of the service-oriented nature of higher education, and reliance on highly skilled workers, a majority of the budget is composed of discretionary costs that can be deployed in a variety of ways. Leadership has the freedom to determine the future direction of the organization and how it allocates resources (and has a responsibility to estimate revenues based on anticipated fluctuations in activity). Service organization budgets are often visually simpler than those in manufacturing or retail environments, because the work is largely intangible (Braun & Tietz, 2013). Budgets are hierarchical in nature, with the various organizational unit operating budgets feeding into the larger master budget (Braun & Tietz, 2013). Stated differently, "No budget or program in an institution of higher education stands alone" (Barr & McClellan, 2011, p. 21). There are two major approaches to budgeting: centralized or decentralized. The degree to which the process is centralized or decentralized is dictated by organizational norms and practices.

The *centralized* budget method is the most widely used method in higher education budgeting. An institution that uses a centralized budget approach brings all of its revenue into the central pool then distributes it according to its internal policies and procedures. This process requires divisions, colleges, departments, etc., to request money from the central administration based on a proposal describing the unit's needs and wants. Budget centralization has a tendency to create a disconnect between the academic authority and fiscal responsibility (Strauss & Curry, 2002). At most institutions, faculty are responsible for the curricular offerings but have no responsibility for the generation of revenue because another administrative unit is responsible for the recruitment of students. This creates difficulty when trying to explain the connection between the revenue source (tuition, grants, endowments, etc.) and the expense items (faculty and staff salaries, office supplies, etc.).

Decentralized or *participatory* budgeting refers to using a decentralized approach to drafting a budget, incorporating all levels of management in the planning process. This can enhance buy-in and improve the accuracy of projections and estimations, but takes more time. It can also lead to units adding wiggle room or bloat into their budget requests (Braun & Tietz, 2013). Regardless of the risk, Lenington (1996) states, "[b]udgets should be a bottom-up exercise" (p. 49), as this will allow for stronger information-gathering and holding units accountable for adhering to the budget, since they had a hand in its development. Decentralization of the budget process implies that the units responsible for generating the revenue are also responsible for distributing the revenue (Figure 6.2), thereby creating a stronger link between responsibility and authority in the budget process. One of the more common methods of decentralized budgeting is *responsibility-centered management* (RCM). The purpose of this approach is to push the decision-making and prioritization to the units that generate the bulk of the institution's revenue. While more entrepreneurial in nature, decentralized budgets do not create additional dollars from new revenues sources; rather, they encourage the development of such new sources.

All budgets involve organizational politics; they are a representation of negotiated exchanges and a shifting of priorities (Goldstein, 2005). It is important to note that

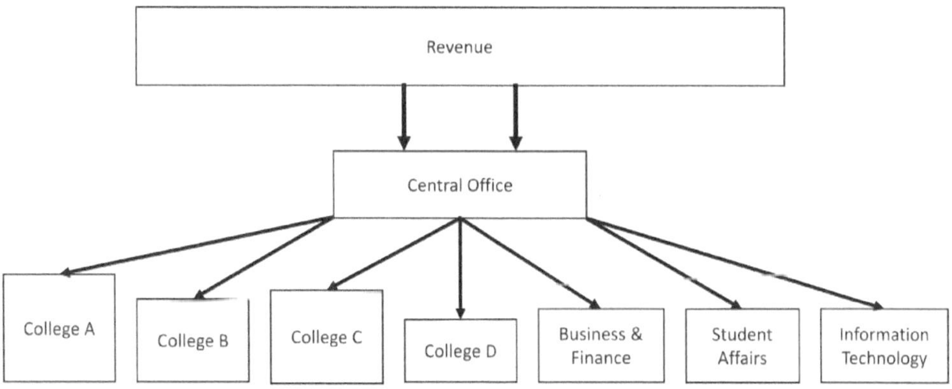

Figure 6.1 Centralized Budget

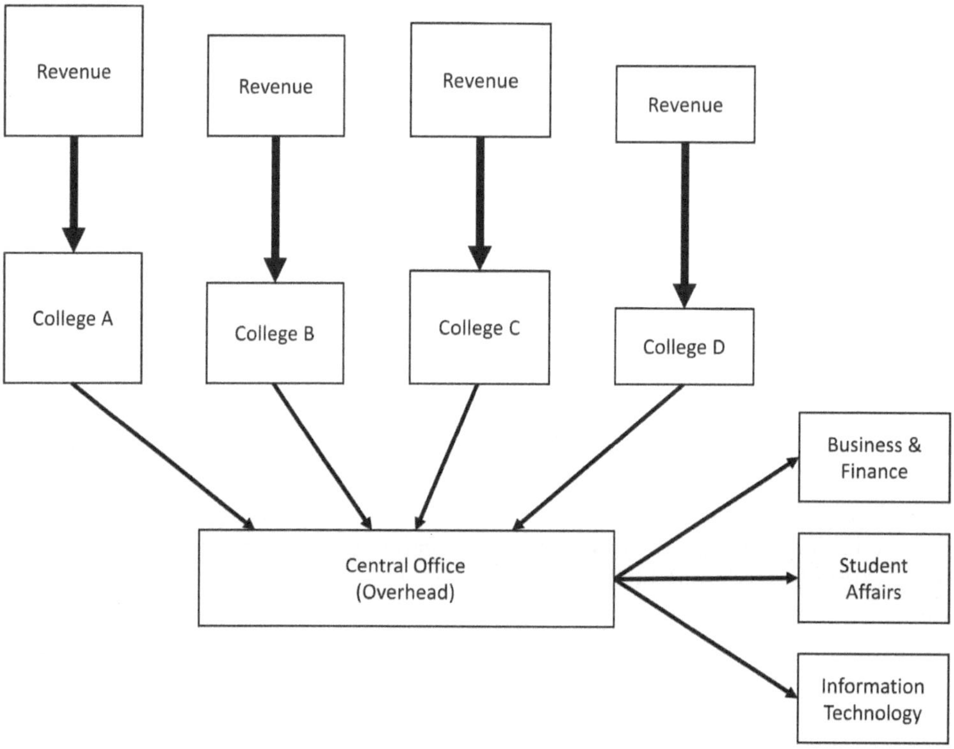

Figure 6.2 Decentralized Budget

senior leadership always has the authority to make adjustments to the budgets, even if developed through a participatory or ground-up process. The president and board have the authority to add, remove, or delay any items they wish (Lenington, 1996). The process of developing a budget will be outlined in subsequent sections, but first, an explanation of budget types and models is necessary.

Budget Types

Budgets can be organized by level (institution-wide, unit or division, auxiliary) and by purpose (operating and capital); this section describes these types. Both public and private institutions construct and adhere to budgets, and the differences between institution types are less evident today than in the past. The key difference between public and private institutions lies in rules about contracts and layers of approvals, and general business practices related to approvals and human resources (Barr & McClellan, 2011). Nearly every institution constructs a *master budget*, which reflects the entire institution's financial plan (absent auxiliary units) and is a representation of its anticipated operations for the next fiscal year. The master budget is a reflection of the budgets for individual units (unit budgets), however organized by the institution.

Revenue Sources	Expenditure Categories
Tuition and Fees (and special fees)	Salaries and Benefits
Sponsored Research Grants, Contracts	Supplies
Patents, Licensing, and Royalties	Capital Equipment
Gifts and Grants	Publications, Printing, Postage
Endowment Support	Professional Development, Travel
Investment Income	Utilities and Facilities Support
State and Local Appropriations (if applicable)	Debt Service Reserve Requirements
Sales and Services, Special Programs	Contingency
Auxiliary Enterprises	Auxiliary Enterprises

Figure 6.3 Revenue and Expenditure

The *operating budget* summarizes activities and planned revenues and expenses stemming from normal business practices, cash on hand, and reserves (Barr & McClellan, 2011; Goldstein, 2012; Serna & Weiler, 2016). The operating budget has categories for revenue sources and expense categories (Figure 6.3).

Public and private institutions differ in their mix of revenue sources (public institutions can count on at least marginal support from their state), but the expenses are largely the same. *Capital equipment* refers to shorter-term or mid-level expenses, such as computers, software, and classroom equipment (Barr & McClellan, 2011; Lenington, 1996). *Reserve requirements* are mandated by external agencies and are also held for planned future expenditures on large items, such as institution-wide data systems. *Contingency* refers to a pool of money held as a cushion against accidental losses or over-spending; if not spent, it can be reinvested in the institution (Goldstein, 2012; Lenington, 1996). Figure 6.4 contains a sample institution-level budget for a private, four-year institution.

Revenues and expenses can be organized by type or purpose—this is referred to natural or functional classification, respectively. If a budget is organized using natural classifications, items that are alike are grouped together in clusters (telecommunication costs, utilities, office supplies). In a functional layout, revenues and expenses are arranged by the purpose through which they were incurred (Barr & McClellan, 2011; Goldstein, 2012). Many institutions use a combination of natural and functional classifications in their operating budgets. Operating budgets are often compiled annually without consideration of multi-year planning or consequences (Balderston, 1995). Figure 6.5 presents division- and unit-level budgets, where the classification system can be more readily seen.

The *capital budget*, by contrast, holds the larger, more permanent assets of the institutions—it documents infrastructure costs, such as buildings (physical plant), building projects, and large-scale equipment with a high replacement cost.

	FY17 Budget	Budget Changes	FY18 Budget	% Change
Revenues ($000s omitted)				
Student Tuition and Fees	234,845	4,171	239,016	1.78%
Residence Halls	21,154	470	21,624	2.22%
Auxiliary Enterprises	18,157	(1,620)	16,537	-8.92%
Investment Income	2,795	108	2,903	3.85%
Unrestricted Gifts	323	(13)	310	-3.88%
Endowment Income	1,914	22	1,935	1.12%
Total Revenue	***279,187***	***3,138***	***282,325***	***1.12%***
Expenditures ($000s omitted)				
Faculty and Staff Salaries	86,487	2,910	89,397	3.37%
Adjunct Faculty Salaries	3,248	(94)	3,154	-2.89%
Part-time Staff	8,001	31	8,032	0.39%
Employee Benefits	27,144	1,465	28,609	5.40%
Salaries and Benefits	***124,880***	***4,313***	***129,192***	***3.45%***
Financial Aid	56,701	3,508	60,209	6.19%
Supplies and Expenses, etc.	47,880	529	48,409	1.10%
Online Programs	10,835	743	11,578	6.86%
Utilities	4,944	-	4,944	0.00%
Technology Capital Funding	8,514	(1,813)	6,701	-21.29%
Deferred Maintenance	6,311	(433)	5,878	-6.87%
Furnishings and Equipment	2,194	(1,377)	817	-62.76%
Facilities Renovation	2,457	(1,257)	1,200	-51.16%
Debt Service	13,398	-	13,398	0.00%
Special Initiatives	1,074	(1,074)	-	-100.00%
Total Expenditures	***279,187***	***3,138***	***282,325***	***1.12%***
Net Surplus/(Deficit)	**0**	**0**	**0**	

Figure 6.4 A Sample University Budget

Capital budgets are multi-year in nature and allow for the *amortization* of assets, which is an accounting term for the slow write-off of a large asset's value over time as it depreciates in value (Serna & Weiler, 2016). While the capital budget is compiled as a separate document (and requires special expertise), it should be considered alongside the operating budget (Balderston, 1995). The creation and implementation of a capital budget is similar in many ways to an operational budget, but

Sterling Arts Institute - Budget Variance Report *Orientation Office*			*Period 3*	
Account	**Description**	**Budget AY**	**Actual YTD**	**Variance**
3200-20114	Orientation Fee	32,000.00	25,412.00	6,588.00
	Total Revenue	***32,000.00***	***25,412.00***	**6,588.00**
3200-30101	Conference Registration	1,200.00	1,500.00	(300.00)
3200-30102	Conference Travel Expenses	3,600.00	2,500.00	1,100.00
3200-30121	Meetings and Meals	680.00	300.00	380.00
3200-30122	Local Travel/Mileage	400.00	684.00	(284.00)
3200-30123	Non-Local Travel/Mileage	250.00	-	250.00
3200-30131	Staff Training	1,200.00	800.00	400.00
3200-30132	Student Training	1,000.00	1,400.00	(400.00)
3200-53010	Supplies	620.00	600.00	20.00
3200-53020	Equipment	1,350.00	1,700.00	(350.00)
3200-57001	Advertising	800.00	800.00	0.00
3200-58001	Special Events	12,000.00	9,487.00	2,513.00
3200-58002	Programming	8,300.00	6,500.00	1,800.00
3200-59301	Copy/Print Cost Allocation	600.00	450.00	150.00
	Total Expenses	***32,000.00***	***26,721.00***	**5,279.00**

Figure 6.5 Art School Budget

generally requires more granular cost estimation and rationale development (Barr & McClellan, 2011). Institutions may choose to acquire capital assets, such as new buildings, by issuing financing (usually in the form of bonds) or pulling from their reserve accounts (or both)—an issue addressed in Chapter 4 (Goldstein, 2012; Serna & Weiler, 2016).

It is important to note that some units on campus are not featured broadly in the institution's operating and capital budgets. Auxiliary units, which are self-sustaining enterprises and are treated like separate entities, have their own budgets and pay the institution service fees for operating and sharing services, such as human resources, payroll, information technology, and maintenance. The *auxiliary budget* (Figure 6.6) is on the same fiscal year as the master budget and is compiled using the same systems (Barr & McClellan, 2011). An institution may also choose to maintain one or more *special fund budgets*, which are used to keep the plans for a special grant or program separate from the institution's overall operating budget.

Budget Models

The budget process and model selected is an important opportunity for an organization; the model selected will strongly influence the status quo and culture around budgeting. In many institutions, "funds are spent as budgeted for fear of losing the funds, rather than saved and reserved for a common need at a later date" (Lenington, 1996, p. 8). Rarely are any of these models used "in their pure form"

Office of Residence Life Budget for FY 2018, Dagny College	FY 2017 Approved Budget	FY 2018 Proposed Budget	$ Increase (Decrease)	% Increase / Decrease
Revenue:				
Operating Income (Room Charges)	31,585,798	32,045,874	460,076.24	1.46%
Facility Rental	186,000	194,000	8,000.00	4.30%
Conference Income	320,000	322,000	2,000.00	0.63%
Other Income	150,000	150,000	-	0.00%
Total Revenue	32,241,798	32,711,874	470,076.24	1.46%
Expense:				
Salaries, Wages, Benefits				
Administrators	1,496,925	1,465,498	(31,426.56)	-2.10%
Staff	255,066	257,617	2,550.66	1.00%
Graduate Assistants	122,320	130,484	8,164.00	6.67%
Resident Assistants	112,402	104,236	(8,166.40)	-7.27%
Student Assistants (Non-RA)	870,451	872,104	1,653.00	0.19%
Wage/Compensation Pool	34,650	33,295	(1,355.20)	-3.91%
Employee Benefits	627,400	623,712	(3,687.68)	-0.59%
Salary, Wages, Benefits Total	3,603,409	3,480,316	(123,093.52)	-3.42%
Operating Expenses				
Supplies	175,885	174,611	(1,273.44)	-0.72%
Travel	224,758	221,704	(3,053.92)	-1.36%
Communication	174,283	183,648	9,364.88	5.37%
Maintenance/Repairs	1,541,350	2,000,115	458,765.08	29.76%
Equipment	1,045,845	1,042,356	(3,488.52)	-0.33%
Utilities	3,007,780	3,059,080	51,299.84	1.71%
Scholarships/Fee Waivers	1,450,075	1,438,788	(11,286.48)	-0.78%
Inter-Department Transfers	4,058,593	4,035,888	(22,704.96)	-0.56%
Operating Expenses Total	11,696,692	12,541,764	845,071.92	7.22%
Fixed Expenses				
Renewals/Replacements	2,001,604	2,257,573	255,968.56	12.79%
Service Charge	2,399,881	2,274,039	(125,842.08)	-5.24%
Debt Service	9,032,537	8,878,743	(153,794.64)	-1.70%
Infrastructure Charge	836,000	836,000	-	0.00%
Insurance	379,526	405,148	25,621.60	6.75%
Fixed Expenses Total	14,649,549	14,562,482	(87,067.20)	-0.59%
Total Expense	28,113,638	28,661,912	548,273.79	1.95%
Net Income	4,128,160	4,049,962	(78,197.55)	-1.89%

Figure 6.6 Auxiliary Budget

(Barr & McClellan, 2011, p. 67). This leads to unending variety: as Goldstein (2005) notes, "there may be as many different budget processes as there are institutions" (p. ix).

Incremental

An incremental budget is historical in nature and is based on the previous year's budget, adjusting it up or down based on changes projected for revenues and expenses. It can be applied across all categories equally, or vary within budgets (known as redistribution), which means each budget unit can decide how the 2 percent cut, for example, will occur (Atkinson et al., 2007; Goldstein, 2012). The advantages of an incremental approach are in its simplicity, and therefore its efficiency of process. This approach assumes costs will vary little year by year and is very popular because it is uncontroversial, fairly quick, and does not lead to major upheaval (Goldstein, 2012).

The disadvantages are many; Goldstein (2005) is a critic of incremental budgeting, noting, "Regardless of the specific approach, incremental budgeting is recognized as producing suboptimal results in terms of resource allocation" (p. 165). Other critics of this budgeting approach note that it completely lacks analysis (Atkinson et al., 2007), magnifies systemic problems, and can compound the effects of bad decisions over time (Barr, 2002; Dickeson, 2010; Goldstein, 2005). It also suggests that the status quo is a *good* thing. Of an incremental process, Goldstein (2012) warns, "Poorly performing units will continue to consume resources that provide little return in terms of enhanced institutional success. At the same time, high-performing and high-potential units do not garner enough resources to leverage their efforts for better results" (p. 97).

Zero-Based

This budget model starts from the ground up, at zero, and is described as the "opposite" of incremental budgeting (Goldstein, 2012, p. 100). Previous budget allocations are wiped away and units must justify every expense planned. As one might imagine, advocates of zero-based budgeting point out that autopilot-like expenses do not live on in perpetuity (Atkinson et al., 2007), but it can also cause mass hysteria on an annual basis (Barr & McClellan, 2011). The advantage of a zero-based model is its intense attention to detail, which may spotlight programs or services no longer contributing to an institution's goals. The disadvantages of zero-based models are grounded in the amount of time it takes to reinvent the wheel, as well as building in time to discuss priorities and goals. Zero-based approaches ignore ongoing costs and disregard organizational history (Goldstein, 2012). Barr and McClellan (2011) suggest that the zero-based approach could instead be used every five or ten years to provide a check on the status quo. It can also be implemented *within* individual units with some positive results (Goldstein, 2012).

Cost Center/Responsibility Center

The RCM budget model relies on responsibility centers (see Chapter 5) and is, by nature, somewhat decentralized (Balderston, 1995). In this model, centers (revenue/profit and cost) manage their own budgets. Data quality and metrics take on extra importance in this model, because shared expenses and revenues (overhead) must be allocated across the institution in a meaningful way (Balderston, 1995; Goldstein, 2012), which is a known area of struggle (Atkinson et al., 1995). Revenue centers (those generating money through enrollment or sales of services) must cover all of their own direct costs while sharing a percentage of their revenue back to central administration to cover their indirect costs—this is typically described as a "tax" (Goldstein, 2012, p. 98). For this approach to work, Balderston (1995) argues, "The unit manager must be able to control costs" while receiving current and accurate information from accounting systems (p. 161). This requirement relies heavily on financial accounting and management accounting systems and practices.

In a decentralized approach, excess revenues or unexpected expenses are the responsibility of the unit, not the central administration. Priest and Boon (2006) suggest "without a budget mechanism like RCM that allows for carefully managed, unit level ways of dealing with surpluses and shortfalls, a university's resource dependence could be the source of its downfall" (p. 184). Unit managers should put in place, where permissible, a carry-over fund which can help the unit even out the ups and downs of its revenue production. These funds can also be applied to larger-scale projects (e.g., a new copier, classroom technology) that cannot be funded directly from yearly operating revenues.

Anthony and Young (1999) provide some useful criteria for the deployment of successful RCM models:

- Degree of influence – while a unit-level or center manager does not have to possess complete control of all decisions related to operations, they should have substantial control over elements such as volume, quality, and costs. Within an academic unit (a college within a university, or school/department within a college, for example), this might be the number of classes and enrollment minimums or maximums, the faculty selected to teach the course, and the tuition charged. The reader may already observe "individual colleges or schools can't set their own tuition, but institutions use this approach." Yes, this is true—and simply demonstrates the idea that a unit manager must be able to manage their operations but does not need complete control of all elements.
- Perception of fairness – the earnings of a unit should correspond in general with actual success. For example, a revenue or profit center that meets its goals or is otherwise successful in light of its mission should be perceived as successful in however the model is measured—if that is meeting enrollment goals, then income for the center should be related to that strong enrollment.
- Absence of dysfunctional incentives – the implemented model should not foster so much competition that the organization is unable to meets its mission and goals, or prevent responsibility centers from reaching their goals. One criticism of RCM is its dividing of interests (Barr & McClellan, 2011) and discouragement of collaboration, since each unit is more or less responsible for its own success. Organizations typically adopt rules to discourage this dysfunctional environment, or provide special incentives for interdepartmental or interdisciplinary collaboration, thereby introducing a hybrid model into the RCM environment.
- Existence of transfer prices – internal service-sharing must be costed and paid appropriately within and across the organization to avoid imbalances of power and responsibility. Institutions have many shared services, such as human resources, information technology, facilities maintenance and support, the Enrollment Management and Student Affairs functions, and many, many others. These units are considered service (or support) centers and would be classified as cost centers, since they have limited ability to generate their own revenue. They are funded

within the RCM environment through the allocation of overheads according to a formula predetermined by institutional leadership. Specific services, such as Residence Life/Housing offering a vacant building for summer office space during a facilities renovation, would generate a transfer pricing event. The academic unit (revenue or profit center displaced) should pay the auxiliary (itself a profit center) for the use of its space in an RCM environment—at fair market value.
- Low record-keeping costs – it should not be an undue burden to use whatever institutional system is in place to document and manage individual responsibility centers' activities. This is similar to the cost-benefit convention discussed in the Financial Statements and Conventions section of Chapter 5; in short, the system needs to be workable for the centers so that the necessary data can be entered and used for timely and accurate performance monitoring and reporting.

The advantages of this model are based in organizational agility and the increase in incentives to perform well within the structures of the model (increased enrollment and grant activity, for example, are rewarded). The responsibility centers are, by nature, closer to the ground on important issues, and have the best information on how to adjust operations to improve. This approach usually makes the use of resources more transparent on campus, which can lead faculty and staff to better understand organizational costs (Goldstein, 2012). Decentralized budget models such as RCM have been championed because of "their potential to hold down overhead costs while advancing the institutional mission" (Priest & Boon, 2006, p. 183). The disadvantages of this model, many of which are noted by Anthony and Young (1999), vary based on how the model is deployed; models built on quantitative factors value things that can be quantified, regardless of quality or strategic priorities. Goldstein (2012) notes this model's history is rooted in private institutions, but "By 2011, nearly half of all independent doctoral universities and more than 20 percent of public doctoral universities" used some form of this model (p. 100).

Project funding (which serves as an alternative to zero-based budgeting) structures the budget as a series of temporary projects on timelines, while elements that live in perpetuity are called programs and re-evaluated periodically (Atkinson et al., 2007).

Program budgeting, also known as the *planning, programming, and budgeting system* (PPBS), was an attempt to depart from more traditional budget models utilized by the U.S. Department of Defense (Balderston, 1995). PPBS splits the budgets into programmatic categories and attempts to establish metrics through which performance can be measured—because of struggles with definitions and measures, the PPBS model has been largely abandoned but informs other present-day approaches. It is not widely used in higher education (Barr, 2002). The strength of this approach is its integration of strategic planning, budgeting, and assessment (Goldstein, 2005).

By contrast, *incentive-based budgeting* requires each unit to contribute a set amount or percentage of operations back into a central pool to support an initiative (new or recurring) of strategic importance (Barr & McClellan, 2011). The units themselves can propose initiatives to receive the central funding. This is generally used for one-time or short-term funding, as continuing funding would impose on other academic units in the long term (Goldstein, 2012).

Formula or Performance

Formula and *performance* models are most frequently applied by states in determining subsidies sent to public institutions or statewide systems, rather than within colleges and universities themselves.

Elements of *formula budgeting* can be found within institutions (particularly those using the responsibility-centered budget approach). In the formula budgeting model, a formula is established by which funds will be awarded, and this model is usually informed by certain performance criteria, such as number of enrolled students, total credit hours enrolled, number of graduates, and so on. The awarding agency will then disburse funds in accordance with the rate input into the formula (Barr & McClellan, 2011; Goldstein, 2012). This model's advantages are clarity, stability, and general simplicity—even if the formula itself is complex. The disadvantages of this model are its reliance on historical information, need to utilize quantitative inputs, and potential for reinforcing the importance of enrollment over strategic aims (Goldstein, 2012).

In a *performance-based budget* model, resources are allocated largely on the basis of meeting specific goals, such as a report card measure, enrollment, or degree attainment (Barr & McClellan, 2011). This model has become increasingly favored in recent years by state agencies (Goldstein, 2012). Goldstein warns that some of the goals or metrics might be inherently meaningless (2005, pp. 168–169) due to a lack of understanding by state agencies of the contributing factors to the output metrics adopted. For a more extended discussion of this topic, see Chapter 4.

Hybrid

This is not so much a model but the blending of the aforementioned models, and is "far and away the common mode of budgeting in higher education" (Barr & McClellan, 2011, p. 77). As evidenced in the responsibility-centered budget model section, rarely are budgets adopted in their pure form—it is a little bit incremental, with occasional zero-based, sprinkled in with something else, such as RCM or formula or program budgeting (Goldstein, 2012). And that is completely acceptable. Budget models are not monolithic in nature, and more than anything need to work for the organization's finances and personnel.

THE BUDGET CYCLE

Developing an institutional, departmental, or programmatic budget is not an event; it is a process. As an administrator prepares for this process, they must understand that the budget represents the allocation of the institution's resources directed toward accomplishing its goals and objectives. Institutional budgets are based on a *fiscal year*, which does not necessarily coincide with the January 1 to December 31 calendar year. Within higher education the vast majority of institutions use July 1 to June 30 as their fiscal year, while the federal government uses October 1 to September 30 for its budgeting purposes. This fiscal year determines the starting and ending points of the budget cycle. According to Balderston (1995), "the greatest practical preoccupation of administrators is the annual budget cycle" (p. 146).

Many scholars have crafted steps to describe the budget cycle. The work of Balderston (1995), Barr and McClellan (2011), Goldstein (2005, 2012), Lenington (1996), Serna and Weiler (2016), and Anthony and Young (1999) informed our twelve-part, two-phase cycle (Figure 6.7). Depending on the degree of centralization, this process occurs within units and moves up the hierarchy to the institution's budget officer or budget management team. These steps are not rigidly sequential, as some jumping backward in the process may need to occur as new information is obtained. This process can span twenty-four months and despite its institution-specific uniqueness, there are enough commonalities to describe the budget cycle in general terms. Figure 6.7 outlines the steps (separated by phase) and provides the direction of the flow of information from the executive level (IHE budget manager(s)) down to the unit budget manager, and then to the personnel within that unit. Note that information can move in both directions—and the unit budget manager is often managing down *and* up during the budget process.

	Information Flow (Top → to ← Bottom)			
	IHE Budget Manager(s)	***Unit Budget Manager***	***Unit Personnel***	***Operating Budget Cycle Steps/Parts***
Planning and Approval Phase	→	→		Guidelines and Timelines
	→	←→	←	Revenue and Expense Projection
	→	←→	←	Information-Gathering and Information-Sharing
		←	←	Development of Requests
	Shared Responsibility			Drafting of Budget
		←→	←	Submission of Budget
		←→	←	Provision of Rationales, Discussion and Approvals
Spending and Adjustment Phase	→	→		Share Budget
	Shared Responsibility			Implement Budget
	Shared Responsibility			Monitor Ongoing Operation and Variance
	Shared Responsibility			Adjustments
	Shared Responsibility			Closing, Analysis and Reporting

Figure 6.7 Budget Flow

Planning and Approval Phase

Guidelines and Timelines

The first step (or steps, if conducted separately) in a budget process is establishing the rules and procedures of the budget planning process as well as the timeline during which it will occur. Guidelines can include boundaries on the planning process, special initiatives, and the budget model itself (Barr & McClellan, 2011). Guidelines help to ensure budget requests are not wildly out of line with what is expected (Goldstein, 2012). The typical budget officer (or person within a unit with budget responsibilities) is engaged in three budgets at once: the previous year budget's closing and analysis, the current year budget, and forecasting and planning the future budget (Balderston, 1995). The issued timeline for the future budget normally includes deadlines for budget request submissions, the response, and revised budget request submissions.

Revenue and Expense Projection

Budgets typically start with last year's figures and begin their estimation points from there, unless a zero-based approach is used. Assumptions must be identified and clarified—such as an increase in enrollment, a decrease in state funding, or salary adjustments promised. Estimates are formulated by working with stakeholders, data from a variety of sources, and variances from last year's budget. Planning for revenue is based on anticipated enrollment, research revenue, endowment earnings, state support (if applicable), income from other investments, and any auxiliary areas (Goldstein, 2012; Lenington, 1996). Estimating expenses requires a hard look at salaries and benefits, which constitute more than half of institutional expenditures. Expenses include supplies, services, travel, and so on—units are usually asked to put forth proposals requesting certain planned expenditures. Planning for revenues and expenses, at its best, is an inexact process (Barr & McClellan, 2011).

Information-Gathering and Information-Sharing, Development of Requests

Information-gathering and information-sharing is a critical component of the budgeting process and it happens throughout the cycle. Budget planning needs to be an open process through which stakeholders can communicate with the budget officer (and the budget officer can share information to stakeholders). To ignore this is to run the risk of operating with insufficient information and buy-in of the unit. At this phase, personnel submit requests for resources to the unit budget officer, who reviews the requests and considers them alongside all other budget requests. Committees may be formed to contemplate options, share information, and review requests. This also involves analyzing last year's budget and performance, and putting the forecasts developed in the last step into tentative estimates of revenues and expenditures along with rationales for those estimates and requests (Barr, 2002).

Drafting of Budget

At this point the budget officer for the unit (and later, institution) puts the work from the information-gathering and requests together and drafts a formal proposed budget (Barr, 2002). As has been stated by numerous scholars, budgets should align with the strategic plan (for more, see Chapter 8). Unit budgets are compiled and submitted upward for the eventual drafting of the institution-level budget in a centralized model (Goldstein, 2012). In a responsibility center model, this occurs at the unit level, but the unit budget is still submitted to executive leadership.

Submission of Budget, Provision of Rationales, Discussions and Approvals

Proposed budgets should be reviewed hierarchically and adjusted based on alignment to priorities and rationales provided (Lenington, 1996). Budget officers (within units and at the institution level) should provide feedback and alternatives to reduce cost, and consider what this budget means for subsequent fiscal years. Implications of unit budgets for other units on campus should also be considered (Barr & McClellan, 2011).

Additional information from units is often requested in support of budget requests, to aid the discussion around budget decision-making. It is not uncommon that a request be adjusted before it is presented to the governing board. Once the budget has gone through the iterative approval process and been approved by the powers-that-be within the institution, it must go to the governing board (or owners) for final approval and adoption. Typically, in a semester-based institution, the allocations are for the fall, spring, and summer terms while institutions on the quarter system will usually have four periods in which allocations take place. This is done primarily because many institutional budgets depend so heavily on tuition dollars (and subsidy dollars for state-supported institutions) which are not finalized until the students are enrolled and actually pay their tuition and fees. Once the budget is approved, it becomes the operating financial plan for the institution and hierarchical units within.

Spending and Adjustments Phase

Share Budget

The master and unit-level budgets likely underwent permutations during the approval process (Barr, 2002), so parties must be notified of what budget they are operating within. Further, the budget has very important communication functions, including the emphasis of institutional priorities and the strategic plan (Anthony & Young, 1999; Balderston, 1995; Lenington, 1996).

Implement Budget

In essence, this is where the budget does its job of executing the plan for expenses and revenues. The budget is put in the accounting system and data are collected

(Goldstein, 2012, p. 123). Lenington (1996) has two recommendations related to this step: first, the operating budget must be implemented in a strong data system that can draw managers' attention to variances; second, the budget must be monitored and adjusted during the fiscal year so issues can be addressed in a timely fashion.

Monitor Ongoing Operation and Variance

The budget, once implemented, must be monitored on an ongoing basis (at least monthly) to ensure spending and earnings are progressing as planned (Barr, 2002). It is not uncommon for enrollment (and, therefore, tuition, fee, and subsidy revenue) to fluctuate; institutions are rapidly changing environments. Unlike most industries, revenues in higher education arrive in large proportions three times a year—the payment deadline for each semester. Therefore, monthly monitoring of revenues may be a bit misleading, while expenses often operate more evenly. It is very important, as noted in the financial and managerial accounting sections, to keep records of how variance from plans occurs, so that it can be anticipated in future planning (Serna & Weiler, 2016). Some variances will be due to cyclical factors that can be forecasted, while others will occur due to structural changes, such as state formula funding changes, or policies.

Adjustments

As actual expenses and revenues are realized, it may become necessary to adjust the budget to reflect this reality. Goldstein (2012) notes, "the ink on the latest budget document will not be dry before circumstances dictate adjustments be made" (p. 9). This may occur due to enrollment shortfalls, or from other revenue variances from what was projected. Further, it is perfectly fine to under-spend on a budget; an authorization to use resources is just that—an authorization, not a requirement. It is always better to under-spend the budget even if that runs contrary to institutional culture and past practices (Lenington, 1996). Over-spending on a budget is more problematic and may require an institution/department to dip into its contingency funds. If a budget is falling short, it must be adjusted to cover the projected deficit (unless it surpasses institutional capabilities for absorbing the shortfall); transfers between accounts running a deficit and accounts with money still remaining can occur (Barr, 2002)—but rules should be in place for when those transfers should occur so that post-closing analysis can take place with reasonable accuracy (Lenington, 1996).

Closing, Analysis, and Reporting

This refers to the process of ending a fiscal year budget by stopping any more items being charged against it. Generally, this happens approximately one month after the last date of the fiscal year for which it serves to enable the full processing of orders, payments, and receipt of goods and services. Placing a stop on new activity within the fiscal year and the closing out of all accounts enables the generation of financial statements (Barr, 2002; Goldstein, 2012).

This is the stage when the accountants get the opportunity to present numbers internally and externally; actual values are checked against the planned expenses and revenues in the budget, and performance is analyzed to inform future budget planning (Goldstein, 2012). Institutions then generate a variety of reports for internal and external consumption (Barr, 2002), including financial statements that can be viewed by accreditors and the U.S. Department of Education. At this point in time, an external audit may also occur.

BUDGETING IN REAL LIFE

In the previous section, the practices of financial accounting and managerial accounting were connected to the practice of budgeting. Regardless of profit status or sector, service or manufacturing focus, having a financial plan is of utmost importance for an organization. This section will connect budgeting with the people responsible—and talk about what happens when things go awry.

As noted, rarely are any budgets implemented exactly according to the plan. Changes are made to models in response to institutional culture and constraints. Steps in the cycle are repeated, skipped to be revisited later, and otherwise re-arranged—and that is a good thing. This section describes considerations budget managers (or those with budget responsibility) need to make in working with a budget or budget development process. As with previous sections, this section is focused more on operating budgets, but can be applied to capital, auxiliary, and special-program budget types.

Common Mistakes

Budget officers and controllers are, above all else, human. If charged with budget responsibility during your career, it is best to keep the following common mistakes in mind as you plan your time and formulate your draft budgets.

Technical Mistakes

- Making incorrect estimates – budget managers engage in forecasting of revenues for planning; it is possible to over-estimate revenue or misunderstand the nature of limited-term revenues (Barr & McClellan, 2011). Serna and Weiler (2016) discuss methods for forecasting revenues: relying on historical averages (and smoothing processes), utilizing correlational analysis, and adopting curvilinear models when necessary—their approaches are outside of the scope of this book.
- Not understanding expenses – budget managers project costs; they may fail to understand the behavior of costs, such as the impact of variable or mixed costs. This can also occur when hidden costs of decisions or projects were not identified properly (Barr & McClellan, 2011). This is why having a strong understanding of accounting principles is so helpful to a budget manager. Goldstein (2012) identifies common culprits of hidden costs: new facilities, new academic programs, elimination of programs and services, human resources, and grant funding programs.

- Math errors – budget managers, not surprisingly, do a lot of math. Math errors can occur through misinterpretation or miscalculation of actual values, and through misjudging multi-year consequences and cross-unit allocations (Barr & McClellan, 2011).

Mistakes of Hubris

- Failure to understand the organization – budget managers need to understand the organization from multiple perspectives; the culture, networks, governance, executive, and mid-level leadership decision-making patterns, history, norms for participation and consultation, and history (Goldstein, 2005). That is a tall order, particularly for a new budget officer. The political environment varies by institution, and is influenced by the complexity of both budgeting processes and the degree of interpersonal connections within the institution (Goldstein, 2012). Further, a failure to link the budget to the institution's strategic plan or priorities can leave an institution unable to meet its goals.
- Failure to understand capabilities – this can arise in four ways: a failure to understand the organization's level of risk tolerance, its communication needs and expectations, the governance structures involved, and the amount of time required for collaboration within the organization. This is related to, but not the same as, culture. The budget officer also needs to gauge the knowledge and technical skill of the members within the organization (Goldstein, 2005).
- Failure to manage information – a good budget officer is careful to communicate clearly, make information available, and welcome dialogue about the budget planning process (Barr & McClellan, 2011). That being said, not all requests have equal weight, and multiple scenarios will compete alongside each other. The budget officer should avoid making commitments to advance any particular request; they should also avoid raising their colleagues' hopes related to particular issues (Goldstein, 2012).
- Not taking problems seriously – budget officers need to develop a sense of the severity of problems, and know when to address them. Waiting too long to identify problems limits the remedies available. Budget officers often need to develop both short- and long-term solutions for budgetary problems (Barr & McClellan, 2011).
- Rocking the boat too hard – this can arise from a variety of actions, but at the core it is about managing change in a way that works for the organization (Barr & McClellan, 2011). Few organizations can withstand dramatic changes to budgeting models—and it is important to be able to manage incremental change appropriately to meet goals. This is of critical importance when making cuts to budgets.
- Letting your ego lead – budget officers are a critical aspect of any organization, but it is important to not act in a way that makes others frustrated. It is critical to demonstrate your integrity and mitigate frustration with a tense and important process as much as possible. Further, letting your ego lead can make it hard to ask questions, explore long-held assumptions, and request clarification or help before it is too late (Barr & McClellan, 2011).

KEEPING A BUDGET ON TRACK . . . AND REASONS WHY YOU CANNOT

Holding people accountable at *all levels* is critical to successful implementation of a budget (Lenington, 1996). Many institutions, through their budget models and norms, establish a "spend it or lose it" attitude, which leads to padded or bloated budget requests and last-minute spending sprees just prior to the close of a fiscal year (Goldstein, 2005). To keep units and the people within on track, Lenington (1996) suggests rules be established when resources can (and cannot) be transferred between accounts. This is important because taking corrective action to remedy an over- or under-allocation may prevent important analysis from taking place at the end of a budget cycle. Additionally, Goldstein (2005) recommends budget managers build flexibility into the budget by relying on several strategies. Flexibility is important to allow adjustments in response to changing conditions *or* to take advantage of unexpected opportunities. Goldstein (2005) also recommends allocating contingencies by expense type or group and making mid- and upper-level managers responsible for these pockets of resources so they can be monitored

Why Budgets (Have to) Change

Budgets are influenced by internal and external conditions; a good economic situation in the state usually means appropriations increase or remain stable, but institutions are still influenced by demographics of demand which affect the number and composition of potential and current students, human resource costs, competition with other institutions for students and staff, and the ever-increasing costs of goods, technology, and deferred maintenance (Goldstein, 2012; Serna & Weiler, 2016). If any of these factors change, it is likely that your institution's budget will, too. The degree of change will vary according to the change in condition and its severity.

Federal regulations and social programs have an impact on institutions, along with state and local shifts (Goldstein, 2005), as described in Chapter 4. Examples of these regulations and programs are safety laws (working conditions, lab safety, crime reporting), non-discrimination laws and their related reporting and administrative requirements, environmental protection laws, privacy and due process laws, and laws related to the protection and participation of individuals with disabilities—to name just a few. One recent example that never quite came to fruition was a 2016 change to the Fair Labor Standards Act, requiring (among other things) the payment of overtime to employees making less than $47,000 annually. Many institutions adjusted their pay scales to exempt employees from those rules, only to have the policy rolled back at a later date.

Within institutions, revenues suffer when enrollment drops (particularly in smaller institutions), when fundraising success falters, and in response to natural disasters (Barr, 2002). Budgets are often adjusted during their implementation cycle due to changing circumstances (Goldstein, 2005), such as in response to a new opportunity (or challenge). Regarding shifting conditions, Serna and Weiler (2016) and Barr and McClellan (2011) stress the importance of integrating the institutional mission within the strategies used to mitigate financial stresses, recommend taking the human cost of budget cuts into consideration, and advise budget managers to use strategies that minimize the demoralizing of employees. The approaches in the next section will affect both the mission and employee morale in varying ways and degrees.

Budgeting in Tough Times

It is important to note that the proper time to plan for financial problems is *before* they happen, says Goldstein (2005), with both short-term (one to three years) and long-term (more than three years) strategies. Goldstein notes that larger institutions are more able to absorb the impact of funding or revenue reductions because they are able to shift resources around, while Barr (2002) notes that smaller institutions are more sensitive to enrollment fluctuations.

A recent study conducted by the *Chronicle of Higher Education* in partnership with the Council of Independent Colleges and the American Association of State Colleges and Universities found 44 percent of public institutions failed to meet their enrollment goals, while 52 percent of private institutions fell short (Carlson, 2018), often even after they lowered their goals. More than half the institutions responding to the survey fell short of their tuition revenue goals. Interestingly, of the institutions surveyed, many highlighted efforts to boost enrollment through offering new programs and enhancing marketing, rather than reducing costs. While institutional characteristics and the severity of cuts will adjust approaches, the strategies adopted to respond to changes need to match the magnitude of the change (Balderston, 1995; Barr & McClellan, 2011).

Freezes

Put most simply, a freeze is the stopping of expenditures—but rarely is it this simple. Some institutions may opt to stop expenditures within a certain type of expense (travel, for example) or to stop hiring people for recently vacated positions, utilizing the savings to offset reduced revenue. While the decision not to hire or to stop pay increases is frustrating, these types of changes are less disruptive and demoralizing than layoffs (Balderston, 1995). Rather than implementing a hiring freeze, some institutions pursue early-retirement incentives for faculty and/or staff, but Goldstein notes that high-performing employees are more apt to take those incentive programs. Another strategy, if organizationally appropriate, is to allow full-time staff members to drop down to part-time status (Goldstein, 2005).

While a budget freeze may seem like a reasonable idea at the time, it unfortunately "singles out a budget component for example, office supplies or unfilled faculty or administrative positions" (Balderston, 1995, p. 167), and may have a disproportional impact on the institution's stronger programs. Cutting core programs or institutional strengths will have long-lasting negative effects. It is imperative that these decisions involve input from a broad array of internal and external stakeholders. Institutions wishing to remain strong or to become stronger during economic tough times must make these decisions based on data and institutional objectives. Strategic cuts during an economic downturn, while difficult, can in fact position an institution so it will be much stronger when the slump is over.

Across-the-Board Cuts

This is the practice of asking all units to cut their budget by a specified percentage. This approach is popular, in part, because it is politically expedient and less controversial than other methods to reduce the overall budget. While it may be the easiest or simplest solution, it is one of the worst alternatives because of the disproportional impact on the most fiscally responsible programs. No unit is specifically highlighted for reductions—everyone shares in the collective pain (Balderston, 1995, p. 169). Dickeson despises flat, across-the-board cuts and believes they "tend toward mediocrity for all programs" (2010, p. 14). This approach indicates an unwillingness among administrators to make difficult decisions, which may be an indicator as to why the institution could be experiencing difficulties.

Targeted Cuts

One way to handle a changing environment is to change the rules of the game. Balderston (1995) notes that you can adjust how a model is implemented, or the underlying assumptions on which the model is built (such as using certain ratios to allocate revenues and expenses). Institutions in financial trouble tend to re-centralize decision-making (Barr, 2002). The term "targeted cuts" refers to an institution considering specific program or service areas for reduction or elimination. Units are treated differently, and this requires an institution to understand the costs and income generated by a program, along with its effectiveness (Balderston, 1995; Barr, 2002). It is much more controversial in nature than across-the-board cuts or hiring freezes and requires the institution to revisit its mission and values.

Restructuring

"Restructuring," or "retrenchment," is the term generally used when a combination of targeted cuts is made as part of an overarching long-term strategy to deal with budget shortfalls. They can be painful but improve processes and efficiency (Barr, 2002). They usually come with a high time and morale cost (p. 101). Cutting programs and services is considered a long-term solution (Goldstein, 2012) and takes significant time and planning (Dickeson, 2010). Generally, academic programs can only be cut when a financial crisis is declared by the institution—per American Association of University Professors guidelines. Further, institutions are often limited by regulations and other constraints, such as policies (institution- or state-based), collective bargaining (union) contracts, and financial and procurement rules regulations (Goldstein, 2005).

Reducing the Impact of Cuts on Morale

To reduce the impact of budget cuts on the institution's morale, Goldstein (citing O'Neil) suggests involving a variety of stakeholders, maintaining as much transparency as possible about the process, communicating information internally and externally, honoring the institution's culture, involving the board, considering long-term implications, and maintaining contact with the state legislature (if a state institution) (Goldstein, 2005). The following list of insightful recommendations for handling budget reductions while preserving morale was adapted from Barr and McClellan (2011) and Goldstein (2012):

- Start small – smaller changes can add up to large savings; this approach includes some of the smaller targeted mechanisms described by Goldstein (2012), such as allowing employees to move from full- to part-time positions, adjustments of workload, and retirement incentives. This strategy is not as appropriate when large and sudden cuts are required.
- Remember to communicate – transparency is a theme many scholars cited in this chapter have touched upon—Serna and Weiler (2016) even recommend going beyond simple transparency and working toward active collaboration. Much of the panic caused by budget cuts can be mitigated by simply sharing information about the magnitude of the cuts and the strategies the institution plans to implement.
- Cast a wide net – the units closest to the business processes often have the most precise information available. An institution's faculty, staff, and students likely have constructive ideas on where money can be saved—providing a venue for suggestions to be provided can prove beneficial for both the ideas it will generate and the openness to participation and transparency it evidences.
- Build in budget flexibility – as Goldstein (2005, 2012) noted, institutions should build some flexibility into the budget for necessary adjustments and changing circumstances; delaying expenditures is another strategy. In leaner times, it is important to evaluate potential expenses in relation to their closeness to the core purposes of the institution.
- Establish and maintain integrity – as referenced earlier, budget managers must maintain a reputation of integrity and credibility. It can be a politically fraught role, with many individuals seeking to game the system or gain information others do not have. While it is never fun to say no, it *is* important to avoid over-promising or playing favorites. Budget managers must maintain their integrity in tough times, and work to share information consistently and avoid being perceived as playing favorites.
- Outsource if it makes sense – outsourcing can be a powerful way to reduce costs, but is not the only reason to outsource. Dickeson (2010) presents several reasons to outsource, which can indirectly reduce costs. Outsourcing can increase customer satisfaction and reduce the time staff spend handling complaints (thereby reducing costs).
- Find a way to increase revenues – budget shortfalls or reductions in funding sources can inspire creativity on both the expense *and* revenue side—strategies will be discussed in Chapter 4.
- Tough times require tough calls – budget managers and leaders must remember their role as organizational stewards; at times, unpopular or uncomfortable decisions will need to be made to serve the institution's interests. It is critical that appropriate legal advice is sought to ensure decisions are made in consideration of the law and policies of the institution.
- Learn something from this experience – while a budget cutting process can be painful, it is also a learning experience for the institution. To ensure something beyond cost-savings emerges from it, the choices, processes, and results need to be documented for future review and analysis.

This section provided a brief overview of common errors and reasons for budget shortfalls, as well as strategies to mitigate them. The lessons were presented in a budget context, but are broadly applicable to the practice of administration in general. Strong budget officers do their best to check their egos, educate themselves, and act carefully in response to changing conditions—while doing their best to be transparent, fair, and honest (Barr & McClellan, 2011; Serna & Weiler, 2016). While practitioners cannot control all aspects of their unit or institution's financial future, they can work to control costs, estimate revenues carefully, and collaborate effectively to enhance a unit or institution's chances of success. Doing this well is difficult, but pays dividends in terms of employee morale and perceptions of good stewardship.

CONCLUDING COMMENTS

Every administrator who remains in higher education long enough will experience an economic downturn. At some point in your career, you will probably have to cut a budget. In fact, it is likely you will be tasked with reducing expenses with far greater frequency than you will be trying to figure out how you are going to allocate excess revenue. Dickeson (2010) notes that colleges and universities have always focused more on generating revenue than they have on reducing expenses, but at some point tuition *will* simply hit a ceiling. Tuition increases have eclipsed all other indexes of economic change for several years—it is time to focus on understanding costs and being more efficient while increasing quality of our programs and services.

This work is not easy—not-for-profit organizations have lagged behind their for-profit counterparts in utilizing information to understand the costs of delivering services. The orientation of higher education further complicates understanding costs: we rely on highly skilled staff to deliver services that are difficult to measure with any precision. All of the decisions related to budget reductions are challenging, but are made harder when financial information is not available or of sufficient quality to be confidently used to make decisions.

Budgets should be linked to strategic plans, but few really are due to the difference in their cycles (operating budgets are usually annual, and strategic plans usually cover several years), but this may also be due to how strategic plans are developed as aspirational documents. What is important to remember is that budgets communicate priorities—and the message they send can either complement or detract from the strategic plan, which will be discussed in Chapter 8. Budgets and strategic plans tell stakeholders a lot about the institution's true priorities, intended or unintended. Further, accreditors and ratings agencies review budgets (via actual financial statements) and strategic plans to evaluate the health and future potential of organizations, and that process has substantial consequences for the institution.

Budget managers will be well served to demonstrate integrity, openness, honesty, and technical skill as they work to analyze the past, project the future, and work with stakeholders to bridge the two. The conditions acting on and within institutions are highly complex and often politicized. It is important, however, to remember that higher education is a somewhat unique environment, says Dickeson (2010): "I can not emphasize too strongly that politics as usual on the campus will bear no resemblance to the standards of accountability expected by the external publics—parents, donors, policymakers, the general public—who support higher education" (p. 100). As colleges and universities compete against other organizations for resources at a macro level, and face ever-increasing costs internally for technology, health care, and physical facilities, we will have to get leaner and more efficient.

Shattock (2003) lists five principles (Figure 6.8) which he believes to be important for the successful financial management of an institution. These principles connect to the budget or budgeting process of institutions of higher education. Administrators and institutions embracing these principles and putting them into practice are typically more responsive to stakeholder needs, more flexible in turbulent economic times, more fluid in decision-making processes, more consistent in financial decision-making, and more transparent in budget policies and procedures.

Reducing expenses is challenging, as many colleges and universities are subject to policies that make many cost-saving measures nearly unattainable—and salaries and benefits can comprise up to 70 percent of the operating budget at most institutions, and facilities and maintenance costs represent an additional 10–15 percent of the budget (Goldstein, 2012). Strategies, both long- and short-term, were presented in this chapter for handling budget cuts, including strategies for reducing the portion of the budget devoted to salaries and benefits. In reality, most of those directives usually come from the central administration or state level. A majority of administrators' involvement with the budget is limited to the unit or divisional level, where decisions related to the smaller portion of non-salary expenses can be managed.

Finally, this chapter contained advice on the human side of budgeting: the value of communication and the importance of involving stakeholders. Using knowledge of the budget and its history, as well as techniques for working with your colleagues,

1) Financial stability – nothing can be more destructive as a financial crisis

2) Financial management is too important to be left to the central office. Financial literacy needs to be widely distributed through the institution at all administrative levels.

3) Spending patterns at the top sends a message throughout the institution. Senior university officers who do not automatically travel first class, do not claim named parking spaces on campus, and have modest lifestyles can set a tone for economy and plain living...Institutional thriftiness emphasizes that financial probity and transparency represent traditional characteristics of university life and sits well with the moral standards of scholarship which the academic community aspires to... [The opposite destroys a commitment to institutional economy]

4) Risks should be examined carefully but when accepted the investment should be generous to ensure a successful outcome.

5) Good financial management requires that where financial messages such as failure to meet financial targets, shortfalls in particular areas and over expenditures in others, should be acted upon in an alert and effective manner. Financial analysis and efficient accounting will only take you so far...unless they are backed up by decision-making processes which command respect, by effective implementation skills, and by a management style that can be interventionist when things go wrong

Figure 6.8 Principles of Financial Management

will enable you to be an active participant in conversations about increasing efficiency or reducing costs in general. Whether or not you are a budget manager, a person who handles the budget as part of your job, or your involvement with the budget is limited to spending it, you have an imperative to be a good steward of resources. It is important not to be afraid of the budget. Instead, engage with it, evaluate changes from year to year. You will likely gain insight (intended or unintended) into your organization and how it works.

REFLECTIVE QUESTIONS

1. What is a budget, and what makes it important?
2. What are some important steps in the budget cycle, and what makes them important?
3. How does the degree of centralization of an organization impact the budget creation and implementation processes?
4. What does the person managing the budget need to know? Why?
5. How did/does your institution handle budgeting in tough times?
6. What are some actions that reduce the pain associated with budget cuts?
7. Why are across-the-board cuts a bad idea? What are some creative alternatives that could work better for your institution?

PART 3

People and Processes

CHAPTER 7

Management Principles

We present several management principles, theories, and approaches that help guide decision-making and action in many organizations, including colleges and universities. It is important to note no single principle, theory, or approach is best suited for every institution. What works for one institution will not be as effective at many others. It is up to the administrators of each institution to determine the managerial styles, processes, and strategies best suited for them and their respective institutions based on their institutional mission, vision, and values, as well as the organizational structure and culture. We believe applying sound management principles will help and is definitely a step in the right direction. The following pages are meant to provide you with a better understanding of management functions, strategic planning, quality management (QM) and improvement, organizational change, organizational learning, and how management concepts can be successfully integrated together and applied within higher educational settings.

BACKGROUND

For many the study of management began in the early twentieth century with the work of Frederick Taylor and his concept of scientific management. Taylor's work brought time-and-motion studies to business and industry and was credited for simultaneously increasing production, raising wages, and lowering costs (Birnbaum, 2000, p. 14). His work was followed by numerous studies on efficiency and effectiveness which revolutionized modern industrial practices. While some of these studies provided managers with alternatives to the status quo, according to Birnbaum (2000), none seemed to live up to the expectations set forth. Birnbaum described a number of management practices that had been implemented within higher education over the last several decades of the twentieth century. His contention is that these practices were fads in the business world, which happened to find their way into higher education because of a lack of public confidence, and therefore were destined to fail. We disagree.

This chapter will argue that many of these practices have had a profound impact on the way higher education operates, and while few, if any, of the management practices described in this chapter are 100 percent in use at any one institution, pieces of them are in place at the vast majority of institutions. As administrators, it is important to understand that the management of resources is a critical activity of any institution of higher education. Management does not, however, occur in a vacuum. Previous chapters presented financial and budgetary aspects of the enterprise, as well as the organizational structures within institutions which typically are different from the communication channels in an institution. It is through these communication channels that the work of an institution is successfully accomplished.

The organizational structure provides a guide as to who should be responsible for what activities, but does not necessarily provide information as to who actually performs the work. The financial patterns and budgetary processes have important implications for present and future decision-making. Savvy administrators understand who makes particular decisions and how those decisions are implemented. Management and managerial processes are not incompatible with the shared governance structures present on many of today's college and university campuses; in fact, they can be used to support them.

MANAGERIAL FUNCTIONS

There are four basic functions which serve as the heart of management practices: planning, organizing, leading, and controlling (Nickels, McHugh, & McHugh, 2008). These four functions will be used to organize this chapter, and each is briefly described below.

Planning means looking toward the future and determining how your institution will meet the needs of its current and future stakeholders. This is accomplished through the development of organizational goals, and strategies to reach those goals. A good plan, while of critical importance, cannot ensure success without proper support. Therefore, the planning process also includes determining what resources are needed to ensure success and how the organization will go about acquiring the needed resources.

Organizing involves the creation or adjustment and implementation of an organizational structure conducive to achieving organizational goals. This includes efficient and effective allocation of institutional resources. Chapters 2 and 5 contained discussion of centralized and decentralized organizations, as well as models for resource allocation. Organization can be further accomplished by recruiting employees who fit within the organizational culture and values and assigning staff to positions that allow each staff member to maximize his or her potential (see Chapter 9). Organizing also entails the establishment or adjustment of policies, procedures, and systems that permit the staff to operate in an efficient and effective manner. Successful organization makes achievement of organizational goals and objectives set via planning more likely.

Leading requires administrators to create a vision for the institution that internal and external stakeholders can support. Leading is distinct from managing day-to-day operations, because to lead, one must be forward-thinking and create an environment that empowers employees to excel. Leaders must be able to motivate, guide, and coach staff throughout the organization to work collaboratively and effectively while working toward accomplishing the institution's goals and objectives.

These goals should have been established via planning and implemented in the organization processes. Leading also includes providing clear directions and expectations as to what is to be accomplished, and providing feedback on employee performance along the way. Leaders must also manage conflict and successfully implement important organizational changes.

Controlling is the process of assessing the progress of the institution in meeting its stated goals and objectives. In order to effectively assess the institution's progress, it is important to ensure that the standards, goals, and objectives are clearly stated and easily understood. Corrective action to address problems is also a major component of controlling. Quality and efficiency are often part of an organization's goals (i.e., approaches to continually improve) and can be understood as part of a controlling function. Controlling is often accomplished through the chain of command and span of control of the administrative team.

College and university administrators carry out the four functions of management to varying degrees depending on their location within the hierarchy in their respective institutions. The functions are not mutually exclusive, and often rely on each other in important ways. The four functions will be addressed in pairs to structure a majority of this chapter, but it is important to note these concepts are broad in range and overlap quite a bit. Before diving into the discussion of the functions of a manager, another important term must be defined before proceeding: strategy.

WHAT IS STRATEGY?

The word "strategic" is perhaps one of the most over-used and inappropriately applied words in organizations today. To be strategic is to be intentional. Martinez and Wolverton (2009) define strategy as "the planning and analysis that allows an organization to fulfill its purpose and reach its goals" (p. xi). Alfred (2006) describes strategy as "a systematic way of positioning an institution . . . in its environment to create value that differentiates it from competitors" keeping both its stakeholders and the larger market in mind (p. 6). What these definitions have in common is attention to *context*, intentionality in planning, and achievement of a goal—be it differentiation from peers or strategic goals. To create strategy, an organization must connect many dots, understand those connections, and formulate an approach that addresses the strategy(ies) through pursuit of a plan or position, which can be accomplished through a pattern of actions. The unifying theme is that the organization is trying to do something significant to advance itself.

Alfred (2006) warns administrators to be mindful of the difference between strategy and tactics—indicating that tactics are everyday actions to keep the organization moving, while strategies are bigger-picture, longer-range, and propel the organization forward to achieving its vision. Most leaders spend their time focusing on tactics—the day-to-day management of business activities and operational problems—rather than thinking about strategy and meeting the challenges and opportunities provided by the environment. This is unsurprising, as day-to-day operations can be sufficiently chaotic to require continuous tactical management. There is a cost, however, to focusing at the day-to-day operational level. If an organization does not pay attention to the big picture, it might not be around very long (Rowley & Sherman, 2001). Administrators who are focused on strategy tend to concentrate on the institution's values as a source that drives its competitive advantage. They engage with and monitor a constantly changing constellation of stakeholders, regulatory concerns, competitors, and evolving technology. Institutions need both strategists and tacticians, but must know which administrators are assuming each role.

Martinez and Wolverton (2009) propose a three-stage schema for determining and adopting strategy: traditional analysis, competitive analysis, and innovation.

- Traditional analysis focuses on mission, goals, and objectives, as well as evaluation of internal capacity and organizational systems (strengths and weaknesses), as well as the external environment (opportunities and threats). This is the phase in which strategic plan development typically rests.
- Competitive analysis relies on industry analysis, which incorporates the evaluation of "buyers, suppliers, substitutes, new entrants, and intensity of rivalry" (Martinez & Wolverton, 2009, p. 6), an idea from Michael Porter (1980). Competitive analysis also calls for the determination of competitive strategies, such as serving as the lowest-cost provider of a service, or focusing on a particular niche (e.g., offering distinctive experiences or the very highest quality). Together, industry analysis and competitive strategy development can result in what is known as a "competitive advantage" (Alfred, 2006; Martinez & Wolverton, 2009).
- The final stage in Martinez and Wolverton's strategy-making schema is innovation, which relies on techniques and tools to understand an industry, the different possible points of distinction, and where a service provider might find unexploited opportunities or improve their position. Innovation and new ideas do not typically strike out of the blue—they are informed by the careful analysis of an evolving environment that presents new opportunities, unaddressed needs in the market, changes in demographics or perception, and new or emerging knowledge.

Alfred (2006) takes a different but complementary approach by providing a set of four questions an organization should ask itself as it formulates strategy (p. 6):

1. "Who are the stakeholders?"
2. "What kind of value is created for these stakeholders?"
3. "Does the value created lead to advantage by differentiating the institution from its competitors?"
4. "Is the advantage sustainable?"

Value, in Alfred's model, refers to understanding what students hope to obtain from their experience—is it superior quality, convenience, variety, cost-effectiveness, or something else?

In essence, what is described here is *strategic thinking* which requires consideration and analysis of the environment and understanding big-picture issues in order to draw conclusions about the future (Ellis, 2010). McGee (2015) warns there is much commonality among colleges and universities, suggesting "98 percent of our organizational DNA is shared with other peer and competitor institutions" and "the 2 percentage points need to make a difference" (p. 114). Institutions that "assume the future will simply be a reflection of the past will be hit hard by the changing realities of a dynamic world that is full of both challenge and opportunity" (Martinez & Wolverton, 2009, p. xi). This translates to strategic planning. When developed and implemented properly, Alfred (2006) believes that the composition of a strategic plan can differentiate a unit from its competitors and lead to a "sustainable advantage" in the future (p. 6). A sustainable (competitive) advantage is something that differentiates one institution from another long-term. Organizational strategy making is key to creating that difference.

In practice, *strategy* (as it is phrased in this section) refers to setting a vision and a broad means to achieve it. Within a strategic plan, the word "strategies" may be used to indicate lower-level groups of actions or objectives. This is a confusing turn of phrase, but important to point out here. When formulating strategy, Goldstein (2012) advises organizations to be focused instead of trying to please everyone: "Too often . . . plans ignore the practical realities that institutions simply can't afford to spread their resources across more than a handful of major areas" (p. 75). Continuing, he concedes that colleges and universities are engaged in many important works, "but they cannot all be strategic priorities at the same time" (Goldstein, 2012, p. 75). Auer (2016) echoes this, noting "If priority setting is done properly, it necessarily means that choices are made to do some things and not do other things" (p. 4).

As discussed in Chapter 8, changes in strategy and strategic plans are sometimes inspired by changes in leadership or a rough accreditation visit (Atkins, 2010; Gorman, 2016; Paris, 2004). Originally, strategic planning was a rigid, lock-step, and formulaic process (Dooris, Kelly, & Trainer, 2004). Teams were formed, an analysis of strengths and weaknesses (internal factors) as well as opportunities and threats (external factors) was conducted, and goals were determined. If the plan was done well, goals were then further subdivided into strategies or objectives, and specific people or teams were assigned to complete the items. If the plan was actually conducted through to completion, it went back on a shelf and collected dust rather than being the source of learning and growth for future planning. Plans today have the same parts, but can have much larger reach and impact if a more modern approach to planning is taken.

PLANNING AND ORGANIZING: PLANNING, IMPLEMENTATION, AND STRATEGIC MANAGEMENT

The first two functions of management, planning and organizing, are often defined in terms of being strategic—consider, for example, the terms "strategic planning" and "strategic management". Deming (1986) noted, "failure of management to plan for the future and to foresee problems has brought about waste of manpower, of materials, and of machine time, all of which raise the cost and price that must be paid" (p. ix). These inefficiencies can be moderated when an appropriate level of planning takes place. Organizations who know who they are and where they are going (planning) are better equipped to respond to changes (organizing) in their environment successfully (Ellis, 2010; Rowley & Sherman, 2001).

Within higher education, the planning process must be taken seriously, and institutions need to continuously look toward the future while maintaining a degree of fluidity in their planning processes. It is imperative that administrators, faculty, and staff understand that planning is a process, not a single event. Managers must use their organizational skills to implement the plan by maintaining reasonable and effective policies, processes, staffing, and resources in a position to achieve the goals and objectives set in the planning process.

Planning: Strategic Planning in Higher Education

Strategic planning originated in the 1950s and 1960s in governmental organizations and was introduced to higher education in the early 1970s (Dooris et al., 2004; Freed & Klugman, 1997). It became more popular as institutions struggled with increased variability in enrollment, funding, and student demographics in the 1980s (Dooris et al., 2004; Langham & Fifolt, 2014). Strategic planning remains an integral part of numerous institutions today—although it is not a simple process for colleges and universities because of their multiple roles, constituencies, and the changing environment (Gorman, 2016).

According to Nickels et al. (2008), strategic planning is a process to determine the major goals of an institution and to provide a foundation for the policies, procedures, and strategies for obtaining and using resources necessary to achieve those goals. It should move the organization toward the strategy it seeks to achieve. Tromp and Ruben (2010) and Stephens (2017) note strategic planning's ability to initiate and manage change within higher education. It is a foundational component to continuous improvement (Seymour, Kelly, & Jasinski, 2004). A strength of the strategic planning process is that it forces members of an organization to take a step back and look at their present capabilities along with the external environment—and have tough conversations about what is important and where the organization should direct its efforts to achieve its vision (Paraska, 2013). Strategic planning should also align an organization's goals with the ever-changing market in which it operates (Nauffal & Nasser, 2016; Rowley & Sherman, 2001). Gorman (2016) states, "When planning in higher education institutions is done well, it can be transformative; when it is done poorly, it can be disastrous" (p. 18).

Countless authors have provided different takes on the components of a strategic plan; most agree a strategic plan will contain:

- A mission (current state)
- A vision (desired future state)
- Core values (underlying assumptions or beliefs of the organization)
- Some combination of themes, priorities, objectives, goals, strategies, and tactics, as well as plans for achieving them
- Metrics or key performance indicators related to plan progress
- Assessment and evaluation provisions for the plan (SCUP, 2018)

The specific language, organization, and pieces of the plans may vary, but at the core a strategic plan is pretty standard. The plan is really only one part of the story, though—how it is formulated can be just as important as the plan itself (Ellis, 2010; Rowley & Sherman, 2001).

Regional accreditors became interested in institutional strategic plans in the 1990s, and rely on them as a signal that institutions are interested in continuous improvement of institutional effectiveness (Dooris et al., 2004; Paris, 2004). From their perspective, a strategic plan is an institution's attempt to read the signals provided by the environment as well as its own capabilities and strengths, and formulate a series of goals that it intends to pursue to best serve its stakeholders (Dodd, 2004; Paraska, 2013). Strategic plans are not set in stone but rather should serve the institution flexibly for several years, with adjustments taking place as needed based on a periodic review of the changing environment and stakeholder needs (Hinton, 2012; Shattock, 2003; Thomas, 1996).

Organizing: Implementation and Strategic Management

A to-do list, no matter how well developed, is just a to-do list. The organizing function of management is key to making the plan a reality through wise use of organizational resources. While managers engage in planning, the concept of management is most often associated with the implementation of a plan. Nickels et al. (2008) define management as a "process used to accomplish organizational goals" with resources (pp. 182–183). *Strategic* management, according to David (1996), is "the art and science of formulating, implementing, and evaluating cross functional decisions that enable an organization to fulfill its objectives" (as cited in Shattock, 2003, p. 24). The distinction, while small, is important—strategic management is focused on achievement of goals in an interconnected interdependent system.

In a strategic environment, an organization's objectives (the institution, or a unit within) must be connected to the institutional mission and institutional goals in order for strategic management to occur (Sadler, 2003). Applying this notion to higher education, Shattock (2003) suggests that the objective of strategic management must be to achieve and sustain institutional success:

> Managing universities is a holistic process in which all the interlocking elements need to work together: for example, a concentration on academic success, to the exclusion of concern about effective financial management, is as short sighted as a concentration on the physical refurbishment of a campus to the exclusion of continuing to refresh academic performance.
>
> (p. 25)

A strategic manager is one who recognizes a need to transform an organization or unit to meet important goals, and has the capability to do just that (Sadler, 2003). Strategic implementation is a set of "actions taken by a college or university to put their positioning plans into action by either changing their mission, changing their environment, or changing their resources, capabilities, and internal operations" (Rowley & Sherman, 2001, p. 202). Strategic managers organize resources, policies, and procedures to create approaches to deal with new concerns, problems, and opportunities while being mindful of organizational politics (Harper, 2013). In a strategic planning context, this is the implementation planning phase. Strategic managers focus on the connections of their work (regardless of their level within the organization) and make decisions in consideration of how those decisions will impact the achievement of their unit- and organization-level goals.

Potential opportunities for strategic implementation include: accreditation changes, regulatory changes, the addition of new programs or services in response to a state mandate, the discontinuation of a program or service, attempting to welcome students from a nearby institution that closes, the retirement or departure of a senior leader, and so on. Strategic management can be evidenced through the presence and implementation of an integrated strategic plan (Dooris et al., 2004). Aspects of strategic management are suffused into the strategic planning process itself. Strategic plans, generally speaking, require fairly substantial changes in order to achieve the goals outlined in the plan to advance the organization. Prioritization of organizational goals is key to effective strategic management and change (Goldstein, 2012; Rowley & Sherman, 2001).

CONTROLLING AND LEADING

The remaining two functions of management are grouped together in what might be a counter-intuitive way: controlling and leading. In a management context *controlling* refers to ensuring operations produce efficient and quality results, and the function of *leading* refers to moving the organization forward in line with its vision and guiding principles—through supporting organizational learning and making changes as necessary to achieve goals.

Controlling: QM and Continuous Improvement

Higher education institutions need to be mission-driven and strategic. If it is not part of your mission or strategic plan, then why do it? Often newly hired administrators feel the need to leave their mark on the institution, so they decide to create a new program or add a new major, a department, or even a college. These new administrators usually neglect to ask "Does this fit in with the institutional mission?" and instead ask staff "How can we *make* this fit?" This is the opposite of demonstrating control. Change for change's sake is rarely a good thing. As Pfeffer (1992) advises, administrators must learn to submerge their ego and focus on their institution's reputation instead of their personal reputations. A great way to enhance an institution's reputation is to enhance its quality. If the institution is successful, the administrator is usually viewed as successful. This section addresses theory and approaches to enhancing quality and engaging in continuous improvement.

The QM Movement

Elements of process improvement and control can be found dating back to the construction of the pyramids in Egypt (Burton, 2016), but more recently the QM movement is best described as a transition from quantity to quality. When a

QM philosophy is implemented in such a way that the entire organization shifts in practice and culture, it can be a transformative experience.

QM practices became popular in the United States due to the success of Toyota, which overtook American automakers in the 1970s and 1980s. Toyota built its manufacturing empire using principles introduced to it by W. Edwards Deming and Joseph Juran, and combined them with its own philosophy (Freed & Klugman, 1997; Seymour, 1993; Sims & Sims, 1995). The Toyota Production System enabled Toyota to produce higher-quality products while also producing them in sufficient quantity. This was due in large part to a total commitment to eliminating flaws in the manufacturing process, and therefore defects—a concept that would later be called Lean thinking (Balzer, 2010).

The QM movement is informed by numerous scholars, but Deming is considered by many to be the founder of the quality movement with his fourteen points (Figure 7.1). In essence, Deming posits that organizations should work smarter, not harder—and the way to do this is to infuse quality throughout the process and empower the workforce with a sense of ownership. To provide guidance on how organizations could transition to a quality-over-quantity philosophy and process, Deming created principles (Figure 7.1) organizations should adopt; they still guide the quality movement today. His principles focus on reducing fear; dissolving silos; changing from quota-based to quality-focused goals; incorporating employees' perspectives; focusing on the processes and inputs; and educating, developing, and improving the lives of employees.

Complementing Deming's work, Joseph Juran identified contexts in which quality could be managed: planning, control, and improvement (Juran & Godfrey, 1998). Quality is an amorphous concept. Philip Crosby (1984) created the "Four Absolutes" to better define QM in a manufacturing context, following Deming's lead (Figure 7.2). Deming, Crosby, and Juran contend that a focus on quality will lower costs of delivering goods and services in the long run, and that failing to do so will increase the costs of doing business (low quality means high costs).

1)	Create constancy of purpose
2)	Adopt the new philosophy
3)	Cease dependence on inspection to achieve quality
4)	End the practice of awarding business on the basis of price tag
5)	Improve constantly and forever the system of production and service
6)	Institute training on the job
7)	Institute leadership. The aim of supervision should be to help people do a better job
8)	Drive out fear
9)	Break down barriers between departments
10)	Eliminate slogans, exhortations, and targets for the work force
11a)	Eliminate work standards/quotas...substitute leadership
11b)	Eliminate management by objective. Eliminate management by numbers
12a)	Remove barriers that rob the hourly worker of his right to the joy of workmanship
12b)	Remove barriers that rob people in management of their right to the joy of workmanship
13)	Institute a vigorous program of education and self-improvement
14)	Put everybody in the company to work to accomplish the transformation

Figure 7.1 Deming's Fourteen Points

- Quality is defined as conformance to requirements, not as 'goodness' or 'elegance'.
- The system for causing quality is prevention, not appraisal.
- The performance standard must be Zero Defects, not "that's close enough".
- The measurement of quality is the Price of Nonconformance, not indices.

Figure 7.2 Crosby's Four Absolutes

Quality management is known by many names: Total Quality Management (TQM), Total Quality Control, Strategic Quality Management, Continuous Quality Improvement, and Quality at the Source, all of which mean essentially the same thing but may employ different approaches (Freed & Klugman, 1997; Seymour et al., 2004; Sims & Sims, 1995). The use of the word "total" simply refers to the idea that all aspects of the enterprise should be considered (i.e., not just the machines building the final product). Seymour (1993), acknowledging the numerous terms and models, summarizes QM this way: addressing the needs of customers through ensuring quality is part of everyone's job, and relying on leadership, teamwork, education, problem solving, recognition of effort, and measurement to make it happen.

QM efforts can incorporate many tools and approaches which may overlap and be somewhat indistinct from one another (except to management scholars). They include Statistical Controls, Six Sigma, Systems Thinking, Kaizen, Kanban, Just-In-Time (JIT), and Lean, among others (Burton, 2016; Chase, Aquilano, & Jacobs, 2001). What sets the QM movement apart from prior practices is its grounding in functionality, process, and outcomes, rather than leaving it as an abstract concept. Ultimately, Deming's points focus on the setting, expectations, and personnel, Crosby's absolutes define the standards for quality, and Juran's processes identify the spheres in which QM activities should be incorporated. While these points, absolutes, and key processes were written for the manufacturing sector, Deming (1986) suggested its utility for other sectors, stating "improvement of quality is a method transferable to different problems and circumstances" (p. 128).

QM in Higher Education

Rowley and Sherman (2001) describe TQM as "a philosophy, a mindset, and a method of operationalizing strategic planning that will have many long-term benefits for the campus" (p. 294). Seymour (1993) proposed a model for QM in higher education that includes seeing quality as more than just student–faculty interactions in the classroom or accreditation. Seymour agrees with Crosby (1979), who advocated for seeing quality as a long-term commitment:

> Quality improvement is not a goal to be accomplished; it is a journey, not a destination. It is a never ending process that requires constant attention by everyone at all levels of the organization from the most sophisticated technical unit to food service, and the maintenance of the buildings and grounds.
>
> (p. 509)

To pursue this philosophy, structural elements of the organization must be addressed to create an organization that learns from itself. The pursuit of continuous improvement can bind the organization into a more "integrated, purposeful whole" (p. 31). Institutions that recognize the importance of incorporating QM into long-range strategic planning are more apt to make this paradigm shift than organizations that do not (Jelinek, Foster, & Sauser, 1995).

In a higher education context, Deming's fourteen points can be applied by ensuring personnel are well prepared to do their jobs through clear purpose and expectations, and provided with sufficient training and autonomy, and leadership focuses on eliminating barriers that impede progress. This approach matches with higher education's shared governance roots, as QM focuses on the people *and* the processes simultaneously. Crosby's absolutes could be envisioned through minding the process, rather than making errors and resolving them at the end—and having a high standard for performance. Juran's contexts, while written for manufacturing, are easily transferred to higher education—planning to ensure high-quality education and co-curricular services are delivered, controlling for problems, and working to improve education and services over time.

The focus of QM, therefore, is necessarily two-fold: processes and people. Both are critical elements within higher education. Colleges and universities are complex organizations that have multiple processes involving students, faculty, and staff. Figure 7.3 summarizes what institutions should concentrate on when beginning their journey toward implementing QM on their respective campuses.

Deming (1986) suggested that while it is helpful, the support of top management (president, vice-president, provost) by itself is not sufficient to improve the quality of an institution. For institutions applying quality principles, it is important to understand that these principles were never meant to be considered "cookbook procedures on file ready for specific application" (Deming, 1986, p. 128). Seymour (1993) notes, "The philosophy and tools of Total Quality management are not a magic potion able to turn a poorly-run, noncompetitive organization into one that operates with awe-inspiring efficiency and effectiveness" (p. ix). In other words, every institution must review the principles and adapt them to the institutional mission, vision, and values, structures, culture, politics, while also getting all levels of the organization involved (Birnbaum, 2000; Jelinek et al., 1995).

Focus on Processes	**Focus on People**
• Adhere to its mission • Eliminate redundancy within its systems and its curriculum • Develop and implement transparent decision making processes • Make data-based decisions • Collect data that will help answer the questions asked • Practice what it teaches	• Involve all stakeholders in the improvement of processes • Measure student learning outcomes throughout the institution • Differentiate between stakeholder needs and student wants • Emphasize leadership • Communicate effectively throughout all level of the institution • Commit to the long term

Figure 7.3 Focus of QM Practice

Institutions that follow their mission and have a consistent purpose that involves quality, efficiency, and effectiveness have the greatest potential for success. Those who lose sight of this will struggle because they have difficulty explaining their identity. This can be seen today in many mid-sized to large institutions that are experiencing an identity crisis. They may have been founded with a very specific mission to meet the needs of their stakeholders and now are trying to meet the needs of everyone by becoming all things to all people. This type of mission creep has created numerous problems for institutional administrators. Dickeson (2010) states, "Colleges and universities have evolved to the point where the bloated curriculum is receiving inadequate resources to accomplish its purposes" (pp. 22–23), and "The price for academic program bloat is the impoverishment of each" (p. 23).

As Crosby (1979) pointed out over three decades ago, "Quality is free . . . what costs money are the unquality things – all the actions that involve not doing the job right the first time" (p. 1). Schein (1999) notes the challenge in shifting culture to QM, stating, "new cultures can be imagined, but they will only be created by experienced success over a long time" (p. 170). In summary, QM should be viewed as a way of running an institution. When done well, QM adds value to the institution, its employees, and its students. The tools mentioned earlier, such as Six Sigma (using statistics to evaluate outcomes), Kaizen (concerted efforts to identify and solve problems, sometimes in quick bursts), and Lean can be very useful when implementing a QM program (Sodhi & Sodhi, 2008).

Lean Higher Education

Lean is one of many lenses available through which QM can be viewed, and is increasingly popular in higher education today (Carlson, 2018). The Lean philosophy originated with Toyota in Japan, as it paired Deming's process for improving quality with a JIT manufacturing process (English, 2012; Myerson, 2014). This became known as the Toyota Production System, as mentioned above, and was later termed "Lean" by scholars at MIT (Balzer, 2010; Burton, 2016). "Lean is a team-based form of continuous improvement that is focused on the identification and elimination of waste from the customer's perspective" (Myerson, 2014, p. 23). Balzer (2010) suggests Lean is a superior approach to QM due to its comprehensive nature, scalability to organizations of all sizes, practicality, reliance on evidence, and empowerment and inclusion of employees.

While Lean's origins are clearly in the manufacturing sector, at the turn of the twenty-first century the principles of Lean started to be applied to the office environment. Employing the Lean methodology can create flexibility and better response times, reduce mistakes, simplify business processes, increase efficiency in processing transactions, and make better use of staff talents (Myerson, 2014). Balzer (2010) extolls the virtues of Lean in higher education, stating it:

> holds great promise for helping colleges and universities do a better job of meeting the needs of those they serve, improving the efficiency and effectiveness of the critical processes and services that allow them to achieve their mission and goals, and providing faculty and staff with more enriching and rewarding experiences at work. (p. xiv)

Lean can also serve as a response to calls for increased accountability, redouble focus on specific outcomes, and help institutions survive in a tough competitive climate (Balzer, 2010). Practitioners of Lean work to achieve a better flow of processes through the identification and elimination of waste in the process—but it is important to note that the concept of waste is considered from the point of view of the customer (or "beneficiary").

Waste is defined as activities or steps during a process that do not add value for the beneficiary (Balzer, 2010; Myerson, 2014). Processes can range from simple to complex, and include all aspects of the institution—every division, unit, department, or program. When applying Lean principles to processes, the critical factor is consideration of the perspective of the beneficiary of a given process (Balzer, 2010).

Practitioners of Lean principles generally look for eight wastes, although Balzer (2010) presents a great model with four groupings consisting of twenty-six wastes in total. In the interests of brevity, the traditional eight wastes will be presented here, with examples specific to higher education informed by Balzer (2010), Burton (2016), English (2012), and Myerson (2014):

- Transportation – refers to unnecessary movement of inventory/supplies and people; Myerson (2014) notes, "Ideally, when material is received, it should be touched only twice: once to put it away and another time to pull it for consumption" (p. 45). This type of waste refers to the product, not the people producing it.
    - In higher education, this could refer a document that requires multiple (possibly unnecessary) layers of approval via sign-offs, ineffective storage practices, and office or building layouts that make the sharing or circulation of important technologies difficult. Another example is having multiple meetings to make a decision when one should have sufficed.
- Inventory – refers to any excess supplies being held in stock for future use. In manufacturing, this is avoided by using a JIT process—supplies are delivered on site as they are needed. This is considered a waste because storing items requires space, which costs money. In the service sector, this is less of an issue, although certainly applies to technology that could become obsolete over time if held for future use.
    - In higher education, this could refer to maintaining stockpiles of office supplies, printed materials, pre-fabricated forms, and technology hardware. Documents and data are other areas in which this can be seen in higher education—data are expensive to store (physically and on the cloud), but we have a very hard time getting rid of them (in case we need them later). It can also refer to library holdings that are underutilized when better use of the space could be made (especially with the prevalence of e-books today).
- Motion – refers to the motion required by an individual to accomplish a task; more movement means reduced efficiency.
    - In higher education, this could refer to a poor office layout, requiring a person to travel to multiple places to complete a single task; this can be mitigated by co-locating important resources and relying on virtual meetings.

Another example is data stored in such a way that it becomes hard to fulfill a reporting request, perhaps because the data must be cobbled together from different sources that do not match up very well. Essentially, this refers to instances where the duration of a process is extended because a person has to go to multiple locations to get something done.

- Waiting – refers to any instance when production or service cannot begin because the materials or information are not ready. This is, according to English (2012), the most complaint-generating waste.
  - In higher education the examples are *endless*. Approvals for purchasing, travel, reimbursement, hiring, and promotion are excellent examples. Any time there is a bottleneck, there is a waiting waste. Breakdowns in technology are another important culprit for this type of waste.
- (Over)processing – refers to "any effort expended on a product or service that does not add value" (English, 2012, p. 61). This waste can be hard to identify, but is insidious. It essentially includes any work done on a project or instance in excess of what is necessary—and it is therefore tough to identify.
  - In higher education, this could refer to a variety of things—but is signaled by any effort where the person working on it feels compelled to go "above and beyond" the requirements. (That said, it is still a great way to impress your boss—*as long as you can get your other stuff done.*) Because services are largely intangible in nature, over-processing waste is rarely openly discouraged. Another example can be found in the selection of software or services—when a unit is seeking a product with bells and whistles that may never be put to good use, but will take a lot longer to design or implement as a result.
- Over-production – refers to the most easily recognized form of waste: producing too much of something. In manufacturing, this refers to making too much of something—which is problematic not only because storing excess product costs money, but also because the time spent producing things not yet needed takes time away the work that really needs to be done.
  - In higher education, this may include: creating programs that are not yet in demand, opening too many sections of a course, printing too many admissions viewbooks, and maintaining too high a level of faculty and staff to deliver programs and services. Over-production can also manifest through duplication of products or services (for example, four different offices on campus purchasing online survey tools or the maintenance of separate customer relationship management systems).
- Correction/defects – refers to the time and goodwill wasted when mistakes are made and must be corrected; this can result from a lack of understanding, a lack of oversight, insufficient or inconsistent understanding, or policies and procedures being changed but not communicated. This type of waste also includes producing the *wrong* thing or failing to address customer needs.

  - In higher education, this could be providing incorrect information to parents and families, data entry or data reporting errors, accidentally mailing admission acceptance letters to applicants who were denied admission, providing services or programs nobody wants (or focusing on work that does not align to overarching mission or goals), or missing out on a needed service or program offering.

- Intellectual/underutilized people – refers to the intellectual capital wasted when an organization does not sufficiently leverage its workers' talents, knowledge, and skills. This can also refer to an organization that does not promote idea-sharing and learning, which will be discussed in the *Leading* section. Both the organization and the employee suffer when they are not able to fully benefit from one another.

Wastes are identified through understanding processes; this can be accomplished through an activity called a *value stream map* (VSM) (Balzer, 2010; English, 2012). To create a VSM, the steps of a process (such as registration for courses from a student's point of view) are laid out in detail. Each step is evaluated as "value-added" or "non-value-added." Steps that add value are those that students believe make it better (or would pay for). Everything else is non-value-added. The goal in Lean is to reduce the non-value-added steps in number or time, or both—although it is acknowledged that many processes must contain non-value-added steps for compliance or administrative purposes. VSMs can be completed through Kaizen blitz events, where all possible stakeholders are essentially locked in a room (with snacks) to fully map the process in excruciating detail. Through this work, a current-state VSM is created, and then a future map can be created, with the intended improvements.

Lean is much more than simply steps and identification of waste in a process (or sets of processes). In a Lean environment, all employees are empowered to immediately bring production (or work) to a halt to address an emerging quality problem (English, 2012). Standardization of work, visual monitoring of operations, use of appropriate technology, teamwork, and development of employees to uphold the Lean philosophy are critical components of a Lean enterprise. English (2012) stresses the commitment required to the Lean approach, stating, "Remember, Lean is a way of thinking and used to change the culture. One principle or value will not work without the other" (p. 49).

Lean is an approach that can be used to rethink important processes. Balzer (2010) notes that it is a system that promotes organizational improvement by changing culture through guidelines and tools. That said, Burton (2016) notes the peril of "improvement toolitis," which is described as focusing on the tools and not the greater purpose of what one is trying to accomplish. It is critical, before engaging in the important work of Lean, to identify a clear-cut problem to solve, and only then should the process of improving flow be engaged (p. 37). Implementation of Lean requires a culture shift, which is best accomplished through formulating teams, establishing expectations, evaluating processes and mapping them out, identifying wastes to improve flow, and continuing to hone the process over time. This advice reflects the history of QM principles, and the influence of the ideas of Deming, Juran, and Crosby is evident. Like all other described QM frameworks, Lean will not work without the buy-in and explicit support of leadership (Balzer, 2010).

QM principles have permeated the higher education landscape at the program, department, and institutional levels, and they are now being implemented at the regional and national levels through the accreditation process, which will be discussed shortly. Regardless of the lens and tools used in a QM approach, measurement is key. This has been a driving force behind the assessment movement within higher education. In a manufacturing context, QM work involves measuring the number of defects, time spent on processes, and other elements that contribute to understanding quality. In higher education, quality can also be measured by tracking errors and time spent, and through measuring specific goals or intended outcomes.

Deming (1986) cautions administrators to not focus on measures alone as, he states, "measures of productivity do not lead to improvements in productivity." There must also be "important meaningful comparisons" (p. 19) before quality can be achieved. In order to accurately measure something, you must decide what it means—and that is no easy task, especially in higher education. Inputs and outputs are easy to measure from a quantity standpoint, but quality is far more difficult. As with any organizational change, this approach has met with resistance from within the academy. Birnbaum (2000) expressed concerns that the emphasis on measurement is leading higher education to essentially lower the goals; he comments "if we cannot measure what is valuable, we will come to value what is measurable" (p. 198). Further, as Balderston (1995) points out, institutions of higher education are much better with "measures of activity or size than of results" (p. 4), especially with regard to learning outcomes. But progress is being made. The assessment movement within higher education has proven that if it is important a way will be found to measure it.

Assessment and Accreditation

QM is focused on leveraging people and processes to deliver a better, higher-quality product or service—assessment and QM are naturally aligned with each other. In fact, at least one regional accrediting body had standards that referenced "improvement" in its criteria as early as the 1930s (Dodd, 2004). Wheeler et al. (2008) point out that QM "has caused institutions to become far more intentional and systematic in the design and delivery of their curricula and far more diligent in measuring the results of what they say they do and what they actually do" (p. 210). Ultimately, assessment in higher education is about developing and measuring intentional learning outcomes, and is an important component of institutional accreditation requirements. Accreditation will be discussed here as it relates to both improvement and assertions of quality.

The system of accreditation in the United States evolved from groups of member organizations formed to discuss common issues and to provide a measure of legitimacy to established colleges against a barrage of start-up diploma mills in the late 1800s and the early 1900s. Brittingham (2009) notes,

> Between 1950 and 1965, the regional accrediting organizations developed and adopted what are considered today's fundamentals in the accreditation process: a mission-based approach, standards, a self-study prepared by the institution, a visit by a team of peers who produced a report, and a decision by a commission overseeing a process of periodic review.
>
> (pp. 14–15)

As the process has evolved, so have the standards. Accreditors have transitioned from a focus on basic inputs and quantitative measures (such as the number of books in the library) to more important measures focused on processes, outcomes, and institutional integrity (Brittingham, 2009; Kretovics & McCambridge, 1998; Wolff, 2005). Accreditation has evolved from a means to fend off diploma mills to become one of demonstrating quality.

During the 1980s and 1990s, the quality movement within higher education focused on administrative processes within the individual institutions (billing, procurement, student registration, etc.) and did not necessarily concentrate on the curriculum or learning outcomes of said curricular offerings (Balderston, 1995). However, organizations such as the American Association of Colleges & Universities, National Institute for Learning Outcomes Assessment, and Council for the Advancement of Standards have been heavily involved in developing ways to assess or measure student learning. Many of these efforts have chosen to emphasize proxies for student learning because of the ease of measurement (standardized tools such as the National Survey on Student Engagement), or they may have confused activity for productivity. However, there are others who have been challenging administrators and faculty to establish alternative measures that are in fact direct measures of student learning.

It is important to point out that measurement for the sake of measurement will not help improve an institution. Up until recently (and some would argue, this is still ongoing), the data required by accreditation agencies were not leading to true improvement. As a consequence, there are far too many colleges and universities with shelves full of data and reports that are not used to make improvements. Similarly, states are increasingly requiring their public institutions to provide "accountability" reports that contain data with very little connection to actual effectiveness. Further, when institutions collect too much data or the wrong data, administrators may find themselves looking for a problem to fit their data (Cohen & March, 1974). Data should be collected to help administrators answer questions. But unfortunately, as Cohen and March point out, all too often administrators appear to be in a hurry to solve a problem that may not exist. Keep in mind, data cannot make the decision; rather, they are used to inform the decision-making process.

Accreditation can appear to be "an episodic exercise leading to a volcanic eruption of activity every ten years, involving the formulation of informal self-study committees and the preparation of large reports, often with many useful recommendations" (Wolff, 2005, p. 91). However, with the shift toward a continuous improvement model, that perception is also changing. Brittingham (2009) notes the many academics expressing a newfound appreciation of being part of a self-study writing team, as it enables them to learn about their institution in a way no other opportunity would provide. The analysis of an institution's processes and outcomes that occurs during the accreditation process can create learning opportunities for organizations and lead to important changes (continuous improvement). A QM mindset promotes the utilization data for continuous improvement, a bedrock component of assessment for accreditation. Although there are many well-known barriers to assessment (time, complexity, data management), it has great potential for improvement of organizations. When institutions "close the loop"—that is, use the data gleaned from the assessment process to have important conversations—the organization can learn from assessment and make meaningful changes (Suskie, 2014).

Leading: Organizational Learning and Change Management

The discussion of organizational learning follows QM both in the management timeline and in practice. According to Terziovski, Howell, Sohal, and Morrison (2000), "TQM principles and concepts underpin the evolution of the learning organization" (p. 30). Organizational learning simply does not occur without a QM mindset. Further, organizational learning impacts the sustainability of an organization's competitive advantage in a crowded marketplace (Chase et al., 2001). Along with moving an organization forward through learning, managers must also manage change—some of the changes are by choice, and others by mandate.

Organizational Learning

The concept of organizational learning was introduced to the business world by Chris Argyris and Donald Schön's *Organizational Learning: A Theory of Action Perspective* in 1978, although it was not until Peter Senge's book *The Fifth Discipline: The Art and Practice of the Learning Organization* that the concept became popular. Organizational learning is an essential component of QM practice. Argyris and Schön emphasize, "organizational learning is not merely individual learning, yet organizations learn only through the experience and actions of individuals" (1978, p. 9). In essence, the whole (organization) can be more than the sum of its parts (individual employees), when the parts themselves are engaged in learning and self-reflection.

Administrators and faculty may make the assumption that because colleges and universities employ highly intelligent people and are designed to deliver education, they must be learning organizations. This is not the always the case. In reality, the intellectual capacity of the employees may contribute to the ability of an organization to learn but by itself cannot create a learning organization. An institution must engage in sufficient reflection and examination of its actions to become a learning organization. Argyris and Schön present two concepts that help define prerequisites to establishing a learning organization: a *theory of action* and *single- and double-loop learning.*

Theory of Action

To help frame the concept of organizational learning, Argyris and Schön (1978) introduce the concept of a theory of action, which they define as "a theory of deliberate human behavior which is for the agent a theory of control but which, when attributed to the agent, also serves to explain or predict his behavior" (p. 11). A theory of action has two distinct parts: an espoused theory and a theory-in-use.

- Espoused theory is the theory of action individuals *believe* they use to govern their lives (and would communicate to others). Espoused theory, however, is not what most people actually use.
- Theory-in-use is what actually governs a person's actions, and it "may or may not be compatible with the espoused theory" and the person may not even realize it (Argyris and Schön, 1978, p. 11).

Considered another way, espoused theory could be thought of as "what we say we do" while the theory-in-use is "what we actually do." The two may be similar . . . or vastly different. For example, senior administrators espouse their value for collaboration and consensus-building and may actually *pride* themselves on how much they incorporate this into their leadership styles. However, when faced with important decisions, they revert to their theory-in-action, which is to quickly check in with one or two trusted colleagues, make a decision, and move on in the name of efficiency. In their minds, they believe they are building consensus and collaborating with a variety of stakeholders before making a decision . . . but in reality that is not the case.

Applied to higher education, the vision, mission, goals, and objectives of a college or university will guide its theory of action. These formal corporate documents define "the norms, strategies, and assumptions embedded in the company's . . . practices" (Argyris & Schön, 1978, p. 14). This theory of action, which is the institution's espoused theory, oftentimes will conflict with the theory-in-use or what is actually observed. For example, there are numerous institutions that profess to have selective admissions (espoused theory), and yet, for a variety of reasons, continue to admit and enroll students who fail to meet the stated requirements (theory-in-use). This theory-in-use, in turn, creates problems within the institution as these underprepared students require attention that the faculty and staff are not prepared, or are ill equipped, to provide. There are also aspects of theory-in-use that live outside formal documents, such as in persistent organizational norms.

Single- and Double-Loop Learning

Members of organizations typically rely on theory-in-use until prompted to do otherwise. Argyris and Schön (1978) refer to this as single-loop thinking, where "members of the organization respond to changes in the internal and external environments of the organization by detecting errors which they then correct so as to maintain the central features of organizational theory-in-use" (p. 18). This is not necessarily a bad thing—the individual is engaging in inquiry and finding a solution to the error. But the organization misses out on a chance to learn when this type of thinking occurs. This single-loop learning is primarily concerned with effectiveness (and is referred to as a Model O-I or Model I). Model I thinking is focused on finding quick solutions within the organization's norms.

To explain, Argyris and Schön use an example of a thermostat to demonstrate a Model I. A thermostat is set at a specific temperature. When the room temperature drops below the specified temperature (error detected), the thermostat turns the heat on until the room temperature reaches that specified (error corrected). The thermostat does not spend any time pondering whether its set point is at a reasonable level—in part because it is a thermostat and not a person. Many individuals operate this way: they see a problem, correct it, and move forward without looking into the root cause.

While new strategies or assumptions may be developed to address errors, they will always be developed within the organization's existing governing norms. Stacey (2007) warns that single-loop learning environments can lead to "skilled incompetence," because assumptions and practices are not carefully questioned. One of the more dysfunctional attributes to Model I organizations is that the governing variables are often considered "undiscussable" (Argyris & Schön, 1978, p. 35). Employees of the institution are either afraid of or prohibited from talking about the problems at hand. This is visible in institutions that will not publicly embrace their respective theories-in-use, but instead cling to the rhetoric of their espoused theories without upholding them.

If the organization is to break free from single-loop learning and the Model I thinking, it must have employees who are reflective thinkers and managers who support them in engaging in reflection. Model I behaviors are more likely to cease when employees must reflect on a problem and realize that they cannot correct it by doing more of the same thing, or simply trying to do the same thing better. This type of reflective practice results in double-loop learning and creates a Model O-II theory-in-use, or Model II learning, which involves the "restructuring of organizational norms" (Argyris & Schön, 1978, p. 22). When norms are changed, often the accompanying strategies and assumptions change as well. Encouraging double-loop thinking, rather than single-loop thinking, is the role of a leader who wishes to enhance organizational learning.

Using the thermostat example again, instead of permitting the thermostat to turn the heat on automatically when the temperature drops below the specified degree, the managers would first need to determine if, at this time, the original setting was appropriate for the institution (i.e., examine the underlying assumptions and institutional values). Connecting this to the admissions process, the institution's faculty and staff would question the failure to adhere to the policy and in addition request that the original policy be discussed openly. This open discussion will permit the faculty and staff to reflect upon the policy and determine if it is indeed the correct policy for the institution at this time.

In higher education, one might imagine a scenario where a small, private liberal arts college is exploring options to remain solvent in a tough market. To recruit more students, the enrollment management office has hired more admissions staff and increased the emphasis on marketing and the amount of money allocated for institutional grants (tuition discounts). The administration has encouraged the creation of new programs to try to pique the interest of Generation Z students, and has added an e-sports coach to start a program on campus. If the chief academic officer (CAO) encourages the creation of strategies that only function within the existing system (more students, more shiny objects), Model I learning will occur. If the CAO encourages employees to "think outside the box" and question the very nature of the problem, it is encouraging Model II learning (as long as it actually follows through with it). Inquiry in a Model II environment might allow for such questions as: Do we need more students, or *different* students? Is *less* actually *more*? Should we solicit deep partnerships with other institutions? Should we discontinue our residential program, or should we move to fully online delivery?

Becoming a Learning Organization

Freed and Klugman (1997) encapsulate why an organization would want to be a Model II environment: "Learning organizations are able to weave a continuous and enhanced ability to learn, adapt, and change into their culture. The organizational values, policies, practices, systems, and structures encourage, support, and accelerate learning for all employees" (p. 55). This approach combines continuous improvement of quality with creating a better workplace through learning, trust, and empowerment. If the organization has not established an environment that values honesty and fosters trust, it will be impossible to establish a Model II process (Stacey, 2007). Employees must feel confident that disagreement will not be viewed as a challenge to authority but rather questions about processes.

Colleges and universities are the ideal institutions within which to develop a Model II learning culture. Most of these institutions have been structured around a concept of shared governance which demands participation of all organizational members. This, combined with the inherent nature of reflective practice among faculty, sets a foundation for a learning organization. Within every organization, there are multiple levels of hierarchy or bureaucratic structure. The individuals occupying these levels have varying degrees of responsibility in ensuring the organization operates as a Model II learning organization. Teare and Dealtry (1998) present four roles managers should adopt in order to promote a Model II environment (Figure 7.4).

According to Garvin (2000), "a learning organization is an organization skilled at creating, acquiring, and transferring knowledge, and at modifying its behavior to reflect the new knowledge and insights" (p. 282). By its very nature, a learning organization changes—and this is a good thing. Dixon (1998) notes "it is a responsibility of organizational members to engage in the continual re-examination of their organization's purpose" (p. 162). In a Model II learning organization, this process will be completed regularly. When connected with QM principles, organizational learning has the potential to vastly improve organizational outcomes.

ORGANIZATIONAL CHANGE

If anything is certain within higher education, it is that it will continue to operate in an environment of change. There is no doubt that higher education systems and individual institutions must continue to meet the needs of the local, state, national, and international communities. Those needs continue to change. As mentioned

1. Role model – demonstrate personal enthusiasm for learning and development.
2. Provider – be a conscious and generous provider of learning and development opportunities for others and an active supporter and encourager whenever opportunities are taken.
3. System builder – build learning into the system so that it is integrated with normal work processes and embedded in the conscious agenda.
4. Champion – the importance of learning for other parts and the organization as a whole.

Figure 7.4 Four Roles

previously, institutions of higher education are not designed to respond to every minor change in society, but rather to educate and prepare the next generation of leaders, who in turn will be responsible for guiding these changes. Within colleges and universities, change may be quite obvious, or rather subtle. There are essentially two dimensions of change (Figure 7.5). On one axis, the change is either planned or unplanned, and on the other the change is either structural or cosmetic. The source of the change can be internally driven by the staff and faculty or thrust upon the institution through outside pressure from any number of external stakeholders.

An example of an unplanned change at the institutional level could be the sudden departure of the institution's president or other senior leader. The institution must prepare for the arrival of a new administrator with a new agenda (and likely new strategic plan). At the state level, an unplanned change can be the creation of a new supervisory board or the appointment of a new government official as the chair of the coordinating board. Both of these changes create a great deal of uncertainty within an institution or a system, and both of these changes are cosmetic rather than structural. The individuals in charge have changed, and some policies may change, but the institutions themselves will remain pretty much the same.

If the change is planned, the institution has time to adapt or adjust to the change prior to its implementation. For example, in the 1970s, many colleges and universities changed from the quarter system of scheduling classes to the semester system. This change did not occur quickly but rather was discussed over time, and its implementation was planned well in advance. All stakeholders were given plenty of advanced notice of the change, so no one was surprised when the transition took effect. This change was also structural in that it required the institutions to make changes to degree requirements, course schedules, and the institutional calendar. These changes

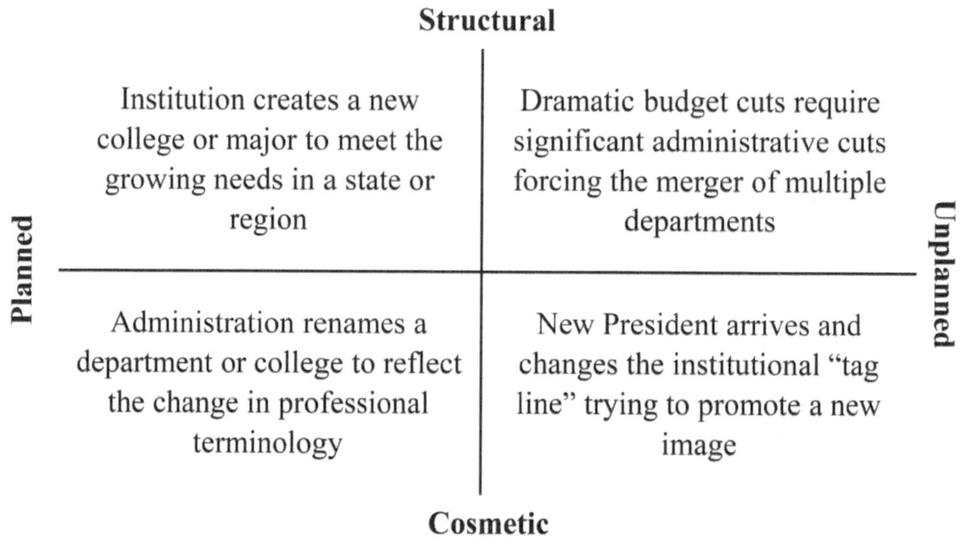

Figure 7.5 Types of Change

will have a great impact on the institutional environment; in the case of substantial changes managers can and should leverage change to reset or renew an organization in response to a changing environment (Stephens, 2017, p. 119).

If change within higher education is inevitable, it becomes important for administrators to understand how to implement change in an effective manner. A leader's success or failure is judged largely by their ability to manage change, and communication is among the most important tools a leader can use (Clawson, 2003; Rowley & Sherman, 2001; Sadler, 2003). That being said, change is hard! Clawson (2003) discusses the challenges of change management, explaining that employees fall into routines with their work—and those routines aid in both efficiency and feelings of comfort. When employees are asked to change routines, uncertainty and discomfort can follow—much like changing from single- to double-loop learning. Leaders should promote change by (1) presenting data on why the change is necessary; (2) building a team to plan for the change (with the best people possible on that team); (3) explaining the planned changes thoroughly; (4) testing out the changes in process/procedures before implementing them organization-wide, if possible; and (5) providing positive reinforcement to those who accept the changes (Clawson, 2003).

There are numerous models for implementing organizational change that can be applied in the for-profit or not-for-profit sectors. One of the easiest to understand is Kurt Lewin's change model of unfreezing, changing, and re-freezing.

Unfreezing is about understanding the organization's (or individuals') readiness for change, and preparing the stakeholders for a change by demonstrating the need and showing that the status quo will not suffice for the future success of the institution. This awareness may come about through dissatisfaction with the status quo (internally motivated change), unplanned internal or external changes (such as a new president or regulations), or a planned internal or external changes (movement from quarters to semesters or changing demographics in the market served). Change may also be inspired by costs of healthcare, employee retirements (buy-outs or surprises), newly-available technologies, regulations or accreditation, competitor institutions, and so on. Citing the work of Michael Beer at Harvard Business School, Clawson (2003) notes that the more unhappy people are with the status quo, the more accepting of change they will be—although that is influenced by the extent of the change, how it will be implemented, and its perceived benefit.

Changing can only occur after the individuals within the institution have agreed to proceed with the change. This agreement can be obtained through the acknowledgment that there is a need for a change, or it can be coerced by threats. Rowley and Sherman (2001) present approaches to implementing successful change, stressing that some are better than others. Divided into immediate and long-term, the approaches summarized in Figure 7.6 should be adapted to the specific change and culture when deployed.

Immediate (Working within norms)	• Communicate frequently and clearly, face-to-face if possible • Incentivize change through budget allocations • Rely on collaboration (more voices = better process) • Set goals and select key performance indicators or metrics • Adjust the work (work with human resources to modifying job descriptions, reassign personnel, avoid downsizing if possible) • Reward behaviors supportive of the change • Use force (this is a bad idea, but is *an* approach)
Long-Term (Changing the norms)	• Change the culture (professional development, shifting norms) • Leverage existing traditions, introduce new ones • Count on champions to promote the change • Use early/easy changes to foster support for additional changes • Rely on the things that are going well and be selective about the order of changes to achieve success in the long term • Continue to communicate thoughtfully and comprehensively throughout the organization

Figure 7.6 Change Approaches

Re-freezing is the process by which the change is adopted by the institution and becomes part of the institution's processes or a part of the new institutional culture. Most administrators will agree that change is easier to accept when there is greater representation in the process. The shared governance model of colleges and universities is an excellent framework from which to build such a representative model. However, not all changes will go smoothly, nor will they be supported by 100 percent of the stakeholders. This dissent should not be seen as a setback or viewed in a negative light, but rather acknowledged and used in a proactive and productive manner to strengthen the change.

Opposition to change, to a degree, is unavoidable. If an organization can afford it, taking time to implement gradual changes is best for long-term acceptance (Rowley & Sherman, 2001). Clawson (2003) notes that individuals asked to change how they work or what they do (*changees*) go through stages similar to the stages of grief. Changees start with anger, and move to bargaining and then despair. Changees in the despair phase should be allowed to vent their frustrations for a short period of time. After despair, most changees will then move on to more productive stages, where they begin to get on board with the changes. Organizations can and should rely on practices associated with organizational learning to enhance the adoption of changes. Leaders should encourage meaningful conversation, including disagreement and assumption-checking, so the impact of the changes on different groups can be considered (Rowley & Sherman, 2001).

Change is not financially neutral to an institution's budget. While in the long run a change may be expected to result in some savings, administrators must understand that change has financial and political costs (Rowley & Sherman, 2001). Whether cosmetic or structural, any type of reorganization will "disrupt current processes and relationships and create greater uncertainty, as new players establish their authority, priorities, and rules of interaction" (Zusman, 2005, p. 149). Change can be fraught with troubles, and leaders would do well to heed a warning from Rowley and Sherman (2001): "campus leaders often feel that their own personal leadership abilities are far more important in the implementation process than the culture. This is a mistake, because the strength of a culture usually overpowers the change tactics of leadership" (p. 191). If part of the change requires the changing of cultures, leaders must provide examples of the behavior they wish to see (Sadler, 2003).

To be effective and long-lasting, organizational change takes leadership, and needs to be implemented with a culture of mutual respect. Organizations tend to guard their traditions and patterns fiercely, and in a higher education environment you may encounter faculty, administrators, staff, students, and alumni who have a deep attachment to "the way things have always been." It is important to recognize that change is not about destroying the past, but rather about creating a new future. As Pfeffer and Sutton (2006) stated, "the only thing more dangerous than changing an organization is never changing it at all" (p. 233).

CONCLUDING COMMENTS

The effective management of higher education institutions is of paramount importance. Although persistent questioning continues on why colleges and universities rely on management principles, theories, and approaches derived from business and industry, "The best answer is that these institutions were, and still are, facing the same problems that business and industry had experienced" (Freed & Klugman, 1997, p. x). These challenges include competition with other institutions, competition for students, increasing demands for quality, concerns about cost, accountability, and so on (Freed & Klugman, 1997; Sims & Sims, 1995).

Today's college and university administrators must be more than academic leaders. They must plan for the future with their internal capabilities and external environment in mind, leverage resources carefully to achieve their plans, and strive to ensure the quality of their programs and services, while also trying to improve. Taken together, they must emulate a skill set similar to corporate managers. Shattock (2003) stresses that

> a university that has a corporate self-confidence will expect to be able to manage risks, to bend circumstances to fit the framework it wishes to establish, to motivate entrepreneurial individuals and thus carry through development which would probably fail at other institutions.
>
> (p. 39)

It is also important that administrators resist fads (Birnbaum, 2000), because all too often new and exciting ideas grab attention even when they are vastly inferior to old ideas (Pfeffer and Sutton, 2006, p. 228). Burton (2016) notes approximately 80 percent of management fads fail due to a lack of commitment and infusion into the organization's culture and practices, rendering them unsustainable. Colleges and universities are replete with new initiatives that have no record of success or no data to support their claims.

Serving in an administrative role can be quite challenging as there are numerous contradictions built into the structure of higher education systems and the institutions designed to facilitate the educational process. Administrators are required to balance competing and often conflicting needs within an institution. Most of these administrators have risen through the ranks and have little or no formal training in management or leadership. They are thrust into roles

> in which others expect them to do things that make a difference, yet at the same time find their discretion to act constrained by existing structures, ongoing routines, the professional prerogatives of others, the lack of slack resources, and the loose coupling that characterizes academic governance.
>
> (Birnbaum, 2000, p. 182)

Stakeholders expect that colleges and universities need to encourage a climate of innovation and development, where new ideas are supported and initiative is rewarded (Shattock, 2003, p. 41); however, as Balderston (1995) points out, these "approaches to management run counter to the university tradition" (p. 4).

There are two clichés regarding management that apply to higher education and should be shared at this point. The first rule of management is you *must accept responsibility for everything beneath you in the hierarchy*. All too often administrators criticize their staff or suggest that certain problems occurred because of staff mishandling a situation. Effective managers understand that what happens within their unit of the institution is their responsibility. They are the individuals who hired or currently supervise the staff responsible for implementing the policies and procedures that have been implemented. Remember that the higher one is in the institutional hierarchy the more responsibility one has.

The second rule of management is *poor planning on your part does not constitute a crisis for me*. It is not uncommon for an administrator to make a panicked phone call to a staff member to request a report or set of data that is needed immediately. Responsible administrators plan ahead and also understand the difference between an emergency and an inconvenience. That is the difference between a tactician (living in the present, not planning ahead) and a strategist. The best manager plans for what is actually needed, organizes specific tasks around the best-suited people and resources, and connects work to institutional and personal priorities. Administrators who fail to understand these two rules risk damaging their credibility, to say nothing of their relationships with colleagues and the quality of their work.

It is also true that management and leadership styles and processes change whenever there is a change in institutional leadership, which happens quite regularly. Many college and university presidents enjoy a tenure of five years or less. According to the American Council of Education, in 2016 the average tenure of a college president was "6.5 years, down from 7 years in 2011 and 8.5 in 2006" (Stripling, 2017, para. 12). This frequent changing of institutional leadership can have a detrimental impact on any institution because as Bosner (1992) points out,

> [r]esume building by higher education executives has been elevated to a fine art. Many do not remain anywhere long enough to be really evaluated for their contributions to an institution's quality growth. Long-term is not really part of their consciousness.
>
> (p. 507)

This revolving door at the upper administrative levels is a breeding ground for fad adaptation, which Birnbaum has repeatedly warned against.

Although higher education has been changing for years, the upcoming decades will bring about exceptional challenges. To thrive, colleges and universities will have to rely on planning, organizing, and increasing quality while dealing with seismic changes. To address these changes in a sustainable way, it is critical that individual institutions strive to become learning organizations which are more flexible and adaptable. Learning organizations create an environment that is supportive and forgiving, which encourages administrators to be open to criticism or bad news (Garvin, 2000). Learning organizations are better equipped to engage in the deep inquiry and important conversations that will be required to meet tomorrow's challenges.

Birnbaum (2000) groused, "higher education does not need more good management techniques; it needs more good managers" (p. 239). That is true, but one cannot be a good manager without understanding both good management techniques and how to apply those techniques. This is why doing the hard work—focusing on strategy, using resources carefully, monitoring quality, and adapting to changing conditions—is so important. When it comes to being an effective administrator, perhaps Deming (1986) said it best: "best efforts are essential – but not enough" (p. ix).

REFLECTIVE QUESTIONS

1. What are the four functions of a management? What are the most identifiable in your department/unit? Why?
2. What does it mean to be strategic?
3. What is the relationship between QM practices, assessment and accreditation, and quality assurance?
4. How can managers support a changing organization to help it meet its strategic goals?
5. How can Lean, one lens for looking at QM, be useful in identifying wastes in your department/unit?

CHAPTER 8

Strategic Planning

Parsing the four functions of management can be challenging, as they are often overlapping or at least mutually reinforcing. Similarly, approaches that illustrate the functions are similarly broad. Strategic planning has been popular in higher education since the 1970s and 1980s. Ideally, colleges and universities are creating thoughtful and reasonable strategic plans and aligning resources *with* those plans. As an administrator, you will likely be involved in several strategic planning processes during your career, and this section will familiarize you with important steps, techniques, and considerations you should incorporate should you be tapped to take a leadership role in the planning process. In this section, you will notice the word "organization" is used, in order to reflect the different ways planning can be applied—an organization can be an academic college, administrative division, department or office, academic program, and so on. When the word "institution" is used, that will refer to the entire college or university, rather than a portion of it. At this time, it is relevant to provide a few definitions.

MISSION

An organization's mission (or mission statement) is a current-state, functional description of what it aims to achieve. Scott (2006) describes it as "the broadest word used to define a university's basic purpose" (p. 1). It can cite major activities, and sometimes puts forward certain values on which the institution prides itself or that make it different from others (Hinton, 2012; Sanaghan, 2009). Missions have evolved over time in reaction to changes within and outside academe. They first began appearing in the catalogs of American universities in the 1930s (Scott, 2006). At the institution level, they typically span three basic areas: teaching, research, and public service, although the balance varies by institution type (Scott, 2006; Weisbrod, Ballou, & Asch, 2008).

Missions can and do change—for example, institutions are increasingly incorporating internationalization into their mission statements (Scott, 2006). An institution may also modify its mission to reflect a new population served, a change in focus, or the expansion of its reach. There will always be tension between mission and solvency—many colleges and universities wish to operate completely independently of financial support, but must ensure they can secure it, regardless (Weisbrod et al., 2008). In all cases, a mission should communicate accurately what the institution's purpose is.

Scott (2006) and Hinton (2012) suggest good mission statements are concise, hit on the core function or purposes without using jargon or trendy language, are used to make decisions, communicate internally and externally, inform marketing strategy, serve as a foundation to overall strategy, are developed by a team (but not the whole community), and can be aspirational in nature. Most other authors agree on these points, but recommend keeping the mission focused on where an institution is now, rather than focusing on the future (Nauffal & Nasser, 2016; Tromp & Ruben, 2010). In many organizations, a mission is a long, detailed statement that includes a lot of extraneous information. Long wandering mission statements can be problematic because it is harder to create consensus around them, and "mission creep" becomes more likely (Hinton, 2012, p. 9).

VISION

A vision statement describes where the institution is headed, its aspirations, and its aims for the future. Sanaghan (2009) notes, "The best visions are vivid, compelling, and well-understood and build on the institution's strengths and values" (p. 9). It also serves as the future a strategic plan aspires to achieve (Hinton, 2012). A vision can be phrased in terms of characteristics the organization will emulate, or achievements it will make—it serves to inspire and motivate, and should state in clear terms an intended impact or change. The vision can be set by a leader but is usually reviewed and revised by the campus community (or strategic planning committee). A properly crafted vision statement sets the stage for the determination of strategic planning priorities or themes.

VALUES

An organization may choose to present a list of its values or guiding principles, which are described as "the ideals and behaviors deemed important by the organization" (Nauffal & Nasser, 2016, p. 33). They can also be core beliefs "that govern daily behavior, communication, decision-making, and leadership within an organization. These are considered non-negotiable" (Sanaghan, 2009, p. 9). Values are baked into the culture of an organization and can be hard to describe—they are a part of the culture and are enduring. They should be a part of the strategic plan, and the best way to ensure this occurs is for the planning team to investigate what these values are early in the planning process. At times, it is easier for a newcomer or outsider to discern these values (Cook, 2010). Dickeson (2015) emphasizes the centrality of values in higher education planning—and that academic programs must always be at the core of a strategic plan.

STRATEGIC PLANNING TERMS AND PROCESS MODELS

Strategic planning is a process in which members of an organization engage in deep analysis of its mission, vision, and values, scan the environment for context, and create a document that establishes its future priorities. The strategic plan must also contain realistic plans to pursue the priorities in a specific timeframe, and should be deeply connected to other plans across the organization (i.e., academic plan, enrollment management plan, facilities master plan, and financial plan). Strategic plans serve as "the governing document that directs the efforts within and the resources of an organization" (Paraska, 2013, p. 1).

The language of strategic planning is important but disagreement on terminology is prevalent. Terms like *directions*, *themes*, *priorities*, *strategies*, *strategic goals*, *goals*, *outcomes*, *objectives*, *tactics*, and *actions* can be found in plans throughout higher education, and their definitions vary by plan. But do not get too caught up in this. Hinton (2012) notes, "as long as everyone involved in the planning process agrees to a definitional hierarchy, any combination of words can be used" (p. 11). Simply discuss and settle on definitions for each term and move on. In this chapter, we use the following terminology (informed by Hinton, 2012, and Sanaghan, 2009):

- Priority – an institution-level, broad effort to focus activity toward the achievement of the vision. (May also be known as "themes" or "directions.") A priority will have multiple aligned goals.
    - This term is only to be used at the institution level; corresponding plans (college, divisional, or departmental plans) will align to these priorities.
- Goal – a component of a priority that serves to direct activity more specifically toward the corresponding priority's achievement. Goals are measurable, and may have associated target metrics.
    - At the institutional level, a goal will have multiple aligned strategies.
    - At the college, division, or departmental level, these are the top-most level of the plan and should align to institutional priorities. As in institution-level plans, a goal will have multiple aligned strategies.
- Strategy – a component of a goal that serves to direct activity more specifically toward the corresponding goal's achievement. Strategies are measurable, and may have associated target metrics.
    - At the institution-level, strategies tend to be the most specifically defined outcome.
    - At the college, divisional, or departmental level, a strategy will have multiple aligned tactics.
- Tactic – an activity that is undertaken to achieve a strategy (in college, division, and departmental plans). Tactics are measurable, and may have associated target metrics.
- Action plans – written plans for how priorities, goals, and/or strategies will be achieved; may contain tactics, timelines, responsible parties, and resource allocations.

Strategic plans are multi-year in nature—usually between five and ten years in range. The longer the period of the plan, the more restrictive it becomes (Goldstein, 2012). The process for developing a plan should be inclusive and representative, allowing for individuals at all levels of the organization to participate and give feedback. This type of approach is critical in integrated planning, which "is a sustainable approach to planning that builds relationships, aligns the institution, and emphasizes preparedness for change" (SCUP, 2018). Using an integrated planning approach will increase the plan's likelihood of acceptance and incorporation into the culture of the organization.

Dooris, Kelly, and Trainer (2004) detail how strategic planning has evolved in higher education; first, it has evolved from a "rational-deductive, formulaic approach" to one that incorporates culture, environment, and political factors (p. 7). Second, strategic planning processes today have put an increased emphasis on the adaptability and creativity of strategic plans. Finally, there has been a shift from seeing the plan as the goal to instead seeing successful implementation as the goal—in fact, some practitioners shy away from using the term "strategic planning" in favor of another: "strategic management".

There is no single "right" model to strategic planning for higher education. Numerous options exist: a five-phase model (Sanaghan, 2009), a seven-phase model (Tromp & Ruben, 2010), a nine-step sequence for Student Affairs (Ellis, 2010), and the Society for College and University Planning's five-phase, fifteen-step model (SCUP, 2018). Some authors have declined to propose a model, instead offering practical advice on the individual elements and dos and don'ts of strategic planning—and they will be synthesized in this section. Before jumping into those models and advice, it seems appropriate at this time to talk about how the mission, vision, and values factor into the planning process.

In most cases, an organization's mission should be set prior to beginning the strategic planning process. The benefit to having an established mission is its role in serving as the foundation for the plan. To ensure the plan is grounded in reality, it should be derived from the mission and move an institution closer to its vision. In some cases, particularly if an institution's survival is in question, the mission may be revised or completely changed as part of a strategic planning process (Cherrey & Clark, 2010; Gorman, 2016). Most authors agree that consideration and revision of an organization's vision is an important part of the planning process, as a strategic plan should be focused on moving the organization in that direction. An organization's values will exist well in advance of any strategic planning process, but impact it greatly—Cook (2010) recommends a study of the values in advance of the process to enhance collaboration (and avoid a mismatch). A good strategic plan should reflect the organization's values. In most models, a review of the mission, an examination or confirmation of the organization's values, and a revision of the vision is incorporated into the early stages of the planning process.

Among the best-known strategic planning models in higher education is Sanaghan's (2009) Collaborative Strategic Planning process. He advises a (flexible) five-phase approach to collaborative planning that can be used for strategic planning and other projects, summarized here:

I. Organizing – a strategic planning task force is formed, resources to support the process are committed, general timelines are set, a communication plan is established, training and development of team members is provided, and the importance of the planning effort is communicated.

II. Data collection and discussion – ideas are generated via face-to-face interaction and discussion of values with stakeholders at all levels to inform the planning task force's work.
III. Data review and interpretation – based on Phase II data, the task force pinpoints major strategic priorities or themes and develops concept papers for them. The papers should document background information, important trends, and important takeaways from Phase II, and lay out options for the institution along with costs and plans.
IV. Vision conference – using the work of Phase III, a collaborative and interactive one-day meeting called a "vision conference" brings a wide variety of internal and external stakeholders together with the planning task force to discuss the concept papers and create a "preferred future" (p. 2).
V. Goals conference – using the data gathered in Phase IV, the planning task force creates a set of goals for each of the strategic priorities discussed in Phase IV. In addition to the planning task force, this meeting, called a "goals conference", should include important institutional decision-makers because the strategic goals form the basis for an action plan and a detailed implementation plan (p. 2).

Tromp and Ruben (2010) present a seven-phase process that rests on four critical concepts: leadership (collaborative, engaged), communication (two-way, sensitive to stakeholder needs and perspectives), assessment (for monitoring and performance improvement), and culture (understand and address/incorporate it). Without proper treatment of the four areas, the seven-phase process will not be successful. The seven phases, summarized, are:

1. Review of mission, vision, and values
2. Exploration of stakeholders and collaborators
3. Environmental scanning
4. Selection of goals
5. Identification of strategies and action plans
6. Creation of the plan documents
7. Determination of outcomes and achievements

Their process, like Sanaghan's, has a pre-planning phase that calls for selection of the planning team, evaluating readiness for change, communication about the need for strategic planning and the process, and so on.

Ellis (2010) recommends a nine-step sequence for strategic planning—and while the advice is directed at Student Affairs, it is applicable for institution-level plans as well. Stressing the importance of a ground-up process, Ellis' sequence includes:

1. Establishing an understanding of current issues and problems
2. Review and adjustment of mission and core values
3. Engaging in stakeholder identification and environmental scanning (internal and external)
4. Clarification of organizational vision
5. Establishment of key performance indicators

6. Selection of measurable goals
7. Creation of strategies and implementation of action plans
8. Evaluation of results to the in-progress plan
9. Provision of a finished planning document

SCUP pioneered an integrated planning model specific to higher education that consists of five phases and fifteen steps that span the foundations of the plan to post-plan evaluation. The earlier phases of the model are focused on building the team, understanding contextual factors and stakeholder needs, and ensuring the process is conducted in a way that will support buy-in, including communication. The plan-drafting phase consists of writing a vision and identification of goals, strategies, tactics, and measures. The last two phases are implementation (the creation and alignment of lower-level plans, the allocation of resources, and addressing implementation road-blocks) and evaluation (SCUP, 2018). SCUP's model builds on those before it by introducing a specific focus on integration of plans up, down, and across the institution.

RECOMMENDED PLANNING PROCESS

Of course, the planning process is more than just a series of steps. Building on these models, along with advice from several authors, we propose a strategic planning model along with guidance on how to use the process to maximize its acceptance by stake-holders. Communication is incorporated within each phase due to its importance. As with other models, this model may be adapted to meet an organization's needs. We recommend one of the following two approaches for the management of the process:

- The formation of a planning team or task force, composed of fifteen to twenty-five people (depending on organizational size, complexity, culture) who will carry the process through from the end of the "foundation" stage to the evaluation phase, obtaining appropriate feedback throughout the process from the whole organization; or,
- The selection and training of four to seven facilitators who will lead short-term planning groups through a series of discussions and idea-generation activities connected to already-proposed priorities (such as student success, research excellence, and globalization). This model is intended to work with college-, division-, or departmental-level plans that are intended to align with a larger institution-level plan's priorities and goals. Each group will identify themes within its priority area. The work generated by each group will be provided to the larger organization (college, division, or department) for feedback. Once the feedback is received, a smaller planning team (the facilitators or the senior leaders—the "leadership group") will select the themes and identify strategies to achieve them.

The planning-team approach is an excellent one, and is recommended by many strategic planning experts. It requires a deep commitment of time and energy from the members, with time built in for training and development, numerous meetings, presence at feedback sessions, and a role in implementation planning and monitoring.

This approach can be appropriate at the institution level as well as the college, division, and departmental level. The facilitator-led approach requires a large time commitment from a smaller number of people. When using a facilitator-led approach, four to seven facilitators are selected and trained to engage participant groups in planning exercises. While the planning-team approach involves fifteen to twenty-five people in the deep-dive on planning, the facilitator approach can reasonably accommodate around 100 participants split into different groups (usually by priority or issue; e.g., student success, research excellence, and internationalization). It is important in both approaches to ensure the groups are composed of representative and diverse individuals. Both approaches also rely on a coordinator who manages schedules, shepherds the process, and serves as a member of the planning team or group. In the planning-team model, team members are involved from beginning to end. In the facilitator-led model, the majority of participants are involved in the beginning of the process, with multiple feedback loops after the major planning event.

Building the Foundation

Prior to the public kickoff of the planning process, organizational leaders (the "leadership group") need to make decisions on how the process will be handled, from logistical details (timelines, responsible parties, and resources) to the interpersonal aspects of planning. This phase, although behind the scenes, sets the stage for the rest of the process. The level of honesty, transparency, and fit to the culture of the organization is critical. The elements listed below will help foster faith in the process:

- Completion of a self-study, if necessary (internal factors research, made available publicly)
- Review of mission, if not subject to revision via a strategic planning process
- Description of strategic plan sponsorship/necessity (an explanation from leadership)
- Readiness-for-change assessment
- Identification of process coordinator or external consultant
- Establishment of the planning team's role and decision-making power, and role in implementation
- Timeline for the planning process
- Communication: announcement of intent to create as strategic plan; includes:
    - Statement of sponsorship/necessity
    - Timeline
    - Brief summary of self-study, link to full self-study (if completed)
    - Call for volunteers (if applicable)

Team or Group Selection, Preparation for Planning Retreat

If planning teams are being selected (rather than taken from a pool of volunteers), that can be completed in the previous phase. In this phase, the planning team or facilitators are selected and trained, and the background work for environmental scanning is completed. Do not underestimate the amount of work necessary to train the team/facilitators and prepare for a retreat.

- Selection of planning-team members (via invitation or volunteering) or facilitators and their group members
- Training of planning team or facilitators on strategic planning (the concept of integrated planning, environmental scanning concepts, and language and terminology of planning)
- Compilation of critical research on internal and external factors (includes recent self-study, if completed; external factors research is conducted by coordinator and members of the planning team/facilitators; sent to planning retreat participants in advance for review)
- Creation of a full-process communication plan
- Logistical preparation for strategic planning retreat (supplies, materials, food)
- Communication:
    - Invitations to selected team members or group members
    - After acceptance of invitation/pre-retreat: critical research on internal and external factors (self-study, other relevant internal documents, external factors and trends)

Planning Retreat

At the retreat, the planning team will complete important tasks and activities during the course of one or two intensive days. Environmental scanning is a deep look at internal conditions, market characteristics and trends, public conditions (financial, media, government, local, and general public), competing institutions or substitutes for postsecondary education, and the "macro environment (demographic, economic, political, technological, and cultural)" (Nauffal & Nasser, 2016, p. 33). In a group setting, it is helpful to use activities to engage in this work; the most popular is SWOT analysis (strengths, weaknesses, threats, and opportunities). Other approaches include PEST analysis (political, economic, social, technological) or STEEP analysis (social, technological, economic, environmental, political). A more complete description of environmental scanning activities is presented in the "success factors" section. Members of the planning teams or group must connect the mission, vision (unless re-written as part of this process), environmental scan, and organization's values when determining in which direction(s) the organization should move. The end result of the retreat should be the identification of a select number of themes or priorities (defined below), along with general strategies for achieving them.

- Identification of organizational values and assumptions (vision, if applicable; vision can also be reviewed later in the process)
- Environmental scanning (internal and external), stakeholder analysis
- Preliminary identification of strategic priorities (if applicable), goals, and strategies (tactics and action planning is completed in a later phase)

- Communication:
  - Acknowledgement of efforts of the planning team, or facilitators and groups
  - Creation of a summary document, reporting on the proceedings of the day, with descriptions of the outcomes of activities, and how they informed the selection of priorities (if applicable), goals, and strategies
  - Creation of an executive summary of a larger summary document for widespread distribution (with links to longer-form summary document)

Organizational Input

Once a draft of the priorities (if applicable), goals, strategies, and tactics (if applicable) is ready, it should be shared widely with the members of the organization for feedback using a variety of methods. It is important to ensure everyone has a chance to provide feedback. Ensure that a mix of days and times are selected, allowing for individuals who work different shifts (or class schedules) to find a session they can attend. This also means that the emerging plan must be worded in non-technical, jargon-free language, and written to accommodate a variety of reading comprehension levels. Feedback may be obtained through surveys, town halls, drop-in sessions, and other means.

- Communication:
  - Upon conclusion of the feedback period, a document summarizing results should be compiled and posted on the organization's website
  - An announcement of the availability of the feedback summary document should be sent out through email or other appropriate channels

Plan Refinement

After the members of the organization have provided feedback and it has been compiled into a document, it should be provided back to the planning team or facilitators (and members of the leadership team). It is likely that a large amount of feedback will be provided, and this phase will require substantial review time. Once the reviewers have a chance make sense of the feedback, the priorities and/or goals and strategies can be refined. At this point, the planning team or facilitator/leadership group should begin thinking about tactics and action plans.

- Communication: a revised document detailing the priorities, goals, and strategies should be prepared and distributed (or, at the very least, made available).

Implementation Planning

Simply creating a beautiful strategic plan with a bunch of goals, strategies, and tactics does not guarantee action. The recent history of higher education is littered with strategic plans that never came to fruition because they were set aside or the organization was not on board with the plan and ready to change (Rowley & Sherman, 2001). Sanaghan (2009) notes that strategic plans are most likely to fail in this phase.

Implementation requires thinking about your internal stakeholders and the external forces that are involved. In fact, at some institutions the team that plans the implementation may be different from the one that writes the previous sections of the plan. Senior leaders must have a hand in creating the implementation plan—so if the planning team does not have them in sufficient numbers, this is a good time to bring in additional viewpoints. The implementation plan should include:

- Action plans, which include tactics, assigned responsible individual(s), resources allocated to the plans, and timelines; ensuing activity is across multiple plan phases (if the planning team lacks expertise to fully develop the plans, consultation with functional units is appropriate)
- An explanation of how the plan will be connected to the budget; indicate if special budget requests are required to be linked to priorities or goals, the entire budget is to be linked to the achievement of priorities or goals, or some other connection will be made
- Guidelines and timelines for the alignment of the plans of colleges, divisions, and departments across campus; all plans must articulate how institutional priorities are supported (and the institutional plans should be informed by and reflective of, to the extent possible, this support)
- Principles or guidelines to ensure the strategic plan is infused into ongoing operations and planning—these can include: presentation of the strategic plan at important meetings (and in prominent locations); linking institution-level budget allocations to strategic plan priorities or goals, requiring alignment of college, divisional, and department plans; a statement of accountability; and plans for continual review of the plan progress (Brodnick & Norris, 2016; Paris, 2004; Sanaghan, 2009)
- Key performance indicators or other important metrics that will be used to monitor plan performance, as well as the individuals or committees tasked with monitoring the implementation
- Communication:
    - Provision of the "final" planning document, which incorporates discussion of all phases of the plan (the statement of sponsorship, mission, vision, and values; a summary of environmental scanning work; priorities (if applicable); goals and strategies; action plans with tactics; and guiding principles or standards of the implementation process; key performance indicators, metrics, and provisions for assessment should also be included)
    - A smaller version of the plan, with less detail, will also aid in implementation and should be shared (Paris, 2004)—perhaps in infographic form, which will help people remember the major points of the plan

Monitoring, Assessment, and Promotion of Plan

Metrics and measures for priorities, plans, and, where necessary, strategies should be developed as part of the implementation phase. In this phase, the plan is set in motion and these items are monitored to ensure progress is being made. Bresciani (2010) provides a model for data-driven strategic planning in Student Affairs, which begins after the institution's strategic plan has been created. Bresciani's model, which can be used beyond Student Affairs, focuses on using data to adjust resources to ensure plan priorities and goals are realized. If a measure reveals a problem, the group or individuals monitoring the progress must take action to adjust their course. Further, the model emphasizes the "systematic" nature of data usage in both initial planning and the monitoring of plan progress. Plan performance assessment must become second-nature to the organization, and this happens by putting it on a schedule, engaging with data regularly, and forming productive and collaborating working relationships across departments.

The planning team or facilitator group (if a standing committee) can continue to review and monitor plan progress—but if the team or group has disbanded, this responsibility must be assigned elsewhere. Goldstein (2012), Hinton (2012), and Clagett (2004) discussed the utility of having a group with long-range responsibility for plan monitoring (this group could also have budget oversight responsibilities)—but this approach is not feasible in every context. If a single person is responsible for plan monitoring and reporting, ensure that he or she has enough time to conduct this work. Key performance indicators and measures must be regularly aggregated and shared with key stakeholders. More in-depth assessment of plan progress will be required. It is crucial that the planning committee (however comprised), the plan coordinator, and the leadership group of the organization keep the plan at the front of operations to see it through. This occurs via promotion of the plan, ensuring it is visible, and keeping it on the agenda at important meetings. The implementation plan should have laid the groundwork for this. In this phase, the implementation plan is simply carried through.

- Communication:
    - Key indicators with current data
    - Interim reports on overall progress at varying levels of specificity depending on target audience

Review of Efficacy, Final Report

At the conclusion of the planning cycle, an overall assessment of achievement of plan goals should be made. This should be conducted by a group (this could be the planning team, the facilitators, or another group altogether) and focus on the extent to which the plan's priorities, goals, and strategies were achieved. The planning process itself should also be reviewed for "lessons learned." At the conclusion of the review process, a final report (with executive summary) should be compiled and shared to enhance organizational learning and success.

STRATEGIC PLANNING SUCCESS FACTORS

Commitment, Support, and Communication from Leadership, Understanding of Organizational Culture

Of course, as with many other things, there is no single "best" way for a leader to communicate, support, and commit to strategic planning. An organization's leader must engage with the planning team—they are a champion for the process but not the author of the plan. They have a critical role in signaling the importance of the planning process and can motivate people to get involved, as well as ensuring the appropriate resources are allocated to the planning process (Sanaghan, 2009; Stephens, 2017). Leaders must get involved in planning and work to understand their employees and the political context in which they operate (Billups, 2015). Nauffal and Nasser (2016) found that both a top-down or bottom-up approach can work, as long as stakeholders are truly involved and communicated with, and evidence is used to make decisions. That said, avoidance of a top-down approach can be very important depending on why a strategic plan is being created—particularly if the institution is in major distress (Gorman, 2016).

Communication regarding the plan is of critical importance; note Rowley and Sherman (2001) say, "many of the failures attributed to strategic planning have little to do with the strategic planning process and much more to do with misconceptions and false expectations about strategic planning" (p. 6). During the *Building the Foundation* phase, the organization's leader must provide a public "charge" to the committee, which should include:

- Size and composition of committee—identify permanent members and representation areas; membership terms; leadership role should be specified (as member, leader, or consultant) (Hinton, 2012)
- Expectations for each member (attendance, contributions, communication, etc.)
- Scope of responsibilities (specify level of authority, be clear)
- Planning timeline
- Identification of the project coordinator (or consultant, if using) and description of their qualifications

Hinton (2012) emphasizes the importance of having a well-prepared coordinator: "Lack of experience and training can lead to plans that are only partially developed, not implementable, or skewed by the domination of one part of the institution" (p. 39).

Another leadership success factor in strategic planning is behavioral commitment. Leaders must signal commitment through emulating behavior consistent with the plan (Broadnick & Norris, 2016). Campus leaders would be served best by not overthinking things—ditch the "visionary president" or transformational leader and instead seek out a collaborative, inclusive process that uses "good information, diverse perspectives, and shared values" (Sanaghan, 2009, p. 1). They must also ensure members of the organization have sufficient knowledge and time to engage in the planning process so that it is truly an open process.

To signal commitment to an open, integrated process, it may be useful to put forward a set of principles to which all planning will align. Both Carroll Community College and the University of Central Florida saw fit to create a set of standards for strategic planning to help set expectations and manage culture (Clagett, 2004; Hope, 2018). Summarized, these principles were:

1. Planning should be guided by vision, informed by data, and collaborative.
2. Everyone shares in the responsibility of strategic planning success and should participate in planning.

3. Budgeting serves to facilitate the achievement of strategic plan objectives.
4. All other plans should align with and focus on achievement of the strategic plan.
5. Strategic plan implementation and effectiveness is assessed and results are used for improvement.
6. Transparency, accountability, and recognition of achievements is critical.

Inclusiveness and Appropriateness of Planning Team

The planning team (or planning groups) should be composed of individuals with "excellent reputations" and a strong work ethic—they will be doing a lot of work and making important decisions (Sanaghan, 2009, p. 6). It should contain representatives from major stakeholder groups. A lack of participation or inclusivity can ruin buy-in, and "How the planning team is constituted and who participates is no less important than the integration of budgetary concerns and institutional priorities" (Auer, 2016, p. 6). Estimates on the "best" number of individuals to include vary; what is *most* appropriate for your organization depends on the level at which the plan is being developed (institution versus department) and the culture. Tromp and Ruben (2010) emphasize, "inclusive planning efforts are generally more successful than those undertaken by a small, exclusive group, and generally have longer-lasting effects on plan implementation and the culture itself" (p. 17).

Hinton (2012) recommends the creation of a standing planning committee, with ongoing strategic planning responsibilities rather than a task force approach. A standing planning committee approach allows for deeper training, development, and continued engagement. If this approach is taken, rotation of members is a good idea (it spreads knowledge and communication), but ensuring there is some continuity with trained members is important. Further, this committee can be the body that evaluates and monitors plan progress (Clagett, 2004; Hinton, 2012). At the institution level, special attention must be paid to ensuring faculty are well represented (Dickeson, 2015). Whitney (2010) recommends inclusion of groups from within and outside the unit when creating divisional or departmental strategic plans. Specifically, Whitney calls on student affairs to include faculty in their planning processes, as it can increase knowledge of organizational culture, stimulate collaboration, and encourage mutual understanding across divisions.

Quality of Communication

The breadth and quality of communication to engage with stakeholders, get feedback, and relay decisions is critical (Broadnick & Norris, 2016). Communication must be clear and consistent, and include internal and external stakeholders (including the board of trustees) (Sanaghan, 2009). Good communication throughout the process increases the likelihood of buy-in and participation (Gorman, 2016; Nauffal & Nasser, 2016). Communication is critical for change management; Rowley and Sherman (2001) advocate for "openness of the process, honesty, building trust, listening, choosing the proper forms of discussion, and agreeing that it may be OK to disagree" (p. 161).

There are many ways to communicate with stakeholders, and utilizing multiple methods can assist in the spread of information (Stephens, 2017). The language used in communication is important as well—pleasing visual layouts and appropriate wording for a variety of audiences is key. Planning terminology must be discussed, defined, and agreed upon; do not take for granted that everyone shares the same definitions for these important elements. Making assumptions that everyone is on the same page can lead to wasted time due to miscommunication or misunderstanding (Sanaghan, 2009).

Something that is often forgotten by leaders is that communication is a two-way street. Leaders must understand how members feel about change just as much as the members need clear, timely, and readable information (regardless of role). Communication is especially important during times of change (process or cultural); and the culture of the organization should influence the selection of the medium and approach to communication (Tromp & Ruben, 2010). Sanaghan (2009) recommends an emphasis on face-to-face interactions and focusing on transparency throughout the process (including financial data). To ensure communication occurs in this manner, it is best to assign one person to oversee communication and serve as "the face" of the planning process. The work of "integrating data collection, document management, scheduling, and disseminating" takes a lot of time (Hinton, 2012, p. 21).

Quality of Internal and Environmental Analysis

The difference between "planning" and "strategic planning" is a big one—to truly engage in strategic planning, an organization must do proper research to understand itself as well as the environment it operates within. This should be treated as an opportunity for organizational learning and discovery (Sanaghan, 2009). Strategic plans must be grounded in reality and achievable, which requires careful study of the environment and the organization's own capacity (Rowley & Sherman, 2001). When engaged in environmental scanning, Alfred recommends leaders work to understand:

- trends, forces, and conditions in the external environment that impact the institution
- competitors, both known and unknown, seeking market share
- stakeholders served by the institution, both current and potential
- value created by the institution for its stakeholders
- differentiation in value created for stakeholders that distinguishes the institution from its competitors
- advantage over competitors that is created through differentiation
- sustainability, or the longevity of advantage

(2006, p. 61)

Data collection in support of environmental scanning can be conducted in a variety of ways. For internal capacity analysis, a self-study is often helpful. While a self-study is its own topic, such studies usually contain an appraisal of the current state (mission, vision, and values; demographics of students, faculty, and staff), a description of the organization, and an indication of budgetary resources and history, as well as descriptions of administrative and/or academic units within the organization. The self-study may also contain policy and procedure documents, indicators of faculty productivity and scholarly achievements, data pertaining to student satisfaction and learning, and numerous other elements, depending on the unit submitting the self-study. Planning subsequent to an accreditation visit can be helpful, as much of the background research work was likely completed as part of an accreditation self-study (Paris, 2004).

Further study can be completed by engaging in interviews with important stakeholders. It may be useful to meet with community leaders, local and regional professional association presidents, and experts in specific areas aligned with institution-level priorities, as well as other stakeholders you would like to include in the planning process but cannot due to limits on the number of participants, time, or availability. Reports and publications from organizations focused on the study of higher education can inform planning processes; SCUP (via the Trends Report) and the Association of American Colleges and Universities are just two examples of wide-interest organizations focused on higher education in general. There are numerous organizations to look at, depending on the area of interest. The *Chronicle of Higher Education* and Inside Higher Ed are continually publishing timely and relevant pieces to signal the direction the higher education market is headed, as well as areas of concern for the future. A good environmental scanning process incorporates all of these things.

It is important to note that the information will never be perfect—nearly all of the items listed by Alfred require estimation, approximation, and opinions. And that is okay, notes Hinton (2012):

> A good environmental scan does not attempt to develop detailed data or market analysis, and does not use projections based on current trends, unless those trends are seen to be evolving into a larger issue. The scan is used to inform the organization's vision and identify the broad strategic objectives that will become a guideline for an action plan.
>
> (p. 33)

To scan is to look internally and externally, and find an alignment. If one does not exist, then the strategic plan can bring the two more closely together.

Shortcuts in this phase will jeopardize the quality of the plan's selected priorities or themes, as well as the contributing strategies or outcomes. Entire books have been written on activities used for strategic planning, and we will not duplicate them here (see, for example, Gray, Brown, & Macanufo, 2010). A few of the most popular and useful tools are:

- PEST/STEEP analysis – an environmental scanning activity that can lead to the identification of important present and looming issues. This is sometimes referred to as PEST analysis (political, economic, social, and technological). Another version is STEEP analysis, which focuses on social, technological, environmental, economic, and political forces that may disrupt or change an institution's future state (Gorman, 2016; SCUP, 2018). Any number of forces can be considered (Martinez & Wolverton, 2009). In any version, participants brainstorm forces or phenomena that will affect the environment. There is often overlap among the categories—and that is not a problem. It can be followed by other tools, such as SWOT analysis.

- SWOT analysis – As mentioned above, a SWOT analysis is a careful examination of the organization's strengths, weaknesses, opportunities, and threats (Trainer, 2004). This analysis must encompass both internal and external environments. Internally, the institution examines its strengths and weaknesses, which may include academic programs, quality of faculty, physical facilities, and location. Externally, the institution must look at what opportunities and threats (economic and social trends/conditions) exist, such as local economic needs, training needs, competing institutions, and demographic changes (Alfred, 2006; Ferrell & Hartline, 2005). A common mistake administrators make when conducting a SWOT analysis is to complete one overarching analysis for the entire institution. This type of analysis does little to add to the planning process (Ferrell & Hartline, 2005).
- TOWS analysis – a SWOT analysis can be converted into a TOWS analysis ("turning opportunities and weaknesses into strengths") by simply flipping a completed SWOT analysis (Trainer, 2004). Administrators should have the ability (authority) to transform a unit's strengths into capabilities by matching those strengths with opportunities in the environment. This process converts strengths into an institution's competitive advantages. Similarly, administrators must have the ability (authority) to convert a unit's weaknesses to strengths.
- Decision maps – these allow people to see outcomes and effort together (McGee, 2015, p. 104). SCUP (2018) recommends the use of these diagrams with solutions for the issues identified by STEEP analysis to allow consideration of multiple factors and courses of action at the same time. One way to use this tool is to organize potential strategies by "amount of effort required" and "anticipated impact." To do this, a horizontal and vertical axis would be drawn, like the example in Figure 8.1.
- Fishbone/Ishikawa diagrams – cause-and-effect diagrams participants create to identify factors that influence or cause a given effect on an outcome.
- Other tools to consider: affinity diagrams, force field analysis, nominal group techniques, flowcharting of processes, use of SMART (specific, measurable, attainable, relevant, time-bound) language, resource allocation exercises (e.g., the $100 Test), dot voting, and stakeholder analysis (see Gray et al., 2010).

Quality of Feedback Opportunities

A lack of opportunity to participate in providing feedback can wreck buy-in, and it is important to welcome feedback, good or bad (Auer, 2016; Broadnick & Norris, 2016). Both the amount and the representativeness of feedback matter. Strategic plans can fail because of a disconnect between the plan and internal stakeholders. "Often, people feel as if the plan is something done *to* or *for* them but not *with* them" (Sanaghan, 2009, p. 1). Sanaghan (2009) has many recommendations for enhancing the quality of feedback, including engaging with stakeholders face to face, soliciting diverse perspectives and ideas, and building in extra time to reflect, ruminate, and make sense of important issues. Enabling an open discussion and feedback process (as well as picking the right planning team) is an important way to get people involved and give them a voice—but their feedback must actually be used. Conflict is not always a bad thing—the strategic planning process should "Allow for and even

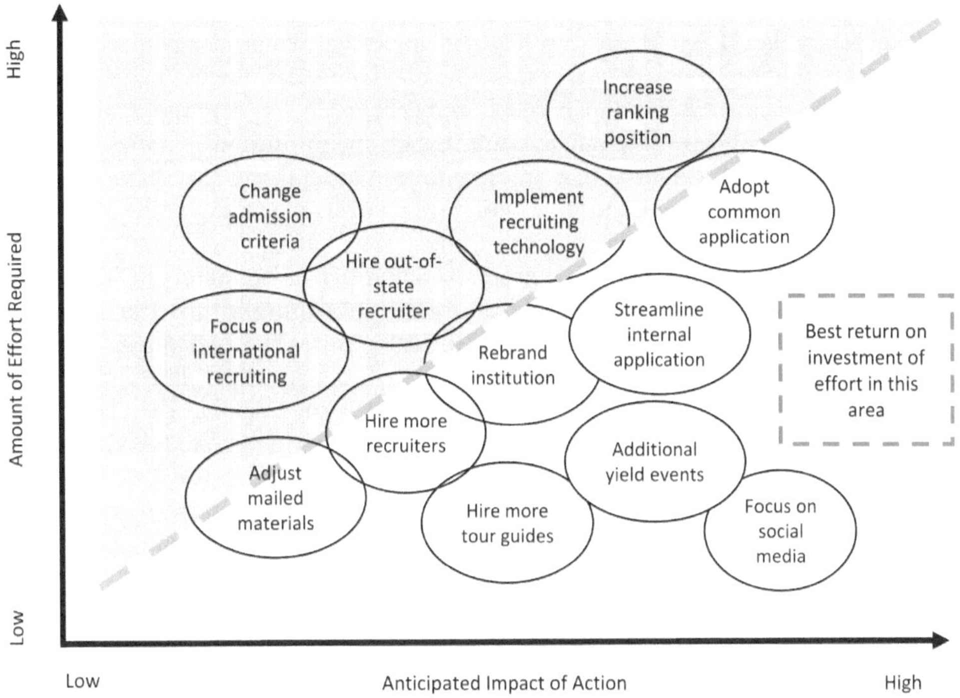

Figure 8.1 Decision Map

encourage productive conflict . . . a polite process may not be worth your time and effort" (Billups, 2015, p. 42).

Quality of Selected Themes/Priorities

A strategic plan is built as a way to support the accomplishment of an overarching strategy (or strategies) via priorities, goals, and objectives. Alfred (2006) states that

> implementation without an articulated strategy to it is essentially meaningless. Strategy fails when thinking is disassociated from doing. Successful strategy depends as much on the tactics used to enact it as it does on the process used to formulate it.
>
> (p. 64)

For example, administrators failing to heed this warning may run the risk of setting unrealistic admissions goals or sending conflicting messages regarding academic standards as they continue to admit underprepared students without a plan to support them.

Whatever the term used, a strategic plan should have a limited number of top-hierarchy priorities. Clagett (2004) suggests ten or fewer, while Goldstein (2012) recommends five or six. Every theme or priority should have a champion (Paris, 2004). Rather than starting off with a number, it is recommended that the planning teams or groups talk through what they believe is most important, and then cluster like-items together. If the themes are very broad, a smaller number is appropriate. If the themes are more focused or spread across disparate areas, then it makes sense to have more. A plan needs to be manageable and achievable—so it must be both realistic and focused while also reaching forward toward the institution's vision.

What is most important is that an organization accepts the fact that everything cannot be a priority at the same time. Pointing to ever-expanding college and university missions, McGee (2015) cautions institutions to focus on what they do well, ensure they are sufficiently different from competitors, and remember "[t]he value of the expected outcome must exceed the cost of obtaining it" (p. 106). Citing a study of fifty senior academic officers, Auer (2016) notes the two things they had the hardest time doing: integrating the budget with the strategic plan, and limiting the number of priorities in the plan. Dickeson (2015) suggests that the plan should bring the mission into everyday operations, and that the process should rely on data to ensure the creation of a realistic plan that addresses "the real issues" (p. 2). He also warns institutions to stay in their lane and avoid using a strategic plan to expand into areas they cannot deliver effectively . . . and that may mean discontinuing programs or initiatives.

Quality of Implementation Strategy

The creation of an implementation plan is an opportunity to bring together various on-campus units to determine how they will carry out their work. Implementation planning should identify the units or individuals responsible for actions and specify timelines and deadlines. The planning team (or facilitators) and organizational leadership may realize that they lack the specific expertise to determine the exact strategies (or tactics, if the plan is being completed at a college, division, or departmental level). It is critical in these moments to communicate and consult with the units best equipped to inform the strategy or tactic to determine how an action plan should be crafted. This will also enhance feelings of participation and buy-in. Specific individuals should be tasked with action plans or tactics (in charge, if not solely responsible) to promote accountability when possible (Hinton, 2012; Sanaghan, 2009). This aids in communication and management of implementation.

An implementation plan is more than just identifying overarching phases and in-phase timelines, and assigning individuals or groups to tactics. Implementation planning is where necessary change management practices (discussed in Chapter 7) are incorporated, and strategies to move the organizational culture are embedded. Project management techniques can be helpful during the implementation phase, but will not make up for a flawed process (Chase, Aquilano, & Jacobs, 2001; Paraska, 2013). Further, in an integrated planning approach, creating a strategic plan at the institutional level is not the end of the story. For a planning process to be integrated, the development of an institution-level plan is just the beginning. After the institution-level plan is set, all plans within the organization need to work together, which will further aid in overall implementation (Bresciani, 2010; Hinton, 2012). Factors that may impede implementation are too many to name; Alfred (2006) and others provide a selection to consider, summarized in Figure 8.2.

Planning Problems (address in advance)	Missing Elements (incorporate in planning)
History of failed strategic plan implementation(s) Use of a flawed, non-inclusive planning process Disagreement with priorities, strategies Unrealistic or flawed priorities or strategies selected Leadership style mismatch (too strict, too loose) Unclear criteria for success Failure to actively measure, monitor, share results	Lack of communication, solicitation of feedback during process Lack of proactive change management Lack of clarity in responsibilities Lack of senior leadership support Lack of resources required to execute plan Lack of alignment with lower unit plans Lack of culture shift/congruence

Figure 8.2 Barriers to Implementation

Degree to Which Plan Is Integrated

As discussed in Chapter 6, a budget is the truest reflection of what an institution truly values. Hinton (2012) suggests a core purpose of the strategic plan is to guide on how resources should be allocated. Strategic plans that are linked to the budget are more likely to be realized (Conneely, 2010; Goldstein, 2012). Therefore, it is critical to leverage the budget to support the strategic plan—both as a signal of its importance and to ensure sufficient resources (financial and personnel) are available to achieve its aims (Atkins, 2010; Hinton, 2012). The relationship between the strategic plan and the budget is two-way: a strategic plan should both inform the budget, but also be informed *by* the budget to ensure it is achievable (Dickeson, 2015; Tromp & Ruben, 2010). Dickeson (2015) and Conneely (2010) also stress the importance of aligning fiscal resources with the strategic plan's goals, and Conneely notes a difference between ongoing and one-time expenses when doing so.

A deeper connection between budget and planning can happen in a variety of ways. Requiring that budget request narratives incorporate their connection to the strategic plan is a fairly straightforward way to accomplish this. Taking it a step further, Goldstein (2012) and Clagett (2004) advocate for the formation of a representative committee that maintains both the budget and the institution's strategic plan. If planning, budgeting, and assessment of plan progress do not operate together, the institution is less likely to achieve its goals (Goldstein, 2012, pp. 87–88). Conneely (2010) and Paris (2004) also note that if the financial environment changes drastically, the strategic plan must be instrumental in determining how funds will be reallocated to support overarching goals in a time of budget cuts. The connection between budget and the strategic plan needs to be more than clerical in nature—Auer (2016) cautions, "Detailed budgets alone do not make a plan strategic or integrated" (p. 4).

As previously mentioned, the institution-level strategic plan must also have alignment with (and drive alignment of) college, division, and departmental plans. Because universities are so complex, different units (silos) develop their own plans to keep things manageable and applied in context. Hinton (2012) notes, "keeping track of all the plans can rapidly become an exercise in herding cats" (Hinton, 2012, p. 34). The degree to which this occurs indicates the level of integration, vertically and horizontally (Broadnick & Norris, 2016). Good strategic plans also align with other requirements or mandates (Paraska, 2013).

Assessment/Measurement and Evaluation, Results Sharing

Strategic plans should be connected to measures and assessed to determine implementation progress. Data from assessment of the plan's progress can be used as evidence of institutional effectiveness for accreditation processes (Paraska, 2013; Paris, 2004). Hinton (2012) suggests a two-pronged approach of annual review and a full-cycle review (at the plan's conclusion). Clagett (2004) described an annual review model in which tasks were rated according to progress—including statuses such as *in-progress*, *behind schedule*, *complete*, and *deleted* or *retired* (due to changing priorities or incorporation into other priorities). The strength of an annual review is its focus on the previous year's achievements to inform any necessary adjustments to the actions for the upcoming year. The annual review can also include a mid-year review to check on in-progress actions where problems can be identified and addressed (Hinton, 2012; Paris, 2004). Langham and Fifolt (2014) note, "To be truly effective, strategic planning must incorporate methods for measuring the effectiveness of the strategies selected" (not just the accomplishment of the goals) (p. 15). Further, if data are not collected to measure the effectiveness of implementation, leadership will not be able to conclusively determine if plan goals or objectives were achieved.

Management of Culture(s) and Organizational Characteristics

Peter Drucker, a well-known expert in the field of management, is credited with saying "Culture eats strategy for breakfast," to indicate its intractability and potential for disrupting even the best-laid plans. Culture includes organizational norms, risk tolerance, and formality of hierarchies, among other things. A strategic planning team *must* understand and plan for campus culture in the process—from plan formation through implementation and measurement (Billups, 2015, p. 41). The culture of colleges and universities is complex, in part because of the variety of groups within; faculty, administrators, staff, students, and the governing board all have distinct perspectives. Proposed changes will all affect groups differently, which makes them more difficult. This is particularly true with changes that could result in program changes and/or eliminations, and job losses (Rowley & Sherman, 2001; Tromp & Ruben, 2010). Adding to the complexity, higher education, by its very nature and history, is tough to change (McGee, 2015; Rowley & Sherman, 2001). After all, if educational institutions were to make rapid changes every time politicians or business leaders demanded, it would not take long for the institutions to lose their focus and subsequently their identity. Being "slow to change" does not always mean "opposed to change."

A significant hurdle in a strategic planning process is choosing the right model for your organization, bearing in mind its history, shared governance model, mission, tolerance for risk, and culture. Planning and plan integration can be helped or hindered by elements such as institutional size, the degree of decentralization, control (public or private), status (for-profit vs not-for-profit), mission, and financial position (Broadnick & Norris, 2016; Hinton 2012). Institutions that are large are often more complex, and decentralization adds to organizational complexity. Public institutions may have different concerns than private institutions—as may not-for-profit and for-profit colleges. Institutions with more specific or specialist missions have an easier time integrating planning, while wealthy institutions are less motivated to do the hard work of integrating plans.

Failure to understand the culture of an institution (how people work, behaviors, norms, assumptions) can also sink a plan; cultures vary in strength and are often more obvious to newcomers who are not immersed in their pull (Hinton, 2012; Rowley & Sherman, 2001). An institution's history and development, its current mission, and its culture have major impacts on the kinds of things an institution will expect from the planning process (level of inclusiveness, representation of stakeholders, openness to administrative structure changes, priorities) (Hinton, 2012). Because every organization is different, there is no single way to make an implementation work properly (Sanaghan, 2009, p. 93). Decision-making processes should match the culture, where possible—top-down, bottom-up, and consensus decision-making models all have pros and cons (Nauffal & Nasser, 2016).

Hinton (2012) advises,

> Organizations that do not achieve the commitment and organizational will to use the planning process as a tool will not be able to successfully complete a plan. This need for collective commitment is the difference between a planning process that works and one that does not.
>
> (p. 24)

Senior leaders *must* be committed, and that must stream downward across the organization. The actual work of changing a culture must come from within, often led at the mid-organization level or by respected faculty and staff (Rowley & Sherman, 2001). Describing a planning process at an institution under severe financial duress, Gorman (2016) discussed the utility of creating multidisciplinary committees to get people involved to carry out the work, and monitoring the plan's progress. Engaging in a participatory approach appears to be the strongest strategy for bringing the culture in line with the vision. This must be matched by "operationalizing" the plan into everyday business and decision-making (Hinton, 2012, p. 26).

CONCLUDING COMMENTS

The process of strategic planning has changed over time, and it has become even more valuable in our current environment. In a review of eighteen strategic plans, Stephens (2017) noted eight themes that signal how strategic planning has changed: shorter plan lengths (a median of six years), broad plan positioning (allowing for flexibility), a focus on communication, jargon-free language, reliance on data to support selected priorities and plan metrics, differentiation from competitors, intentional alignment across the organization, and the power of leadership in driving the process. Planning has come a long way from the days where a small group of leaders created a plan for the future and released it to the organization without input or discussion. In an increasingly complex higher education environment, an integrated, open approach has many benefits.

While the obvious benefit to developing a strategic plan is the creation of the plan itself, there are other consequences. Ellis (2010) describes positive influences a strategic planning process can have on a Student Affairs unit:

1. It makes the division or functional area examine current trends and issues, its current capabilities, and the needs of its stakeholders
2. It encourages Student Affairs to specifically address how it supports institutional goals
3. It can serve as a communication tool to explain the role and value of Student Affairs to others in the organization
4. It stimulates important conversations and can uncover issues and concerns
5. It can bring members of an organization together

Of course, these benefits are not exclusive to Student Affairs—they can be experienced by any institution, division, department, or unit that partakes in the process.

The approaches and considerations described in this chapter can be adapted to all levels of an organization. If engaging in integrated planning, a unit (no matter what the level) must look around to see what else is happening in the organization so that it may be incorporated into its planning. Inclusivity, communication, and use of feedback are of paramount importance. As should be obvious at this point, the construction of the plan is only one component—there are myriad decisions to make before a word of the plan is written. Further, a great plan can fail before it starts, due to a lack of clarity in the implementation and assessment phases of its life. While the process may seem daunting, the benefits outweigh the obstacles. As a management tool, it sets the stage for achievement of a specific vision. The strategic planning encourages organizations to study themselves as well as the environment in which they operate to make the best decisions they can with their limited resources.

In closing, strategic process planning is of critical importance in mission-driven organizations. It can and should help guide important decisions about the scope and focus of services, and how resources are used, and bring the organization closer to its vision. Dooris et al. (2004) may have said it best: "When we strip away the models, schema, and paradigms; when we discard the PowerPoint presentations; and when we look beyond the grids, scorecards, and matrices, we confront our ability to think with intention" (p. 5). At its core, strategic planning is about choosing to be intentional in our work to do better than before and be distinctive in a crowded higher education market. As colleges and universities continue to struggle with increasing costs and declining college-age student populations, it will be ever more critical that they act in line with who they are and what they are organized to do.

REFLECTIVE QUESTIONS

1. What is the relationship between mission, vision, values, and strategic plan priorities?
2. What are the most critical interpersonal aspects of strategic planning?
3. How is an environmental scan conducted?
4. Where do strategic plans tend to fail, and why?
5. What are some key practices for fostering implementation success?
6. What are the benefits of the strategic plan planning process and strategic plan implementation?
7. Review your institutional strategic plan. How is your department/unit represented?

CHAPTER 9

Managing Human Resources

Recruitment, Selection, and Retention of Competent Staff

Human resource (HR) management in colleges and universities encompasses more than just staffing the institution with high-quality employees. Functions such as compensation and benefits, training and development, affirmative action, and employee resource programs are typically housed in the HR office. These services are necessary for the successful operation of any complex organization. However, unlike much of the for-profit world, HR within higher education typically does not play an active role in the recruitment and retention of professional staff and faculty. Its role, while still important, is usually one of support and guidance rather than one of decision-making.

Within most institutions of higher education, hiring decisions are made by administrative *hiring managers* within the individual units. The hiring manager is most often the supervisor or the director of the unit. The talent acquisition department within the HR division is responsible for ensuring that those hiring decisions are the best for the units and ultimately for the institution. This office assists search committees, department chairs, directors, or other hiring managers in the hiring process by ensuring compliance with institutional policies and local, state, and federal laws. Even though HR may not make the decision as to who gets interviewed or hired, it plays an important role in the process. The HR office is far more active in the recruitment and selection of support staff, and at some institutions this extends to some entry-level professional staff.

HR becomes more actively involved once the hiring decision is made, in handling the paperwork for the new hires and providing these new employees with information about benefits plans and additional support services available, such as employee assistance programs and wellness activities. HR is also an important resource when employees are separating from the institution, whether voluntarily (retiring, accepted a new position elsewhere, etc.) or involuntarily (terminated or laid off).

Recruiting and retaining employees are perhaps the most important functions of a manager or administrator in any organization. "The ultimate success of any college or university depends on the quality of the people it hires" (Hochel & Wilson, 2007, p. 1). McCaffery (2004) points out that

> [i]n management parlance, the quality of a company's people is the only significant strategic variable for any enterprise. It is their contribution that most affects 'bottom line' performance. Additionally, Hoffman (2000) suggests there is a clear link between employee turnover and student dissatisfaction making the recruitment and training of front-line personnel imperative (p. 299). The surprise is that it has taken the university sector so long, not just to acknowledge it but rather to recognize and act on it.
>
> (p. 134)

The processes described in the pages that follow coincide with the staffing model described by Janosik et al. (2003). This model includes six interlinked and overlapping functions: (a) recruitment and selection, (b) orientation, (c) supervision, (d) staff development, (e) performance appraisal, and (f) separating (p. 8).

THE RECRUITING PROCESS

There is no more important decision that a supervisor makes than a personnel decision. "In spite of the importance of the hiring process, few of us in academia are trained in employment selection" (Hochel & Wilson, 2007, p. 3). Within higher education institutions, hiring a new employee is the beginning of a significant investment of both time and financial resources. The higher education work environment tends to be quite accommodating and is often far more flexible than private sector business enterprises. This collegial environment lends itself well to a high number of long-term employees within our institutions. A young tenure-track faculty member may stay at an institution for upwards of 35 years if successful in the tenure process. Other administrators may work their way through the bureaucratic structure holding a variety of positions throughout an equally lengthy career at a single institution. For each of these individuals, the host institution will invest well over $2 million in salary and benefits in addition to the other resources it commits during their tenure.

Whether looking for an entry-level or seasoned professional, you need to develop a recruitment plan (see Figure 9.1).

This plan will provide you with a framework from within which you can hire the individuals necessary to fill your organizational needs. Hiring staff is not necessarily about hiring the most qualified candidate, but rather is about hiring the candidate who is the "best fit" for the organization at this point in time. The closer the individual's values and goals align with those of the unit/institution, the better the fit. Recruitment as defined by Nickels, McHugh, and McHugh (2008) "is the set of activities used to obtain a sufficient number of the right people at the right time: its purpose is to select those who best meet the needs of the organization" (p. 292). Below, several of the activities in the hiring process have been outlined. Your institution's process may vary slightly or combine some of the steps listed, and you may have to change the order or

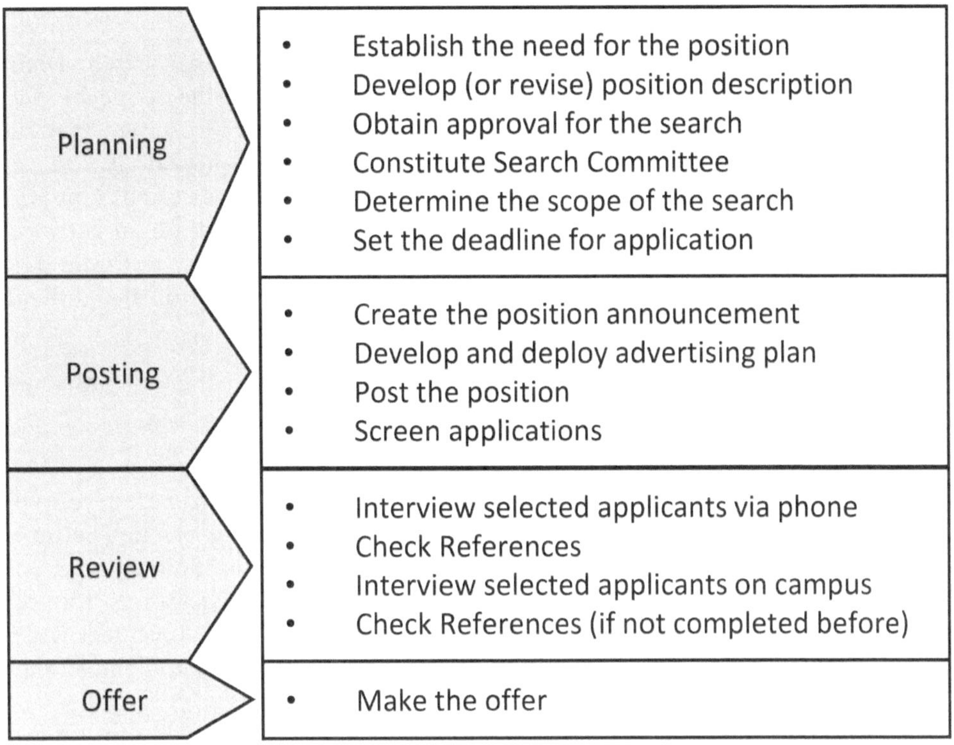

Figure 9.1 Hiring Steps

double back at times. This is simply one process that institutions can use as a guide for their respective search processes. It is important to understand that there is no single best way to recruit staff and that each institution needs to structure a system that best fits its circumstances. The outline below is a hybrid of the plans from various institutions of higher education throughout the United States.

Establish the Need for the Position

Whether a new position or hiring to fill a vacancy, it is incumbent upon the supervisor/hiring manager to justify the need for this position. That said, the departure of a staff member should not automatically generate a rehiring for the position. Organizations that run effectively and efficiently ensure, to the best of their ability, that each position for which they are recruiting is actually needed. This may seem to be obvious, but there are more than a few instances in institutions where individuals have been hired in an effort to increase one's fiefdom rather than because of an institutional need. It takes a confident and sometimes courageous administrator to admit the vacant position is no longer needed within the organization when duties can be reshuffled.

Determine the Scope of the Search

Will this be an internal, local, regional, national, or international search? Many institutions have specific criteria that are used to determine the scope of each search. Typically, for administrative and faculty positions it is assumed that the search will be national or international unless otherwise requested. If you can demonstrate that there is a sufficiently talented/qualified and diverse applicant pool in the area, you may be able to conduct a local or regional search for an entry- or mid-level administrative position or for a non-tenure-track faculty position. This decision may be made for monetary reasons as well, especially during difficult financial times.

Establish the Timeline for the Search Process

Once the position has been approved and you have been cleared to begin, you will need to establish the timeline in which you hope to complete the search. The timelines for searches will differ based on position type as well as institutional type, and they can also be impacted by the scope of the search. Working backwards from the start date is the best approach to developing your timeline. HR involvement (especially at state institutions) can significantly increase the time it takes to complete the hiring process, so check with them before you confirm any dates.

Before you contact potential search committee members, you will want to have an idea as to the approximate timeframe of the search and when (at least tentative dates) critical events such as the review of application materials, telephone interviews, or on-campus visits will take place. Most of the committee members will be busy people, and the more notice you can give them to block dates on their calendars, the better off everyone will be. Whether you have six months or three weeks before the new person starts makes a big difference for potential committee members. We encourage you not to rush the search process; rather, you will need to be thoughtful and deliberate in your planning to ensure the best possible outcome. Figure 9.2 shows an example of a typical administrative or faculty search timeline. The particulars for your searches may differ, but this figure should give you an understanding of the time involved in the search process.

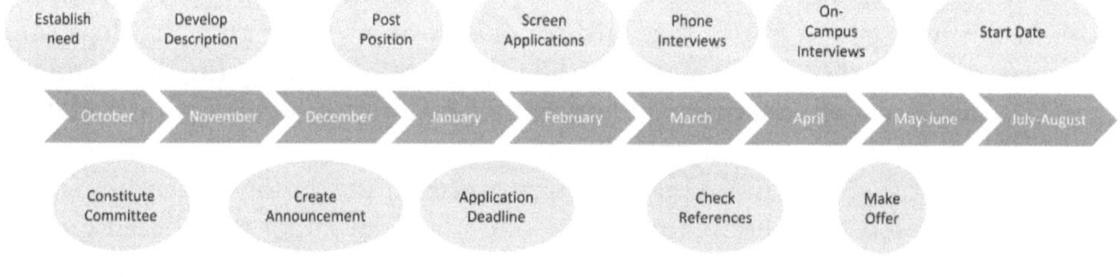

Figure 9.2 Search Timeline

Set the Deadline for Applications

As part of the timeline, you will need to determine when you will begin to review the applicant files. There are benefits to keeping your timeline open rather than having a hard deadline. You will still need to specify a date on which the review of applications will begin, but leave the ending date as "the position will be open until filled." Wording such as this permits individuals to send their materials in after the review process begins and allows you to continue recruiting qualified applicants without having to re-advertise the position. If you set a firm deadline you may eliminate candidates who may have a letter or transcript that was delayed or someone who may not have thought about making a move until later in the semester. Building flexibility into your search can help you and the committee when narrowing the pool of applicants.

Develop the Position Description

Typically, the "job description specifies the objectives of the job, the type of work to be done, the responsibilities and duties, the working conditions, and the relationship of the job to other functions" within the institution (Nickels et al., 2008, p. 291). This document is primarily used for internal purposes and is *not* the same as the position announcement (described later). For replacement positions, there should be an existing position description that may serve as a good starting point for your recruitment efforts. The description may be current, or it may be several years old and out of date. Regardless of its currency, it is important to review this document to ensure that it represents the position for which you are recruiting. Ensure that the description reflects what is currently needed, and reflects the position's essential tasks within the institution as it exists now. If this is a new position and a position description must be created, you should contact other institutions with similar positions to see if they would be willing to share a position description to help you get started.

When developing any position description, it is always a good idea to think about the knowledge, skills, abilities, and competencies needed to be successful in the position. These competencies should be measurable because eventually you will need to evaluate the new hire and it is always helpful to have the ability to measure one's performance based on the expectations set forth in the position. As you start writing the statements, avoid the use of specific language that is too restrictive unless absolutely necessary (e.g., "must have two years of experience with Banner"). You will eliminate anyone with experience using another enterprise resource planning (ERP) system. The question you have to ask is whether you really need the specific knowledge (Banner) or the competency (ERP) in this initial hiring process, or can the new hire be trained in this area? The full position description should be posted on the institution's web site (usually found in the HR section) and also on the departmental site. This link should be provided to all applicants and potential applicants, so each candidate has a full understanding of the position and the institution.

Lastly, for the full position description, it is in your best interest to have one all-encompassing phrase at the end of the responsibilities and duties section: "other duties as assigned." This simple phrase provides the hiring manager with a great deal of flexibility as time moves forward and the needs of this position begin to change. This helps avoid conflict with individuals who like to mention that what is being asked of them is not in the job description.

Constitute a Search Committee

The search committee structure can be critical in some searches and pretty much irrelevant in others. The higher in the organization, the more political the search process will be, and therefore the more important and political the appointment of the committee members. You want to make sure that the individuals on the committee have a vested interest in the hiring decision, and that they can contribute to the conversation regarding the qualifications, skills, and abilities of the candidates. You must understand who your internal and external stakeholders are and which ones are most important to have on which searches at which levels.

The size of the committee will vary depending on your institutional practices. Typically, the higher you go on the organizational chart, the more people involved on the search committee. Entry-level faculty and staff committees can be as small as three to five while dean and presidential committees can include over twenty from across the enterprise. Search committees are usually composed of individuals from the department or program with the vacancy and most often will have at least one person from a different department within the institution.

For entry- and mid-level positions, it is typically not necessary to involve personnel from outside the institution, and in most institutions you can stay within your operational area. For example, in Residential Life, when recruiting for a hall director, you probably do not need to be concerned about involving faculty or members of the development office on your search committee. Your committee could easily consist of current hall directors, perhaps an area coordinator or assistant director, and of course students (at least one). However, when recruiting for a director-level position, you should consider other departments within the Student Affairs area to be represented as well as a faculty member or two. There may also be a need to involve others from outside the institution especially for director-level positions in departments such as Career Services, Alumni Relations, or Admissions, among others.

When recruiting for faculty, there will be different needs depending upon the department. For example, for an Educational Administration program where the institution prepares graduates to be principals or superintendents, you may want to involve someone from one of the local school districts, or for a Management or Accounting position, you may want to involve a member or two from the college's advisory board or a local business. When searching for academic administrators such as a college dean, it may be very important to request development and business office representation as well as other external stakeholders (depending on the college and its involvement), and of course members of the college faculty and student body.

There are two schools of thought on the selection of a search chair. First, there are individuals who believe the hiring manager should chair the committee, enabling her participation in all committee discussions about the applicants, giving her more information relevant to the hiring decision. Second, others believe that it is best not to have the hiring manager on the committee since she will be making the final decision. If the hiring manager appoints the appropriate members to the committee and she has confidence and trust in the membership, there is no need to be so intimately involved. If that is the case, it is best to select a chair who is at or above the level of the position for which you are recruiting (i.e., a director chairs a director-level search, a dean chairs a dean's search, etc.). It is *not* appropriate to have a future subordinate chair the search committee.

Create the Position Announcement

The position announcement is *not the same* as the position description. This announcement will provide information about the job specifications which differs from the description in that "job descriptions are statements about the job, whereas job specifications are about the person who does the job" (Nickels et al., 2008, p. 291). Additionally, the announcement is much shorter than the actual position description, and often includes information about the institution. There are a few standard sections of announcements: position title, institution and departmental names, required qualifications, preferred qualifications, a brief listing of duties or responsibilities, materials needed to apply, application deadline or date on which application reviews will begin, method for sending in the application materials, and a web address where applicants can view the full position description and learn more about the department and institution. Whether you include the salary or salary range is usually an institutional decision (check with your HR office). Additionally, if your institution is an Affirmative Action and Equal Employment Opportunity employer a statement indicating such should appear in this document.

When recruiting for administrative positions, the more complex the position the more detail is necessary in the announcement to convey such complexity to your potential applicant pool. For faculty positions, make sure you understand at what rank you are permitted to recruit (usually dictated by budget), what experience is necessary, and what courses are available to teach. Regardless of the position, for professional positions there are typically two parts for the qualifications section: required qualifications and preferred qualifications. In both parts the qualifications listed need to match the competencies listed in the position description. Also, realize that the more requirements you have, the greater likelihood you will be limiting the applicant pool.

Required Qualifications

When trying to decide what the requirements are for the position, it is necessary to consult the position description and review the duties, responsibilities, and competencies. Then ask yourself and the other committee members what it takes to be successful in a position like this. In this section, you are stating the *minimum* qualifications necessary to be considered as a viable candidate. It will be these requirements on which you will conduct the initial applicant screening, so you want to be confident that everything listed is absolutely necessary. Some of the typical requirements for administrative positions include but are not limited to:

- Academic degree: content area (related majors too?) and level (bachelor, master doctoral: Ph.D, Ed.D, JD, etc.)
- Years of experience – be specific. Do not give a range such as "3–5 years," because you are stating a minimum, which in this case would be three years of experience. Also, does the experience have to be in the same type of position? In the same field? In a related field?
- Years of supervisory experience (same comments as above)
- Budgeting experience
- Demonstrated communication skills: writing and public speaking
- Demonstrated interpersonal skills: understanding group dynamics
- Experience with ERP software

When hiring for an entry-level position in Student Affairs, is a master's degree in higher education or student personnel required? Does the candidate really need supervisory experience? When recruiting for a faculty position, is the terminal degree required or will you consider candidates working on their dissertation? How much teaching or research experience is necessary? Do applicants have to have published in peer-reviewed journals? Do the applicants need to have held non-faculty positions—administrative experience, business experience, etc.?

Preferred Qualifications

These are the qualifications that you would like the candidates to possess, but you believe that if required could severely limit the diversity and depth of your applicant pool. These can include new items as well as some of the same areas as above, but can be more restrictive, such as:

- Academic degree – e.g., master's required, doctorate preferred
- Five years of supervisory experience
- Demonstrated research and assessment skills
- Experience with Banner
- Experience with fund accounting or perhaps with a minimum dollar amount for budgeting

For faculty positions, you may want to specify some of the research areas you are targeting or the topics to be covered in the courses you hope this person will be able to teach. Additionally, the type of research methodology preferred, quantitative or qualitative, may be helpful, among other requirements.

Application Materials

For each position, it is important to make certain that the materials required from applicants will provide the committee members with the information necessary to successfully screen the applicant pool to a reasonable number with which to begin the interview process. Only require what you are going to use as evidence that the candidates are qualified (see Figure 9.3). Regarding references, there are two approaches:

one is to request letters of recommendation as part of the application and the other is to request names and contact information for at least three individuals. The latter makes the committee's work a little easier (less to read during the initial screening) and it is easier on the candidates. Remember, you need only check the references of the individuals you are serious about inviting to campus.

Create and Implement an Advertising Plan

Where you post your announcement is going to depend on whether this will be a local, regional, national, or international search. Also, it is important for you to understand exactly who is in your target market. These decisions need to be made before you can proceed with any advertising. At many institutions, the HR office will have a list of required publications or web sites where your ad will appear. What HR cannot provide are the specific professional publications, web sites, or conferences where your target market is most likely to view this announcement. For every position vacancy, it makes sense to complete a targeted mailing (or emailing) to relevant departments (academic and administrative) and professional organizations' listservs or member directories, and alumni in the field. In many instances, the informal networks bring in high-quality applicants, so it is important to keep lines of communication open.

Establish the Schedule for Interviews

This may be a tentative plan, but if you are planning to conduct phone interviews, it is prudent to establish several dates in advance when the committee members will

Administrative positions

- Cover letter addressing how the candidate meets the qualifications
- Detailed resume
- Names and contact information of at least three references
- Statement of managerial or leadership philosophy (supervisory positions)

Faculty positions

- Cover letter addressing how the candidate meets the qualifications
- Detailed curriculum vitae
- Statement of teaching philosophy (two pages maximum)
- Sample course syllabi
- Copies of student evaluations of teaching (all from the most recent year)
- Writing sample (publications preferred)
- Names and contact information of at least three professional references

Figure 9.3 Materials Required

be available. It also makes sense to set some preliminary dates for your on-campus interviews to ensure that you get on the schedules of individuals who need to see each candidate (deans, department chairs, directors, VPs, etc.). Many of the people on your campus travel during the peak recruiting periods, so you want to ensure those needed are indeed available or that they designate someone to fill in for the interviews. (You do not want a new staff member to start off on the wrong foot because you failed to schedule a VIP for the on-campus interview).

Screen Applications

There are at least two distinct levels of screening: the initial screen for qualifications and the advanced screen to determine which applicants progress to the next step of the search. The initial screening can be done by one or two committee members to ensure that all applications passed on to the other committee members do indeed meet the minimum qualifications stated in the advertisement. This screening should take place as the files arrive so that the full committee sees the files of qualified candidates only. As the hiring manager or committee chair it is a good idea to encourage committee members to schedule a couple of times to review the candidate files prior to the review date stated in the announcement. This will permit the committee members to review the files in manageable pieces rather than all at once. This will also permit you to schedule a committee meeting to discuss the candidates shortly after the review date posted.

Typically, there are at least two evaluation tools used for screening purposes. The first is for the initial screening, and it should contain all of the required qualifications with a simple yes (the candidate meets the minimum) and no (the candidate does not meet the minimum) option for each evaluator. This form is to be used by the two committee members designated to conduct this portion of the review. If a candidate does not meet all of the minimum qualifications, then the file is not forwarded to the entire committee. If there is disagreement between the two initial screeners on any of the requirements, then a third member or the committee chair should review the file and serve as the tie breaker.

The second form (see Figure 9.4) should contain all of the required qualifications and preferred qualifications with a numerical rating for each qualification and enough room under each so committee members can comment on the qualifications. The numerical rating is not meant to be a definitive screening tool but rather a way to structure the committee's conversation about the candidates. For example, in Figure 9.4 this scale permits each committee member to rate the doctoral degree based on their individual perception as to the quality of the department or institution from which the degree was awarded. A doctorate from Stanford University or the University of Wisconsin–Madison may be viewed as having a higher level of rigor than a doctorate from Capella University or Nova Southeastern. Likewise, candidates' years of experience could range from the required three to perhaps fifteen or more. Each committee member can evaluate that experience and assign it a score. As long as each committee member is consistent in his or her independent ratings, it will not matter if one member rates the applications tougher or looser because the scores will be averaged among all members.

Candidate Name	Reviewer Initials			
Required Qualifications				
	Poor Evidence	Fair Evidence	Good Evidence	Excellent Evidence
Doctoral Degree Comments:	1	2	3	4
Prior Experience (Min 3 Years) Comments:	1	2	3	4
Communication Skills Demonstrated Comments:	1	2	3	4
Leadership Skills Demonstrated Comments	1	2	3	4
ERP Software Experience Comments:	1	2	3	4
Preferred Qualifications				
Banner ERP Software Experience Comments:	1	2	3	4
Commitment to Diversity Demonstrated Comments:	1	2	3	4
Total Points	Recommended for an interview: ❑ Yes ❑ No			
Additional Comments				

Figure 9.4 Candidate Review Form

During your reviews, do not read too much into the individual applications. It is up to each of the applicants to convince you that they are qualified for this position. Avoid making assumptions about the candidates and simply evaluate the materials as they have been presented. Remember, if you have a sufficient applicant pool you need only one or two people who are good fits, so do not go out of your way to bring people into the pool. In fact, it is in your best interest to screen out as many people as possible, leaving only the most/best qualified applicants in the pool. Each member of the committee will have his or her preferences, and each one will have the opportunity to discuss why the candidates selected should be invited for an interview. If the committee has enough diverse views and opinions, you should end up with a well-qualified diverse selection of candidates.

Here is a simple strategy that may be of assistance to you when reviewing files, assuming that there is a sizable pool of applicants who meet the minimum qualifications. As you read the files, separate the applications into three piles, A, B, and C. The A pile is for the applications that you definitely want to take a closer look at; the B pile is for those that look like they could fit but they do not *jump out* at you or *wow* you, and the C pile is for the applications that meet the minimum but do not have many, if any, of the preferred qualifications and will be removed from consideration. Once you have completed the review of all applications and you have at least ten applications in the A pile, move all of the applications in the B pile to the C pile. If you do not have at least ten in your A pile, re-evaluate the B pile, taking the best candidates from this pile and reclassifying as many files as A as are needed to meet your goal. Not every applicant deserves an interview, and you need only one person to fill the position. If the candidates do not make it easy for you to see that they meet or exceed your requirements, move on to the next file.

Conduct Telephone Interviews

Once you have narrowed the pool down to five to ten qualified candidates, we encourage you to conduct brief (30 minutes maximum) telephone interviews. (This is an optional step in the process but highly recommended if you have more than three well-qualified applicants for the vacant position.) These interviews will give you the opportunity to find out a little more about the candidates and how well they might fit into your department and your institution. It is recommended that you develop a set of standard questions that will be asked of each candidate to ensure that the same basic information is gathered from all those interviewed. There should be an opportunity for follow-up questions if needed where the committee can probe deeper into areas of interest or concern. This step in recruitment is the first opportunity for the committee to interact with the candidates, and it also gives each applicant the opportunity to ask a few questions of the committee. The questions asked by the candidate can be very revealing as to each candidate's priorities and concerns.

Reference Checks

Before you spend the money to bring a candidate to campus, it is in your best interest to conduct a reference check. Be sure to notify candidates that references are going to be called. Similar to the telephone interviews, you should develop a few standard questions that each committee member can use when making these calls. These questions will be asked of each individual, ensuring consistency in the process.

Invite Candidates to Campus and Conduct On-Site Interviews

It is difficult to imagine hiring a new faculty member or administrator without having that person visit the campus and interact with a variety of internal and possibly external stakeholders. Typically, the two or three highest-rated candidates are invited to campus for a series of interviews. The length of the visit and who is involved in the on-campus process is dependent upon the level and scope of the position. For faculty and mid- to senior-level administrators, a one- or two-day interview process should be adequate. This allows enough time for a variety of individuals and groups to interact with the candidate, and it gives the candidate enough time to develop an informed opinion of the campus and its community. For entry-level positions, one half-day to a full day should suffice. As you develop the itinerary for each of the candidates, make sure that everyone expected to participate in the process is available to do so. It is always a good idea to schedule the VIPs (deans, VPs, etc.) prior to contacting your candidates.

Each of the candidates invited to campus should have a similar experience on their respective visits, but they do not have to be exactly the same. For example, you may require all faculty candidates to teach a class during their visit. It makes sense to schedule the candidates for the classes they are most likely going to teach, which may not be the same for all candidates based on their strengths. The nature of higher education is such that no two days on a campus are the same, so we should not overly stress trying to make every schedule look the same. The on-campus visit is an opportunity for the college community to interact with the candidates and help evaluate each based on those interactions. Input from these stakeholders should be solicited and considered during the final evaluation process. While the candidate is interviewing for a position within your department, the one chosen is also going to be a member of the greater college community.

Interview Questions

It is critical that you develop interview questions that will permit you to assess the strengths and weaknesses of each candidate. Your first step should be to request a list of illegal questions (see Figure 9.5) from your HR staff; you do not want to jeopardize a search process because you or a committee member asked an illegal question. Next, you begin to develop the content questions for this position. A simple rule is to ask only questions that are relevant to the position and its functions, and to which you really need to know the answer to make the best decision.

That may seem obvious, but we have been involved with numerous committees in which a question or two was asked and most of the committee members looked on in

- Are you married?
- Do you have children?
- Do you plan to have children?
- Do you have any disabilities?
- Do you have any ongoing medical conditions?
- Where were you born?
- What nationality are you?
- Are you a U.S. citizen?
- What church do you attend?
- What is your sexual preference?
- To what social clubs do you belong?
- How old are you?
- How much longer do you intend to work before you retire?

Figure 9.5 Illegal Questions

- Give us an example of a difficult decision you have recently made at work
- Tell us about a time when you disagreed you with your supervisor
- Tell us about a mistake you made in your current position
- Give us an example of a time when you had to confront a colleague
- Give us an example of a time when you had to talk with a disgruntled student/parent/colleague/subordinate
- Tell us about a time when you had to compromise
- Give an example of a situation in which you were unable to accomplish your goal
- Tell us about a time when you successfully motivated a colleague
- Give us an example of time when you were successful in accomplishing your stated goal

Figure 9.6 Behavioral Questions

disbelief because it had no relationship to the position or to the discipline. For example, in one instance during a search for an activities coordinator, a colleague asked a young female candidate if her husband was okay with her working full-time. On another occasion a candidate for a senior-level position was asked what was her religion.

For specific questions to ask, we recommended that behavioral interviewing be used. This is a process during which candidates are asked very specific questions requiring them to demonstrate their skills and abilities as they relate to the position. For example, when interviewing Director of Residential Life candidates, instead of asking the candidates how they would handle an angry parent, you ask them to provide you with an example of a time when they had to deal with an angry parent. You can then follow up with other questions to get at the details if they are lacking. What you want the candidates to do is to describe the *situation* and any *tasks* that were involved, tell you what *actions* were taken, and describe the *results* of those actions. This STAR concept gives the committee an understanding of how candidates reacted in a situation, rather than hearing the candidates' opinion or beliefs as to how they might react.

Make Your Recommendation to the Hiring Manager

Does the committee make a recommendation or simply provide information to the hiring manager? This is an area that can be very tricky. A hiring manager may prefer the search committee to forward the names of the *acceptable* candidates in no particular rank order. If a candidate is unacceptable to the committee, this should be documented and submitted to the hiring manager as well. Regardless of which option is chosen, it needs to be stated up front at the first committee meeting so that there are no false expectations created for any of the parties involved. This also needs to be reinforced prior to the last on-campus interview.

Making the Offer

"Employment is a mutual exchange in which employees provide contributions that meet an organization's expectations in return for inducements that meet the expectations of the job holder" (Rosse & Levin, 2003, p. 33). As you prepare to make the offer, it is apparent that you have determined this candidate meets your needs/requirements, and now it is up to the candidate to determine if the institution meets his or her expectations.

If you are the hiring manager and have the authority to make the official offer, here are a few tips to assist you in this process. This is a transaction and is not personal. When you communicate the offer to the candidate, make certain the you are very clear as to what the offer entails: salary, benefits, moving expenses, parking (if applicable), etc. If you listed a salary range in your advertisement, understand that most people believe they should receive the high end of that range. If you are intending to offer at the lower end, it is suggested that the entire range not be stated in the advertisement but simply state that the starting salary is the minimum amount, e.g., if your range is $40,000 to $60,000, simply state that the starting salary is $40,000. That gives you a little room if you have an outstanding candidate that you believe would take the position for a little more than your minimum.

Be prepared to negotiate. If your candidate of choice wants to negotiate, you must be clear as to what is or is not negotiable. If you have no room for negotiating, be very specific in the initial communication with the candidate that this is a *non-negotiable* offer. As candidates prepare for the job search, many mentors encourage them to go into the process believing that everything is negotiable unless otherwise stated. Candidates mean no disrespect to you or the institution. They realize that the salary with which they start the position is the base on which any future raises will be calculated. If the candidates are savvy, they will negotiate by asking questions, such as "I was anticipating a salary closer to $60,000—how close do you think you can come to that figure?" By asking questions instead of making statements the candidate sends the signal that this is an open negotiation and not a demand or deal-breaker. Your response needs to be honest and firm, not defensive or angry.

As you consider the salary being offered to new hires, you must be cognizant of two issues: equity and salary compression. *Equity* refers to the perceived equality of pay among individuals in similar positions or positions at the same level within your institution (e.g., academic advisors in different departments and career advisors). *Salary compression* is the unfortunate circumstance that occurs when new hires are offered a salary that is equal to or greater than that of an existing employee with similar credentials doing the same job (e.g., an assistant professor in Finance being offered more than a current associate professor in Finance). This has become quite common in higher education during the past few decades. The frequency of this issue does not make it any easier to explain salary discrepancies to your current employees.

After making the offer, if your top candidate does not accept the position, do not take it personally. Simply move on to the next acceptable candidate. If there are no others, you will need to repeat or re-open the search process. Do not get discouraged when you lose strong candidates; it is simply the nature of our business—there are numerous institutions competing for the same talent. Sometimes we win and sometimes we lose.

Handling Internal Candidates

Internal candidates need to be treated fairly throughout the search process. Because of their presence on the campus we know more about them than the rest of the applicant pool, and they know more about the department and the institution than other candidates. This knowledge can be advantageous to the candidates, or it can hurt them in the selection process. As the hiring manager or search chair, it is your responsibility to discuss with the search committee the importance of evaluating only the application materials presented by each candidate when choosing whom to advance in the process. If the credentials of the internal candidates are equal to or better than the rest of the pool, the candidates should be allowed to continue. However, if they are lacking, they should be eliminated along with the others whose credentials fell short. Extending a "courtesy interview" to internal candidates is a waste of everyone's time and should not occur. If you have multiple internal candidates each needs to be reviewed on his or her individual qualifications, and if you decide one candidate should be interviewed you do not need to invite the other(s). This is about treating people fairly, not equally.

If one or more of the internal candidates are successful in making the pool of finalists invited to campus, you must be cognizant of your insider information. While we have witnessed their strengths, we also understand more about their limitations as well. When other candidates are brought to campus, we typically see them on their best behavior and do not get a true picture as to their limitations. There are pros and cons to every hiring decision that is made, but there is no more politically charged decision as one that includes an internal candidate. Pfeffer and Sutton (2006) suggest that organizations that are performing well should consider promoting from within if there is a well-qualified person who can continue moving the institution along the same path. Conversely, if the organization is in need of a change, it will most likely be better off hiring an outsider who can act as a change agent.

Using Search Firms or Executive Recruiters

In the last couple of decades, there has been an increase in the use of search firms to fill mid- and senior-level positions on campuses throughout the United States. Whether this is a good trend or a bad one depends on how you view this process and how you view the value these firms bring. This is a case where the phrase "*caveat emptor*" (let the buyer beware) is important to keep in mind when selecting a firm. A search for an academic dean can cost the institution $150,000 or more, while a presidential search can be well over $250,000. We have found no data indicating that search firms do a better job than internal committees at finding well-qualified candidates.

Sometimes it appears as though institutions contract with a search firm so they can have some external source to blame if the hiring decision is a poor one and the candidate does not work out as expected. If instead of spending the money to hire the recruiters you put it to use internally to provide additional support to the search committee, or perhaps a very modest stipend for the committee members, you would probably be better off. One of the major problems with using search firms is trying to determine the commitment of the candidates. Are they really interested in *your institution* or do they just want to be a senior executive at *any institution*?

RETAINING EMPLOYEES

Reducing employee turnover saves institutions money and in most cases increases productivity. Therefore, it is important for every college and university to pay attention to employee retention, at all levels. Employee retention begins with the recruitment process as described above. If as an institution you do a good job in the recruitment and selection process, retention efforts tend to go a little smoother as there are fewer unexpected or unanticipated conflicts between the new hire and the institution. The next few sections will give you a brief understanding of how colleges and universities can potentially increase employee retention. We believe three of the processes identified in the Janosik et al. (2003) staffing model—orientation, supervision, and evaluation—are directly connected to employee retention. Additionally, a section on mentoring has been added as this has become a necessity for retaining high-quality professional employees.

Orienting New Hires

The orientation process for faculty and staff needs to be an explicit and thorough process that can be accomplished formally and informally. This process includes inculcating new professionals with the educational and operational philosophy and the culture of the institution (Janosik et al., 2003, p. 5). A highly effective orientation process will begin simultaneously with the recruitment process. As you communicate with candidates and potential candidates, you are conveying information about the institution and its culture, which is an integral part of the institution's orientation process. Janosik et al. go on to suggest that "orientation is not just the activities scheduled for the first morning of the staff member's first day at work. It begins when the vacant position is advertised and application materials are developed. Orientation begins with the position announcement" (p. 7). The impression given in the announcement begins to help the potential candidates form their perception of the institution (see Figure 9.7).

As your new employees arrive on campus, the orientation must continue in a systematic and comprehensive manner for up to the first year on the job. We create all of these wonderful first-year experience programs for our students but seem to frequently neglect the first-year experience of our faculty and staff. Whether the new employees are external hires or internal hires, they all need orientation—new responsibilities, duties and relationships, and policies and procedures will seem quite different in their new role. Where you sit in the organization determines how the organization looks (Janosik & et al., 2003).

Supervising Employees

Supervision, based on the definition of several authors, is the systematic and ongoing process of ensuring that all subordinate staff members efficiently and effectively accomplish duties and tasks progressing toward the achievement of organizational

Basic campus information

- Campus maps and directions
- Email account, listservs, and office phone number and mailing address
- Web links to policies and procedures (department handbook if available)
- Salary and benefits fully explained including deferred compensation programs (retirement accounts)
- Parking policies, permit instructions, closest parking to one's office or classroom building(s)

Position-specific

- Direct supervisor contact information (email, phone, mailing address)
- Colleague contact information

Community information

- Banking information
- House/apartment-hunting tips
- Connect with a realtor if necessary
- Local area maps
- Local points of interest
- Airport information

Figure 9.7 Orientation

goals and objectives. It also ensures the necessary developmental and growth opportunities for the staff members to accomplish their professional and personal goals while establishing or maintaining their respective career path.

When working with staff, it is important to understand that you have two essential responsibilities: (1) to ensure that all staff hired perform the duties and responsibilities of their positions to the best of their abilities, and (2) to ensure that the staff under your supervision receive professional development and job enrichment activities that will help them develop a successful career path.

As a supervisor, you cannot assume that your employees will know exactly what to do. Whether they are stepping into their new roles as a faculty member, department chair, academic advisor, or director of a functional area, they most likely have not performed all of the duties and responsibilities associated with their new positions. It is your responsibility to ensure that each new hire has the administrative and technical support and resources (to the best of your ability) to do the job properly.

According to Bolam (2002), "professional development is widely accepted as fundamental to the improvement of organizational performance and therefore, as a core task of management and leadership" (p. 113). As a supervisor, you should be genuinely interested in the development of all of your employees. It is your responsibility to have an understanding of the professional development needs of your staff so you can encourage their participation in the most appropriate professional development activities, such as conferences, classes, workshops, and publishing. There may be opportunities to cross-train staff or permit them to volunteer in other departments.

Supervisors need to develop an open and trusting relationship with staff so as to encourage honest conversations about career aspirations on an ongoing basis, not annually. The more you understand about their needs and career goals, the better you will be prepared to delegate responsibilities or to encourage specific activities. Asking your direct reports where they see themselves in five or ten years can help you develop a plan that can maximize their skill development so they can achieve their goals while performing at a high level in their current position.

Every supervisor desires to keep competent staff for as long as possible. However, it is not in anyone's best interest to coerce them to stay beyond the point where they are actively interested in remaining. Former employees are quite often an excellent resource for attracting new employees. If they have respect for you as a supervisor and believe that you trusted them and demonstrated confidence in their abilities, they will be far more likely to be of assistance down the road in referring potential employees and perhaps in creating collaborative efforts.

What Makes an Effective Supervisor?

Becoming an effective supervisor is a challenge regardless of one's academic training. Because supervisors are dealing with human beings and the diverse nature of personalities, all within the incredibly diverse field of higher education, it is safe to say that there is no single, most effective way to supervise employees. However, there are some key skills and personality characteristics that are particularly helpful in the supervision process within institutions of higher education. The following are a few such skills and abilities:

STRONG COMMUNICATION SKILLS

Every supervisor within higher education should have solid communication skills. Much of what you do involves interacting with your staff or peers throughout the day. You will need to make formal and informal presentations, represent your department at meetings, interview prospective employees, and write reports, among other tasks requiring effective communication skills. Supervisors need to fine-tune their writing, presentation, and interpersonal skills, and, most importantly, a good supervisor needs to be a good listener, not necessarily in the sense of being a counselor but rather a person who listens for content and affect and adapts communication to meets the needs of the situation or people involved. You need to be able to understand the situations being brought to you before you develop a plan or strategy to resolve the issue.

HONEST AND ETHICAL

This should go without saying; however, hardly a semester goes by where we do not read in the *Chronicle of Higher Education* or other news source about a misguided administrator who decided to circumvent a policy or law. Unfortunately, we have our share of administrators and faculty who seem to have lost sight of honest and ethical behavior. Virtually every professional organization/association involved with higher education has an established code of ethics which is intended to guide the actions of its membership. As a supervisor, you serve as a role model to your staff and in most instances are assumed to be honest until proven otherwise. Do not give your staff a reason to doubt your honesty, your motives, or your ethics. Regardless of how your colleagues or supervisors act, you must respect yourself enough to act with integrity and honesty.

SUPPORTIVE

As a supervisor, you need to be supportive of your staff, helping them to grow as professionals in their chosen fields. It is your responsibility to assist your staff through the bureaucratic processes at your institution, help them understand the power and political dynamics of the institution, recognize them publicly for their accomplishments, and help them to learn how to recover from setbacks when they occur. Being supportive does not mean always providing positive feedback. In many instances, it is necessary to provide corrective feedback to help your staff grow professionally. A simple guideline for providing feedback is: publicly praise and privately correct.

FLEXIBLE AND FAIR

Being fair does not mean treating everyone equally. You must be flexible in your supervision style, recognizing that not all of your staff members have equal talents; nor do they all perform the exact same duties in the exact same ways. Staff members need to be treated based on their performance, attitudes, and abilities. Treat them fairly, not equally. You also need to be receptive to the unique communication styles of your staff so you can determine the most appropriate way to interact.

CHALLENGING

As a supervisor, one of your roles is to ensure that your staff develop as professionals. This cannot occur if the individuals are not challenged to be professionals. This may require you, as the supervisor, to take some risks with regard to assignment of duties and responsibilities.

DELEGATOR

You have hired competent professionals. Let them grow and mature as professionals by sharing as much responsibility and authority as possible. If you do not have confidence in your staff, you need to do one of two things: (1) change your staff, or (2) learn to trust them. If you cannot do either, then it is time for *you* to look for another position.

MENTORING

Being a mentor involves coaching and guiding individuals (Nickels et al., 2008, p. 299) through the political and power dynamics within your institution, and being supportive in their professional and career development processes. Supervisors do not always make the best mentors for their employees. More often than not it is in the best interest of the staff member to be mentored by someone from outside the department or a senior staff member (non-supervisor) within the department.

BEING SELF-REFLECTIVE

You should constantly reflect upon your practice and evaluate your performance. Examining your interactions with subordinates, peers, and superiors, paying attention to your attitudes and behaviors, can be very enlightening. The more you know about your managerial and leadership styles, the better you can perform in these roles. Do not be afraid to ask others to provide feedback about you and your performance.

Evaluations and Performance Appraisals

Evaluating employees can be very stressful for the individual employees and the supervisor. To make this task a little easier, it is strongly recommended that the tools used for the evaluation be directly connected to the position description. If the position of the individuals being evaluated has changed during the evaluation period, all changes should be noted on the evaluation form/document.

A performance appraisal is an evaluation in which the performance level of employees is measured against established standards to make decisions about promotions, compensation, and additional training (Nickels et al., 2008). Performance evaluations should not be used to "rank" employees. While many of us might like to witness healthy competition among our staff, Pfeffer and Sutton (2006) indicates that "forced employee rankings resulted in lower productivity, inequity and skepticism, negative effects on employee engagement, reduced collaborations, and damage to morale and mistrust in leadership" (p. 106).

According to David Middlewood (2002), there are two elements to every performance appraisal: accountability and development (Figure 9.8). Understanding these elements will help you develop an evaluation tool that will meet the needs of the employee, the supervisor, and the institution.

When conducting a performance evaluation, regardless of the tool(s) chosen, it is important to operate within a climate of trust—the subordinate needs to trust the

Elements of a Performance Appraisal	
Evaluation for Accountability	Evaluation for Development
• Focus on organizational needs • Focus on transactional elements • Focus on measurable outcomes • Focus on need for quantitative data	• Focus on individual needs • Recognition of transformational elements • Focus on educational value added outcomes • Focus on need for qualitative data

Figure 9.8 Performance Appraisal Elements

supervisor and have confidence that the supervisor is concerned about the individual's professional development in addition to the well-being of the department or institution. This can be partially accomplished by ensuring that the tool(s) utilized have a balance between meeting the accountability needs and the professional development needs. These evaluation sessions should be conducted in an environment that values learning and growth, not one that is designed to be punitive or intimidating.

If the performance evaluation tools are available at the time of hire, it is beneficial to share them with each new employee. It is helpful for staff members to understand from the beginning what criteria are going to be used to evaluate their performance. If the tools have not been developed, then it is in everyone's best interests to include the staff in the development process. If the staff members have the opportunity to assist in preparing the tools, they will have a much better understanding of what is expected and hopefully a greater appreciation for the role of the supervisor.

When conducting an evaluation, it is also important to consider the financial and physical resources available for use by the faculty and staff. It has been shown that "people's performance depends on the resources they have to work with, including the help they get from colleagues, and the infrastructure that supports their work" (Pfeffer & Sutton, 2006, p. 96). Additionally, Pfeffer and Sutton go on to point out that "it is impossible for even the most talented people to do competent, let alone brilliant, work in a flawed system. Yet a well-designed system filled with ordinary – but well trained – people can consistently achieve stunning performance levels" (2006, p. 96).

SEPARATING

There are two types of separation from an organization: voluntary and involuntary. Each type of separation must be handled in slightly differing ways.

Voluntary Separation

Assuming that you have established an environment of trust and openness and that you have made it clear to your employees that their career development is important, you should be well aware of any staff member's intention of leaving the institution. Leaving for career development or professional advancement opportunities are two of many positive reasons for departing an institution. If during conversations with a staff member it becomes apparent that the individual is considering employment options elsewhere, your role as the supervisor is twofold: (1) you want to ensure that this is the right decision for this employee professionally and personally, and (2) you want to find out what changes could have been made to keep the individual with your institution. This is not the time to make counter offers or imply changes will be made. There are many institutions that have a *counter-offer policy* whereby, if employees present a bona fide offer, the institution will make a reasonable counter offer in an effort to retain that employee. We believe this policy is counterproductive and actually encourages employees to search for positions with the sole intent of receiving a raise. If you have the appropriate structures in place and you provide the necessary support, supervision, and professional development there is no need for a counter-offer policy. When employees approach with an offer, we recommend that you simply acknowledge their opportunity and offer to help them evaluate the offer/decision and do everything you can to show your support. It is their decision, not yours.

Involuntary Separation

At some point in your administrative career, you will be involved with an involuntary separation from your institution (either you or one of your staff). Having to terminate a staff member is neither an easy nor pleasant task, but more often than not it becomes a necessary one. There are two major types of involuntary separation: for cause and for financial exigency. If your institution is experiencing financial difficulties, you are encouraged to be creative and explore other alternatives before deciding to lay-off employees.

If the departure is for cause, the supervisor should have exhausted all other options before deciding on termination. If you have worked with the employee to improve his or her performance and after a reasonable time there is no improvement, termination may be your only option. This is where you need to consult your HR staff and possibly the institution's legal counsel. The legal implications of employee termination are far beyond the scope of this text, as there are entire books written on employment law. You should ensure that you have done everything possible to avoid this action and that all of your efforts have been documented. We have witnessed situations where a supervisor started the termination process only to have it halted because the employee in question had received stellar employment reviews for the past several years. If you need to terminate for cause, you must ensure that you have the documentation to support your recommendation.

SPECIAL CIRCUMSTANCES

Post-Tenure Review

While still a controversial topic within the academy and a topic that many of our colleagues prefer not to discuss, it is one that needs to be reconsidered on a regular basis. Repeatedly, faculty members argue that post-tenure review is unnecessary and it impinges upon their academic freedom. The other side of this argument is that post-tenure review has become necessary to protect academic freedom and that everyone, including faculty, should be evaluated on a regular basis to ensure adequate professional development. Tenure has come under fire and is often looked upon as an archaic tradition whose time has long since passed. If higher education continues to resist post-tenure review, it runs the risk of losing tenure altogether. This is a case where political powers-that-be will find few objections among the voting public if they propose the elimination of tenure at public colleges and universities. No other working group has the protections that are perceived to come with indefinite tenure. So, if for no other reason than to avoid losing tenure, public higher education institutions should seriously consider some type of post-tenure review process. We believe it will serve the academy better if the faculty define the process rather than leaving it to the politicians.

Originally, tenure was instituted to protect faculty from wrongful termination and to protect their freedom of speech in the classroom and in their writings. As you will notice in the American Association of University Professors (AAUP) 1940 statement, tenure was not intended to protect a faculty member from termination for cause (poor performance):

> After the expiration of a probationary period, teachers or investigators should have permanent or continuous tenure, and their service should be terminated only for adequate cause, except in the case of retirement for age, or under extraordinary circumstances because of financial exigencies.
>
> (AAUP, 1940 Statement www.aaup.org/AAUP/pubsres/policydocs/contents/1940statement.htm)

The key phrase in that statement is "should be terminated only for adequate cause," which in recent times has been misinterpreted to mean that you cannot terminate a faculty member with tenure. The AAUP does not detail what is meant by "adequate cause," leaving that up to the individual institutions, and the courts if necessary.

We are not advocating the elimination of tenure, but rather that colleges and universities find ways in which all faculty and staff members can be held accountable to its mission. If that means keeping current with research and publications, then one should do so. If it means providing high-quality teaching, then one should do so. Regardless of the interpretation, if it is documented and applied fairly across the institution all parties are equally protected. In its current state, the faculty tend to hold the upper hand, and unproductive, and in some cases incompetent, faculty are retained because they have indefinite tenure.

Collective Bargaining

According to the Bureau of Labor Statistics the unionized share of the workforce has declined to just 10.5 percent in 2018. Yet this trend is bucked in the ranks of education, training, and library occupations boasting a union representation of 33.8% (www.bls.gov/news.release/union2.nr0.htm).

If you are to take an administrative position in higher education, especially public higher education, you will have a high probability of encountering a union. These unions, while an outgrowth of the industrial revolution of the late 1800s and early 1900s, do not operate in the same adversarial way. The major issues facing today's workforce in higher education, with few exceptions, are not about working conditions but rather concern salaries and benefits. Work stoppage is infrequent, and violence is almost non-existent. In many states, right-to-work laws give workers the option to join or not join a union if one is present in the workplace. Furthermore, if the employees choose not to join, they cannot be forced to pay a fee or dues to the union (Nickels et al., 2008, p. 329).

If you do find yourself in a "union shop" as an administrator, regardless of your opinion of unions, you need to familiarize yourself with the contract and its stipulations.

Most collective bargaining agreements are quite detailed as to what can and cannot take place on the job and the union representatives try to ensure that their members are well versed as to their rights. You also need to be as well versed, so you better understand your responsibilities and your limitations. Whether it is a faculty union, staff union, or trade union, its members are also employees of the institution and need to be valued as such.

CONCLUDING COMMENTS

People are the backbone of any organization, and they also consume the bulk of the financial resources in every institution of higher education. As an administrator at an institution of higher education, you have tremendous responsibility placed upon you. The recruiting and retaining of quality faculty and staff is of paramount importance in higher education. Many of these individuals have opportunities outside of academe that pay significantly better salaries, but they choose to stay within higher education because of the collegial environment, which leads to very favorable working conditions. Part of your responsibility is to ensure that these conditions persist throughout your tenure as an administrator.

The HR department does not exist to make sure you get what you need or want, but rather to make sure administrators like you comply with institutional policies and local, state, and federal laws. Because of this role, it may in fact appear to be working against you when you are attempting to make a hiring decision. It becomes extremely important that as a supervisor you learn to be patient! You must understand, as a manager/administrator, that while however well intended, HR is not always your friend but it can serve as a valued resource.

If you take your role as a supervisor seriously, you will find that recruiting and retaining quality staff will consume a significant portion of your time on task. Regardless of your leadership or managerial style, you must stay connected with your staff. Your support and encouragement will help to maximize their engagement within the institution and hopefully will maximize their tenure with the institution.

Finally, when considering the replacement of a staff member or creating a new position, it may be in the best interest of the institution to consider the possibility of one individual serving multiple roles. Cross-training staff or hiring individuals who can perform multiple tasks may be what is needed. One example of this is academic advising professionals and career counseling. Because of the overlap between selection of majors and courses and eventual employment, much of what advisors do is actually career counseling: helping the student differentiate between elective courses that may benefit them in their intended major, or trying to help the student decide on a major or career path. It may make sense to combine the advising and career counseling functions so that students do not get bounced around between departments. This may be difficult, as in many institutions the career functions report to the Student Services side of the organization while academic advising reports through the Academic Affairs portion. The question that needs to be asked is which is more important to the student: to whom the advisor reports or the quality of the advising provided? If you look closely at the staffing within your institution, you should be able to find several opportunities to cross-train staff, which can in turn improve their efficiency and effectiveness. Many of the smaller liberal arts colleges and community colleges have been doing this for years.

REFLECTIVE QUESTIONS

1. During a hiring freeze every position must be approved by the powers-that-be. Briefly justify the filling of your position if you were to leave.
2. Write ten behavior-based interview questions based on your current position.
3. What are the key considerations for determining membership of a search committee? Does level of position matter? Why?
4. Rate yourself from 1–6 (Poor to Outstanding) on the eight skills and abilities of an effective supervisor, and describe why you believe you deserve those ratings.
5. Review your current performance appraisal document. How do the criteria connect to what you actually do in your current position?

CHAPTER 10

Marketing Basics

Marketing is one of the more recognizable business practices being used within higher education. Driving through town or across the country you see billboards touting "academic excellence" or "athletic achievement" for the local college or university. There are social media blasts, television ads, radio announcements, and advertisements in newspapers and national magazines. Additionally, you will see current students, alumni, and "friends" of the institution sporting university logo apparel. This was not always the case. From the founding of Harvard College in 1636 through the 1960s, higher education in the United States experienced over 300 years of growth (Lenington, 1996). During that time most institutions of higher education did not perceive a need to "market" themselves to attract students. The continued population growth combined with a relatively strong economy (with a few exceptions) made for a steady stream of students.

After World War II and the GI Bill, there was an explosion of potential college-bound students. Then came the baby boom generation with the largest-ever cohort of college-aged students. With so many students knocking at the door, most administrators failed to see the need for developing a sound marketing strategy for their respective institutions. In the 1970s, however, the aggressive expansion of higher education met the baby bust as high school graduation rates began to decline after the baby boom generation worked its way through the systems, and there was now a shortage of available students. Many institutions saw the need to compete for the traditional-aged students (recent high school graduates) while others decided to try to expand the market by recruiting veterans, international students, and "returning adults" to their campuses. Additional strategies included expanding into evening and weekend programs; adding graduate programs, especially in business and education; and increasing part-time enrollments. It was during this period that institutions of higher education began to accept the role that marketing plays in recruitment and retention efforts.

While perhaps the most visible aspect of marketing, advertising is only one piece of the greater institutional marketing picture. According to Shimp (2000) there are six basic marketing tools available for use in an integrated marketing strategy: personal selling, advertising, publicity, sales promotion, sponsorship, and point-of-purchase (typically found in retail environments). These tools are utilized by a variety of offices on our campuses and may not be as visible to the public, or even a majority of the institution's employees, as the broad-based advertising. Marketing is one of the most important ways in which institutions of higher education connect to the outside world, and informs the public exactly what we do and what we are about. Unlike producers of consumer goods, colleges and universities do not have a tangible product that can be distributed through retail outlets or online shopping. Most institutions are marketing the college experience and one's engagement in the process of learning, not simply a degree. Furthermore, an education cannot be purchased. It has to be co-produced between the student and the institution's faculty and staff.

Hossler (2006) notes that

> the marketing and the commodification of colleges and universities has become widespread in the United States and now all sectors of higher education (including the for-profits) compete with each other on the following dimensions:
>
> 1. Range of academic programs
> 2. Perceived quality and reputation
> 3. Tuition and financial aid packages
> 4. Locations in which they offer courses and degree programs
> 5. When courses are offered (day, evening, weekends, on-line)
> 6. Quality of student life and out-of-class facilities and activities
> 7. Early application and early admissions practices in some instances
>
> (p. 113)

The more frequently people see your institution's name, the more likely they will be to consider you when ranking institutions. This necessitates an understanding of marketing and marketing principles used today within the business sector, and an understanding as to how those principles can be applied to higher education.

We will take a closer look at the marketing practices employed throughout higher education and frame those practices using two different models: the product model and the services model. You will be introduced to the variety of marketing arms of individual institutions and gain an understanding of strategic and integrated marketing approaches. From an institutional perspective it will become clear that the authors, among many others, believe that *marketing is everyone's responsibility*, from the president down to your current students.

Before we jump into all of the areas of marketing and how they fit within higher education, let us first look at a usable definition. *Marketing*, as defined by the American Marketing Association, "is the activity, set of institutions, and processes for creating, communicating, delivering, and exchanging offerings that have value for customers, clients, partners, and society at large" (www.marketingpower.com/AboutAMA/Pages/DefinitionofMarketing.aspx). This definition does not single out the customer; nor does it specify a marketing tool. This definition is broad because marketing is broad.

MARKETING BASICS

Going beyond the definition of marketing, we must look at some of the guiding principles that underlie this function. The following sections will describe many of these marketing principles and give you an idea as to how those principles can be applied within the higher education sector.

What Is a Market?

A market is simply "a collection of buyers and sellers" (Ferrell & Hartline, 2005, p. 5). From a higher education perspective, the institutions are the sellers and the students are the buyers. For higher education, there are actually a couple of distinct markets that must be considered. There is the *macro* level, in which we look at higher education as an industry, or the *micro* level, in which consider the individual institution.

Whether at the macro or micro level, there are buyers (current and potential students) and there are sellers (the plethora of institutions of higher education). Potential students interested in pursuing higher education will find plenty of opportunities to further their education. There truly is an institution for everyone and anyone. Therefore, a market exists because options exist, as individuals can choose between the alternatives present (Foskett, 2002, p. 243). While every potential student may not qualify for admission into the institution of first choice, each student will almost certainly qualify for admission into at least one institution of higher education. We are living in a time in which we are fast approaching "universal access" to higher education. Here in the United States, opportunities to continue one's education are abundant, and it is difficult to believe people who say they do not have the opportunity to continue their education. It appears to be that what they really are saying is that at this point in time higher education is not as high a priority as other goods or services.

Exchange

An exchange takes place in a market where buyers want what the sellers have and they are willing to "pay" for those goods or services. This transaction is an exchange. According to Dickson (2000), "Marketing is based on the principle of exchange. Marketing exchanges exist because they are beneficial to both parties" (p. 8).

Using the exchange as a lens, Ferrell and Hartline go on to describe a product as "something that can be acquired via exchange to satisfy a need or want" (2005, p. 8). This definition does not specify a "manufactured good," and therefore, we believe, can include services such as higher education. As discussed in Chapter 1, students can be viewed as products, customers, or co-producers. Regardless of how you choose to describe the "parties" involved, the fact is an exchange takes place: students pay tuition and in turn are given the opportunity to participate in the educational process.

Figure 10.1 depicts the relationship between the approaches to marketing (product or services), the strategy employed, and the tools used to carry out the strategy. Marketing is a strategic process that requires an institution to conduct an appropriate self-analysis similar to that of a self-study for accreditation. If the institution is to continue to be successful through the next several decades or at least until the next technological revolution, it must be deliberate in its approach to and implementation of its marketing strategy.

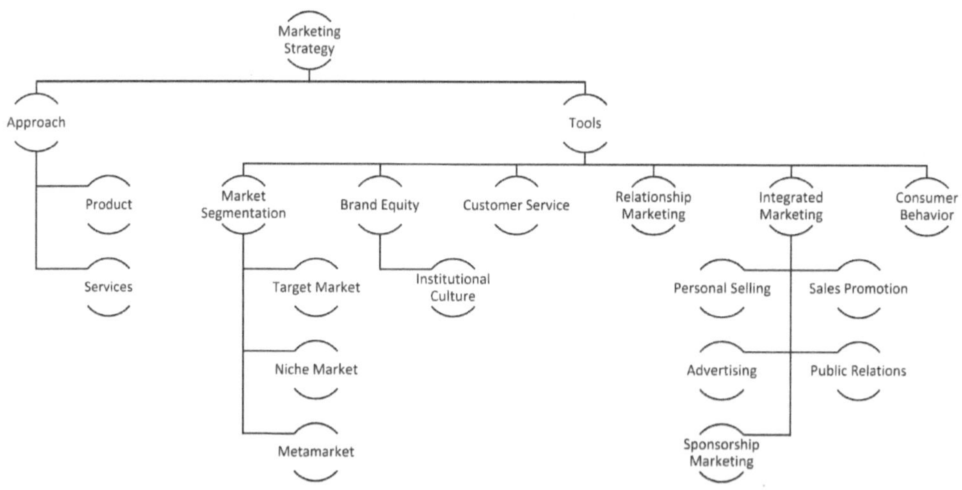

Figure 10.1 Marketing Concepts

SERVICES MARKETING

Historically, there are two ways to approach marketing strategy: the product approach ("the Four Ps") or the services approach ("the Four Cs"). We believe that the services approach best fits higher education because, as noted earlier, students are not products. Viewing higher education as a service requires one to reconceptualize the marketing mix from the product metaphor to the service metaphor. The services marketing mix consists of the Four Cs—cost, customer, convenience, and communication—which seem a bit more intuitive and easier to connect with for administrators and faculty.

Cost

Cost in the higher education perspective is essentially the cost of attendance for the student, not simply the tuition price listed. This is not the same as the cost to the institution to educate each student. Institutional costs were discussed earlier in Part 2 of this book. There are numerous components to cost, as students are typically not charged a flat fee for attending our institutions. For example, students incur a variety of expenses from the institution, including tuition, room and board, and a myriad of fees associated with everything from athletics and activities to laboratory and technology fees. Each institution is somewhat unique in how it structures its fees, and the sum of all of these student expenses is what is commonly called the *sticker price*. This is the price that is advertised on an institution's web site. It seems that today few students actually pay the *sticker price* of an institution. Institutions have numerous ways to reduce the actual cost to the individual students. Students may receive financial aid from the federal government (Pell Grants, loans, work-study), state subsidies (grants to students or direct payments to the institution), institutional sources of funding (scholarships, grants, employment, or other forms of tuition discounts), or from external sources (private foundation grants/scholarships, alternative loans, etc.), making it rather difficult for institutional personnel to quote the actual cost to prospective students.

Customer (Co-producer)

In the services approach there are multiple customers for each institution of higher education. The most obvious customers are the prospective students and the current students (co-producers) attending our individual institutions. However, institutions of higher education have many other customers, several of which are worth mentioning here. In higher education we need to concern ourselves with parents (primarily of traditional-aged applicants and students), employers that hire our graduates, community members who take advantage of our facilities and utilize the services and activities we provide, and taxpayers (primarily for state-supported institutions), among others.

Convenience

Ease of access can play an important role in the selection of some services. The majority of students enrolling in higher education in the United States will attend an institution within 100 miles of their home, reinforcing the regional or local nature of most higher education institutions. Additionally, ease of access to a campus can make prospective students feel more comfortable about their choice of an institution. Online learning has slowly increased over the past decade as some students prefer the convenience of taking a class while enjoying the comforts of home or perhaps while on the road traveling for business. Institutions such as Arizona State University, Southern New Hampshire University, and many for-profits like Capella University and the University of Phoenix have made online learning more mainstream.

Communication

How effectively you communicate with your prospective students, current students, and other customers will make a significant difference in their level of satisfaction with the services you provide. Communicating with your customers is more than what you say: it is also how and how often you say it. As students change, so must our communication tools. While print media may still an important tool in marketing, other tools can be more effective depending on the message being sent. Communicating through social media platforms (Instagram, Twitter, Facebook, etc.) and using text messaging can be more effective if speed or timing is critical. As an administrator in a service sector industry, understanding how to communicate with your customer base is a necessity.

SERVICES APPROACH

In addition to the Four Cs being different from the Four Ps of the product metaphor, services marketing takes a different approach to marketing strategy because it is not concerned with manufactured goods but rather focuses on the service industries, of which higher education is one. Hoffman (2000) defines *services* as deeds, efforts, or performances where the primary difference between goods and services is the property of tangibility. They are "intangible dominant", and therefore lack physical properties that can be evaluated by customers prior to purchase (p. 292). Services possess three types of attributes: search attributes, experience attributes, and credence attributes. Hoffman defines these attributes as follows:

- Search attributes – can be determined prior to purchase, such as tuition or the campus setting
- Experience attributes – can be evaluated only during and after the co-production process, such as a lecture or small group discussion or the quality of the residence hall meals
- Credence attributes – cannot be evaluated confidently even immediately after receipt, such as guidance from your faculty advisor or career counselor (p. 312)

A large proportion of properties possessed by services can be discovered only during and after the consumption of the service; these are experience attributes. Other properties of services cannot be assessed even after the service is complete, because customers lack the technical or specialized expertise to conduct such an evaluation (these are credence attributes); hence services are evaluated differently than goods. This inability of the customer to conduct an evaluation places services in a *trust market*, which means that this consumer must rely on the service provider's expertise, honesty, and integrity. When you get the oil changed in your car, you cannot ask for a sample before committing to the service. Likewise, when renting a hotel room you do not have the opportunity to sample the room prior to registering. Higher education is no different; even though prospective students visit the campus and may have the opportunity to sit in on a class, they cannot sample the student experience for a few weeks before deciding to register.

In another contrast to goods, Hoffman (2000) points out that

> services deliver a bundle of benefits through the experience that is created for the consumer . . . the most profound implication of the service experience is that it demonstrates that customers are an integral part of the service process. Their participation may be active or passive, but they are always involved in the service delivery process.
>
> (p. 300)

Hoffman and Kretovics (2003) suggest that education can clearly be described as a service encounter. As such, it is characterized by the four unique characteristics that distinguish the provision of goods from services: intangibility, inseparability, heterogeneity, and perishability (Zeithaml, Parasuraman, & Berry, 1985).

Intangibility

Service encounters, such as education, are said to be intangible because they are performances rather than objects. They cannot be touched or seen in the same manner as goods and are therefore evaluated differently. For example, students do not have the expertise to evaluate the true quality of their education; consequently, evaluations of their educational experience are predominantly based on the tangible evidence that surrounds the experience, such as classroom environment, peers, technology, campus, and school rankings.

Inseparability

Inseparability of production and consumption refers to the fact that whereas goods are first produced, then sold, and then consumed, services are sold first and then produced and consumed simultaneously. For example, students first purchase education through the payment of tuition, and the colleges or universities agree to provide the education through their curricular offerings. The education is then consumed by the students while it is being simultaneously produced by the faculty and students in the classroom.

Heterogeneity

Heterogeneity refers to the potential for service performance to vary from one service transaction to the next. Within a given academic institution, the quality of instruction varies from one course to the next and may even vary day to day from the same instructor within a single course. Additionally, the knowledge, skills, and abilities acquired by each student will differ significantly based upon the programmatic goals of the specific majors, departments, and colleges within the same institution.

Perishability

Finally, *perishability* means that services cannot be saved; unused capacity in services cannot be reserved, and services themselves cannot be inventoried. Within a traditional educational setting, if a student misses a class or if enrollment is less than capacity, the instruction provided that day is gone forever. While students may be able to make up the required work, they are deprived of participating in the learning that took place in the class session(s) missed (Hoffman & Kretovics, 2003).

When considering higher education as a service encounter, the concept of inseparability is the characteristic that we believe deserves the most attention. *Inseparability* refers to: (1) the provider's physical connection to the education being provided, (2) the student's involvement in the learning process (co-production), and (3) the involvement of other students throughout the education encounter. Unlike the manufacturers, who rarely if ever see an actual consumer of their goods while producing those goods in a factory, higher education providers are often in constant contact with their students and must construct their service operations with the students' physical presence in mind. This interaction between student and education provider defines a *critical incident*. Within the services marketing literature, critical incidents represent the greatest opportunity for both gains and losses in regard to customer satisfaction and retention (Hoffman & Bateson, 2002).

Co-production

Due to the student's direct involvement in the learning process, students are often viewed as "partial employees" (co-producers) of their learning (Bettencourt, Ostrom, Brown & Roundtree, 2002; Keh & Teo, 2001; Mills & Morris, 1986). Partial employees are a special breed of service customers who are responsible for the co-production of the service encounter out of necessity or by design. This same symbiotic relationship exists for a multitude of services, such as hairstyling, counseling, accounting, insurance, dentistry, taxi services, and, most importantly, education. Similarly, colleges and universities have learned that as students increase their participation in the educational experience, labor costs decline and/or enhanced services can be provided as employee labor is shifted from tasks now completed by students to new added-value services. For example, students self-register for classes, make room and roommate selections online, and schedule advising appointments, among other tasks. This has permitted the registrar's staff and housing employees to focus their efforts on other aspects of the educational process. In addition to lowering labor costs, intentionally transforming students into co-producers can also enhance the effectiveness of the learning process. Students as co-producers are more adept at explaining their specific needs to service providers within the institution and thereby have a greater likelihood of being satisfied with the final results. However, tradeoffs do exist. The more responsibility that is transferred to the student for the co-production of their education, the greater the cost savings to the organization; but if the student's co-production efforts are "substandard, disruptive or require remedial action by the institution, potential costs are increased" (Mills & Morris, 1986, p. 732) such as academically underprepared students needing tutoring or other developmental services.

We believe that viewing students as co-producers of their educational experience better explains the students' relationship with the institution and the academic process. Most if not all employees within higher education will agree that students must actively co-produce the learning process if they hope to get the most out of their experiences. We can think of no other industry where the old adage "you get out of it what you put into it" is truer than in higher education. If students do not actively engage in their learning process they will not maximize their educational outcomes.

STRATEGIC MARKETING

Strategic marketing is not the same thing as strategic planning (Chapter 8); while many of the concepts are the same or very similar, they are two distinct processes. It is hoped that the institution has a strategic plan in place and that said plan will inform the marketing strategy. The institution does not want to develop a marketing plan that runs contrary to the institution's strategic plan. Consider the strategic plan as the road map which provides the traveler with the big picture of the city in which he or she is trying to navigate. The marketing plan then would be the more specific route drawn out with specific directions as to how to get from point "A" to point "B" dependent upon the mode of transportation. A well-defined marketing strategy describes how the institution will fulfill the needs and wants of its students (Ferrell & Hartline, 2005, p. 12).

For marketing to be effective the institution needs to "have a clear understanding of the needs and wants of all the people whom it serves, particularly students" (Maust, 1985, p. 16). This requires research to be conducted by various departments or individuals within the institution. The more complex your institution, the more individuals involved in this research effort. Chapter 8 discusses the types of environmental analyses that can structure this effort. We have adapted Ferrell and Hartline's (2005) list based on the needs of higher education institutions and listed them in Figure 10.2. This type of situation analysis is similar to performing an environmental scan which "identifies important trends in the environment and then considers the potential impact of those changes on the firms marketing strategy" (Dickson, 2000, p. 17).

After taking a closer look at your particular situation, you should have the data necessary to realistically determine your key strengths and weaknesses institutionally and departmentally. Make sure that you, or the powers-that-be, are using the appropriate data in the decision-making process. A common mistake at the departmental or divisional level is using institutional-level data when conducting your assessment. This level of data will not give you the information needed to conduct an effective analysis at the department level, and vice versa. When analyzing this data, it is very important to examine all these issues from the students' and the institutional perspectives. Looking at one and failing to consider the other can be a costly mistake. Ferrell and Hartline (2005, p. 77) suggest asking a few simple questions:

- What do students (and non-students) believe about us as an institution of higher education?
- What do students (and non-students) think of our service/educational quality, customer service, price and overall value, convenience, and promotional messages in comparison to our competitors?
- What is the relative importance of these issues: not as we see them but as students see them?

A marketing strategy, which should address these questions, is not a static document. Rather, it must be dynamic and flexible. There is no single strategy for higher education, and there is no single way to implement any given strategy. A strategy is unique to the institution or organization and is not transferable to others without serious modifications—there are no "best practices" for strategy. As the environments around us change, so should one's implementation plan.

Internal Marketing

Marketing is not for external audiences only, especially when considering large, complex institutions of higher education. How many times have administrators commented that others within the institution simply do not understand what they do or what they are trying to accomplish? One of the most important considerations in implementing and controlling marketing activities involves gaining the support of employees (Ferrell & Hartline, 2005, p. 257). This internal marketing should not be overlooked. Do not make the assumption that the rest of the institutional employees

The internal environment

- Review of current objectives, strategy, and performance – is your department/program/area acting in a manner that is consistent with the institutional mission?
- Availability of resources – what resources do you currently have control over? What additional resources are needed to accomplish your goals and objectives? What can you "live without" if the budget gets tight?
- Organizational culture and structure – where do you fit within the institution? Are you central to the institution? Are you supportive of the central functions of the institution?

The student environment

- Who are your current and potential students?
    - Demographics – grades, test scores, residence status, etc.
- Where and how do students learn about your institution?
- When do students commit to your institution?
    - November, March, June, August?
    - Are you a school of first choice?
    - Are you a school of last resort?
- Why and how do students select your institution?
    - What are your more desirable majors?
    - Are you in a preferred location?
    - Price? (including any financial aid or tuition discounts)
- Why do admitted students choose not to attend your institution?
- Why do other potential students choose not to apply?
- What do graduates do with a degree from your institution?
    - Who employs them? (companies, government, not-for-profit, etc.)
    - Where do they live?

The external environment

- Competition – with whom are you currently competing? (Be honest with yourself.) What are viable substitutes?
- Economic growth and stability – is your region/state growing or declining in population? Is there a net immigration or migration of college educated citizens? What is the current and projected economic climate?
- Political trends – is the state, region, country becoming more conservative? Liberal?
- Legal and regulatory issues – are the governments becoming more or less restrictive? DOE policies, accreditation changes
- Technological changes – How will they impact your institution?
    - Distance/online delivery of courses/degrees.
    - Enterprise resource planning systems such as Banner or PeopleSoft
    - Social networking such as Facebook and Twitter
    - Socio-cultural trends – demographic/values/population shifts.

Figure 10.2 Marketing-focused Situation Analysis

understand the responsibilities or functions of any department or office. The larger the institution, the more important internal marketing becomes.

Throughout our careers in higher education we have witnessed much disbelief on campuses about the actions taken by institutional colleagues. We have heard faculty criticize administrators, administrators criticize faculty, and students criticize both. A favorite complaint of faculty concerns administrators "wasting time" in endless meetings; administrators in turn accuse faculty of not working (teaching) enough; and students will criticize faculty for not being available or even on campus. Much of this criticism could be eliminated or at least toned down if each group understood just what the others do on their respective campuses.

According to Ferrell and Hartline (2005) internal marketing is an approach to motivate, coordinate, and integrate employees toward the implementation of the firm's marketing strategy. There are five important considerations to successful internal marketing:

1. Internal marketing begins with employee recruitment, selection, orientation, and training (see Chapter 9).
2. Senior administrators must be completely committed to the strategy.
3. Employee compensation programs must be linked to the implementation of the marketing strategy. This means employees should be rewarded on the basis of behaviors consistent with the strategy.
4. There must be open communication throughout the organization.
5. Structures, policies, and processes should match the marketing strategy (Ferrell & Hartline, 2005, p. 272).

An effective internal marketing campaign can assist in the development of an institutional culture. The marketing messages being sent should reinforce the institution's academic integrity and correspond with the culture that exists or the culture toward which the institution aspires to move.

TOOLS FOR STRATEGIC MARKETING IMPLEMENTATION

Market Segmentation

Institutions of higher education typically do not attempt to market to everyone (even though many of our mission statements profess to be all things to all people), but rather segment the market. The process of market segmentation is simply a process of dividing the larger market into smaller, more manageable groups of a somewhat homogeneous population whose members have similar needs, wants, or characteristics (Ferrell & Hartline, 2005; Nickels, McHugh, & McHugh, 2008). This segmentation can occur on several levels, as outlined by Simpson (2000, pp. 217–224):

- Geographic – country, region, city, county, etc.
- Demographic – age, gender, race, ethnicity, income, education . . .
- Psychographic – personality, values (grad school implications?)

- Benefit sought – comfort, convenience, durability, economy, luxury, status
- Situation – physical surroundings, social surroundings, temporal perspective, task definition, and pre-purchase attitude
- Behavior or usage – patterns of use, loyalty, status

It is not uncommon for institutions of higher education to consider multiple market segments in their recruiting processes. Taking these market segments and determining which group(s) your institution can serve profitably is called *target marketing* (Ferrell & Hartline, 2005, p. 13; Nickels et al., 2008, p. 362). Typically, institutions will use this type of target marketing when assigning admissions counselors to specific geographic areas, or focusing direct mail campaigns on specific demographic characteristics (scores on the ACT/SAT, GPA, Athletics, etc.), or using special marketing tools for siblings of current students or children of graduates. Those are just a few examples of the use of market segmentation and target marketing.

When we market to the larger market this is called *mass marketing*. For many institutions, that is precisely what many advertisements such as billboards, television advertisements, and other ads are geared toward: a more general audience. *Mass customization* is used primarily in direct mail campaigns, such as when the institution sends out a postcard or flyer and inserts the prospective student's name into the body of the card, giving it the appearance of being printed especially for that person. However, the more customized our ads or the more focused our audience, the more targeted is our marketing. A subset of target marketing is *niche marketing*. This is when we focus on finding small, but profitable, market segments (Nickels et al., 2008, p. 364). Niche marketing is usually done at the program level or in some cases for specific-purpose institutions such as art schools, music conservatories, or seminaries.

Before concluding the discussion on markets, it seems appropriate to briefly mention the *metamarket*, which Ferrell and Hartline (2005) define as "a cluster of closely related goods and services that center around a specific consumer activity" (p. 5). While not necessarily the major factor in our marketing efforts, this concept is particularly relevant in higher education. Imagine an institution of 5,000 students. These students at minimum will need to purchase textbooks for their classes (from the university bookstore and competing local stores); they will need a place to stay while attending campus (residence halls, apartments, other rentals); they will need to eat (food service on campus, fast-food establishments, local grocery stores); and they will need transportation to and from class (bicycles, cars, public transportation, parking services, etc.). These complementary services represent a metamarket that can be used when addressing your potential student body. How easy will it be for students and potential students to access the other markets? These metamarkets are also important to many of the communities in which our institutions are located as they provide a significant boost to the local economy (the multiplier effect in Chapter 3).

Branding and Brand Equity

Apple, Facebook, Pepsi, Google, Kleenex, and Scotch Tape are all brand names of one form or another. When you see these names they invoke an image or emotion and you immediately associate them with a specific product or company. What about these: CSU, KSU, MSU, OSU, Cal, Cornell, Stanford, Northwestern? What thoughts or images come to mind? Are these brands as well? Do institutions of higher education have brand equity? Perhaps the best way to answer this question is to ask other questions: when you think of the best institutions of higher education, which schools come to mind? Why did you choose these schools? Have you ever been to their campuses or met anyone who graduated from there? How did you come by your perception of high-quality education?

Brand equity is the value associated with having a name or symbol that differentiates the services of one provider from another (Aaker, 1991, cited in Toma, Dubrow, & Hartley, 2005; Nickels et al., 2008). Brand equity, as applied to higher education, includes awareness of an institution, recognition of what an institution is known for, a sense of loyalty toward the institution, an understanding of the institution's worth, and the desire to pay a premium price to be associated with it (Shimp, 2000; Toma et al., 2005). Brands do not have to be national or international; many are local or regional. This is very true for higher education. For example, take a few of the institutions listed above. Depending on where you live in the country, *OSU* can mean Ohio State University, Oregon State University, or Oklahoma State University; *KSU* can be Kent State University, Kennesaw State University, or Kansas State University; and *CSU* can be Colorado State University, Cleveland State University, Chicago State University, or California State University. You get the point—regionalism does play a part in brand or name recognition.

One cannot simply state that "X" institution is the best in the country and expect people to accept that as fact. Building a reputation and brand equity takes time, and this type of institutional identification is one of the tangible results of institutional culture. Toma et al. (2005) note "the best performing (not necessarily the most prestigious) institutions typically have well-defined norms, values, and beliefs and clear symbols, language, narratives, and practices to articulate them" (p. 7). This is a *culture*. Toma et al. further suggest "culture is not just something to have, but is more accurately something to use" (p. 3). Culture can become instrumental in helping the institution create a "brand" that in turn will help to enhance the institution's external image as well. The more clearly identifiable the institution's culture, the easier it becomes to market.

Additionally, according to Shimp (2000), brand equity is a function of brand awareness and brand image. Awareness comes from getting your brand out in front of potential students, hoping to draw their attention. To do this you must first understand who your potential students are, where they are located, and what is their current situation. This may seem trivial, but for many institutions of higher education which aspire to be great national institutions, they seem to forget that for the present time they may be local or regional institutions and are struggling in that market. We have heard many a president declare that he or she would make their institution one of the great research institutions (or liberal arts colleges) in the country without giving any indication as to what resources are needed to help realize this vision. Institutions must have a plan in place for developing brand awareness (name recognition) at the level at which they hope to compete. Simultaneously, the institution must develop its brand image. In other words, when the institution is named to a group of potential or perhaps even current students, what are their perceptions? What comes to mind first?

Cultivating a brand image begins with "shaping a distinctive identity and projecting a coherent and consistent set of images to the public" (Toma et al., 2005, p. 27). Developing this clear and consistent message is a starting point, not the end. A strong brand image can be very powerful in a competitive market; however, unlike a consumer product your brand must be consistent with what is going on within your institution. A well-crafted external image can become worthless if it does not correspond with the reality of the situation or institution (Toma et al., p. 4), meaning that the brand you have worked so hard at crafting for your external audiences must match the culture that permeates your campus. Institutions must understand themselves before members can rally around their purposes and aspirations and before a campus can frame itself to be appealing to outsiders (Toma et al., p. 7).

For example, a college or university may market its small class sizes and its low student-to-faculty ratio. But if the first class a student enters is a large lecture taught by a graduate assistant or adjunct faculty member, the marketing was for naught. What the student experiences is not what was advertised.

Often a new administration will come to a campus with the intent of changing the institutional image. Being very naïve, many of these administrators assume that a catchy new tag line—"Excellence in Action" or "Symbol of Academic Excellence"—will automatically change the image and reputation of the institution; but simply saying it out loud does not make it so. It takes years for an institution's reputation to change, and many believe that such a change must begin internally with the faculty, staff, and students. Toma et al. (2005) suggest that strong brands are also linked to institutions having clear values that they articulate through a variety of forms (p. 34), such as consistently applied admissions standards, a core curriculum, or strong developmental education programs. The key here is that the actions the institution takes simultaneously with changing its tag line must accurately reflect the image one is attempting to portray—actions really do speak louder than words.

INTEGRATED MARKETING

Integrated marketing communications are a set of tools used in the establishment of internal and external relationships and in the development of brand equity (Shimp, 2000). Those tools include: personal selling, advertising, publicity, sales promotion, sponsorship, and point-of-purchase (not used in higher education). The mix of tools to be used is dependent upon the marketing strategy, brand awareness, and brand equity. Below we have taken each tool and briefly described it and its higher education equivalent

Personal selling is the face-to-face or at least person-to-person interaction in which one party tries to convince the other that the product or service in question is something that is needed or wanted (Siguaw, 2000). There are three basic types of personal selling: inside sales (seen most often in retail environments), outside sales (old-fashioned door-to-door), and telemarketing (those annoying calls at dinner time). In higher education, we use all three of these approaches. While in the not-for-profit sector we typically do not hire a sales force, we do have several positions whose primary responsibilities fall within the sales functions: admissions counselors, development officers, and alumni relations staff.

Advertising is by far the most recognized of the integrated marketing tools. Its primary purpose is to add value to brands by influencing consumers' perceptions (Shimp, 2000) of the products or services being provided. Two types of advertising are most used in higher education: mass-media advertising, which is trying to target as many people through one advertisement as possible; and direct advertising, which typically targets a single individual or business. While television advertising in the not-for-profit sector is usually limited to commercials during televised sporting events (football bowl games or the National Collegiate Athletic Association basketball tournament), there are some institutions that regularly advertise their programs through local television stations. The web has also become an excellent place for colleges and universities to advertise. Most institutions still stick with the tried-and-true direct advertising techniques of direct mailings and telemarketing. Ask any junior or senior high school student who has taken the ACT or SAT just how many text messages or direct mail pieces they receive each month.

Public relations (PR) is the marketing tool that is used primarily to build goodwill between the institution and its local or regional communities (Shimp, 2000). PR is another form of mass communication that is geared to bringing about a favorable impression of the organization and its mission. In higher education we use PR regularly when we send announcements to hometown newspapers about successful students; when we submit press releases about an activity or function on the campus, such as a renowned speaker; when we have articles published about the institution or the accomplishments of its students, faculty, or staff; and even unsolicited reports about the achievements of sports teams and athletes or research activities by faculty or students. Another lower-profile form of PR is when faculty, staff, or students present at conferences or publish articles or books. Any time something goes out with the institution's name it can be considered PR. Unfortunately, PR can also be seen as damage control when something goes wrong on a campus. It is usually the responsibility of the PR staff (or person) to initially handle the media requests.

Sales promotion is the use of any incentive to induce consumers to buy a particular brand or to encourage the sales force to aggressively sell it (Shimp, 2000). We see this on television and other mass-media tools pushing "zero percent financing," "no interest for a year," "no money down," etc. Similarly, our newspapers and direct mail will often carry coupons for 50 cents off or a "buy one get one free" incentive. Within higher education we are not above such practices. Many institutions practice some form of tuition discounting (see Chapter 4) or waiving of the application fee, attempting to entice greater enrollments. When done effectively, sales promotion may change the students' perceptions of the value of the education they are receiving.

Sponsorship marketing has been around for quite some time, but previously many people classified it as PR. Some of the more notable sponsorships are the "FedEx Orange Bowl," the "Tostitos Fiesta Bowl," and of course the naming rights for scoreboards or on sports venues throughout the world. It is rare that higher education institutions engage in sponsorships of commercial ventures. However, it is worth noting that one for-profit institution went so far as to purchase the naming rights to a professional football stadium. Typically, colleges and universities will lend their names and financial support to charitable causes such as local golf outings to raise money for a local hospital or college department, or sponsorship of a National Public Radio or Public Broadcasting System program and in some instances the entire station. These types of sponsorships put the institution's name in front of potential students and potential donors while connecting it to a worthy cause. Institutions must be careful with promotions so they do not appear to be acts of desperation on their part.

Integrated marketing communications combine all of the promotional tools into one comprehensive, unified promotional strategy. The idea behind this promotional mix is to use these promotional tools and additional company resources to create a positive brand image and to meet the strategic marketing and promotional goals of the organization (Nickels et al., 2008). Institutions typically meet these goals through the use of an effective promotional campaign. Nickels et al. go on to discuss the six steps in establishing a promotional campaign. They believe that in order to be effective an organization must:

1. Identify the target market
2. Determine the objectives – goals are clear and measurable
3. Determine the promotional budget
4. Develop a unifying message
5. Implement the plan
6. Evaluate the effectiveness (p. 432)

Not only does the overall effectiveness of the campaign need to be evaluated but every individual tool's use should also be evaluated. One way to do this is to look at the actual results and compare those to the results projected prior to initiating the campaign. For example, if the institution is trying to increase enrollment from a particular region of the state or country, how successful was it compared to what was projected? If the development office decides to launch a new campaign or is trying to increase donations to the annual fund, it will need to compare the actual proceeds with the projected. This type of evaluation can provide useful data and can also help administrators with making realistic projections.

CONSUMER BEHAVIOR

While we believe that our students are co-producers and not customers, there is much we can glean from the consumer behavior literature that can assist us in making our institution the institution of choice. As defined by Sheth (2000), "consumer behavior is the mental and physical activities undertaken by household and business customers that result in decisions and actions to pay for, purchase, and use products" (p. 138). Prior to arriving on campuses students and their parents make decisions and take actions with regard to enrollment. They decide which institution to attend, which major to declare, whether to live on campus or commute, which financial aid to accept, and which payment method or plan to use. These decisions are based on their perceptions of their alternatives and as Sheth points out, "the objective reality of a product matters little; what matters is the consumer's perception of a product [service] or a brand" (p. 142). As you try to influence the perceptions of your institution, you must understand what helps shape those perceptions. Sheth (2000) suggests that perceptions are predicated on three factors: stimulus characteristics, context, and consumer characteristics (p. 144), which are described below.

Stimulus characteristics revolve around the nature of the information from the surrounding environments, which is subdivided into two distinct areas: sensory characteristics and informational characteristics. *Sensory* characteristics are anything that stimulates one or more of the five senses, such as the use of texts sent to prospective students. When potential students make a campus visit, what sights, sounds, and smells do they encounter? If your buildings and grounds are in a state of disrepair, what message is being sent? The other stimulus, *informational characteristics*, are messages (intended and unintended) conveyed in your promotional efforts. This information gives prospective students the opportunity to interpret your brand image and to determine what your institution is about and how they might fit on your campus. The photos and images you present on your promotional materials should reflect the institutional culture and be directed toward the needs and to some extent the wants of your target market.

Context is the setting in which the information is received and plays a role in every interaction with the potential students. This includes texting, the institutional web site, personal visits by admissions personnel, and phone calls by current students. If you send representatives to high schools and college fairs, what kind of image do they present to your prospective students? Are they friendly, knowledgeable, and articulate? The institutional location—an urban, suburban, or rural campus—also plays a role in how it is perceived by these prospects. The aura of your campus plays an important part in how your campus is perceived. It is also important to note that the staff and faculty who interact with potential students play a vital role in their perception of your institution. If a prospect's first encounter is a less-than-friendly person there is a good chance you will lose that particular individual. Proper training of institutional representatives is the key to their success. Another aspect of the context includes external factors such as the state of the economy (higher education is typically counter-cyclical, so we tend to see enrollment increases during downturns), which can influence how prospective students and their families perceive institutional affordability.

Consumer characteristics include the personal knowledge and experiences of the potential students, including their prior experience with higher education: *Can we afford this institution? Is it too far from (or close to) home? Do I feel like I belong? Does it have my intended major?* If the students are first-generation, you will need to understand that their parents may not be able to assist in narrowing the alternatives. Additionally, parents who have attended college may make assumptions that while true when they were in school do not apply today.

Understanding how potential and current students perceive your institution plays an important role in developing an institutional marketing strategy. If you know how you are perceived, you will be in a better position to effectively recruit your target market. If you are interested in expanding your market you will have an idea as to how best to approach your new target markets. If you wish to change an institutional perception you will need to look at changing promotional materials and also at changing the institutional culture and or brand image.

CUSTOMER SERVICE IN HIGHER EDUCATION

The customer services movement of the 1970s and 1980s has had a profound impact on higher education. Whether this is considered a positive force for change, or a negative influence on the academy, is not being debated at this time. We believe the student-as-customer metaphor has been utilized to one degree or another in higher education for quite some time.

In looking at many of the "frontline" or "first person" positions within higher education it is apparent that good customer service skills are important for the incumbent personnel. A smiling face and helpful personality can go a long way in reassuring a disenchanted student. After all, for the most part good customer service skills are not much more than being polite, helpful, and respectful. When students need assistance they do not need the extra aggravation of a rude faculty or staff member. Additionally, ignorance is not an excuse to be unprofessional. As noted in Chapter 2, higher education institutions may have large bureaucratic structures in which the division of labor may or may not make sense to the students. Therefore, while you may not know the correct answer or appropriate office for the referral, you can still be polite and helpful by pointing the student in the direction where her or his question can be properly addressed.

As with most things in life, anything taken to the extreme is not necessarily good and more often than not will have a negative impact. As Michael put it (2005, p. 3), "Universities are in a knowledge industry and their cardinal mission is achieving excellence. Unfortunately, excellence does not lend itself to quick fixes, to convenience, to drive-by dispensation, crass commercialization, and to unbridled customer satisfaction." Good customer service in higher education must not equate to giving students everything they want, but rather should focus on making sure they have what they need to be successful at their respective institutions. The "customer knows best" mentality encourages administrators, faculty, and staff to go against written policies or procedures. For example, a student complains about a grade or a parent calls to request a room change, or any of the hundreds of examples one can recall, and the "powers-that-be" make a decision that is contrary to policy to "please the customer" sitting in front of him or her. This may appear to be serving the customer, but in actuality these decisions ultimately undermine the authority of subordinates and undercut the policies and procedures currently in place. If a policy needs adjustment then so be it, but do not re-write policy because you want to provide "good customer service" to the student sitting in front of you at that moment. The customer is not always right, and in higher education it is the exception and should not be the rule. Good customer service means treating students with respect and treating students fairly.

Satisfaction

Hoffman (2000) points out that as a central theme of the marketing concept, customer satisfaction should not be absent from any service organization. Institutions of higher education must also be concerned with student satisfaction by proactively defining what it means and finding ways to appropriately measure it. Satisfaction results are more important for internal use than for external comparisons. Every institution is unique in the way in which its classes are delivered and its services are provided. Therefore, off-the-shelf forms may be of some limited value but rarely do those instruments measure what your institution is most concerned about. Waiting for students to complain in order to identify problems within the institution or gauging institutional progress in achieving student satisfaction based on the number of complaints is naïve. Students will not necessarily complain to the source of the problem but instead will voice their dissatisfaction through social media or with their feet. They may drop out or transfer, and tell other students and potential students exactly how they were mistreated by the institution (Hoffman, 2000, p. 313). It is common knowledge in the marketing area that negative news travels much faster than positive news.

By utilizing the information obtained from the "home grown" satisfaction surveys or assessments, each institution can develop plans or implement programs that address student needs. Students are often willing to pay more and stay with an institution that meets their needs than to take the risk associated with moving to a lower-priced offering. Institutions that pride themselves on their student satisfaction efforts generally provide better environments in which to work, and therefore have increased their chances to attract the best and brightest employees (Hoffman, 2000, p. 314) and students.

Ultimately, on college and university campuses good customer service is achieved through the effective management of student perceptions and experiences—student satisfaction can be increased either by lowering expectations or by enhancing perceptions. In which direction does your institution intend to head?

SERVICESCAPE

The term "servicescape" refers to the nonliving physical evidence that is used to create the service environment, including ambient conditions (room temperature, air quality, noise level, music, orders); space function (layout, equipment, furnishings); and signs, symbols, and artifacts (signage, personal artifacts, style, and décor) (Hoffman, 2000). As you look around your respective campuses, how would you describe the servicescape? How would your students describe it? If there are gaps in these two descriptions, how can they be resolved?

According to Strange and Banning (2001), the physical environment of a campus has a definite impact on students' decisions to attend one institution over another, and it is also important in their willingness to stay. The physical environment communicates intentionally and unintentionally. Considering the outdoor environment, Eckert (2012) found students placed high importance on campus cleanliness, the appearance of a "planned design," maintenance, lighting, and walkways when evaluating their campus environments. Other elements that were important included trees, green space, landscaping, parking, trash and recycling containers, signage, building exteriors, benches and other seating, outdoor meeting spaces, and water features. The physical environment is an area in which actions speak louder than words. If there is visible evidence of deferred maintenance, if the grounds are not clean and well groomed, if the furnishings are old and in disrepair, what messages are being sent to current and prospective students? Take a closer look at your campus' physical environment; what messages are being sent to your students and visitors, intended and unintended?

Relationship Marketing

Relationship marketing connects directly with retention efforts on our campuses; its "goal is to keep individual [students] overtime by offering them new products [or services] that exactly meet their requirements" (Hoffman, 2000, p. 365). For student retention efforts this refers to focusing the institution's marketing efforts toward the existing student population, intent on developing long-term relationships with those current students (Hoffman, p. 318), thereby encouraging them to persist through graduation. When one takes a closer look at the National Survey of Student Engagement, used by several hundred institutions annually, much of what you will find revolves around the concept of relationships and indirectly relationship marketing.

The key behind relationship marketing is building trust between the student and the institution and its employees. Customizing Hoffman's (2000) approach to fit higher education, *trust* can be defined as an individual's belief in the honesty, integrity, and reliability of another person. In the service environment, three major components of trust are: (1) the institution's expertise, (2) the institution's reliability, and (3) the institution's concern for the student.

Hoffman (2000) also suggests six strategies for building trust (adapted for higher education institutions):

1. Protect confidential information – the Family Educational Rights for Protection Act helps higher education institutions by requiring them to keep student information confidential. Additionally, institutions should refrain from selling directory information such as student names and contact information to companies, as this violates their trust.
2. Refrain from making disparaging remarks about other students and competitors – friendly rivalries should be just that, friendly. If you constantly put down your competitors to your students you will be undermining their trust. Institutional pride is a great characteristic and it assists in the development of institutional culture. So instead, continue to promote your institution and its successes but not at the expense of others.
3. Telling the student the truth even when it hurts – if you do not have the desired major or if the student needs to take remedial courses, explain it to the student and present them with several options, including attending another institution (even if it is considered a competitor).
4. Providing the student with full information – explain the pros and cons to students and their parents so they can make the best decision for their respective needs.
5. Being dependable, courteous, and considerate with all students – this means everyone at the institution, from the president on down the line. When people do not know the answer they need to make the appropriate referral rather than giving it their best guess. Frontline staff need to be courteous and respectful of the students and campus visitors.

6. Being actively involved in community affairs – town–gown relationships are important for almost every institution of higher education. Institutions need to be good corporate citizens and provide leadership in the community when appropriate. Poor relations with the local community hurt everyone (p. 319).

WHO IS RESPONSIBLE FOR MARKETING?

While there are several offices whose main responsibility is to market the institution, the simple answer to this question is: everyone employed at the institution is responsible for marketing the institution. As noted above, word of mouth is one of the more effective marketing tools that can be employed by an institution. Every person working at an institution communicates with potential students on a daily basis. If the employees communicate a favorable image, there is greater likelihood that greater interest in the institution will accrue, as will institutional *goodwill*. The offices and departments listed below are examples of how different areas within an institution help with its marketing efforts.

Admissions

Admissions counselors recruit students (through personal selling) to their respective institutions. The admissions office is usually the largest source of direct mail provided by the institution and is one of the top offices in the use of telephone solicitations. This office often sets the tone for further interactions by other units on the campus.

University Communications (Marketing)

This office or a similar one is usually responsible for the "big picture" aspects of the institutional marketing and will be the coordinating group on campus ensuring that the messages being communicated are consistent and coherent. An institution of higher education can ill afford inarticulate or incoherent messages to the general public.

Development

Although they are organized to raise money for the institution, one of the most important aspects of development personnel's activities is promoting the institution, and promotion is one of the most important marketing tools available to an institution. Institutions that struggle with brand image will also have difficulty in fundraising. It is hard to convince someone to donate money when the person asking cannot clearly and coherently articulate the cause.

Alumni Affairs

Institutions must consider what perceptions these graduates had while they were students, and they must also be cognizant to what has transpired at the institution since these students graduated. Every institution has a story to tell, and it must begin telling that story as early as possible, which is why we are seeing "student chapters" of the alumni association. If we can convince them how great we are while they are students, it is much easier to keep them involved once they leave the campus.

Student Affairs

The Student Affairs division consists of several departments, each with its own set of stakeholders. Each department plays a role in the marketing efforts of the institution, some internal and some external. Housing, Residential Life, and Recreation Services are three of the most visible Student Affairs offices with regard to their marketing efforts (books and newsletters). Additionally, Student Affairs divisions sponsor activities such as alternative spring breaks, concerts, community service projects, and nationally known speakers open to the public.

Academic Programs and Colleges

Academic programs contribute to the marketing efforts of the institution in more ways than departmental brochures or course offerings. Student internships, faculty consulting, staff volunteer time, and class projects are a few of the many ways in which the academic departments participate.

Human Resources

The job search process at any institution involves advertising the position to a broad audience of potential applicants. This advertising is not promoting the position only, but rather is promoting the entire institution. When your institution places a vacancy announcement in the *Chronicle of Higher Education* or any other national media, it is representing the entire institution and needs to be reflective of the mission and culture of said institution.

CONCLUDING COMMENTS

Higher education is in a "trust" market in which the potential students must rely on the institutions to be honest and forthcoming in their marketing efforts. If institutions mislead potential students into believing they will be getting something different than what they will actually receive, this does neither party any good. The student will drop out or transfer and the institution will have missed an opportunity. We recall hearing a college dean, addressing an audience of faculty and staff, tell this group that "with over 250 majors at this institution we should be able to find something for every student." This implies that the students actually want what is being offered or will settle for something less than what is desired. Many students start at one institution and finish their academic career at another; there is absolutely nothing wrong with students transferring. In fact, if we market ourselves appropriately, we should be happy to assist any student in the transfer process. If students are tricked or coerced into staying at an institution and graduating with a degree they did not really want, what do you think is the likelihood that that they will speak favorably about that particular institution? We would much rather have a satisfied dropout or transfer than a disgruntled alum. After all, word of mouth is one of the most powerful advertising modes there is, and it does not cost a dime.

When the economy takes a downward turn, you cannot afford to cut your marketing efforts. Remember: marketing is your access to potential students and donors. If you reduce your marketing efforts, you will reduce your visibility and risk losing students and donors to competing institutions. A word of caution: it is important that the mission of the institution drives the marketing strategy and not the other way around. In tough economic times, it becomes tempting for an institution to compromise its mission by altering the standards for admission as well as retention. If prospective students have a low probability of success at the institution, do not admit them. Compromising your standards may solve some short-term problems but it will inevitably create other, potentially more costly, short- and long-term problems for the institution. Similarly, if current students are not performing up to the academic (or disciplinary) standards set forth, do not hesitate to dismiss them. Poorly performing students tend to have a negative impact on the larger community and they tend to lower the reputation of the institution. If their grades are too low, their bills remain unpaid, they violate the codes of conduct, they treat faculty and staff poorly, etc., the institution is going to be better off without them. Similarly, if faculty and staff are not happy at the institution or do not respect the institution, it may be in their best interest as well as the institution's for them to seek employment where the fit is tighter. As an employee you should be proud of the institution at which you work. If you are embarrassed to mention it by name, it is time for you to leave. Employees are an integral part of the marketing of the institution and they need to be confident in representing it fairly to potential students and their parents as well as potential donors. Marketing truly is everyone's job.

REFLECTIVE QUESTIONS

1. What institutions are competitors for your institution, and why?
2. Can you describe the Four Cs and how they apply to your institution? Your department/unit?
3. Analyze your institutional marketing, branding, and internal marketing. What is being communicated? How does this differ by intended audience?
4. Who (which offices) on your campus is/are held accountable for marketing?
5. Higher education is a trust market. How do institutions recover from a breach in trust (scandal)?

PART 4

Perspectives on the Future

CHAPTER 11

Fundraising

American higher education has always relied on the generosity of benefactors, from Harvard's beginnings in 1636 through the twenty-first century's challenges (Brittingham & Pezullo, 1990). Colleges and universities of all types employ individuals tasked with the responsibility of connecting and communicating with alumni and other individuals to obtain gifts for the institution (Council for Advancement and Support of Education (CASE), 2018; Drezner & Huehls, 2015; Proper & Caboni, 2014). The work of institutional advancement personnel (also known as development) is ever more important as institutions struggle to survive in an increasingly complex and competitive environment (Gasman & Drezner, 2008). Fundraising dollars, note Drezner and Huehls (2015), "provide support for nearly every aspect of our institutions, from keeping the lights on, to constructing new buildings, to supporting students, to allowing new lines of research" (p. 104). The Council for Aid to Education (CAE; 2018) reported colleges and universities raised 43.6 *billion* dollars in 2017—the highest number recorded since 1957 and a 6.3 percent increase from the previous year.

Philanthropy, the practice of supporting causes by individuals or organizations, has a long history. Evidence of philanthropy dates back to 4000 BC in Egypt's Book of the Dead, which commended altruists for giving food and drink to the needy (Brittingham & Pezullo, 1990). The word "philanthropy" refers to more than just the giving of money—it refers to any type of resource shared by an individual or group of individuals (time, services, physical property, etc.) to benefit the public (Walton & Gasman, 2008). Administrators within colleges and universities often see fundraising as critical but do not understand how it works (Cook, 2008a). This chapter will provide a brief history of philanthropy, provide an overview of important concepts and roles, outline the fundraising process, and discuss trends seen in higher education. Most importantly, this chapter will illustrate why any discomfort with the idea of engaging in fundraising is counter-productive to advancing the cause of higher education.

HISTORY OF FUNDRAISING IN AMERICAN HIGHER EDUCATION

Higher education in the United States may have been informed by the Oxford model, but developed a distinctive character from its inception. It is impossible to truly understand the history of American higher education without also understanding the impact of philanthropy on its emergence and evolution (Backer & Haddad, 2016; Walton & Gasman, 2008). Early Americans placed a high value on supporting their emerging colleges, seeing it as more than charity—they saw it as investment that could bring about a better future (Brittingham & Pezzullo, 1990). The colonists valued a localized approach to education and saw institutions as an important component to local identity. As such, early institutions of higher education got their start through important donations of land, books, and supplies (candles and blankets)—in addition to funds to pay faculty and support operations (Geiger, 2008; Walton, 2008). Most of the early donations of money were considered unrestricted, meaning they could be used as the institution saw fit (Dodge, 2016). As education evolved and fortunes grew, private donations by individuals continued to sustain education in new, more specific ways: advancing research, providing support for specific disciplines, and providing access through scholarships (Walton, 2008). Philanthropy has had a large, diversifying impact on the types of colleges and universities in the United States (Drezner, 2011).

Organizations known as *foundations* emerged in the late nineteenth century—these organizations sought to support important social and policy issues in line with their ideology. Many early foundations chose to support colleges and universities, as they saw their causes were aligned (Backer & Haddad, 2016; Karl & Katz, 2008). Andrew Carnegie, a steel magnate of the late nineteenth century, was among the first of the industrialists to begin pouring money into organizations such as colleges and universities to achieve mutually-agreed-upon aims through his Carnegie Foundation for the Advancement of Teaching (Carnegie Foundation, 2018; Geiger, 2008; Karl & Katz, 2008). Initially, foundations were met with criticism for taking too active a role in the directions pursued by postsecondary institutions. But as the support became more and more critical to ongoing operations in the mid-twentieth century, the criticism died down (Karl & Katz, 2008). The funds provided by foundations (and individuals) in the early twentieth century provided for facilities, research centers, and specific support to cutting-edge disciplines and professional programs (Cash, 2008; Dodge, 2016). In the present day, colleges and universities rely on foundations as a major form of support, as they are capable of giving at levels above most, if not all, alumni, for better or worse (Clevenger & MacGregor, 2016).

Private institutions of higher education had been actively raising money from friends and foundations from their early days; Brown, Colgate, Colby College, Harvard, Rutgers, Tufts, and Yale are named after individuals and families to honor their important early contributions (Brittingham & Pezzullo, 1990). Public and non-elite private four-year institutions ventured into fundraising in the early and mid-twentieth century. Public institutions largely modeled their efforts after their private colleges and universities, who had greater experience in this area (Oliver, 2008). Over time, sophistication in fundraising efforts increased and dedicated personnel were hired to better solicit a greater variety of gifts from individuals and foundations (Drezner, 2011). Public colleges and universities at all levels face the additional hurdle of motivating donors to give when they are perceived to be state-supported (Gardner, 2018).

Regional public institutions (Gardner, 2018) and two-year institutions (Akin, 2008) began their fundraising efforts well after the elite private and flagship public institutions. As a consequence, these institutions are at a distinct disadvantage as they establish a giving culture (Drezner, 2011; Gardner, 2018). Public community colleges largely did not engage in fundraising activities until the 1970s (Akin, 2008). For both two- and four-year institutions, fundraising has become critical for institutional survival as state and local support declines (Chan, 2016; Gardner, 2018). Community colleges have an especially difficult task, as their alumni base is very different than baccalaureate and graduate institutions (Akin, 2008). Community colleges and urban regional four-year institutions have been successful in raising *friends* (interested non-alumni individual donors) and engaging with foundations and area organizations to meet their goals (Akin, 2008).

CONCEPTS, ROLES, DEFINITIONS

Development and *advancement* are terms used to describe the activities associated with fundraising; the term "development" was coined in the 1920s at Northwestern University. Fundraising and marketing are similar disciplines—both are focused on developing relationships by establishing an understanding of client needs and matching them (Lindahl, 2010). They were originally conducted by outside firms, before institutions began hiring their own staff to manage affairs (Oliver, 2008). The term "advancement" was introduced later, to be more descriptive and specific to higher education (Chan, 2016). Organizations soliciting gifts must be appropriately organized, registered, and approved at the federal, state, and local levels, depending on where they operate. The success of a fundraising operation, according to Brittingham and Pezzullo (1990) tends to rest on three factors: fundraising capacity (access to donors, the maximum the institution could raise from that pool of donors, institutional prestige and current success, and the institution's ability to pursue donations), history (culture of giving, alumni engagement and norms, actual practice with fundraising), and effort (the staff time and resources devoted to fundraising, institutional prioritization of fundraising).

Donors are individuals, foundations, and, to some degree, corporations that choose to provide resources (money, time, services, and property of various types) to organizations. This is an action known as *philanthropy*. Donors (also known as *benefactors*) care about improving the world, and typically do so by supporting causes or activities that align with their world view (Whillans, 2016). Donors' motivations to provide support have been studied by many authors, and are a mix of internal and external factors (Lindahl, 2010). Drezner and Huehls (2015) and Whillans (2016) outline a mix of altruistic and self-interested motives, noting the rarity of a donor wishing to provide resources without benefit being returned through one or more of the following: recognition, tax implications, gaining entrée to like-minded and/or powerful individuals who also contribute, or using the experience to model appropriate philanthropic behavior to others. The source of motivation for a given donor has important implications for the type of appeal that will work best.

Donors *must* believe in and agree with the mission in order to be truly compelled to give; often they see themselves as co-producers of the program or service being supported, and able to bring about significant change (Cook, 2008a).

Schervish (2008) summarized twelve years of research with two points about donor motivations: first, regardless of wealth, the motivation to give is the same; second, wealthy donors intend to "shape, rather than merely support a charitable cause" (p. 747). Gifts are made at all income levels—but wealthier donors tend to have higher expectations regarding both the impact their gifts will make and the proof of that impact provided in return (Lindahl, 2012; Schervish, 2008).

Institutional leadership matters greatly to donors at all levels of wealth. Cook (2008a) notes "Leaders . . . set the tone, style and focus . . . through their attitudes, values, and decisions, as well as personal involvement and time" (p. 744). Clevenger (2016) agrees, indicating that the emphasis senior leaders put on fundraising has a vast impact on the success of fundraising work. Gifts to colleges and universities come from alumni, friends, corporations, foundations, and other sources. The gifts provided can be utilized on current operations and for capital purposes, depending on the wishes of the donor. A variety of research on donor behavior has been conducted, but is outside of the scope of this chapter.

The donor is always in a position of power when making a contribution, but the extent of the power difference varies based on the potential impact of the gift (Ostrander & Schervish, 2008). Donors can and do approach organizations to initiate relationships, but they also may work with colleagues, peers, and friends to raise a pool of resources and simply present it to an organization. Notable examples of this are workplace donation drives or requesting donations for an outside organization. One example of this is the recent Ice Bucket Challenge for the ALS Association (to fight Lou Gehrig's Disease, or amyotrophic lateral sclerosis). Whillans (2016) notes the runaway success of the Ice Bucket Challenge campaign—the ALS Association gained 739,000 new donors who gave $41.8 million—up from $19.4 million raised in the previous year. That said, it is important to realize that this is not a normal outcome of a fundraising initiative.

Donors (individuals, foundations, and corporations) can be very tricky to work with: they can be temperamental or drag their feet, they can change their minds, and they may ask for special favors or seek too much involvement in the affairs of the institution (Cook, 2008b). Lindahl (2010) notes the many ways organizations can lose donors. The donor perceptions of the organization are crucial: if an organization is perceived as being irresponsible, having a poor image, misusing funds, or simply taking actions a donor disagrees with, they may withdraw their support. Organizations can also bungle relationships with donors just like people do: providing a garbled or ineffective case for support, not providing enough information, and poor or haphazard communication are common ways to lose donors. Strong fundraisers develop a clear understanding of their donors, and work to match interests carefully.

Donors are much more likely to support organizations with which they have strong ties, which explains why alumni giving is a major focus of most institutions of higher education (Dodge, 2016; Drezner, 2011; Schervish, 2008). Alumni provided 26 percent of the total donations given to colleges and universities in 2017, but only 10 percent of undergraduate alumni solicited actually provided donations (CAE, 2018). The socialization process for alumni giving is more effective if it begins when they are students; undergraduates engaged in alumni or fundraising activities as students are more likely to become donors (Drezner, 2011). Alumni giving rates are a component of many popular media college-ranking methodologies (Dodge, 2016; Shafer, 2016). Dodge (2016) notes that alumni *do* appear to respond to the perception of being able to help the institution in a time of need, which supported the notion of social exchange theory—the idea of "giving back." Dodge also found giving rates were correlated with certain institutional characteristics: selectivity, average student debt, demographic profile, control (public or private), value of the endowment, and satisfaction with the undergraduate experience. Alumni participation rates in 2017 were generally higher at private institutions than public institutions of the same level (CAE, 2018).

Despite ever-increasing numbers of alumni, the alumni-giving participation rate has declined since 1992, having climbed in fits and starts from 1977 (~16 percent) to approximately 19 percent in 1992, down to around 8 percent in 2016 and 2017 (CAE, 2018). In short, it is complicated—and it is hard to study broadly. Figure 11.1 presents the sources of 2017 donations from the CAE's Voluntary Support of Education (VSE) survey.

Foundations are organizations that make grant awards to organizations to advance important initiatives (Backer & Haddad, 2016; Karl & Katz, 2008). Foundations are not-for-profit organizations that exist to take in money and distribute it to other organizations they deem worthy of supporting—and they are a very popular form of tax avoidance in the United States (Clevenger & MacGregor, 2016; Shafer, 2016). In short, anyone can form a foundation and funnel excess income into that organization (thereby avoiding taxes on personal or business income). Donations to foundations are tax-deductible, and serve as a holding pen for charitable giving—foundations are required by law to disburse a set percentage of their earnings from investments on an annual basis.

Foundations can be described as donors, as they make a decision to provide funds as a body much like an individual would—but the decision is likely more complex

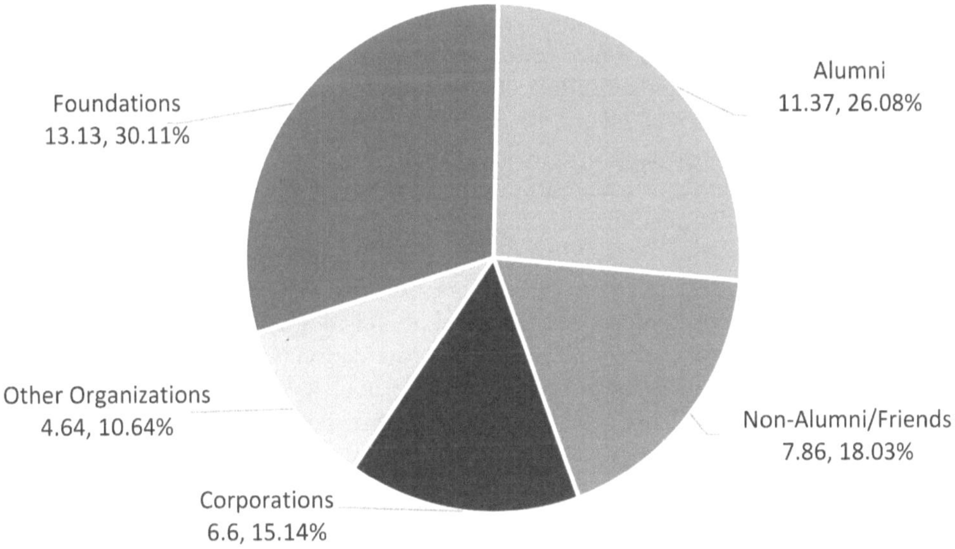

Figure 11.1 Voluntary Support Billions (2017)

(Clevenger & MacGregor, 2016). Many foundations have the capacity to make massive gifts and engage in what is known as "strategic philanthropy" (Backer & Haddad, 2016, p. 30). Put simply, strategic philanthropy is providing resources to organizations that align with the foundation's ideology. Backer and Haddad (2016) note the power of foundations today, and describe them as capable of influencing institutional decision-making processes related to "faculty hires, course offerings, pedagogy and academic programs" (p. 30) in addition to governance structures. The process of pursuing and accepting gifts or grants from foundations often requires complex paperwork (Lindahl, 2010).

The Internal Revenue Service defines four types of foundations in the United States: independent (controlled by a family or an individual), corporate (the foundation arm of a corporation), community (held by the public to support area-based needs), and operating. Operating foundations are founded *by* a recipient organization to channel money for its own interests—many public colleges and universities use these to manage their donations and channel them into the college or university itself (Goldstein, 2012; Lindahl, 2010). Chan (2016) noted there are approximately 72,000 foundations in the United States, many of which are either associated with higher education institutions or foundations that give to higher education institutions, such as the Bill & Melinda Gates Foundation, the Alfred P. Sloan Foundation, and the Andrew W. Mellon Foundation, which supports digital access to research. Like individual donors, foundations can be tricky to work with (Lindahl, 2010).

Corporations are profit-seeking entities owned by shareholders (public or private). Corporate giving to higher education has a relatively short history—prior to 1935 there was little involvement. Brittingham and Pezzullo (1990) noted the sharp increase of giving between 1940 and 1988: from $38 million annually to $1.85 billion annually. Philanthropy has many benefits for corporations, visibility and tax avoidance primary among them. Corporations, like individuals, are motivated both by altruism and self-interest to donate: donations enable corporations to be perceived more positively, engage with other organizations, influence the communities in which they operate, and gain recognition (Lindahl, 2010). Corporations give cash directly to organizations, but may also give in-kind goods or services. Some corporations choose to match the contributions of their employees (Brittingham & Pezzullo, 1990). The process of pursuing and accepting gifts from corporations is quite simple when compared to gifts or grants from foundations (Lindahl, 2010).

Today, it is common to see spaces on campus branded with corporate sponsorships, although this is a relatively recent practice (Brittingham & Pezzullo, 1990). Corporations may give directly to colleges and universities, or elect to make their gifts by channeling their money through an affiliated foundation (Clevenger & MacGregor, 2016). This is not universally positive; the deep pockets of corporations and their support of projects that align with their interests can raise ethical concerns. Basken (2018) notes that federal support of university research dropped 11 percent between 2011 and 2016, with corporate support of university research increasing 26 percent between 2011 and 2016. Academic partnerships with drug manufacturers for research on health-related issues have particularly tricky implications, as the drug manufacturers have a vested interest in the outcomes of the studies being sponsored.

Fundraisers (also known as development or advancement officers) are personnel who work for colleges and universities to connect with alumni and other important contacts (Whillan, 2016). Fundraisers have two clients: the institution for whom they work and their prospective donors. Individuals who raise money for institutions engage in a process to find, collaborate with, and gain a commitment from donors. Despite claims to the contrary by many practitioners, fundraising is a science and can be observed, measured, and analyzed (Cook, 2008a). That is not to say that learning fundraising skills is easy—fundraisers must be adept at donor cultivation behaviors, networking, and planning strategically to best use time and resources (Alphin, Lavine, Stark, & Hocker, 2016). They must also work to achieve institutional priorities with donors who may have very different interests while serving both well (Brittingham & Pezzullo, 1990). Caboni (2014) and Perlmutter (2015) articulate the importance of taking excellent care of both clients—abiding by institutional guidelines, laws, and appropriate codes of ethics.

Shafer (2016) notes a recent increased emphasis on donor development and retention. This is accomplished through proper research and cultivation, as well as stewardship (for current donors). Fundraisers must establish connections with a variety of potential donors and maintain them in order to be successful. Fundraisers do more than solicit funds: they work with donors to secure new instructional technologies (computers, library resources, classroom software and hardware), specialized equipment for programs and service areas (appliances for a culinary program, virtual reality simulators), food and spaces for events, or special-collection items for on-campus museums (B. Braydich, Principal Gifts Manager, Institutional Advancement, Kent State University, personal communication). Fundraisers can connect academic programs with experts who donate their time to host guest lectures or provide mentoring or internship opportunities for students (B. Braydich, personal communication). Institutions that are successful maintaining strong relationships with their donors will likely see additional gifts from those donors in the future.

Clevenger and MacGregor (2016) present a "toolbox" for corporate and foundation development officers, but it is quite applicable across a variety of development roles. To be successful, the authors indicate the following attributes as critical: "relational emphasis, knowledge, ability to create value propositions, political savvy, excellent communications, ethical integrity, professionalism, stewardship, powerful influence, nimbleness, and patience" (p. 272). As fundraising continues to become more and more professionalized, fundraisers are engaging in goal-setting, hosting large events, and using sophisticated systems to research, track, and communicate with prospective donors (Brittingham & Pezzullo, 1990).

A *campaign* is a meticulously planned period of high activity in fundraising, usually spanning multiple years (Drezner, 2011; Shafer, 2016). Cook (2008b) presents four campaign types: traditional, comprehensive, single-purpose, and continuing major gifts. Other experts describe campaigns using slightly different language, but the two most popular terms are "capital" and "comprehensive." A *capital* campaign refers to a focused, intense push to raise resources for campus building projects—the construction of new facilities, or the major renovation of facilities. In recent years, "comprehensive" has emerged as the most common term for campaigns, as it allows for all the previously described narrower-purpose campaigns to occur within them

(Shafer, 2016). Institutions use campaigns to raise a significant amount of money to increase assets, fund building projects, enhance the endowment, or complete special projects/research initiatives.

Today, the notion of a campaign is more marketing than reality. In recent years, campaign periods have gotten longer and longer and may seem never-ending; in a study by CASE, the median length of capital campaigns was ninety-five months (nearly eight years) (Hall, 2018; Scutari, 2018). In a campaign, the donations institutions will accept are the same: "cash, securities, gifts-in-kind, and estate gifts (planned giving)" (Shafer, 2016, p. 207). Institutions also may "reach back" and count donations from earlier periods as part of the campaign—even if the campaign was not yet announced when the donation occurred. Fundraising campaigns have multiple phases (Drezner, 2011):

- Pre-campaign (six to eighteen months) – feasibility studies conducted, often by an outside consulting firm
- Planning (three to six months) – priority-setting, goal identification, leadership identification
- Quiet phase (one to two years) – solicitation of major gifts and leading benefactors to support the campaign; all gifts received in this phase are typically counted toward the campaign goals
- Public phase (three to five years) – the public kick-off of the campaign; most institutions attempt to have 40 to 50 percent of funds raised before the public phase is announced

At the conclusion of the campaign, stock is taken of the efforts and results. Today, it is not uncommon to see the launch of a comprehensive campaign with a goal of $500 million or more. The composition of donors has also changed over time; a smaller and smaller percentage of the donors are doing the vast majority of giving (Drezner, 2011). As income inequality increases, it is estimated that 10 percent of the donors are providing 90 percent of the funds during campaign periods—and the numbers may be restricted further to a 5 percent/95 percent balance in the future.

Tax-exempt organizations are generally "nonprofit organizations that are exempt or excused from paying federal income tax under Section 501(c) of the U.S. Internal Revenue Code" (Lindahl, 2010, p. 110). Within this classification, there are twenty-seven types of tax-exempt organizations—a *charitable organization* is one of these organization types.

DONATION TYPES: ANNUAL/CURRENT, MAJOR, PLANNED, AND GRANTS

Gifts to colleges and universities can be distinguished by three elements (in addition to their source; see Figure 11.2).

Annual gifts are donated funds from alumni and friends as well as real estate, buildings, capital equipment, and services; they may also be called *current gifts* (Lenington, 1996). These are unrestricted donations given to the institution, providing maximum

Donation Types	Flexibility	Focus
• Annual/Current (< \$100,000)	• Unrestricted	• Spendable
• Major (≥ \$100,000)	• Restricted	• Capital
• Planned (Varies)	• Semiunrestricted	• Endowment
• Grants (Varies)		

Figure 11.2 Gift Types

flexibility for administrators, who determine how best to utilize them (Drezner, 2011; Goldstein, 2012). The distinguishing attribute of annual gifts is that they are used in the *current* operating budget, either by adding to current revenues or offsetting current expenses (Association of Fundraising Professionals, 2010; Schroeder, 2001). Drezner (2011) notes that some institutions have begun to allow *some* conditions to be attached to annual giving in order to motivate donors—he refers to these types of current-use gifts as "semiunrestricted" (p. 6). Private institutions have a particularly strong reliance on current gifts to operate (Goldstein, 2012). Annual gifts also tend to be unrestricted—but not always—and are generally less than \$100,000 (Cook, 2008a; Schroeder, 2001). Annual-giving donors tend to make repeat gifts. Cultivation of alumni is critical to establishing and maintaining supportive annual giving. Donors who participate in an annual giving program can be cultivated to make major or planned gifts later in the future (Drezner, 2011; Schroeder, 2001).

Major gifts are higher-value donations given by individuals, corporations, or foundations; while the threshold for calling something a *major* gift varies by institution, many authors have cited \$100,000 as the threshold, although organizational guidelines do vary (Cook, 2008a). Other terms for major gifts are "principal," "impact," and "transformational," and refer to escalating dollar figures of \$1 million or more. Executive leadership is usually involved in the cultivation, solicitation, and stewardship of major gifts. Major gifts deliver a majority of the resources colleges and universities receive from individuals, and have implications far beyond the institution's operating budget. Most major gifts are restricted—that is, designated for a specific purpose—and given by donors who expect to be treated as co-producers in institutional efforts. Donors capable of large donations are more apt to donate to cultural and educational institutions, and see their support as an investment (Cook, 2008a; Schervish, 2008). Institutions are spending more and more time cultivating major donors, as they are seen as most lucrative. Fundraising campaigns are usually spent in pursuit of major gifts, though all are welcome.

Planned gifts are a transfer of wealth from an individual or family to the institution upon their death—although there are variations that allow the institution to receive some benefit before the donor passes (Lenington, 1996). Planned gifts (also known as *bequests*) are usually restricted in nature, and go to the endowment of an institution. There are several types of planned gifts, and each has benefits and drawbacks (Drezner, 2011). Planned gifts are long-term in nature and are not without risk to the institution—the institution must manage the funds to maximize the benefit to both the benefactor and themselves. If properly set up, these gifts can add a revenue stream to the institution for years to come. As the baby boom generation ages, institutions hope that planned giving by alumni will increase. But administrators must understand that donors can change their minds at any time and withdraw or modify the gift.

Grants are financial gifts to an institution in support of a specific goal or program. Grants can come from foundations, government agencies, corporations, or individuals and will have some restrictions on how the money can be spent (Goldstein, 2012; Lenington, 1996; Weisbrod, Ballou, & Asch, 2008). For example, a research grant may agree to pay for a research assistant or to compensate the faculty member involved, or it may cover travel to conferences or other institutions, and it may also cover the purchase of special equipment or the renovation of an existing lab facility. Research grants tend to go to institutions with good track records on a given line of inquiry, and are less apt to be awarded for new or untested ideas (Brittingham & Pezzullo, 1990). Programmatic grants may include the development of new opportunities for under-represented students to participate in pre-college programs or perhaps create an initiative to encourage more undergraduate students to study science, technology, engineering, or mathematics (STEM disciplines). Regardless of the focus, granting agencies demand the institution inform them as to the results of their efforts, and may even require the institution to match some portion of the funds in order to receive the award. Research institutions spend a great deal of time and energy in pursuit of grants (Weisbrod et al., 2008).

FLEXIBILITY: UNRESTRICTED, SEMIUNRESTRICTED, AND RESTRICTED

Early gifts to higher education from benefactors were largely unrestricted, meaning they could be used as the organization saw fit to advance their mission. In present times, large unrestricted donations are fairly rare (Proper & Caboni, 2014). In the 2017 VSE survey results, "only 6.3 percent of [all] contributions reported . . . were completely unrestricted" (p. 16). At the 933 reporting institutions, 10.9 percent of the gifts for current operations were unrestricted; the remainder were restricted (CAE, 2018). This makes sense—donors with the most resources have higher expectations of seeing a specific impact and thus would be more likely to make restricted gifts. Restricted gifts, by contrast, are provided for a specific purpose, including scholarships, endowed faculty positions, research initiatives, and capital property, buildings, or renovations, among other things (Drezner, 2011; Goldstein, 2012). Most of the current gifts with restrictions in 2017 were earmarked for research (32.5 percent) and specific academic divisions (21.3 percent) at the 643 institutions that reported these data (CAE, 2018).

Donors making larger (and more often than not, restricted) donations seek "a deeper sense of involvement in the fundraising process . . . Psychologists have labeled this preference the 'martyrdom effect'" (Whillans, 2016, p. 8). Of the gifts to endowment and other capital purposes, only 3.6 percent were considered income-unrestricted, which means the income from investment earnings could be spent however the institution wished (CAE, 2018). For restricted-income endowment gifts, more than a third of funds were restricted to student financial aid/scholarships (CAE, 2018). Proper and Caboni (2014) note, "Historical research has shown that fundraising has often shaped institutional spending patterns, as institutions adjust their behavior to what donors are willing to contribute to" (p. 6). Institutions have taken notice, even allowing donors to place restrictions on annual giving (which has historically been unrestricted), such as designating a gift to a college or unit within the institution (Drezner, 2011).

FOCUS: SPENDABLE, CAPITAL, ENDOWMENT

The final major distinguishing element of a donation is how it can be used, although the distinctions have some overlap. *Spendable* donations are exactly what they sound like: monies that can be spent right away on institutional needs. Annual giving tends to be spendable, and donors can further define whether the institution can spend the donation as it sees fit (unrestricted) or if the resources should be used in a specific area (semiunrestricted). Donations for *capital* purposes are spendable, but restricted to the building, renovation, or maintenance of physical facilities or equipment. Finally, *endowment* gifts are non-spendable—funds are designated to create a pool of money that will generate revenue through capital gains and interest. In 2017, 42.3 percent of donations were earmarked for endowments (including deferred gifts), capital purposes (property, facilities, equipment), or loans. "Such expenditures cannot be used to directly offset annual expenditures" (CAE, 2018, p. 8). Endowments can be restricted to specific purposes, or unrestricted in nature (Balderston, 1995).

College and universities establish endowment accounts for a variety of specific purposes, such as scholarships, research support, and staffing; however, the overarching general purpose of an endowment account is to provide financial support for the institution (Barr & McClellan, 2011). Gifts (annual, major, and planned) can be restricted to endowments (and if the gift is large enough, can create one). The money placed into an endowment account is invested by the institution, and it is the earnings from these invested dollars (investment income or yield) that are spent by the institution (Barr & McClellan, 2011; Drezner, 2011). Endowments have been described as the "ultimate revenue good" because they sit in place and earn money for the institution, especially if they are unrestricted in nature (Weisbrod et al., 2008). Michael and Kretovics (2005) note,

> there are primarily two strategies for endowment growth: a) investment performance, that is, the extent to which institutional leaders are strategic in investing the sum available, and b) the extent to which these leaders are able to generate new monies.
>
> (p. 48)

Typically, internal policies prohibit the institution from spending the principal amount of the endowed fund (Drezner, 2011; Goldstein, 2012). Rather, the disbursements from the endowment come through the "spend rate," which is set by the managing board. Over the past few decades the standard has been 5 percent of the endowment value. Drezner (2011) observed annual gains in the stock market of approximately 10–11 percent, which leaves room for both disbursement and reinvestment.

For example, a donor wants to establish a scholarship fund for students majoring in horticulture. To do this, they donate $100,000 to the institution, and the institution invests the $100,000 while agreeing to allocate a portion of the investment income toward scholarships. The remaining income is reinvested with the original principal in hopes of growing the endowed fund. Therefore, the $100,000 investment could yield a $5,000 scholarship each year. Investment income above the $5,000 (using the standard 5 percent spend rate) level would be reinvested into the principal, helping the endowment account to grow. There are risks with relying on endowments, however: the earnings from endowment accounts are sensitive to stock market changes (Drezner, 2011; Goldstein, 2012). Endowment earnings declined during the recession beginning in 2008, but returned an average of 12.2 percent on investment during the fiscal year ending in 2017—a substantial uptick, but still not enough to make up for the expected returns *not* earned in leaner years (Wyllie, 2018).

Although giving has increased over time, the relative make-up of total donations has been fairly consistent, as demonstrated in Figure 11.3. Alumni, non-alumni individuals, and foundations provide the majority of donations, although the balance has changed:

> Since 2007, foundation support has exceeded alumni giving as a source of contribution to colleges and universities. Note that many family foundations, corporations, and other organizations can be vehicles for alumni gifts, but gifts from those entities are credited to the organization.
>
> (CAE, 2018, p. 3)

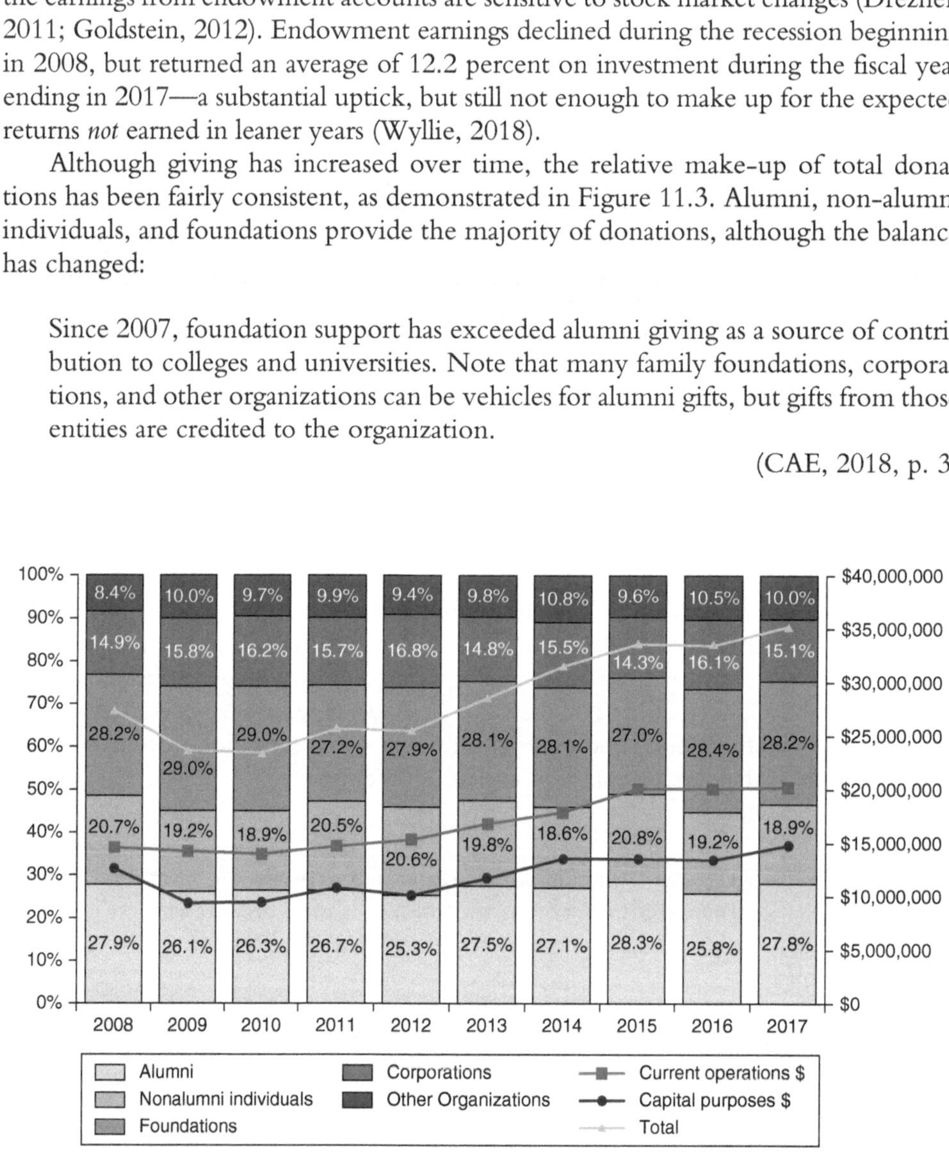

Figure 11.3 Support for Higher Education

Source: CAE, 2018.

Among the 2017 VSE survey respondents, donations funded 10.5 percent of expenditures, though that varies by institution. Within that 10.5 percent, 6.1 percent of donations were for current operations and the balance was for endowments, capital projects, and other longer-term needs. A great deal of work is happening within institutions to amass this kind of support, and the next section will provide a brief overview of the fundraising process.

FUNDRAISING AS A PROCESS

Cook (2008a) summarized several models for fundraising. Smith's "Five I's" model (*identification*, *information*, *interest*, *involvement*, and *investment*) is widely accepted for cultivating major gifts. Other models use different terminology; for example, "research," "cultivation," "solicitation," and "recognition." It is important to note that in nearly all models, solicitation (the step involving "the ask") is very small—a tiny fraction of the lengthy work involved in studying prospects, matching interests, building relationships, and trying to achieve a mutual goal. Lindahl's (2010) model of the fundraising process is both sufficiently broad and specific to higher education. The steps outlined

Step	*Description*
Research	Identify a pool of prospective donors (often referred to as prospects) and compile data on historical giving, current ability to give, and ties to programs or services at the college or university.
Planning, Goal Setting	Engage in a series of activities to formulate overall fundraising (or campaign) goals and the strategies to achieve them.
Cultivation	The process of establishing a relationship with a (potential) donor and figuring out areas of mutual interest. This can be conducted one-on-one, through events, and through passive written or online materials. It is critical to adapt the method of communication to the prospect at this stage; social media or online fundraising mechanisms may be useful here.
Solicitation	Asking for a gift directly or working through a peer-to-peer ask strategy. Peer-to-peer strategies involve asking donors to use *their* networks to generate donations. Social media and online fundraising can be particularly useful if this approach is used.
Stewardship	The act of recognizing and appreciating donors, keeping them engaged, and using their gifts well (as intended, exhibiting careful resource use, smart investing). Common reward structures include a tiered system of recognition (silver, gold, and platinum donors, for example). To be a good steward is to show donors your organization is worthy of continued support, and reporting on the use of gifts and their impact is a critical piece of stewardship.
Evaluation	The process of judging the effectiveness of activities—were goals met? Why or why not? These goals can be financial, administrative, or of other varieties.

Figure 11.4 The Fundraising Process (adapted from Lindahl, 2010)

Approach	*Description*
"Needs-Based Strategy"	Explain to donors what funds are needed for; frame the request for support as a shared responsibility around a worthy cause and worthy beneficiaries.
"Opportunity-Based Strategy"	Promote the mutual benefit of a donation by focusing on the benefit to the donor *and* the uniqueness and impact of the project, program, or service being supported; may involve special access or perks for the donor.
"Agenda-Based Strategy"	Let the donor drive the philanthropy, which potentially alters the direction of the organization; requires careful attention to the donor's interests and conditions for donating.

Figure 11.5 Donor Appeal Strategies

in Figure 11.4 are not necessarily sequential or distinct from one another, and have been adapted to identify where social media could be helpful.

Remembering that donor motivations are complex, it is helpful to consider strategies for cultivation and solicitation of a variety of donors. Every institution has a different mix of donors and channels for giving (Weisbrod et al., 2008). Ostrander and Schervish (2008) noted three strategies (Figure 11.5) would-be recipients can use to appeal for donations).

TRENDS AND ISSUES IN PHILANTHROPY

Philanthropy was not a common area of study until the 1980s (Walton & Gasman, 2008; Whillans, 2016); the notion of whether it qualified as a profession was still being discussed in 2010 (Caboni, 2014). As government support for public higher education dwindles, institutions are relying more and more on the philanthropic gifts of individuals and organizations to make up the difference. A majority of the research on fundraising is not connected to a theory, or if it is, the foundational work was conducted on a largely white and male population (Drezner, 2011). As a consequence, giving by donors in minority groups is not as well-understood as it could be; this has important implications for future fundraising as the United States becomes increasingly diverse. Merrill (2018) noted substantial shifts in donation patterns among millennial-generation donors—namely a hesitance to provide funds for endowments and instead focus on supporting experiences, such as study abroad or experience-based learning. Drezner and Huehls (2015) and others have recommended further study of fundraising, using a variety of theoretical lenses to better understand donor motivation, the timing of gifts, donor engagement, and the effect of philanthropy on mission.

Although giving is occurring at ever-increasing levels, a substantial portion of the funds donated in 2017 (28.1 percent) were given to just twenty institutions (Seltzer, 2018). This is in line with historical trends. Alphin et al. (2016) note the utility of rankings and institutional prestige (as well as successful athletic programs) in generating success in fundraising—lower-prestige institutions simply have a harder time making the case. It is increasingly clear that not all institutions are on equal footing when it comes to soliciting major gifts, and the market for major gifts is changing (Scutari, 2017). "Mega gifts" exceeding $10 million are on the rise, but alumni giving is down, says Scutari—meaning the universities must be careful in how they target prospects, as mega-gifts, by definition, are rare. Only a small number of individuals are able to give at this level, and over-reliance on mega-donors may leave prospects who are well equipped to donate at substantial levels untapped.

The acceptance of philanthropic gifts raises important concerns in shared governance environments; this concern is both current and historic (Drezner, 2011; Proper & Caboni, 2014; Oliver, 2008; Webster, Jakeman, & Swayze, 2016). During the late nineteenth and early twentieth centuries, early skeptics were asking important questions about the ethics of accepting donations from industrialists such as Andrew Carnegie, John D. Rockefeller, and others. Philanthropy, in most cases, comes with a personal agenda from the individual donor or foundation (Drezner, 2011). W. E. B. DuBois was a noted critic of black colleges' acceptance of funds from northern industrialists, stating it was a corrupt instrument of control to keep black students at a disadvantage to white students (Gasman, 2008). Indeed, many donations were intended for practical programs, as the benefactors were prone to believing a liberal arts education lacked value in the black college setting (Drezner, 2011; Gasman, 2008). DuBois believed, as others did, that accepting this money corrupted the system (as well as those who received it).

Scholars today have the same concerns as important nineteenth-century progressive leaders about relying on donations from a system that has the capacity to perpetuate, rather than to reduce, income inequality (Drezner, 2011). Washington Gladden specifically honed in on gifts' sources: donations that may have been resourced "by nefarious methods" (1895/2008, p. 21). Gladden's concerns revolved around accepting money from industrialists whose fortunes were acquired by tactics that included union-busting and unfair practices, asking, "[i]s it not plain that an institution which accepts subsidies from notoriously iniquitous sources, by this act virtually resigns the privilege of bearing testimonies against such iniquities?" (p. 22). Senior leaders must consider carefully the source of a donation; Brittingham and Pezzullo (1990) propose four reasons to refuse a gift:

1. The source of funds influences or appears to influence academic freedom or institutional independence
2. The source of the funds is compromised in the sense Washington Gladden referenced in his important 1895 essay
3. The restrictions on the gift are not compatible with the institution's mission or business processes
4. The gift would make the institution too dependent on one funding source

Colleges and universities today struggle with this on a daily basis. For evidence, one must look no further than controversial gifts, and the returning of gifts to donors who have fallen into disgrace. A recent example from Florida State University is a useful illustration. In the mid-2000s, Florida State accepted a multi-million-dollar gift from the Charles G. Koch Foundation (and a corporate partner) for its economics department (Backer & Haddad, 2016). As a condition of the gift, the Koch

Foundation demanded deep influence over the faculty hiring process and decisions (essentially having veto power on candidates), and provided funds to start two new undergraduate degree programs that aligned with the libertarian ideals of the organization. After the gift was accepted, faculty from other areas of the institution raised alarms about the Koch Foundation's terms and their impact on institutional autonomy and academic freedom. In the end, an ad hoc panel issued a report, leading to changes to institutional policy related to conditions made by donors on gifts—but the gift was not returned. The donor was simply asked to honor a new agreement, which reduced its day-to-day influence on the faculty and programs.

The influence of donations on institutional direction can be of major concern, even if not as overt in the Florida State case. Webster et al. (2016) presented a less controversial example by interviewing key personnel at a private liberal arts and science college that derived nearly all of its income from tuition and endowment income along with philanthropic support. The authors' conversations revealed that philanthropic support was essentially the elephant in the room during strategic planning discussions. The process itself was motivated in part by being able to showcase the institution's plans to donors, and was infused with questions about how the institution's plans would be perceived by donors. It is hard to imagine decisions *not* being influenced by current and prospective donors given the level of attention paid to the donor perspective in this case. Sometimes the focus of a particular gift does *all* of the communicating. The University of Oregon faced internal backlash for the acceptance of a $100 million gift from Phil Knight of Nike which was earmarked entirely for athletics, not academic purposes (Proper & Caboni, 2014). Fundraisers and leadership can attempt, but ultimately do not control, the intentions of donors, which can influence institutional direction or emphasis.

At times, institutions must respond to public pressure to return gifts (Weisbrod et al., 2008). In 2016, Ohio University announced it would return a 2007 donation of $500,000 from Roger Ailes, the former Fox News magnate (Huckabee, 2016). The decision was made in the wake of Ailes being accused of sexual harassment by more than twenty women and the settlement of a sexual harassment case (to the tune of $20 million). Ohio University also removed Ailes' name from a campus classroom facility in its Scripps College of Communication.

Violations of the law are not the only reason for cutting ties with donors. In 2018, Purdue University, the University of Louisville, and the University of Kentucky all elected to remove the name of John Schnatter, the founder and former chair of Papa John's, a national pizza chain, from their facilities in the wake of a public relations scandal involving his use of a racial slur (Berrett, 2018; Kirsch, 2018). In addition to removing his name, Purdue University also returned his $8 million gift. Conversely, Ball State University elected not to distance itself from Schnatter, a donor and alumnus who endowed their John H. Schnatter Institute for Entrepreneurship and Free Enterprise. In a statement to the campus community, the Ball State Board of Trustees chair stated, "Higher education plays a unique role in the support of free speech and the exchange of ideas that lead to better understanding. In that pursuit, it does not mandate perfection" (Ball State, 2018, para. 2).

Senior leaders are charged with more than determining the acceptance (and return) of gifts. Senior leaders are expected to be actively engaged in fundraising because they are of the greatest interest to donors. Their impact on stewardship efforts cannot be understated. Today, college and university presidents are being evaluated on their fundraising prowess. The size of an institutional endowment, or at least its growth, is considered to be a reflection of its leadership. Recently, presidential contracts have begun to include fundraising goals (with bonuses associated). As fundraising becomes increasingly important, more pressure will be placed on other senior and mid-level administrators to raise additional monies. Senior leaders set the agenda of the institution, execute major projects, and can speak to current projects (Clevenger, 2016; Drezner & Huehls, 2015). While the estimates vary, contemporary scholars have estimated college or university presidents spend between 40 and 80 percent of their time on fundraising, with the higher end of the range signifying comprehensive campaign work (Buller, 2015; Cook, 2008b).

Drezner and Huehls (2015) note that boards of trustees (sometimes called boards of directors) often have a major role in fundraising through:

1. Their selection and continued employment of the president
2. By setting a strong and clear institutional path forward
3. Through encouraging potential donors
4. By being donors themselves

Private institutions commonly have larger boards, which can be related to fundraising patterns or goals. The board of trustees has a complex and important influence on an institution. Boards, presidents, and other senior leaders are not doing the ground work for fundraising—or at least, they should not be. Development personnel should be engaging in the research and planning, and bring the senior leader (or leaders) in to close the deal—usually on gifts of $100,000 or more. Within Lindahl's model, senior leaders (including the president) would only be involved in the cultivation, solicitation, and stewardship phases (Clevenger, 2016; Drezner & Huehls, 2015). Increased emphasis on the fundraising role means executive leadership is spending less time on campus, and less time engaged with internal issues (Cook, 2008b). The fundraising role of a president has also made them wary of taking a public stand on issues, lest they offend a potential major donor.

Fundraising has also seen changes through the presence of social media. If employed well, social media can keep people connected to the institution like never before (Alphin et al., 2016; Merrill, 2018). Colleges and universities are turning to social media to maintain connections internally and externally across the institution (admissions, retention, alumni relations, marketing, and fundraising) but may not be employing it to full capacity. Hersey (2016) notes that young alumni, notoriously hard to track due to their mobility, are a perfect audience with which to engage via social media—addresses change but Twitter handles are comparatively stable. Social media is not without challenges—Hersey warns that if an institution is going to utilize social media for fundraising, they should be strategic, consistent, and use it well. Young alumni are particularly critical for cultivation, as lifelong giving habits can be developed. In 2017, 26.3 percent of all first-time alumni donors were current students or graduating seniors (Blackbaud, 2018). To cultivate young alumni, Cal State Los Angeles began asking each graduating student to give a gift equal to the date of their graduating year (i.e., a graduate of 2002 was asked to give $2,002). In the first year this initiative launched, 100 students made the gift; in the next year, 1,400 did. Establishing a climate or cultural norms around giving can have great impact (Gardner, 2018).

Crowd-sourcing or crowd-funded initiatives are another important trend, though one with deep historical roots. Dating back to the 1700s, individuals would pool money together to achieve mutually-beneficial aims (Shafer, 2016). Land-grant universities, established through the Morrill Acts, are another notable example. The Acts granted land to states wishing to open postsecondary institutions focused on "practical education" (Oliver, 2008, p. 618), but the locations had to be approved. Oliver (2008) described the important role local communities played in the selection of sites for these new institutions, noting communities that were able to present resources to accompany the land grant were more likely to be awarded the grant. These resources came in the form of land adjacent to the proposed grant area, proposed issuance of bonds to cover expenses, pledges from wealthy donors, grants from special interest groups, as well as bequests of resources. Shafer (2016) advises institutions interested in crowd-sourced or crowd-funded initiatives to have a strong plan for communicating with donors, a technical platform through with donations are collected, a strong message, and a compelling project. The elements of a strategy, according to Shafer, should include: identification of matching backer, creativity, focusing on spreading the message widely, speed (use a deadline to get people to donate *now*), and using the limited-time nature of the campaign to encourage action. Once the crowd-sourcing campaign is over, it is important to remain engaged with those donors.

To be an effective fundraiser, one must be able to speak clearly and effectively about how resources will and have been used—and explain this without academic "jargon" (Perlmutter, 2014c, para. 6). This requires broad and deep institutional knowledge, and articulating a need to donors. Major donors expect to have an impact and be able to see the impact of their giving, which makes data tracking and reporting very important (Clevenger, 2016; Whillans, 2016). Whillans states,

> As it turns out, one of the best ways to engage donors is to show them their actions matter. Blood donation organizations often provide donors with a text message each time they have saved a life. Fundraising offices often provide donors with emails documenting the buildings, research and people their donations have supported. Although impact-focused campaigns can sometimes take more effort than business-as-usual recognition efforts, research suggests that these costs are balanced with benefits for both charities and donors.
>
> (2016, p. 6)

Wealthy donors, as well as millennial-generation donors, see their support as an investment, and expect to see evidence of a return on their investment (Lindahl, 2010; Merrill, 2018). Foundations, like individual donors, are starting to attach performance or accountability measures to their support of institutions (Goldstein, 2012; Merrill, 2018). Reporting and accountability are becoming increasingly important components of donor stewardship (Merrill, 2018; Perlmutter, 2014d).

CONCLUDING COMMENTS

In the seminal work of campus fundraising, *The Campus Green*, Brittingham and Pezullo (1990) make several recommendations for planting the seeds of long-term fundraising success. They urge leaders to be strategic in pursuing private support from individuals, corporations, and foundations—achieving alignment of interests bodes well for future collaboration and donation or funding requests. Further, they advise institutions to ensure students understand the role that philanthropy plays in the quality of their on-campus experience to foster appreciation and a pay-it-forward mindset. The authors remind leaders to be ready to wrestle with important issues of institutional values and fundraising ethics while enhancing a tradition of philanthropy within campus stakeholders. Finally, they advise leaders to study institutional fundraising efforts to learn and improve over time. Fundraising may feel awkward and uncomfortable, but that should not impede efforts. It is too critical an activity to be avoided.

Leaders and fundraisers must keep their focus on the benefit fundraising will bring as governmental support and other revenue sources become compromised. Fundraising must support college and university priorities—not the other way around (Brittingham & Pezzullo, 1990; Perlmutter, 2014b). "The ideal of the university represents an autonomous generator of knowledge, free from external constraints, allowing the flow of knowledge to disseminate freely for the advancement of the public good" (Backer & Haddad, 2016, p. 52). Anyone who has spent time in higher education appreciates this lofty goal for what it is—an ideal. In order to achieve lofty goals, an institution must engage in the work of being financially sustainable (Alstete, 2014). Private funding enables higher education to continue pursuing this ideal, but it does not come without risks to consider (Backer & Haddad, 2016). Institutions must know who they are and what they want to accomplish and seek gifts that honor those intentions (Perlmutter, 2014b).

Leaders must be cognizant of the message sent by the acceptance of certain gifts. Donors (individual, foundation, and corporate) should not write the agenda of an organization. There has been a push for accountability in recent years as misdeeds at the very top of the corporations (Enron, Tyco) and charitable organizations (United Way) compromised or outright destroyed their future. In order to promote integrity in accepting donations, organizations must understand their values, establish sound practices and procedures, stick to them, and be transparent about fundraising operations (Brittingham & Pezzullo, 1990; Lindahl, 2010). The presence of well-written policies will give senior leaders more than guidance—they provide something to point to when a proposed donation could be seen as counter to or manipulative of the mission and vision of the institution.

Finally, many college and university presidents are nervous about engaging in fundraising—they are afraid to be seen "as a beggar" (Cook, 2008b, p. 640), of being rejected, being too intrusive, or offending prospects. Fundraising *is not* begging, admonishes Perlmutter (2014a); it is knowing important stakeholders and influencers, and yes, asking them to support something—but they are already likely expecting to be asked to contribute or they would not have engaged in the first place. The finesse is in when and how you cultivate, and the eventual request for support. Schervish (2008) notes that there is untapped capacity out there—that donors are out there, just waiting to be contacted with the "right" opportunity. He notes that fundraisers are either not finding (the right) opportunities, or not cultivating donors well enough, which is why senior leadership needs to be involved. Fundraisers are critical in framing the value proposition for potential donors in an authentic way that will motivate them to make the impact they are capable of making. Whillans (2016) agrees, stating, "In the context of donations to universities, research has revealed that simple framing—such as informing donors about seed money being contributed by the university—can increase charitable donations as much as sixfold" (p. 5). Put simply, it is the job of senior leaders to engage in this work to ensure the future financial sustainability of the institution.

REFLECTIVE QUESTIONS

1. Describe the relevance of fundraising in today's higher education market. How does it differ by type of institution?
2. Who donates to colleges and universities (your institution)? What motivates donors?
3. What are the key components of the fundraising process? How are they represented on your campus?
4. What are different types of donations? How are they used on your campus?
5. Why are all gifts not equally welcome? When should an institution return a donation?

CHAPTER 12

Where Do We Go from Here?

What Is Next?

Unfortunately, many in the general public and numerous politicians view higher education as a "bloated sector [of the economy], where professors engage in minimal teaching and groundless research, where administrations engage in an unbridled waste of resources, and where students were ill-prepared for the world of work" (Michael, 2005, p. 17). State and national politicians along with the media continue to throw barbs at individual institutions as well as the higher education industry as a whole. The charges brought forth include institutions of higher education being inefficient and ineffective. As current or future administrators it is going to be up to you to turn this tide of criticism into an effort to support the most productive *non-system* of higher education in the world. Wholesale adoption of business practices will not cure all of higher education's ills, but recognizing some of the inefficiencies and ineffective practices can be a start.

Higher education is an industry in and of itself, and each institution within this industry must wrestle with its multiple purposes, conflicting agendas, and declining resource base. Institutional leaders must be prepared for an endless balancing act of competing and conflicting forces (Michael & Kretovics, 2005). The previous chapters have been designed to demonstrate how higher education institutions utilize many current business practices and to provide the reader with an introductory understanding of the language of business. It is intended that this understanding of how these practices relate to higher education (and hopefully your particular institution) will provide you, one of tomorrow's academic leaders, with the knowledge to more effectively communicate with higher education's multiple stakeholder groups.

This chapter takes a look at some of the ongoing issues that will continue to impact higher education in the future, and frames them within a business perspective.

EDUCATION VERSUS TRAINING

Debate continues as to the mission of higher education within the United States and to some extent throughout the industrialized world. There are some who view education as a means to an end—a college degree provides one with access to a good job, which in turn provides access to the middle or upper socio-economic class. Others contend that a college education is meant to prepare individuals to be knowledgeable and responsible citizens of an ever-increasingly interdependent world.

Providing one with the skills and abilities necessary to perform certain tasks for a specific job is an important role and has a place in the world of postsecondary education. However, empowering individuals to think critically, engage in problem-solving activities, communicate effectively, and act responsibly is, in our opinion, more important and precisely what is needed to ensure an ethical and civil society.

The heart and soul of a democratic society is an educated populace. Therefore, it is critical that higher education administrators and leaders resist the temptation of bowing to the pressures of consumer demands, and continue to focus on societal needs, creating new knowledge, discovering new truths, and challenging and expanding the minds of today's youth and tomorrow's leaders.

FOR-PROFIT HIGHER EDUCATION

For-profit higher education is here to stay. As of 2016, the for-profit sector enrolled over 1 million students and this number is expected to increase as these institutions continue to aggressively market themselves. The for-profit institutions have established their niche and will continue to thrive as long as they are perceived by students and prospective students as meeting their needs. As market-driven institutions they recognize that failure to provide a reasonable quality service for their customers will eventually spell their demise. This financial incentive is what keeps these institutions solvent.

According to Breneman (2005), for-profit institutions within the U.S. market have extended the higher education market to students who otherwise would not have enrolled. The market niche captured by these institutions continues to expand and is beginning to erode the traditional base away from not-for-profit institutions as more 18- to 21-year-old students enroll in for-profit institutions, especially at the two-year level. We believe these three points help contextualize the role of the for-profits in the U.S. market. The not-for-profit sector can learn a great deal from the for-profit institutions and one of the most important points to learn is that every institution is a competitor as well as a potential collaborator (Breneman, 2005, p. 7).

It has been argued that when institutions of higher education become market-driven, "their role as public agencies significantly diminishes—as does their capacity to provide venues for the testing of new ideas and agendas for public action" (Zusman, 2005, p. 150). We do not disagree with this point, but rather submit that the for-profit sector makes no claim to testing new ideas or setting an agenda for public action. Its mission is to provide a service (education or training) at a price that will provide a reasonable return for its investors. Consideration of the greater good or preparing an educated populace is a by-product if anything at all.

GLOBALIZATION: EDUCATION WITHOUT BORDERS

In 1999, the process of restructuring European higher education began in Bologna, Italy when twenty-nine education ministers met and agreed to begin the process to eliminate educational borders much like the European Economic Union did for economic borders (Adelman, 2009; Gaston, 2010). Since that initial meeting this venture has become known as the Bologna Process, and this restructuring effort has caught the attention of the rest of the world.

Two components of the Bologna Process worth mentioning here are the qualifications frameworks and the tuning project. The qualifications framework is an attempt to establish a common understanding of what each level of a degree represents. In the United States, colleges and universities use the Carnegie Unit or credit hour as the basic metric. There is a common understanding that a bachelor's degree requires a minimum of 120 credit hours, a master's degree requires a minimum of an additional thirty credit hours and the doctoral degree represents ninety credit hours of study beyond the bachelor's degree. The European Union had no common metric as each country had differing measures to certify degree attainment. The qualifications framework is trying to change that by clarifying what each academic credential represents.

The tuning project, according to Adelman (2009), is an effort to "establish a common language for expressing what a specific institution aims to do, but not prescribe the means of doing it" (p. 48). Discipline-specific learning outcomes and competencies will then become transparent so students and employers alike can make comparisons between institutions.

These developments are important for administrators to track. For example, presently the European degrees are structured into three cycles which equate to the bachelor's, master's, and doctoral level in the United States (Adelman, 2009; Gaston, 2010). The short cycle, equivalent to the U.S. bachelor's degree, is a three-year degree. This has provided some momentum in the United States to shorten the average time to a degree. For some, this means reducing the number of credits; for others, it means increasing the number of credits taken each year. Either way, this has financial implications for U.S. institutions, especially those that are tuition-driven. Additionally, with the support of the Lumina Foundation, three states within the United States—Indiana, Minnesota, and Utah—are participating in a version of the European "tuning project" which may result in new calls for a centralized educational system in the United States.

GOVERNMENT INTERVENTION

Federal, state, and local governments have been involved in funding, and to some degree regulating, postsecondary education for quite some time and there is no indication that their involvement will diminish anytime soon. In fact, with every passing year there is more evidence of increasing government involvement. With every change in administration, the Department of Education (DOE) issues new rules and modified interpretations of existing rules, and of course there is the reauthorization of the Higher Education Opportunity Act/Higher Education Act. Two of the primary factors fueling this increased government presence are the commodification and commercialization of institutions and their degrees, and the globalization mentioned in the previous section.

First, Derrik Bok (2003) warned that the commercialization of higher education taking place was inviting greater government oversight and regulation. His warning appears to have been an accurate prediction. These government interventions have moved higher education, ever so slightly, down the path toward a single system of higher education within the United States in which education is viewed as a commodity rather than a process. One of the key strengths of higher education in the United States has been its entrepreneurial nature and institutions having the ability to differentiate themselves from one another.

As discussed in Chapter 2, most states in this country have multiple systems of higher education within their borders. There exists political pressure within many states to reduce the number of systems and in some instances to reduce the bureaucracy surrounding these systems, which brings us to the second point, globalization. As described previously, Europe is moving toward a more transparent system of higher education in which students are not restricted to educational opportunities based upon the country where they reside. Many in the United States believe we should do something very similar. This movement, in the United States, toward a single system of higher education is not in the best interests of higher education nor the country. However, colleges and universities as well as state systems must be careful: more federal dollars mean more federal involvement, which ultimately means more federal control.

ACCREDITATION

Calls for accountability, fluctuations in funding, and enrollment swings contribute to the uncertainty in the higher education marketplace and support the need for a strong system of accreditation. This need has never been greater. Accrediting bodies are not-for-profit organizations with a relatively small core staff whose functions are carried out, primarily, by volunteers. These volunteers make up the teams of individuals who review self-studies, make campus visits, and write accreditation reports detailing their findings, and in some instances recommend specific actions to be taken by the college or university. Over the past few decades, accreditation has been viewed by many within higher education as a chore necessary for the institution to maintain its ability to offer federal financial aid. This attitude toward and use of accreditation must change.

For higher education in the United States to truly become accountable, accrediting bodies must become more forceful in their oversight, and they must be adamant about ensuring the quality of the education being delivered. Creating a culture of assessment and continuous improvement is just the beginning of a process that will move individual institutions to unprecedented levels of performance. Colleges and universities and systems of higher education must take more seriously their self-evaluation process, and use meaningful measures that people outside higher education will understand. The days of the eight- or ten-year review must end, and colleges and universities must commit themselves to an ongoing process of assessment and continuous improvement. This active commitment will provide the framework within which every institution can live its unique mission.

The accreditation system in the United States is voluntary and is based on a peer review process.

Wolff (2005) refers to the accreditation system as "the oldest and best known vehicle for providing external accountability and quality assurance" (p. 82). Unfortunately, there are many who believe that the current system is not living up to its previous reputation. There is another large contingent who believe accreditation is failing; not because it is a bad process, but because the individuals (volunteers) and institutions involved do not take their roles and responsibilities seriously enough, leading to a wait-and-see attitude. Accreditation needs to be viewed as a proactive process of institutional change rather than a reactive process of improvements that must be made.

MISSION CREEP

Every year more and more institutions adopt a very generic mission to *be all things to all people*. As these institutions continue to proliferate, one cannot help but witness the disappearance of the private liberal arts college from the higher education landscape. Former liberal arts colleges have added graduate or "career-related" majors such as business, nursing, and education, or they have established weekend colleges for non-traditional students, all in an attempt to maintain or expand enrollments. Similarly, a number of the four-year colleges have changed their identities from colleges to universities in an effort to attract a different type of student and to expedite their quest for greater prestige. Unfortunately, these changes have hastened the demise of the once-great tradition of liberal education. While many of the larger private and the majority of public institutions profess to provide a broad-based or liberal education, they fall considerably short of this goal when compared with the traditional four-year liberal arts education. The general education requirements or core requirements at the vast majority of universities are nothing more than a cafeteria-style collection of unrelated course offerings that do not encourage students to connect their learning and thinking from one course to another. Why is this occurring? The research literature and the popular press support three reasons for the mission shifts: quest for prestige (rankings), financial stability, and administrative ego.

Quest for Prestige

One of the reasons institutions drift from their previously stated missions is in an attempt to be viewed as more prestigious. This quest for prestige has become synonymous with being highly ranked in one of the national or international rankings of higher education institutions. The proliferation of institutional rankings and the quest to become number one has encouraged many institutional leaders to add graduate or professional programs. As Balderston (1995) notes, "a university's general reputation rests largely on achievements in graduate education and research" (p. 247), and reputation plays a significant role in the rankings game. The addition of these programs comes at a cost, both financially and to its mission.

Pursuit of Financial Stability

In recent years numerous liberal arts colleges have announced name changes, from *colleges* to *universities*. A driving force behind this move has been a desire for increased enrollments or an attempt to stabilize their enrollments. As institutions witness a decline in the high-school-aged population, reducing the number of traditional-aged students, many struggle to maintain current enrollment figures. Others that are tuition-driven realize that sustained enrollment growth is necessary to meet the increasing costs of providing the personalized education they market. The lack of financial stability has most institutions turning to external sources of funding. These external sources can be institutional alumni or friends donating to the endowments, government sources of grant funding, or private foundations such as the Lumina Foundation or Bill and Melinda Gates'. Institutions must be careful to not let these external sources of revenues alter their respective missions or change their identities.

In the past, when financial difficulties arose most institutions believed they could simply grow their enrollments, thereby increasing tuition revenue, which ultimately addressed the financial problem. However, today, with the demographic shifts discussed in Chapter 1, institutions must realize they cannot expect to grow themselves out of financial trouble—the prospective students are no longer there. Cost cutting and establishing reserve funds must become the norm. It is also critical for institutions to closely control their desires to expand their physical plants. Being a good fiscal steward of other people's money (students) is a long-term commitment, not a short-term fix. College and university administrators must become more creative in their solutions, and they have to be more vigilant in sticking to their respective missions. The mission creep described above has contributed to the escalating costs of higher education and it is time to stem that tide. Strategic thinking and sound fiscal controls are necessary for institutions to navigate during times of financial difficulty or instability.

Administrative Ego

Virtually all leaders prefer to leave an institution in a better position (financially or prestige-related) than when they arrived; they strive to create a new tradition or take the institution to new heights. However, pursuing this path without a complete understanding of (or in some instances, in spite of) the values and culture of the institution is utterly irresponsible. Cohen and March (1974) suggest that most academic leaders want to leave their mark on their respective institutions. Doing so does not require transforming the institution from a liberal arts college to a comprehensive college or from a regional university to a research university. In many instances, it simply means providing an organizational framework within which the institution can fulfill its stated mission.

When hiring new presidents or other senior leaders, institutions must consider whether the potential administrator is a short- or long-term thinker. The short-term thinkers will typically be looking to make a big splash in as short a period of time so he or she can leave a legacy, usually some physical improvement(s) to campus, for all to admire. A long-term thinker will consider the mission of the institution and perform a comprehensive environmental scan and perhaps develop a strategic plan before making any long-term financial commitments. In many instances a long-term thinker's legacy is a financially sound institution with a mission and vision that has been embraced by the faculty, staff, and students.

State coordinating boards and institutional boards of trustees must be more thoughtful in their oversight of institutions attempting to modify their missions. The change of mission should not be taken lightly and needs to demonstrate that it is in the best interests of the institution, the state, and its stakeholders. Too many institutions have ended up in serious financial difficulty because an overzealous president wanted to leave a legacy in the form of a major building spree. Boards need to be looking at the long-term, not the short-term. While financial stability may appear to be boring, it will help preserve an institution's future.

INTERCOLLEGIATE ATHLETICS

There is no doubt that high-profile athletic programs bring attention to colleges and universities. The real question is whether or not such attention is desirable for the academic mission of the institution. To many, it appears that the media places more emphasis on the high-priced coaches for Division I football and basketball, several earning in excess of $1 million annually, along with lavish new athletic facilities complete with luxury boxes for corporate sponsors and potential donors, than it does to the academic successes of colleges and universities.

The enormous budgets combined with the negative news accounts of student athletes in legal trouble, and in some instances academic difficulty, has spawned severe criticism of colleges and universities and the promotion of their athletic programs. Trying to take a reasoned approach, the NCAA continues to revise its academic standards in an effort to place more emphasis on the student in collegiate athletics. These reforms are considered by many to be a step in the right direction, but to some it is a façade that obscures the loss of control over athletics programs within the major athletic conferences. For example, one of the more recent egregious examples of academic fraud involving intercollegiate athletics occurred at the University of North Carolina (UNC). Student athletes were disproportionately enrolling in sham courses over an eighteen-year period in which they were guaranteed good grades for little or no academic work, and for some courses there were no scheduled meeting times. According to a series of articles in the *Chronicle of Higher Education* and at Inside Higher Ed, the athletic programs feigned ignorance (which is an entirely different problem) and came out unscathed. UNC clearly demonstrated that the athletic programs were/are more important than the academic mission of the institution. To call coaches educators but not hold them accountable for their student athletes' education seems quite hypocritical.

Another example of the NCAA's failure to be proactive in policing the major programs is the recent scandal in college basketball involving Adidas, the sports apparel company, and several high-profile basketball programs. According to Inside Higher Ed and the *Chronicle of Higher Education*, federal investigators charged that Adidas and several NCAA Division I basketball coaches conspired to pay the families of recruits to attend specific institutions. By all accounts the NCAA missed this scandal entirely.

The time has come for individual institutions to take a hard look at how intercollegiate athletics fits within their respective missions. Is intercollegiate athletics extracurricular, or has it become central to the institutional mission? With television contracts in the tens of billions of dollars, has big-time college athletics become too big to fail? These questions will continue to plague colleges and universities, especially public ones, for the near future. Defending this spending as tuition and fees continue to rise and scandals such as those above are made public will become increasingly more difficult. This is yet another example where money has become the driver and institutions of higher education have lost sight of their responsibility to their students and other stakeholders.

It seems inevitable that the larger programs with high-profile, revenue-producing teams will continue to dominate their sports and reap the financial rewards while the smaller programs will continue to struggle as they attempt to keep pace. The majority of NCAA Division I schools must subsidize their athletic programs through student fees or financial transfers. For some the cost is too great. Expect to see more institutions follow the lead of Northeastern and Hofstra and eliminate some of their more expensive programs (Division I football in these cases). These are not Title IX issues but rather, unfortunately, strictly financial-survival issues. It seems as though the *student* appears to be missing in many of the big-time college sports programs and the emphasis is on the athlete and the coaches. That needs to change if college athletics is to survive in the long run. Perhaps encouraging more institutions to adopt a Division III model of non-scholarship athletics could be considered.

PROFESSIONAL ADMINISTRATORS

It is the norm for institutions of higher education to hire former faculty members to serve in administrative roles such as deans, vice-presidents, and presidents. These individuals are typically inexperienced in budgeting and management practices and ill-equipped to run the multi-million-dollar operation effectively. A faculty member's success in an academic career, with an impressive teaching and publication record, does not prepare one for the challenges of academic administration. Many of today's college and university administrators have demonstrated admirable leadership qualities and have enjoyed lengthy careers as institutional leaders. However, far too many others have successfully demonstrated the "Peter Principle" as they have been promoted to their level of incompetence (Peter, 1969). Higher education is a mature industry, and as such it can no longer afford to be managed by well-intended amateurs. The time has come for more deliberate and thoughtful administrative training for educational leaders. According to numerous articles in the *Chronicle of Higher Education* and at Inside Higher Ed, many new administrators lament the fact that they have little or no formal training in leadership/management.

For educational institutions to achieve greater levels of efficiency and effectiveness, they must do a better job of identifying and preparing administrative leaders. Programs such as the American Council on Education's ACE Fellows have been designed to give potential academic administrators leadership development and mentorship as they "spend an extended period of time on another campus working directly with presidents" (www.acenet.edu/leadership/Pages/default.aspx). Unfortunately, not all future presidents, provosts, and deans have the opportunity for such an experience (or choose to pursue one). The reality is, more than likely, current academic leaders have worked their way up through the academic ranks and have little to no academic or practical training in leadership, organizational dynamics, or other business practices. There is no doubt that it is important for institutional leaders to have an understanding of the academic side of higher education, but it is equally important for them to understand the business side of the enterprise before assuming such a critical administrative role.

It is not being advocated that business leaders be hired to fill these positions. In some instances, an institution might be able to find a former corporate vice-president or CEO who can step in and perform well. However, it is more likely that higher education will find what has been demonstrated time and again: a good leader in one industry does not necessarily transfer well to another, and having attended college does not provide expertise on the academic environment.

As an industry, higher education must provide more opportunities for preparing academic administrators and future higher education leaders to think strategically while developing learning organizations. Whether through grow-your-own strategies, state-wide development, or professional associations, this preparation of professional administrators must take place. Succession planning in higher education has never been more important. The future of higher education in the United States depends on the quality of its leaders and their ability to articulate a vision for the future that recognizes the challenges and opportunities for individual institutions and the industry as a whole.

ADMINISTRATIVE SALARIES

For an industry that pays so little attention to the preparation of its leaders, it seems to provide more-than-adequate compensation for this cadre of administrators. As presidential salaries at the leading public institutions top the $1 million mark, politicians and many among the general public are questioning institutional priorities. Boards of trustees have argued that, if in the private sector, these administrators would be compensated at much higher levels than they currently receive. This argument might be effective if these administrators had private-sector options.

College and university administrators have chosen to lead organizations that have a public mission and are responsible for utilizing other people's money for the greater good. As such, it is unreasonable to compare a college president's salary with that of a corporate CEO. If academic administrators wish to pursue careers that are more financially rewarding, let them. For those wishing to stay in the academy and impact future generations, compensate them fairly.

Governing board members, most of whom come from the business world, must realize that higher education is a unique industry, and it is their duty as board members to be good fiscal stewards. These board members, especially those at public institutions, will need to take more of a leadership role with regard to compensation or risk government intervention. It is only a matter of time before state legislators begin to request a ceiling on administrative compensation.

CONTINGENT WORKFORCE

There is no doubt that the most important resource in any institution of higher education is its personnel—the faculty, staff, and administrators employed to carry out the institution's academic mission. These resources, collectively, are also its most expensive. As colleges and universities continue to be called upon to reduce expenses in an effort to hold down the cost of attendance, it becomes apparent that for this reduction to be meaningful there must be a reduction in the costs associated with personnel. One solution adopted by many institutions is to lower personnel costs by reducing the number of full-time employees and replacing them with part-time or contingent workers, the most common of which are adjunct faculty. These faculty are paid less to teach, do not qualify for benefits, and are not required to participate in the governance system; nor is there an expectation that they advise students.

It is important to differentiate between contingent faculty who would prefer to be full-time and those who teach part-time by choice. Not every institution has an available pool of part-time faculty. Higher education has a long history of hiring adjunct faculty to teach classes. Sometimes it is because of hard-to-find specialized training; in other cases it is because the program would like to have a practitioner in the classroom. Whatever the reason, contingent faculty have been around for quite some time. They come to campus, teach their class(es) and move on to the next campus or back to their full-time job in the local community. According to the AAUP, over two-thirds of teaching faculty are contingent faculty. This is neither bad nor good; it just is. However, now their numbers have greatly increased and the rationale has changed considerably. It used to be that contingent faculty were hired for their expertise in the subject area; now it appears that they are being hired as a budget-saving tool.

Contingent faculty is the life blood of most for-profit institutions and the majority of community colleges. One of the primary reasons that the for-profit colleges remain profitable is that the majority of their faculty are adjunct. Their pay is low, and they do not receive benefits through the college, thereby reducing the cost of labor and increasing the profitability of the institution. While this model may work for the for-profit sector and in many community colleges, it has not been received well by the four-year colleges and universities throughout the country.

The issue at hand for academic administrators is to find the balance between the use of contingent faculty and tenure-track faculty. Relying on a contingent workforce comes with significant costs, despite the savings. Institutions need to become increasingly more flexible while simultaneously providing the highest level of education and academic integrity possible.

TECHNOLOGY

One thing that is certain is that technology will continue to change. With every change and with each new technological advancement, colleges and universities will need to make adjustments that will not come without increased costs. According to a 2019 *University Business* (UB) survey of college and university finance administrators, "keeping up with technology" was number three in their top ten concerns for the future. UB reported that almost two-thirds of its survey respondents anticipated spending more on technology this year compared to last (Ezarik, 2019).

For several years distance education grabbed the headlines and was touted as "the way" to reduce the cost of higher education. While there is some evidence that indicates students can learn as effectively through distance education, the results remain mixed. As for reducing the cost of education, there is conflicting evidence as to any cost savings or profitability in these programs.

As the use of technology increases, so does the cost of labor. For every faculty or support staff position eliminated, there appears to be a new technology position created. This makes sense, as every additional opportunity comes with significant risks; information security, student privacy concerns, and data and systems accessibility are among the top concerns of senior information technology personnel (Askren, Berman, Carmean, Gill, & Grajek, 2019). It also seems that for every new system implemented, institutions need to hire teams of technology experts to modify it or the existing infrastructure so the systems can work in harmony. Just ask any institution that has implemented a new enterprise resource planning (ERP) or customer relationship management (CRM) system in the past decade. Colleges and universities will also likely be relying on an emerging technology called Blockchain to certify students' achievements (Tapscott & Tapscott, 2017).

Virtual colleges such as Western Governor's University have yet to live up to the hype, but online programs at Arizona State University and Southern New Hampshire's competency-based programs seem to be making inroads. Given time, there is hope that these models will lead to technological innovation that will permit colleges and universities to offer high-quality programs at reduced costs. Further, the advancement of Blockchain technology has the potential to unseat higher education as the arbiter of advanced knowledge and skills if it becomes a trusted medium through which individuals can provide proof of competence. This area will continue to evolve and change drastically over time, and its future is exceptionally hard to predict.

FUNDRAISING

Fundraising is becoming more important for higher education, private and public alike. As costs continue to increase and state and federal dollars are reduced, colleges and universities must turn to the private sector and to private individuals. While the elite institutions have the billion-dollar endowments, the thousands of other institutions struggle with their financial futures as they continue to strive to reach such a lofty goal for their respective endowments. This quest for more money has every institution of higher education soliciting donations from anyone/everyone who will listen.

As more institutions approach or surpass the $1 billion endowment figures, over 100 as of 2018, there will be increasingly more calls for reform. Institutions will face pressure to spend more of their endowment monies on operating costs to help reduce the out-of-pocket costs to students and their families. Presently, several state and U.S. legislators are threatening to require institutions to spend a specified percentage of their endowments or risk losing their not-for-profit tax status, thereby requiring the institutions to pay taxes on endowment earnings and potentially eliminating the tax incentives to the donor. It will be in higher education's best interest to take a leadership role in this spending issue rather than waiting for a legislative mandate. Whether this comes from professional associations or from the actions of a chosen few institutions, action will need to be taken soon.

DATA-BASED DECISION-MAKING

Academic leaders at the institutional and state-wide system level have an obligation to make decisions based on data and not on the political or personal motives of the individual making the decision. Over the years we have seen far too many administrators base decisions on *administrative ego*, ultimately placing their institutions in financial peril. Acting in an ethical and responsible manner requires individuals to make, whenever possible, data-based decisions. Likewise, data-based decisions are in the best interests of the institution, the state and its population, and not just the administrators of the institution. These types of decisions need to be the norm rather than the exception.

At the institutional level, administrators must take the lead in demonstrating that their decisions are based on current and accurate data. If a new program or college is to be established there needs to be sufficient evidence to support the expansion, such as demand for the program(s) to warrant the allocation of resources. Likewise, if there is little or no demand for current programs and their value to the students or the institution cannot be documented, administrators may need to consider their discontinuation.

Tomorrow's educational leaders have to be equipped with the ability to gather and interpret data. This will require a more concerted effort on behalf of higher education institutions to foster the development of leaders trained in the use of data-based decision-making. Administrators must be able to discern the difference between a crisis at the institution and a normal problem of everyday operations. All too often administrators push for hasty decisions by labeling something a crisis, forcing a decision to be made before the appropriate data can be gathered. Perhaps a way to frame these *institutional crises* is to ask, "Will anyone die or be irreparably harmed if a decision is not made today?" If the answer is no, which it most often is, then delay the decision and gather the appropriate data.

CONCLUDING COMMENTS

"Nations that fail to adequately and appropriately educate their citizenry irrespective of race, gender, and economic backgrounds will not and cannot optimize their workforce returns or maximize their leverage in a global marketplace" (Michael & Kretovics, 2005, p. 68). In other words, higher education is the key to successful participation in the global economy for countries and for individuals.

Postsecondary institutions are in the business of providing venues where students of all ages and abilities can actively engage in educational activities that will enable them to better their lives and improve the human condition. As the world grows smaller and smaller, and as one nation's economic woes infect the global economy, the expectations of higher education have never been greater. Simultaneously, the criticisms of its performance have never been louder. The world looks toward its institutions of higher education for solutions to the economic and social ills of the time. History is replete with examples of societal and economic contributions originating from the ivory tower. However, these past successes do not absolve higher education from its responsibility, its moral obligation, to prepare world leaders equipped to resolve tomorrow's problems. In order to do this, we must stick to our core mission.

Finally, we would like to leave you with a thought about an ongoing threat to higher education in the United States, which comes in the form of undue influence at the institutional and system level. Perhaps the two most dangerous things influencing higher education in the United States are: large corporate foundations such as the Bill and Melinda Gates Foundation and the Lumina Foundation; and the federal government, primarily the DOE. On the one hand, one can argue that these institutions/organizations/agencies provide resources necessary for colleges and universities to conduct research and provide special programs. On the other hand, corporate foundations typically provide funding for programs that the foundations are interested in moving forward which are not always in the best long-term interests of our institutions. If they focused on research funding and comparative studies to determine the best types of programs, their impact could be greater and more positive in nature. Similarly, with every changing of the administration in Washington, DC we have different interpretations of the laws and rules that govern higher education, and, of course, different political agendas that perpetuate the ever-increasing unfunded mandates of the DOE. As the DOE flexes its oversight muscle it becomes more and more dangerous to higher education. If we are not careful, the higher education sector could become as regulated as the Pre-K–12 sector. Ultimately, in our quest for additional resources we may in fact be perpetuating the very problems we are trying to solve.

REFLECTIVE QUESTIONS

1. Does your current institution emphasize education or training? Why do you believe that?
2. How is your institution globalizing its campus?
3. How is your institution preparing to meet the needs of tomorrow's students?
4. How does your department/unit help fulfill the mission of your institution?
5. What factors are leading institutions to change their missions (stated or otherwise) to reflect more of an "all things to all people" approach?

References

Adelman, C. (2009). The Bologna process for U.S. eyes: Re-learning higher education in the age of convergence. Washington, DC: Institute for Higher Education Policy. Retrieved from: www.ihep.org/Research/GlobqlPerformance.cfm.

Akin, S. R. (2008). Institutional advancement and community colleges: A review of the literature. In A. Walton & M. Gasman (Eds.), *ASHE reader on philanthropy, volunteerism & fundraising in higher education* (pp. 698–707). Boston, MA: Pearson Custom.

Alfred, R. L. (2006). *Managing the big picture in colleges and universities*. Westport, CT: ACE/Praeger.

Alphin, H. C., Lavine, J., Stark, S., & Hocker, A. (Eds.) (2016). *Facilitating higher education growth through fundraising and philanthropy*. Hershey, PA: IGI Global.

Alstete, J. W. (2014). *Revenue generation strategies: Leveraging higher education resources for increased income*. ASHE Higher Education Report. DOI: 10.1002/aehe.20019.

Altbach, P. G. (2001). The American academic model in comparative perspective. In P. G. Altbach, P. J. Gumport, & D. B. Johnstone (Eds.), *In defense of American higher education* (pp. 11–37). Baltimore, MD: Johns Hopkins University Press.

Altbach, P. G., Gumport, P. J., & Johnstone, D. B. (Eds.). (2001). *In defense of American higher education*. Baltimore, MD: Johns Hopkins University Press.

Anthony, R. N., & Young, D. W. (1999). *Management control in nonprofit organizations* (6th ed.). Boston, MA: McGraw-Hill.

Archibald, D. H., & Feldman, D. H. (2011). *Why does college cost so much?* New York, NY: Oxford University Press.

Argyris, C., & Schön, D. A. (1978). *Organizational learning: A theory of action perspective*. Reading, MA: Addison-Wesley.

Askren, M., Berman, M., Carmean, C., Gill, C., & Grajek, S. (2019). Top 10 IT issues 2019. [PowerPoint presentation]. Retrieved from: https://events.educause.edu/~/media/files/events/educause-live/2019/live1902/slides.pdf.

Association of Fundraising Professionals. (2010). Glossary of fundraising terms. Retrieved from: www.cfre.org/wp-content/uploads/2013/05/bgloss.pdf.

Astin, A. (1985). *Achieving educational excellence: A critical assessment of priorities and practices in higher education*. San Francisco, CA: Jossey-Bass.

Atkins, K. (2010). Strategically planning to change. In S. E. Ellis (Ed.), *Strategic planning in student affairs* (pp. 17–25). San Francisco, CA: Jossey Bass.

Atkinson, A. A., Banker, R. D., Kaplan, R. S., & Young, S. M. (1995). *Management accounting.* Englewood Cliffs, NJ: Prentice-Hall.

Atkinson, A. A., Kaplan, R. S., Matsumura, E. M., & Young, S. M. (2007). *Management accounting* (5th ed.). Upper Saddle River, NJ: Prentice Hall.

Auer, M. R. (2016). The hardest part of integrated planning. *Planning for Higher Education, 44*(2), 3–8.

Backer, L. C., & Haddad, N. (2016). Philanthropy and the character of the public research university: The intersections of private giving, institutional autonomy, and shared governance. In H. C. Alphin, J. Lavine, S. Stark, & A. Hocker (Eds.), *Facilitating higher education growth through fundraising and philanthropy* (pp. 28–58). Hershey, PA: IGI Global.

Balderston, F. E. (1995). *Managing today's university: Strategies for viability, change, and excellence.* San Francisco, CA: Jossey-Bass.

Ball State University. (2018, August 3). [Newsletter]. Retrieved from: https://mailchi.mp/bsu.edu/message-from-the-board-of-trustees-1271121.

Balzer, W. K. (2010). *Lean higher education: Increasing the value and performance of university processes.* New York, NY: CRC Press.

Barnshaw, J. W., & Dunietz, S. (2015). Busting the myth: The annual report on the economic status of the profession. *Academe*, March–April, 4–19.

Barr, M. (2002). *The Jossey-Bass academic administrator's guide to budgets and financial management.* San Francisco, CA: Jossey-Bass.

Barr, M. J., & McClellan, G. S. (2011). *Budgets and financial management in higher education* (2nd ed.). San Francisco, CA: Jossey-Bass.

Basken, P. (2018, February 25). How to protect your college's research from undue corporate influence. *Chronicle of Higher Education.* Retrieved from: www.chronicle.com/article/How-to-Protect-Your/242616.

Baum, S., Ma, J., Pender, M., & Libassi, C. (2018). Trends in student aid 2018. College Board. Retrieved from: www.collegeboard.org.

Becker, W. E., & Toutkoushian, R. K. (2015). On the meaning of markets in higher education. In J. C. Weidman, J. L. Yeager, L. Cohen, L. T. DeAngelo, K. M. DeLuca, & M. Gunzenhauser (Eds.), *Economics and finance of higher education: ASHE Reader Series* (pp. 5–44). Boston, MA: Pearson Learning Solutions.

Bell, L., & Bush, T. (Eds.). (2002). *The principles and practice of educational management.* London: Sage.

Berliner, D. C., & Biddle, B. J. (1995). *The manufactured crisis: Myths, fraud, and the attack on America's public schools.* Reading, MA: Addison-Wesley.

Berrett, D. (2018, August 3). As colleges distance themselves from Papa John's founder, Ball State U. sticks with him. *Chronicle of Higher Education.* Retrieved from: www.chronicle.com/article/As-Colleges-Distance/244140.

Bettencourt, L. A., Ostrom, A. L., Brown, S. W., & Roundtree, R. I. (2002). Client co-production in knowledge-intensive business services. *California Management Review, 44*, 100–128.

Billups, F. (2015). Strategic planning in the academy: Reflections on what really matters. *Planning for Higher Education, 43*(3), 41–44.

Birnbaum, R. (1988). *How colleges work: The cybernetics of academic organization and leadership.* San Francisco, CA: Jossey-Bass.

Birnbaum, R. (2000). *Management fads in higher education: Where they come from, what they do, why they fail.* San Francisco, CA: Jossey-Bass.

Birnbaum, R., & Shushok, F., Jr. (2001). The "crisis" crisis in higher education: Is that a wolf or pussycat at the academy's door? In P. G. Altbach, P. J. Gumport, & D. B. Johnstone (Eds.), *In defense of American higher education* (pp. 59–84). Baltimore, MD: Johns Hopkins University Press.

Blackbaud. (2018). 2017 donorCentrics annual report on higher education alumni giving. Retrieved from: https://institute.blackbaud.com/asset/2017-donorcentrics-annual-report-on-higher-education-alumni-giving/.

Blumenstyk, G. (2016, September 13). After ITT's demise, more trouble is likely for for-profit colleges. *Chronicle of Higher Education*. Retrieved from: www.chronicle.com/article/After-ITT-s-Demise-More/237765.

Bok, D. (2003). *Universities in the marketplace: The commercialization of higher education*. Princeton, NJ: Princeton University Press.

Bolam, R. (2002). Professional development and professionalism. In L. Bell & T. Bush (Eds.), *The principles and practice of educational management* (pp. 103–118). London: Sage.

Bosner, C. F. (1992). Total quality education? *Public Administration Review*, 52, 506–515.

Boynton, M. (2015, July 23). Former Emory University employee sentenced to prison for stealing tuition payments. CBS Atlanta. Retrieved from: http://atlanta.cbslocal.com/2015/07/23/former-emory-university-employee-sentenced-to-prison-for-stealing-tuition-payments/.

Braun, K. W., & Tietz, W. M. (2013). *Managerial accounting* (3rd ed.). Upper Saddle River, NJ: Prentice Hall.

Breneman, D. W. (2005) Entrepreneurship in higher education. In B. Pusser (Ed.), *Arenas of entrepreneurship: Where nonprofit and for-profit institutions compete* (pp. 3–10). New Directions for Higher Education 129. Hoboken, NJ: Wiley & Sons.

Breneman, D. W., Doti, J. L., & Lapovsky L. (2001). Financing private colleges and universities: The role of tuition discounting. In M. B. Paulsen & J. W. Smart (Eds.), *The finance of higher education: Theory, research, policy, & practice* (pp. 461–479). New York, NY: Agathon.

Bresciani, M. J. (2010). Data-driven planning: Using assessment in strategic planning. In S. E. Ellis (Ed.), *Strategic planning in student affairs* (pp. 39–50). San Francisco, CA: Jossey-Bass.

Brittingham, B. (2009). Accreditation in the United States: How did we get to where we are? *New Directions for Higher Education, 2009*(145), 7–27. DOI: 10.1002/he.331.

Brittingham, B. E., & Pezzullo, T. R. (1990). *The campus green: Fund raising in higher education*. ASHE-ERIC Report. Washington, DC: George Washington University Press.

Brodnick, R., & Norris, D. (2016). Integrated planning as an institutional manifestation. *Planning for Higher Education, 44*(2), 28–37.

Brown, W. A., & Gamber, C. (2002). *Cost containment in higher education: Issues and recommendations*. ASHE-ERIC Higher Education Report, 28(5). San Francisco, CA: Jossey-Bass.

Buller, J. L. (2015). *The essential academic dean or provost* (2nd ed.). San Francisco, CA: Jossey-Bass.

Bureau of Labor Statistics, U.S. Department of Labor. (n.d.a). *Occupational outlook handbook: Postsecondary teachers*. Retrieved from: www.bls.gov/ooh/education-training-and-library/postsecondary-teachers.htm.

Bureau of Labor Statistics, U.S. Department of Labor. (n.d.b). *Occupational outlook handbook: Postsecondary education administrators*. Retrieved from: www.bls.gov/ooh/management/postsecondary-education-administrators.htm.

Burke, J. C. (2002). *Funding public colleges and universities for performance: Popularity, problems, and prospects*. Birmingham, AL: Rockefeller Institute Press.

Burke, J. C. (2005a). The many faces of accountability. In J. C. Burke (Ed.), *Achieving accountability in higher education: Balancing public, academic, and market demands* (pp. 1–24). San Francisco, CA: Jossey-Bass.

Burke, J. C. (2005b). Reinventing accountability: From bureaucratic rules to performance results. In J. C. Burke (Ed.), *Achieving accountability in higher education* (pp. 216–245). San Francisco, CA: Jossey-Bass.

Burton, T. T. (2016). *Global kata: Success through the Lean business system reference model.* New York, NY: McGraw-Hill.

Bush, T. (2002). Educational management: Theory and practice. In L. Bell & T. Bush (Eds.), *The principles and practice of educational management* (pp. 15–33). London: Sage.

Bush, T. (2003). *Theories of educational leadership and management* (3rd ed.). Thousand Oaks, CA: Sage.

Caboni, T. C. (2014). The normative structure of college and university fundraising behaviors. In J. C. Weidman (Ed.), *ASHE reader on economics and finance of higher education* (pp. 733–751). Boston, MA: Pearson Custom.

Carnegie Foundation for the Advancement of Teaching. (2018). Foundation history. Retrieved from: www.carnegiefoundation.org/about-us/foundation-history/.

Carlson, S. (2016, November 27). When college was a public good. *Chronicle of Higher Education.* Retrieved from: www.chronicle.com/article/When-College-Was-a-Public-Good/238501.

Carlson, S. (2018, January 21). How enrollment challenges can spur change. *Chronicle of Higher Education.* Retrieved from: www.chronicle.com.

Campaign for Free College Tuition. (n.d.). www.freecollegenow.org.

Cash, S. G. (2008). Private voluntary support to public universities in the United States: Late nineteenth century developments. In A. Walton & M. Gasman (Eds.), *ASHE reader on philanthropy, volunteerism & fundraising in higher education* (pp. 615–625). Boston, MA: Pearson Custom.

Chan, R. Y. (2016). Studying philanthropy and fundraising in the field of higher education. In H. C. Alphin, J. Lavine, S. Stark, & A. Hocker (Eds.), *Facilitating higher education growth through fundraising and philanthropy* (pp. 1–27). Hershey, PA: IGI Global.

Chase, R. B., Aquilano, N. J., & Jacobs, F. R. (2001). *Operations management for competitive advantage* (9th ed.). New York, NY: McGraw-Hill.

Cherrey, C., & Clark, E. C. (2010). Strategic planning: Renewal and redesign during turbulent times. In S. E. Ellis (Ed.), *Strategic planning in student affairs* (pp. 75–85). San Francisco, CA: Jossey-Bass.

Chronicle of Higher Education Almanac. (2017). Average published and net costs at 4-year public and private nonprofit institutions, 1996–97 to 2016–17. Retrieved from: www.chronicle.com/article/Average-PublishedNet/240817.

Chronicle of Higher Education Almanac. (2018). Average tuition-discount rates at private nonprofit colleges, 2006–7 to 2017–18. Retrieved from www.chronicle.com/article/Average-Tuition-Discount-Rates/244011.

Chu, D. (2006). *The department chair primer: Leading and managing academic departments.* Boston, MA: Anker.

Clagett, C. A. (2004). Strategic planning at Carroll Community College. In M. J. Dooris, J. M. Kelly, & J. F. Trainer (Eds.), *New directions for institutional research No. 123: Successful strategic planning* (pp. 113–119). San Francisco, CA: Jossey-Bass.

Clawson, J. G. (2003). *Level three leadership: Getting below the surface* (2nd ed.). Upper Saddle River, NY: Prentice-Hall.

Clevenger, M. R. (2016). Senior leaders as effective fundraisers: A toolbox for dealing with complexities in the new ecology. In H. C. Alphin, J. Lavine, S. Stark, & A. Hocker (Eds.), *Facilitating higher education growth through fundraising and philanthropy* (pp. 82–107). Hershey, PA: IGI Global.

Clevenger, M. R., & MacGregor, C. J. (2016). The role of corporate and foundation relations development officers. In H. C. Alphin, J. Lavine, S. Stark, & A. Hocker (Eds.), *Facilitating higher education growth through fundraising and philanthropy* (pp. 256–293). Hershey, PA: IGI Global.

Clotfelter, C. T., & Rothschild, M. (1993). Introduction. In C. T. Clotfelter & M. Rothschild (Eds.), *Studies of supply and demand in higher education* (pp. 1–10). Chicago, IL: University of Chicago Press.

Cohen, A. M., & Brawer, F. B. (2008). *The American community college* (5th ed.). San Francisco, CA: Jossey-Bass.

Cohen, M. O., & March, J. G. (1974). *Leadership and ambiguity: The American college president.* New York, NY: McGraw-Hill.

Comesky, R., McCool, S., Byrnes, L., & Weber, R. (1992). *Implementing total quality management in higher education.* Madison, WI: Magna Publications.

Comm, C. L., & LaBay, D. G. (1996). Repositioning colleges using changing student quality perceptions: An exploratory analysis. *Journal of Marketing for Higher Education*, 7(4), 21–34.

Congressional Budget Office. (2018). Federal aid for postsecondary students. Retrieved from: www.cbo.gov/publication/53736.

Conneely, J. F. (2010). Strategic planning and financial management. In S. E. Ellis (Ed.), *Strategic planning in student affairs* (pp. 51–61). San Francisco, CA: Jossey-Bass.

Conway, T., Mackay, S., & Yorke, D. (1994). Strategic planning in higher education: Who are the customers? *Journal of Educational Management*, *8*(6), 29–36.

Cook, L. P. (2010). Values drive the plan. In S. E. Ellis (Ed.), *Strategic planning in student affairs* (pp. 27–38). San Francisco, CA: Jossey-Bass.

Cook, W. B. (2008a). Surveying the major gifts literature: Observations and reflections. In A. Walton & M. Gasman (Eds.), *ASHE reader on philanthropy, volunteerism & fundraising in higher education* (pp. 738–746). Boston, MA: Pearson Custom.

Cook, W. B. (2008b). Fund raising and the college presidency in an era of uncertainty. In A. Walton & M. Gasman (Eds.), *ASHE reader on philanthropy, volunteerism & fundraising in higher education* (pp. 626–646). Boston, MA: Pearson Custom.

Council for Advancement and Support of Education. (2018). About CASE. Retrieved from: www.case.org/About_CASE/About_Advancement.html.

Council for Aid to Education. (2018). *2017 Voluntary Support of Education.* New York, NY: Author.

Council for Higher Education Accreditation. (2019). Home page. Retrieved from: www.chea.org/.

Crosby, P. (1979). *Quality is free: The art of making quality certain.* New York, NY: McGraw-Hill.

Crosby, P. (1984). *Quality without tears: The art of hassle-free management.* New York, NY: McGraw-Hill.

Deming, W. E. (1986). *Out of the crisis.* Cambridge, MA: MIT Center for Advanced Engineering Study.

Dickeson, R. C. (2010). *Prioritizing academic programs and services: Reallocating resources to achieve strategic balance* (2nd ed.). San Francisco, CA: Jossey-Bass.

Dickeson, R. C. (2015). Placing academics at the heart of higher education planning. *Planning for Higher Education*, *43*(2), 1–3.

Dickson, P. R. (2000). Introduction to marketing. In M. R. Czinkota (Ed.), *Marketing best practices* (pp. 2–61). Fort Worth, TX: Dryden Press.

Dixon, N. M. (1998). The responsibilities of members in an organization that is learning. *Learning Organization, 5*(4), 161–167.

Dodd, A. H. (2004). Accreditation as a catalyst for institutional effectiveness. In M. J. Dooris, J. M. Kelly, & J. F. Trainer (Eds.), *New directions for institutional research No. 123: Successful strategic planning* (pp. 13–25). San Francisco, CA: Jossey-Bass.

Dodge, L. E. B. (2016). Alumni giving and social exchange: A study of alumni giving behavior. In H. C. Alphin, J. Lavine, S. Stark, & A. Hocker (Eds.), *Facilitating higher education growth through fundraising and philanthropy* (pp. 294–323). Hershey, PA: IGI Global.

Dooris, M. J., Kelly, J. M., & Trainer, J. F. (2004). Strategic planning in higher education. In M. J. Dooris, J. M. Kelly, & J. F. Trainer (Eds.), *New directions for institutional research No. 123: Successful strategic planning* (pp. 5–11). San Francisco, CA: Jossey-Bass.

Dougherty, K. J., & Natow, R. S. (2015). *The politics of performance funding for higher education: Origins, discontinuations, and transformations.* Baltimore, MD: Johns Hopkins Press.

Dougherty, K. J., Natow, R. S., Bork, R. H., Jones, S. M., & Vega, B. E. (2015). Accounting for higher education accountability: Political origins of state performance funding for higher education. In J. C. Weidman, J. L. Yeager, L. Cohen, L. T. DeAngelo, K. M. DeLuca, & M. Gunzenhauser (Eds.), *Economics and finance of higher education* (pp. 65–98). ASHE Reader Series. Boston, MA: Pearson Learning Solutions.

Drezner, N. D. (2011). *Philanthropy and fundraising in American higher education.* ASHE Higher Education Report, 37(2). Hoboken, NJ: Wiley. DOI: 10.1002/aehe.3702.

Drezner, N. D., & Huehls, F. (2015). *Fundraising and institutional advancement: Theory, practice, and new paradigms.* New York, NY: Routledge.

Eckert, E. (2012). Assessment and the outdoor campus environment. *Planning for Higher Education, 41*(1), 141–156.

Ellis, S. E. (2010). Introduction to strategic planning in student affairs: A model for process and elements of a plan. In S. E. Ellis (Ed.), *Strategic planning in student affairs* (pp. 5–16). San Francisco, CA: Jossey-Bass.

English, P. F. (2012). *Safety performance in a lean environment: A guide to building safety into a process.* Boca Raton, FL: CRC Press.

Ezarik, M. (January 29, 2019). Campus finance leaders have concerns over financial status quo. *University Business.* Retrieved from: https://universitybusiness.com/campus-finance-leaders-have-concerns-over-financial-status-quo.

Ferrell, O. C., & Hartline, M. D. (2005). *Marketing strategy* (3rd ed.). Mason, OH: Thompson/South-Western.

Foskett, N. (2002). Marketing. In L. Bell & T. Bush (Eds.), *The principles and practice of educational management* (pp. 241–257). London: Sage.

Freed, J. E., & Klugman, M. R. (1997). *Quality principles and practices in higher education: Different questions for different times.* Phoenix, AZ: American Council on Education/Oryx Press.

French, J. R. P., & Raven, B. (1968). The bases of social power. In D. Cartwright & A. Zander (Eds.), *Group dynamics* (3rd ed., pp. 259–269). New York, NY: Harper & Row.

Gardner, L. (2018, September 16). In the drive for donors, regional public colleges have a lot of catching up to do. *Chronicle of Higher Education.* Retrieved from: www.chronicle.com/article/In-the-Drive-for-Donors/244523.

Garvin, D. A. (2000). Building a learning organization. In W. L. French, C. H. Bell, & R. A. Zawacki (Eds.), *Organization development and transformation* (pp. 281–294). Boston, MA: McGraw-Hill Higher Education.

Gasman, M. (2008). W. E. B. DuBois and Charles S. Johnson: Differing views on philanthropy in higher education. In A. Walton & M. Gasman (Eds.), *ASHE reader on philanthropy, volunteerism & fundraising in higher education* (pp. 309–324). Boston, MA: Pearson Custom.

Gasman, M., & Drezner, N. D. (2008). Fundraising as an integral part of higher education. In A. Walton & M. Gasman (Eds.), *ASHE reader on philanthropy, volunteerism & fundraising in higher education* (pp. 595–600). Boston, MA: Pearson Custom.

Gaston, P. L. (2010). *The challenge of Bologna.* Sterling VA: Stylus.

Geiger, R. (2008). After the emergence: Voluntary support and the building of American research universities. In A. Walton & M. Gasman (Eds.), *ASHE reader on philanthropy, volunteerism & fundraising in higher education* (pp. 292–300). Boston, MA: Pearson Custom.

Gladden, W. (2008). Tainted money. In A. Walton & M. Gasman (Eds.), *ASHE reader on philanthropy, volunteerism & fundraising in higher education* (pp. 20–23). Boston, MA: Pearson Custom.

Goldstein, L. (2005). *College & university budgeting: An introduction for faculty and academic administrators* (3rd ed.). Washington, DC: National Association of College and University Business Officers.

Goldstein, L. (2012). *A guide to college & university budgeting: Foundations for institutional effectiveness* (4th ed.). Washington, DC: National Association of College and University Business Officers.

Gorman, Y. J. (2016). Integrated planning: One institution's story of transformation. *Planning for Higher Education, 44*(2), 18–27.

Grawe, N. D. (2018). *Demographics and the demand for higher education.* Baltimore, MD: Johns Hopkins University Press.

Gray, D., Brown, S., & Macanufo, J. (2010). *Gamestorming: A playbook for innovators, rulebreakers, and changemakers.* Sebastopol, CA: O'Reilly Media.

Grubb, T. (2017, December 5). Man gets 5 years for embezzling $134K from UNC's Catholic parish. *The Herald-Sun.* Retrieved from: www.heraldsun.com/news/local/counties/orange-county/article188139959.html.

Guyenet, S. J. (2017). *The hungry brain: Outsmarting the instincts that make us overeat.* New York, NY: Flatiron Books.

Hall, H. (2018, February 13). The new normal in higher education: Endless fundraising campaigns. Inside Philanthropy. Retrieved from: www.insidephilanthropy.com/home/2018/2/13/the-new-normal-in-higher-education-endless-fundraising-campaigns.

Harper, V. B. (2013). Strategic management of college resources: A hypothetical walkthrough. *Planning for Higher Education, 41*(2), 158–168.

Harris, A. (2018, January 23). Outlook for higher ed in 2018 is bleak, ratings agency says. *Chronicle of Higher Education.* Retrieved from: www.chronicle.com.

Hearn, J. C. (2006). Alternative revenue sources. In D. M. Priest & E. P. St. John (Eds.), *Privatization and public universities* (pp. 87–108). Bloomington, IN: Indiana University Press.

Heller, D. (2015). The financial aid picture: Realism, surrealism, or cubism? In J. C. Weidman, J. L. Yeager, L. Cohen, L. T. DeAngelo, K. M. DeLuca, & M. Gunzenhauser (Eds.), *Economics and finance of higher education* (pp. 137–163). ASHE Reader Series. Boston, MA: Pearson Learning Solutions.

Hersey, L. N. (2016). Tweeting for donors: How institutions of higher education use social media to raise funds. In H. C. Alphin, J. Lavine, S. Stark, & A. Hocker (Eds.), *Facilitating higher education growth through fundraising and philanthropy* (pp. 59–81). Hershey, PA: IGI Global.

Hinton, K. E. (2012). *A practical guide to strategic planning in higher education*. Ann Arbor, MI: SCUP.

Hochel, S. A., & Wilson, C. (2007). *Hiring right: Conducting successful searches in higher education*. San Francisco, CA: Jossey-Bass.

Hoffman, K. D. (2000). Services marketing. In M. R. Czinkota (Ed.), *Marketing best practices* (pp. 290–331). Fort Worth, TX: Dryden Press.

Hoffman, K. D., & Bateson, J. E. G. (2002). *Essentials of services marketing* (2nd ed.). Fort Worth, TX: Harcourt College Publishers.

Hoffman, K. D., & Kretovics, M. A. (2003). Students as partial employees: A metaphor to describe the student–institution interaction. *Innovative Higher Education, 29*(2), 103–120.

Hope, J. (2018). Achieve culture change to implement your strategic plan. *Planning for Higher Education, 46*(2), 1–4.

Hossler, D. (2006). Students and families as revenue: The impact on institutional behavior. In D. M. Priest & E. P. St. John (Eds.), *Privatization and public universities* (pp. 109–128). Bloomington, IN: Indiana University Press.

Hu, S., & Kuh, G. (2003). Maximizing what students get out of college: Testing a learning productivity model. *Journal of College Student Development, 44*, 185–203.

Huckabee, C. (2016, September 13). Ohio U. will remove Roger Ailes's name from a newsroom. *Chronicle of Higher Education*. Retrieved from: www.chronicle.com/blogs/ticker/ohio-u-will-remove-roger-ailess-name-from-a-newsroom-2/114219.

Ivancevich, D. M., & Ivancevich, S. H. (1992). TQM in the classroom. *Management Accounting, 70*(9), 14–15.

Janosik, S. M., Creamer, D. G., Hirt, J. B., Winston, R. B., Saunders, S. A., & Cooper, D. L. (2003). *Supervising new professionals in student affairs*. New York, NY: Bruner-Routledge.

Jelinek, S. M., Foster, R. S., Jr., & Sauser, W. I., Jr. (1995). A rose by any other name: Applying total quality management to higher education. In S. J. Sims & R. R. Sims (Eds.), *Total quality management in higher education: Is it working? Why or why not?* (pp. 107–126). Westport, CT: Praeger.

Johnson, N. (2016). Aligning student and institutional incentives in higher education finance. Lumina Foundation Report. Retrieved from: www.luminafoundation.org/files/resources/aligning-student-and-institutional-incentives-full-1.pdf.

Juran, J. M., & Godfrey, A. B. (1998). *Juran's quality handbook* (5th ed.). New York, NY: McGraw-Hill.

Karl, B. D., & Katz, S. N. (2008). The American private philanthropic foundation and the public sphere 1890–1930. In A. Walton & M. Gasman (Eds.), *ASHE reader on philanthropy, volunteerism & fundraising in higher education* (pp. 238–260). Boston, MA: Pearson Custom.

Keh, H. T., & Teo, C. W. (2001). Retail customers as partial employees in service provision: A conceptual framework. *International Journal of Retail & Distribution Management, 29*, 370–378.

Kelchen, R. (2018). *Higher education accountability*. Baltimore, MD: Johns Hopkins Press.

Kirsch, N. (2018, July 11). Papa John's founder used N-word on conference call. *Forbes*. Retrieved from: www.forbes.com/sites/noahkirsch/2018/07/11/papa-johns-founder-john-schnatter-allegedly-used-n-word-on-conference-call/#495e044c4cfc.

Kocher, G. (2017, May 19). Former UK physics employee gets no jail time in embezzlement case. *Lexington Herald-Leader*. Retrieved from: www.kentucky.com/news/local/crime/article151504422.html.

Kolb, D. A. (1984). *Experiential learning: Experience as the source of learning development*. Englewood Cliffs, NJ: Prentice-Hall.

Kretovics, M. (1999). Assessing the MBA: What do our students learn? *Journal of Management Development, 18*(2), 125–136.

Kretovics, M., & McCambridge, J. (1998). Determining what employers really want: Conducting regional focus groups. *Journal of Career Planning and Employment, 58*(2), 25–30.

Kuh, G. (1996). Guiding principles for creating seamless learning environments for undergraduate students. *Journal of College Student Development, 37*, 135–148.

Langham, A. T., & Fifolt, M. (2014). Connecting institutional goals with measurable outcomes: Lessons learned from an academic realignment initiative. *Planning for Higher Education, 42*(4), 13–22.

Lenington, R. L. (1996). *Managing higher education as a business*. Westport, CT: Oryx Press.

Lewis, D. R., & Dundar, H. (2001). Costs and productivity in higher education: Theory, evidence, and policy implications. In M. B. Paulsen & J. C. Smart (Eds.), *The finance of higher education: Theory, research, policy, and practice*. New York, NY: Agathon Press.

Lindahl, W. E. (2010). *Principles of fundraising: Theory and practice*. Sudbury, MA: Jones & Bartlett.

Locke Anderson, W. H., Putaliaz, A. F., & Shepherd, W. G. (1983). *Economics*. Englewood Cliffs, NJ: Prentice-Hall.

Marquet, C. T. (2011, July 1). Embezzlement epidemic. *University Business*. Retrieved from: www.universitybusiness.com/article/embezzlement-epidemic.

Martinez, M. C., & Wolverton, M. (2009). *Innovative strategy making in higher education*. Charlotte, NC: Information Age.

Maust, R. N. (1985). Marketing. In Fecher, R. J. (Ed.), *Applying corporate management strategies* (pp. 13–21). New Directions for Higher Education 50. Hoboken, NJ: Wiley & Sons.

McCaffery, P. (2004). *The higher education manager's handbook*. London: RoutledgeFalmer.

McGee, J. (2015). *Breakpoint: The changing marketplace for higher education*. Baltimore, MD: Johns Hopkins University Press.

McGuire, J. (2017, July 10). Former OUPD officer sentenced for embezzlement. Norman Transcript. Retrieved from: www.normantranscript.com/news/oklahoma/former-oupd-officer-sentenced-for-embezzlement/article_42ee4e3b-cc5b-589e-9233-7acbf529b917.html.

McLean, J. (2017, September 11). Kirksville man pleads guilty to stealing thousands from MU fraternity. ABC 17 News. Retrieved from: www.abc17news.com/news/kirksville-man-pleads-guilty-to-stealing-thousands-from-mu-fraternity/619240436.

Measelle, R. L., & Egol, M. (1992). A new system of education: World-class and customer focused. *Ohio CPA Journal, 51*(3), 39–42.

Merrill, J. P. (2018, October 9). 3 ways to reach those elusive millennial donors. *Chronicle of Higher Education*. Retrieved from: www.chronicle.com/article/3-Ways-to-Reach-Those-Elusive/244752.

Michael, S. O. (2005). A contextual background. In S. O. Michael & M. A. Kretovics (Eds.), *Financing higher education in a global market*. New York, NY: Algora Publishing.

Michael, S. O., Holdaway, E. A., & Small, J. M. (1993). The resource-environment of Alberta's post-secondary institutions: A study of administrators' perceptions. *International Journal of Educational Management*, 7(5): 9–20.

Michael, S. O., & Kretovics, M. A. (2005). Financing higher education in the United States of America. In S. O. Michael & M. A. Kretovics (Eds.), *Financing higher education in a global market* (pp. 33–70). New York, NY: Algora Publishing.

Middlewood, D. (2002). Appraisal and performance management. In T. Bell & T. Bush (Eds.), *The principles and practice of educational management* (pp. 119–134). London: Sage.

Mills, P. K., & Morris, J. H. (1986). Clients as "partial" employees of service organizations: Role development in client participation. *Academy of Management Review, 11*, 726–735.

Moody's. (2017, December 5). US higher education sector outlook revised to negative as revenue growth prospects soften. Retrieved from: www.moodys.com/research/Moodys-US-higher-education-sector-outlook-revised-to-negative-as--PR_376587.

Myerson, P. A. (2014). *Lean retail & wholesale*. New York, NY: McGraw-Hill.

National Association of State Student Grant and Aid Programs (NASSGAP) (2016). Full aid data, 1974–2016. Retrieved from: www.nassgapsurvey.com/.

Nauffal, D. I., & Nasser, R. N. (2016). Strategic planning at two levels. *Planning for Higher Education, 40*(4), 32–39.

Needles, B. E., & Powers, M. (1998). *Financial accounting* (6th ed.). Boston, MA: Houghton Mifflin.

Needles, B. E., & Powers, M. (2007). *Financial accounting* (9th ed.). Boston, MA: Houghton Mifflin.

Net Price Calculator Information Center (2018, January 1). Retrieved from: https://nces.ed.gov/ipeds/report-your-data/resource-center-net-price.

Nickels, W. G., McHugh, J. M., & McHugh, S. M. (2008). *Understanding business*. Boston, MA: McGraw-Hill Irwin.

Oliver, F. H. (2008). The roots of academic fundraising. In A. Walton & M. Gasman (Eds.), *ASHE reader on philanthropy, volunteerism & fundraising in higher education* (pp. 602–614). Boston, MA: Pearson Custom.

Ostrander, S. A., & Schervish, P. G. (2008). Giving and getting: Philanthropy as a social relation. In A. Walton & M. Gasman (Eds.), *ASHE reader on philanthropy, volunteerism & fundraising in higher education* (pp. 84–99). Boston, MA: Pearson Custom.

Palmer, J. C. (2009). Trends in state tax support for higher education: Prospects for an entrepreneurial response. In J. C. Knapp & D. J. Siegle (Eds.), *The business of higher education, Volume 2: Management and fiscal strategies* (pp. 1–16). Santa Barbara, CA: Praeger Perspectives.

Paraska, S. E. (2013). Connecting your institution's achievements to demonstrate a culture of compliance. *Planning for Higher Education, 41*(3), 1–9.

Paris, K. A. (2004). Moving the strategic plan off the shelf and into action at the University of Wisconsin-Madison. In M. J. Dooris, J. M. Kelly, & J. F. Trainer (Eds.), *New directions for institutional research No. 123: Successful strategic planning* (pp. 121–127). San Francisco, CA: Jossey-Bass.

Perlmutter, D. D. (2014a, April 7). Don't fear fund raising, part 1. *Chronicle of Higher Education*. Retrieved from: www.chronicle.com/article/Dont-Fear-Fund-Raising-Part/145767.

Perlmutter, D. D. (2014b, July 14). Don't fear fund raising, part 2. *Chronicle of Higher Education*. Retrieved from: www.chronicle.com/article/Dont-Fear-Fund-Raising-Part/147683.

Perlmutter, D. D. (2014c, September 24). Don't fear fund raising, part 3. *Chronicle of Higher Education*. Retrieved from: www.chronicle.com/article/Dont-Fear-Fund-Raising-Part/149021.

Perlmutter, D. D. (2014d, December 1). Don't fear fund raising, part 4. *Chronicle of Higher Education*. Retrieved from: www.chronicle.com/article/Dont-Fear-Fund-Raising-Part/150269.

Perlmutter, D. D. (2015, March 9). Don't fear fund raising, part 5. *Chronicle of Higher Education*. Retrieved from: www.chronicle.com/article/Dont-Fear-Fund-Raising-Part/228235.

Perna, L. (2015). Toward a more complete understanding of the role of financial aid in promoting college enrollment: The importance of context. In J. C. Weidman, J. L. Yeager, L. Cohen, L. T. DeAngelo, K. M. DeLuca, & M. Gunzenhauser (Eds.), *Economics and finance of higher education* (pp. 376–412). ASHE Reader Series. Boston, MA: Pearson Learning Solutions.

Peter, L. J. (1969). *The Peter principle*. Cutchogue, NY: Buccaneer Books.

Pfeffer, J. (1992). *Managing with power: Politics and influence in organizations*. Boston, MA: Harvard Business School Press.

Pfeffer, J., & Sutton, R. I. (2006). *Hard facts, dangerous half truths and total nonsense: Profiting from evidence-based management*. Boston, MA: Harvard Business School Press.

Porter, M. E. (1980). *Competitive strategy: Techniques for analyzing industries and competitors*. New York, NY: Free Press.

Priest, D. M., & Boon, R. D. (2006). Incentive-based budgeting systems in the emerging environment. In D. M. Priest & E. P. St. John (Eds.), *Privatization and public universities* (pp. 175–188). Bloomington, IN: Indiana University Press.

Priest, D. M., & St. John, E. P. (Eds). (2006). *Privatization and public universities*. Bloomington, IN: Indiana University Press.

Proper, E., & Caboni, C. (2014). *Institutional advancement: What we know*. New York, NY: Palgrave Macmillan.

Protopsaltis, S., & Parrott, S. (2017, July 27). Pell grants – a key tool for expanding college access and economic opportunity – need strengthening, not cuts. [Blog post]. Center on Budget and Policy Priorities. Retrieved from: www.cbpp.org/research/federal-budget/pell-grants-a-key-tool-for-expanding-college-access-and-economic-opportunity.

Redd, K. E. (2000). *Discounting toward disaster: Tuition discounting, college, finances, and enrollments of low-income undergraduates*. New Agenda Series, 3(2). Indianapolis, IN: USA Group Foundation. ERIC: ED 447 775.

Rey, J. (2016, July 7). UB vice president Dennis Black resigns. *Buffalo News*. Retrieved from: http://buffalonews.com/2016/07/07/ub-vice-president-dennis-black-retires/.

Rowley, D. J., & Sherman, H. (2001). *From strategy to change: Implementing the plan in higher education*. San Francisco, CA: Jossey-Bass.

Rosse, J. G., & Levin, R. A. (2003). *Academic administrator's guide to hiring*. San Francisco, CA: Jossey-Bass.

Sadler, P. (2003). *Strategic management* (2nd ed.). Sterling, VA: Kogan Page.

Sanaghan, P. (2009). *Collaborative strategic planning in higher education*. Washington, DC: NACUBO.

Schein, E. (1999). Empowerment, coercive persuasion and organizational learning: Do they connect? *Learning Organization*, *6*(4), 163–172.

Schervish, P. G. (2008). Major donors, major motives: The people and purposes behind major gifts. In A. Walton & M. Gasman (Eds.), *ASHE reader on philanthropy, volunteerism & fundraising in higher education* (pp. 747–760). Boston, MA: Pearson Custom.

Schroeder, F. W. (2001). Making peace between annual and major gifts. CASE White Paper. Washington, DC: Council for Advancement and Support of Education. Retrieved from: www.case.org/Publications_and_Products/2001/April_2001/Making_Peace_between_Annual_and_Major_Gifts.html.

Scott, J. D. (2006). The mission of the university: Medieval to postmodern transformations. *Journal of Higher Education*, 77(1), 1–39.

Scutari, M. (2017, April 10). Mega-gifts are rising and alumni giving is shrinking. Which means what, exactly? Inside Philanthropy. Retrieved from: www.insidephilanthropy.com/home/2017/4/10/mega-gifts-universities-fundraising.

Scutari, M. (2018, February 22). Boom times: Universities keep raking in more cash. How long can this last? Inside Philanthropy. Retrieved from: www.insidephilanthropy.com/home/2018/2/22/higher-ed-fundraising-grants-2017-trends.

Selingo, J. (2016). *2026: The Decade Ahead: Chronicle of Higher Education* Special Report. Washington, DC: *Chronicle of Higher Education.*

Selingo, J. (2018, January 27). Higher education is headed for a supply and demand crisis. *Washington Post.* Retrieved from: www.washingtonpost.com/news/grade-point/wp/2018/01/27/higher-education-is-headed-for-a-supply-and-demand-crisis/?noredirect=on&utm_term=.dbf12ac50c99.

Seltzer, R. (2016, May 16). Discounting hits new highs. Inside Higher Ed. Retrieved from: www.insidehighered.com/news/2016/05/16/discount-rates-rise-yet-again-private-colleges-and-universities.

Seltzer, R. (2017, April 28). Diminishing returns for tuition discounting. Inside Higher Ed. Retrieved from: www.insidehighered.com/news/2017/04/28/new-study-demonstrates-rise-tuition-discounting-and-diminishing-returns.

Seltzer, R. (2018, February 6). Giving to colleges rises by 6.3%. Inside Higher Ed. Retrieved from: www.insidehighered.com/news/2018/02/06/personal-giving-pushes-donations-colleges-and-universities-new-level-2017.

Serna, G. R., & Weiler, S. C. (2016). *Higher education, fiscal administration, and budgeting: An applied approach.* Lanham, MD: Rowman & Littlefield.

Seymour, D., Kelly, J. M., & Jasinski, J. (2004). Linking planning, quality improvement, and institutional research. In M. J. Dooris, J. M. Kelly, & J. F. Trainer (Eds.), *New directions for institutional research No. 123: Successful strategic planning* (pp. 49–56). San Francisco, CA: Jossey-Bass.

Seymour, D. T. (1993). *On Q: Causing quality in higher education.* Phoenix, AZ: American Council on Education/Oryx Press.

Shafer, A. A. (2016). Effective approaches in higher education development: A survey of fundraising best practices. In H. C. Alphin, J. Lavine, S. Stark, & A. Hocker (Eds.), *Facilitating higher education growth through fundraising and philanthropy* (pp. 206–227). Hershey, PA: IGI Global.

Shattock, M. (2003). *Managing successful universities.* Maidenhead: Open University Press.

Sheth, J. N. (2000). Consumer behavior. In M. R. Czinkota (Ed.), *Marketing best practices* (pp. 136–175). Fort Worth, TX: Dryden Press.

Shimp, T. A. (2000). Integrated marketing communications: Advertising, promotions, and other tools. In M. R. Czinkota (Ed.), *Marketing best practices* (pp. 416–459). Fort Worth, TX: Dryden Press.

Siguaw, J. A. (2000). Personnel selling and sales management. In M. R. Czinkota (Ed.), *Marketing best practices* (pp. 460–497). Fort Worth, TX: Dryden Press.

Simpson, P. M. (2000). Market segmentation and target markets. In M. R. Czinkota (Ed.), *Marketing best practices* (pp. 210–246). Fort Worth, TX: Dryden Press.

Sims, R. R., & Sims, S. J. (1995). Toward an understanding of total quality management: Its relevance and contribution to higher education. In S. J. Sims & R. R. Sims (Eds.), *Total quality management in higher education: Is it working? Why or why not?* (pp. 1–21). Westport, CT: Praeger.

Society for College and University Planning (SCUP). (2018, Spring). Trends for higher education spring 2018. Retrieved from: www.scup.org/trends.

Sodhi, M. S., & Sodhi, N. S. (2008). *Six Sigma pricing.* Upper Saddle River, NY: FT Press.

Stacey, R. D. (2007). *Strategic management and organisational design* (5th ed.). Essex: FT Press.

Starsoneck, L. (2017, January 19). Defining time, talent, and treasure. [Blog post]. Armstrong McGuire. Retrieved from: www.armstrongmcguire.com/blog/defining-time-talent-and-treasure.

State Higher Education Executive Officers (2018). *State Higher Education Finance (SHEF) FY 2017*. Boulder, CO: Author.

Stephens, J. H. (2017). Eight themes in strategic planning: Reflections from a year of focused learning. *Planning for Higher Education, 45*(4), 118–124.

St. John, E. P., & Priest, D. M. (2006). Privatization in public universities. In D. M. Priest & E. P. St. John (Eds.), *Privatization and public universities* (pp. 271–284). Bloomington, IN: Indiana University Press.

Strange, C. C., & Banning, J. H. (2001). *Education by design: Creating campus learning environments that work*. San Francisco, CA: Jossey-Bass.

Strauss, J. C., & Curry, J. R. (2002). *Responsibility center management: Lessons from 25 years of decentralized management*. Washington, DC: National Association of College and University Business Officers.

Stripling, J. (2017, October 15). The lure of the lazy river. *Chronicle of Higher Education*. Retrieved from: www.chronicle.com/article/The-Lure-of-the-Lazy-River/241434.

Suskie, L. (2014). *Five dimensions of quality: A common sense guide to accreditation and accountability in higher education*. San Francisco, CA: Jossey-Bass.

Tapscott, D., & Tapscott, A. (2017, March 13). The Blockchain revolution and higher education. *Educause Review*. Retrieved from: https://er.educause.edu/articles/2017/3/the-blockchain-revolution-and-higher-education.

Teare, R., & Dealtry, R. (1998). Building and sustaining learning organizations. *Learning Organization, 5*(1), 46–70.

Terziovski, M., Howell, A., Sohal, A., & Morrison, M. (2000). Establishing mutual dependence between TQM and the learning organization: A multiple case study. *Learning Organization*, 7(1), 23–31.

Thomas, H. (1996). Strategic planning. In D. Warner & D. Palfreyman (Eds.), *Higher education management: The key elements* (pp. 33–46). Buckingham: Open University Press.

Tokasz, J., & Besecker, A. (2017, December 6). Former UB vice president pleads guilty to stealing $320,000 from university. *Buffalo News*. Retrieved from: http://buffalonews.com/2017/09/07/longtime-ub-administrator-plead-theft-related-charges-court/.

Toma, J. D., Dubrow, G., & Hartley, M. (2005). *The uses of institutional culture: Strengthening identification and building brand equity in higher education*. ASHE Higher Education Report, 31(2). San Francisco, CA: Jossey-Bass.

Toutkoushian, R. K., & Paulsen, M. B. (2016). *Economics of higher education: Background, concepts, and applications*. Dordrecht: Springer. DOI 10.1007/978-94-017-7506-9.

Trainer, J. F. (2004). Models and tools for strategic planning. In M. J. Dooris, J. M. Kelly, & J. F. Trainer (Eds.), *New directions for institutional research No. 123: Successful strategic planning* (pp. 129–138). San Francisco, CA: Jossey-Bass.

Tromp, S. A., & Ruben, B. D. (2010). *Strategic planning in higher education: A guide for leaders* (2nd ed.). Washington, DC: NACUBO.

U.S. Department of Education (2006). *A test of leadership: Charting the future of U.S. higher education*. Washington, DC: Author.

U.S. Department of Education (2016, August 25). Department of Education bans ITT from enrolling new Title IV students, adds tough new financial oversight. Retrieved from: www.ed.gov/news/press-releases/department-education-bans-itt enrolling-new-title-iv-students-adds-tough-new-financial-oversight.

U.S. Department of Education, National Center for Education Statistics (NCES) (2017). Table 311.15. Number and percentage of students enrolled in degree-granting postsecondary institutions, by distance education participation, location of student, level of enrollment, and control and level of institution: Fall 2015 and fall 2016. In U.S. Department of Education, NCES (Ed.), Digest of Education Statistics (2017 ed.). Retrieved from: http://nces.ed.gov/programs/digest/.

U.S. Department of Education, NCES (2018). Digest of Education Statistics. Retrieved from: https://nces.ed.gov/ipeds.

U.S. Department of Education, NCES (2018). Integrated Postsecondary Education Data System (IPEDS), fall enrollment component (provisional data). In U.S. Department of Education, NCES (Ed.), Digest of Education Statistics (2018 ed.). Retrieved from: http://nces.ed.gov/programs/digest/.

U.S. Department of Education, NCES (2018). Table 302.10. Recent high school completers and their enrollment in college, by sex and level of institution: 1960 through 2017. In U.S. Department of Education, NCES (Ed.), Digest of Education Statistics (2018 ed.). Retrieved from: http://nces.ed.gov/programs/digest/.

U.S. Department of Education, NCES (2018). Table 303.10. Total fall enrollment in degree-granting postsecondary institutions, by attendance status, sex of student, and control of institution: Selected years, 1947 through 2028. In U.S. Department of Education, NCES (Ed.), Digest of Education Statistics (2018 ed.). Retrieved from: http://nces.ed.gov/programs/digest/.

U.S. Department of Education, NCES (2018). Table 306.10. Total fall enrollment in degree-granting postsecondary institutions, by level of enrollment, sex, attendance status, and race/ethnicity or nonresident alien status of student: Selected years, 1976 through 2017. In U.S. Department of Education, NCES (Ed.), Digest of Education Statistics (2018 ed.). Retrieved from: http://nces.ed.gov/programs/digest/.

U.S. Department of Education, NCES (2018). Table 318.10. Degrees conferred by postsecondary institutions, by level of degree and sex of student: Selected years, 1869–70 through 2028–29. In U.S. Department of Education, NCES (Ed.), Digest of Education Statistics (2018 ed.). Retrieved from: http://nces.ed.gov/programs/digest/.

U.S. Department of Education, NCES (2018). Table 330.10. Average undergraduate tuition and fees and room and board rates charged for full-time students in degree-granting postsecondary institutions, by level and control of institution: Selected years, 1963–64 through 2017–18. In U.S. Department of Education, NCES (Ed.), Digest of Education Statistics (2018 ed.). Retrieved from: http://nces.ed.gov/programs/digest/.

U.S. Department of Education, NCES (2018). Table 333.10. Revenues of public degree-granting postsecondary institutions, by source of revenue and level of institution: Selected years, 2007–08 through 2016–17. In U.S. Department of Education, NCES (Ed.), Digest of Education Statistics (2018 ed.). Retrieved from: http://nces.ed.gov/programs/digest/.

U.S. Department of Education, National Center for Education Statistics (2018). Table 333.40. Total revenue of private nonprofit degree-granting postsecondary institutions, by source of funds and level of institution: Selected years, 1999–2000 through 2016–17. In U.S. Department of Education, NCES (Ed.), Digest of Education Statistics (2018 ed.). Retrieved from: http://nces.ed.gov/programs/digest/.

U.S. Department of Education, NCES (2018). Table 333.55. Total revenue of private for-profit degree-granting postsecondary institutions, by source of funds and level of institution: Selected years, 1999–2000 through 2016–17. In U.S. Department of Education, NCES (Ed.), Digest of Education Statistics (2018 ed.). Retrieved from: http://nces.ed.gov/programs/digest/.

Volkwein, J. F., & Grunig, S. D. (2005). Resources and reputation in higher education: Double, double, toil and trouble. In J. C. Burke (Ed.), *Achieving accountability in higher education* (pp. 246–274). San Francisco, CA: Jossey-Bass.

Walton, A. (2008). Philanthropy in higher education: Past and present. In A. Walton & M. Gasman (Eds.), *ASHE reader on philanthropy, volunteerism & fundraising in higher education* (pp. 3–11). Boston, MA: Pearson Custom.

Walton, A., & Gasman, M. (2008). Introduction. In A. Walton & M. Gasman (Eds.), *ASHE reader on philanthropy, volunteerism & fundraising in higher education* (pp. xxiii–xxv). Boston, MA: Pearson Custom.

Warner, D., & Palfreyman, D. (1996). *Higher education management: The key elements.* Buckingham: Open University Press.

Webster, W. P., Jakeman, R. C., & Swayze, S. (2016). The role of philanthropy on the strategic planning process of a selective liberal arts and science college. In H. C. Alphin, J. Lavine, S. Stark, & A. Hocker (Eds.), *Facilitating higher education growth through fundraising and philanthropy* (pp. 228–255). Hershey, PA: IGI Global.

Weisbrod, B. A., Ballou, J. P., & Asch, E. D. (2008). *Mission and money: Understanding the university.* New York, NY: Cambridge University Press.

Wheelan, C. (2010). *Naked economics: Undressing the dismal science.* New York, NY: W. W. Norton & Company.

Wheeler, D. W., Seagren, A. T., Becker, L. W., Kinley, E. R., Mlinek, D. D., & Robson, K. J. (2008). *The academic chair's handbook* (2nd ed.). San Francisco, CA: Jossey-Bass.

Whillans, A. V. (2016). A brief introduction to the science of fundraising. CASE White Paper. Washington, DC: Council for Advancement and Support of Education. Retrieved from: www.case.org/Publications_and_Products/White_Papers.html.

Whitney R. (2010). Involving academic faculty in developing and implementing a strategic plan. In S. E. Ellis (Ed.), *Strategic planning in student affairs* (pp. 63–74). San Francisco, CA: Jossey-Bass.

Wolff, R. (2005). Accountability and accreditation: Can reforms match increasing demands? In J. C. Burke (Ed.), *Achieving accountability in higher education* (pp. 78–103). San Francisco, CA: Jossey-Bass.

Wu, F. H. (2017, September 26). Tuition discounting: The problem, not the remedy. Inside Higher Ed. Retrieved from: www.insidehighered.com/views/2017/09/26/why-tuition-discounting-has-created-more-problems-solutions-essay.

Wyllie, J. (2018, January 25). Endowment returns rebound after a dismal 2016, but the long-term outlook is cloudy. *Chronicle of Higher Education.* Retrieved from: www.chronicle.com/article/Endowment-Returns-Rebound/242327

Zeithaml, V. A., Parasuraman, A., & Berry, L. L. (1985). Problems and strategies in services marketing. *Journal of Marketing, 49*, 33–46.

Zemsky, R. M. (2005). The dog that doesn't bark: Why markets neither limit prices nor promote educational quality. In J. C. Burke (Ed.), *Achieving accountability in higher education* (pp. 275–295). San Francisco, CA: Jossey-Bass.

Zuckerman, R. A., & Kretovics, M. A. (2003). Membership acquisition and retention model, *NASPA Journal, 41*(1), Article 8. Retrieved from: http://publications.naspa.org/naspajournal/vol41/iss1/art8.

Zumeta, W., Breneman, D. W., Callan, P. M., & Finney, J. E. (2012). *Financing American higher education in the era of globalization.* Cambridge, MA: Harvard Education Press.

Zusman, A. (2005). Challenges facing higher education in the twenty-first century. In P. G. Altbach, R. O. Berdhal, & P. J. Gumport (Eds.), *American higher education in the twenty-first century* (2nd ed., pp. 115–160). Baltimore, MD: Johns Hopkins University Press.

Index

Page numbers in *italics* refer to figures; page numbers in **bold** refer to tables

A *Test of Leadership* 8
AACSB International 6
access 4, 7–8, 16–17, 207, 249–50; to higher education 51, 76, 205; marketing and 225; records and 87; tuition and 59, 63, 65
accountability 4–5, 16–18, 60, 67–8, 75–6, 92, 141, 149; accreditation and 252; evaluation and 197–8; and fundraising 246–7; and Institutional Research 29; Lean methodology and 137; and planning 162, 165, 170
accounting 79–93, 95–7, 106, 111, 113; *generally accepted accounting principles* (GAAP) 80; managerial 89–92; System *80*; of University of Wisconsin system *84*; *see also* budgets
accounting equation 80, 82, 85, 93
accounts 82, 112; endowed 239–40; payable 82, 85; receivable 85; reserve 69, 103
accreditation 5, 141, 167, 205, 252–3; and change 129, 132; and QM 134, 140–1; types of 5–6; *see also* Council for Higher Education Accreditation; Higher Learning Commission
adjunct faculty 216, 258; *see also* faculty
administration 24, 28, 119; budget 97–100; Educational 182
administrative ego 132, 253–5, 260
administrative salaries 257
administrators 4, 17, 21, 34, 55–6, 60, 64, 74–7, 136, 140–3, 147–51, 168–9, 195, 249–51, 254; budget and 95–6, 109, 117, 120; and change 132; customer service and 220; finance and funding 80, 92–3; fundraising and 229, 237–8, 245; and human resources 201; and management 172; as managers 125–30; and marketing 203, 206, 211, 213, 216, 218; professional 256–60; and rankings 8; and recruiting 178, 182, 188
admissions 144, 169, 216, 245; basic economic principles and 47–8; marketing and 14, 204, 217, 219, 223; open 49; organizational structures and 30, 32; selective 9, 49, 143; target marketing and 214; *see also* Enrollment Management
advancement 14, 29, *29*, 229, 231, 235; *see also* development; foundations; fundraising; grants
advertising 185, 216–17, 224; recruiting process and 203–4; word of mouth 225
affirmative action 28, 177, 183
affordability 4, 7–8, 76, 219; *see also* cost of attendance; tuition
Ailes, Roger 244
American Association of Colleges and Universities (AAC&U) 141

American Association of University Professors (AAUP) 117, 200
American Council on Education (ACE) 256
American Marketing Association (AMA) 204
anarchical model 34
Argyris, Chris 142–4
assets 80, 82–3, *83*, *84*, *85*, 86, 92–3, 95, 101, 103, 236
assessment 4, 7, 14, 27, 86, 140, 211, 221, 252; program budgeting and 107; and QM 140–1; and strategic planning 130, 157, 159, 162–3, 171–2, 174; *see also* student learning
athletics 61, 206, 214, 244, 255–6
auxiliary services 14, 32, 103, 110; budget *103*, 113; enterprises 69; and RCM 107

balance sheet 82–3, 85
Bill and Melinda Gates Foundation 254, 261
Birnbaum, Robert 16, 20, 22, 34, 125, 135, 140, 149–51
Bloom, Allan 17
Bologna Process 13, 250–1
brand 216–19, 223; awareness 30; equity 214–16
branded 69, 234
budgeting 28, 35, 55, 97–8, 113, 171; lack of faculty experience in 256; process 95–7, 110, 126; and tough economic times 116–18; *see also* finance
budgets 27–8, 40, 48, 79, 82, 96, 98–121, 237; and action plans 162–3, 165–6, 170–1; and auxiliary units 103, *104*; basics 95–121; capital and operating 54, 66, 96–7, *101*, 111–13; centralized and decentralized 90, 92, 99, *99*, *100*, 107; changes and cuts in 115–19, 171; cost center/responsibility center (RCM) 105–7; cycle 108–9; definition of 96, 98; developing 89–90; and elasticity 50; flow *109*; formula or performance 108; freeze 116; hybrid 108; incremental 104–5; indexes *83*; managers 109–19; marginal cost, marginal revenue and 57; master 100; office in organizational chart 27, 97; performance funding 67; planning 79, 89–90, 93, 96–7, 110–11; purpose of 95; spending and adjustments 111; state funding of higher education 18, 66–7, 75; training to manage 21; types of 100–10; zero-based 105; *see also* costs; mission
bureaucratic organizations 20, 21–2, 34, 145, 196, 220, 252
business office 96, 182

cannibalization of program 72
capital budgets 96, 101, 103
career administrators *see* professional administrators
centralized budgeting *see* budgets: centralized
chancellor 20, 22, 26–7; *see also* chief executive officer; president
change in organization *see* organizational change
change model 147–8, *147*
chief executive officer (CEO) 27, 97; *see also* president
Chronicle of Higher Education 11, 88, 116, 167, 195, 224, 255–6
Chronicle of Higher Education Almanac 61, 63, 70
collective bargaining 27, 117, 200–1
collegial model 34
colleges *see* community colleges; for-profit higher education; four-year institutions; not-for-profit institutions; two-year colleges
commodification 204, 251
communication 34, 92, 170, 232; budget and 96, 111, 114, 120; channels of 126; marketing and 30, 206–7, 213, 216–8, 223; makes for an effective administrator 147; and strategic planning 156–66, 174; skills 195; style 196
community colleges 3, 20, 22, 24, *25*, 34, 47, 63, 231; cross-training staff at 202; faculty and 258; *see also* two-year colleges
contingent faculty 257–8; *see also* adjunct faculty
coordinating boards: statewide 20, 66, 74, 146, 255
co-producer: student as 13, 15, 55, 205, 207, 209–10, 218; donors as 231, 237
Continuous Quality Improvement (CQI) 134
controlling 89–90, 96, 211; as a managerial function 92, 126–7, 132, 135

consultants: use of 12, 159, 164
consumer behavior 43, 45, 50, 208, 217–19; *see also* co-producer
cost of attendance 7, 57, 61, 66, 70, 206, 258; *see also* affordability; tuition
costs: associated with rankings 8–9; auxiliary services and 32; budget basics and 98, 101, 105–7, 113–21; fixed 54; for-profit and 32, 34; in higher education 12, 46, 54–6, 70, 81, 89, **91**, 98, 125, 133, 157, 206, 254, 258–9; managerial accounting and 89–90, 93, 95; marginal costs (MC) 55, 57; outsourcing and 12; reducing 71–6; student fees and 32; student labor as co-producers and 210; total 54; tuition and 76; understanding of 55; variable 54; *see also* affordability; finance; grants; price; revenue
Council for Higher Education Accreditation 5
credit: Carnegie unit or 251; hours 34, 41, 43, *43*, *44*, 51–2, Bologna Process and implications of 251; hours and degrees in the US 251; transfer 72
crisis 117, 136, 260; types of 16–17
Crosby, Philip 133–6, *134*, 139
cross-training 201
culture 98, 114, 149–50, 154, 156–7, 159, 172–3, 213, 219; of assessment 252; changing and 147–8; institutional 16, 112–13, 117, 213–16, 222; Lean and 139; model II and 144–5; new hires and institutional 193; organizational 125–6, 133, 135, 163–6; quality management and 136
customer 204, 206–9, 259; as consumer 218; needs 134, 138; perspective 136–7; satisfaction and outsourcing 118; service in higher education 220–1; *see also* students: as customer
cybernetic model 34

data based decision making 260
debt service 54; as sample fixed expense *104*
decentralized budgeting *see* budgets: centralized and decentralized
decision-making 21, 26, 40, *80*, 87, 96, 99, 111, 114, 117, 120, 141, 173, 234; and control 92; data and 55, 72, 141, 211; and management principles 125–6; planning and 89; tough economic times 75; values and 154
demand 4, 41, *43*, *44*, *45*, 47; curve 43, 45, 47, 57; for colleges and universities 19, 46, 53, 59, 64; from outside influences 238, 244; Higher Education Demand Index 48; price elasticity and 41, *49*, 49–51, *52*; shifts in 45–6; supply and 40–1, 43, 47, 49; theory 47
Deming, W. Edwards 7, 129, 133, *133*, 134–5, 140, 15
development 29, *29*, 197, 223, 229, 231, 235; climate of innovation and 150; learning and; of requests 109–10; office representation 182; officers 12, 217, 235, 245; professional 194, 198–9, 256; research and 70–1; training and 70, 156, 158, 165, 177, 194, 256, 260; *see also* advancement; fundraising

earnings 106; budget and 112; endowment funds and 110, 239–40, 259; foundations and 233; retained 82
economics 39–57
economy 4, 46, 55, 64, 69, 97, 225; definition of 41; effect of 49; global 21, 40, 57, 260; student debt and 11; *see also* budgeting: and tough economic times; decision-making
education market *see* market; higher education
educators *see* faculty
elasticity 41, 53; price elasticity of demand 49–51, *49*; price elasticity of supply 51–3, *52*, *53*
employee 70, 115–16, 133, 144–5, 147, 177–202; evaluation; marketing and 211–13, 222–3, 225; orientation 28; recruiting and empowering 126–7, 136, 139, 221; retention 193
endowments 9, 11–12, 60, 76, 110, 233, 236–45, 259; maintenance 74; *see also* development; foundations; grants
Enrollment Management 8–10, *10*, *11*, **12**, 14, 30–1, *30*, 39, 46–9, 51–4, 56, 61, 63–5, *65*, 67, 70, 72, 86, 106–8, 112,

115–16, 155, 254; as counter-cyclical 219; tuition discounting and 56–7, 95; *see also* admissions
enterprise resource planning (ERP) 87, 181, 259
environmental scanning 157, 160, 162, 166–7
equilibrium point 44, 46
espoused theory 142–3
European Union 13, 40, 251; *see also* global economy; globalization
evaluations 4, 158, 172, 189, 208–9, 218; accounting data and 79, 92–3; college self- 252; of employee 193, 197–8, *197*; strategic planning and 128, 130, 158, 172; tools for screening candidate 186
exchange 40, 80, 99, 233; employment as a mutual 190; principle of 205; of value 80, 87
executive vice president 26, *26*; *see also* administrators
expectations gap 8
expense 59, 66, 80–3, 85, 95–97, 99 191, 258; accountability and 87–8; auxiliary services and 32, 69; budget and 89–90, 100–20; fundraising and 237; reducing 72; strategic planning and 171; student 206

faculty 14–15, 71, 99, 107, 116, 138, 144, 149, 172–3, 195, 200–1, 217, 219–20; become administrators 21, 256–7; contingent 258; and an economy of scale 55; financial gifts and 244; institutional research and 29; marketing strategies and 206, 216; organizational learning and 142–5; orientation 193; and planning 118, 130, 165–8; and post-tenure review 199–200; and quality movement 134–6; recruiting 178, 183–4, 188–9; on search committee 182; search timeline *180*; as stakeholders 4, 28; and student learning 141–2, 204
finance 27, 59–78; accountability and 60; *see also* budget; costs; funding
financial aid: and accreditation 5–6, 252; enrollment management and *30*; as public funding 3–5, 60, 62, 64–6, *65*, 76, 218; rankings and 9; student debt and 11, 206, 238; tuition and 63, 204
financial risk 61, 70, 99
financial stability 81, 253–5
firing *see* separation from an organization
fiscal steward 60, 79, 95, 254, 257
fiscal year 83, 96; adjustments 111–12; budgets and 100, 103, 108; spending 115
Florida State University 243–4
for-profit higher education 12–13, 24, 32, 34, 80, 82, 97, 204, 217, 250; faculty and 177, 258; federal financial aid and 66; financial profits and 21, 97; and implementing organizational change 147; increase and decrease in 19; institutional structure in 20–1, 92; marketing and 42, 207; revenues *59*; tuition and *62*; *see also* privatization
foundations 68, 70, 230–4, 237–8, *240*, 246–7, 254, 261; see also advancement; endowments; fundraising; grants
four-year institutions 11, 20–2, 48, 74; fundraising 230–1; mission creep and 22; *see also* for-profit higher education; liberal arts colleges; not-for-profit institutions
Free Application for Federal Student Aid (FAFSA) 66
free college 8, 12
funding 39–57, 59, 62–71, 77, 107, 110, 112, 118, 206, 243, 254, 261; and accountability 4, 18; and accreditation 252; crisis 16; decline in state 12; federal 3, 5–6, 11, 40, 59–60, 64 251; and the global economy 59; institutional 57; performance 67–8; project 107; public 5, 8, 66; shift 10–12; sources 61, 64, 68–70, 247
fundraising 42, 68, 74, 115, 223, 229–48, 259; advancement/development 29; president and 26 ; and rankings 9; *see also* advancement; development; endowments; grants

GI Bill 45, 65, 203
gifts 29, 60, 68, 76, 229–45; *see also* development
global economy 21, 260
globalization 13, 158, 250–2, 260
goals 26, 34, 57, 106, 126–33, 140, 143, 172, 195, 218; fundraising 231, 236, 245; institutional 21, 34, 96, 105, 108, 114, 174; integrated marketing communications and 216, 218; Lean and

136–9; performance-based budget and 108; personal 178, 194; political savvy and 67, 74; strategic planning and 155–63, 171; unrealistic admissions 116, 169
governance 20, 34, 66, 114, 150, 234; adjunct faculty and 258; shared 21, 34, 73–4, 126, 135, 145, 148, 172, 243
government 3–5, 29, 57, 59, 60, 71, 75, 93, 108, 206, 238, 242; control 4; higher education and state 20, 146; institutions and partnerships 70, 254, 261; intervention 7, 251–2, 257
government funding 64–6; *see also* funding: federal
grants 5, 56, 64–6, 68, 70–1, 236, 246; federal 8, 63–4, 70; private 234; state 63; students and 8, 64–5, 206–7

Harvard University 8, 11, 203, 229–30
heterogeneity 208–09
hierarchical institutions *see* bureaucratic organizations
higher education *see* higher education institutions
Higher Education Act 65, 251
higher education administrators 13, 250; *see also* administrators; president; vice-president
higher education institutions *see* community colleges; for-profit higher education; four-year institutions; liberal arts colleges; not-for-profit institutions; research oriented universities; two-year colleges
Higher Education Opportunity Act – 2008 66, 251
Higher Learning Commission (HLC) 6
hiring manager 177, 179, 182–3, 186, 190–2
hiring process 177–192; human resources and 177, 180; reference check 188; search firms and 192; *see also* position description
Hirsch, E. D. 17
Hofstra University 256
human resources 28, *28*, 100, 177–202, 224; as shared services 103, 106, 113

illegal interview questions *see* interview: illegal questions
indirect costs 70, 90, 105
inflation 11, 51, 67; and tuition 62, 90
information technology 73, **91**, 106, 259
inseparability 208–9; effects of 209
institutional culture *see* culture: institutional
institutional rankings 8–9, 209, 242, 253
institutional research 29
intangibility 89, 208–9
integrated marketing 203–4, 217; communications 216–18
intercollegiate athletics 61, 255–6
interview: behavioral *190*; conducting an 188; human resources and an 177, 180; illegal questions in an 189–90, *189*; internal candidate 192; process of the 185–6; questions 146; in the recruitment process 187–8; reference checks and the 185, 188; scheduling 185; and the search committee 136; STAR 190; strategic planning and 167; telephone 180, 185, 188; *see also* hiring
ITT Tech 81

job description *see* position description
junior colleges *see* community colleges; two-year colleges
Juran, Joseph 133–5

Koch, Charles G. 243–4
Kuh, George 15

leading: as a managerial function 126–7, 132, 142
Lean principles 73, 92, 133–4, 136–7, 139
learning organizations 142, 144–5, 151, 257; and loop learning 142–4, 147, 159
Lewin, Kurt 147
liability: accounts 82–3
liberal arts colleges 22; cross training staff and 201; mission creep and 22, 253; *see also* four-year institutions; not-for-profit institutions
listening 165, 195
Lumina Foundation 251, 254, 261

macro 5, 39, 47–8, 51, 53, 120, 160, 205
management 22, 125–51, 153, 158, 170, 172–4, 221, 256; accountant 89–90, 92; budgets 96, 99, 109; change 142–9,

146, 165, 170; financial 79, 120, *120*; functions of 126–7; lean 136–7; practices 125; principles 125–51; and professional development 194; quality 134–6; of resources 126; scientific 125; strategic 127, 129–32, 156; strategy 116; styles 150; as supervisor 150, 194; *see also* administrators
managerial functions *see* management: functions
managers *see* administrators; management: practices
marginal cost (MC) 42, 55, 57
marginal revenue 41, 57
market 42, 53, 73–5, 214, 243, 252, 254; advertising and the target 185, 203; definition of 41–2, 205; higher education 12–13, 16, 21, 40–51, 76, 167, 203–4; higher education supply and demand in the 41, 43–9; institutional culture and the 213, 215, 219; and rankings 9; segmentation 213–14; students and the 14, 219, 224–5; target 214; trust 222, 224; tuition and the 56
marketing 203–25, *206*, *212*, 236; brand 214–216; centralized 69; communications 30; definition 204–5; for-profit institutions and 32, 250; integrated 216–18; internal 211–13; relationship 222–3; responsible for 223–5; services 206–9; strategy 154, 203–5, 210–19; types of 214; *see also* fundraising
measurement 86, 92, 93, 140–1, 172; *see also* accountability
mentoring 191, 196–7, 235, ACE Fellows and 256
metamarket 214
micro 39, 47–8; and elasticity 50–1, 53 *52*, *53*; costs 54; market 205; politics
mission 26, 69, 73, 90, 136, 153, 156, 220, 253–5, 258, 261; accountability and 4, 68; and athletics 255; and auxiliary services 32; and budget 106–7, 115–16; creep 22, 74, 136, 154, 170, 253; difference between not-for-profit and for-profit institutions 21; and donors 231, 243, 247, 254; in higher education 21, 42, 200, 249–50, 252–3; management and 125, 128; marketing strategy and 217, 225; public 257; quality principles and 132–43; rankings and 253; strategic plan and 130–1, 153–6, 159–66, 172–4; tough economic times and 116–17, 225
Moody's Investor Service 81
Morrill Acts 46–7, 246

national accrediting bodies 5–6; *see also* accreditation
National Center for Education Statistics (NCES) 9–19, *10*, **12**, 32, 48–9, 59–62, **59**, *60*, **62**, 97
National Collegiate Athletic Association (NCAA) 217
National Governors' Association 98
National Institute for Learning Outcomes 141
National Public Radio (NPR) 218
National Survey of Student Engagement (NSSE) 141, 222
nature of students 13–16
net assets 82–5, *85*
No Child Left Behind 7
Northwestern University 231
not-for-profit institutions 19–21, 34, 42, 147; accounting and 79–83, 92; budget and 97–119; enrollment **13**; difference between not-for-profit and for-profit 32, 173, 250; foundation as 233; marketing and 217; organizational structure in 20–32; revenues and funding in **59**, 66–78; strategic planning 173; and tax status 259; tuition 11; tuition discounts and 63; *see also* community colleges; four-year institutions; liberal arts colleges; research oriented universities; two-year colleges
notes payable 82

objectives 126, 131, 155, 169, 218; and goals 21, 108, 126–30, 169; and position description 181; *see also* goals; strategy
officers *see* administrators; chief executive officer; executive vice-president; president; provost
operating budget 54, 89, 96–103; categories 101; costs 54; fundraising and 237; state appropriations and 66
organizational change 125, 127, 140, 145–9

organizational chart *see* organizational structure
organizational learning *see* quality management
organizational structure 19–35
organizing: as management function 89–92
outcomes: and accreditation 140–1; learning 7, 14, 141, 251; and performance funding 67; and quality 136–40, 145; *see also* assessment; strategic planning
outsourcing 12, 118
overhead: as fixed costs 54; auxiliary service fees and 69; decentralized budget (RCM) and 105–7; *see also* indirect costs

performance appraisal 197, *197*; *see also* evaluations
perishability 209
personnel *see* human resources
PEST (political, economic, social, technological) analysis 160, 167
Peter Principle 256
planning 89; and the budget 89–90, 96, 110–13; for financial accounting 80–1; for managerial accounting 89; as a function of management 126–7; *see also* strategy; strategic planning
political: budgeting 117–18; environment 114, 160–7; model 34; savvy 235; search process 182, 192; structures 75
position description 181–3; announcement 183; and evaluation 197
postsecondary *see* community colleges; for-profit higher education; four-year institutions; liberal arts colleges; not-for-profit institutions; research oriented universities; two-year colleges
post-tenure review 199–200
power: anchoring 75; donor and 232, 234, 244; imbalance of 106
president 20, 22, 26–7; administrative ego 254–5; and executive recruiters 192; fundraising and the 245, 247; and organizational change 146–7; and power 34; QM and the 135; and salary 257; *see also* chief executive officer; chancellor
price: affordability 4, 7–8, 76, 219; of prestige 9
Princeton Review 8
privatization 12; *see also* for-profit higher education
professional administrators 256–7; *see also* administrators
professional development 194, 198; accountability and 198; counter offer and 199; performance appraisal and *197*; post-tenure review and 199
program: cannibalization 72; development 72
provost 20, *23*, *25*, *26*, 26–7, 135; *see also* administrators; vice-president
Public Broadcasting System 218
public good: higher education as a 64, 247
public-private-partnership 70
Purdue University 244

QM *see* quality management
qualifications 182, *187*; minimum 186; preferred 183–8; required 183–8
qualifications framework 251
quality 57, 89, 106, 127, 151; principles 14; *see also* quality management
quality management (QM) 92, 125, 132–42; Crosby's four absolutes 133–34, *134*; Deming's 14 points 133, *133*; Juran's three key processes 133–34, 139; learning organizations and 142–5; *see also* Total Quality Management

rankings 8–9, 242; and increased costs 9; performance appraisal and 197; and quest for prestige 253
RCM *see responsibility-centered management*
recruiters 192
recruiting process 178–90, *179*, *180*; students and 214; *see also* admissions; enrollment management; hiring
regional accrediting bodies 5–6, 14, 29, 140, 252
registrar 27, 30, 210
research-oriented universities 22, *23*; *see also* not-for-profit institutions
reserve accounts: auxiliary enterprises 69, 100–3, 254; requirement as expense *101*
responsibility-centered management (RCM) 99, 105–8; *see also* budgets: centralized and decentralized

retained earnings 82
retaining employees *see* employee: retention
revenue 59, **59**, 81, 112, 116, 119; and athletics 255; of auxiliary services 32, 56, 69, *104*; budget and 90, 95–99, *99*, *100*, *102*; diversion of 12; generating new 57; fundraising and 237–9; marginal 41, 57; overestimating 113; planning and 89, 110; RCM and 105–7; sources of 60–75, *60*, *101*; and tax status 21: and tuition 61, 64, 71, *61*, 116, 254; *see also* costs; development; grants; tuition
risk 114, 149, 172–3, 221, 259; fundraising and 237, 240, 247; *see also* financial risk

salary compression 191
scarcity: economic condition 41
Schnatter, John 244
scientific management 125
screening: applicants 183–6; tools 186; *see also* hiring process
search committee 177, 180, 182–3, 192: human resources and 177; members 182
self-analysis: and marketing 205
self-interest: and economics 41
self-study 73, 159–60, 166–7; accreditation 5, 140–1, 167, 205
Senge, Peter 142
separation from an organization 198–9
shared governance *see* governance: shared
service encounter 15, 208–10
servicescape 221
situation analysis 211, *212*
Spellings Commission (A Test of Leadership) 8, 98
sponsorship marketing 216–8
staff *see* employee
staffing model 178, 193
stakeholders 11, 28, 79–81, 97 126, 249; change and 146–8; external 4, 14, 29, 81, 93, 96, 116; fundraising and 68, 247; internal 4, 85, 116; mission creep and 255–6; needs 13, 17, 131, 136, 150, 158; planning and 117–20, 128, 139, 143, 157–74; on search committees 182, 189; student affairs and 224
Standard & Poor's (S&P) 81
Stanford University 53, 186
STAR (Situation, Task, Action, Result) concept *see* interview: STAR
STEEP (social, technological. Economic, environmental, political) analysis 160, 167–8
STEM (Science, Technology, Engineering, and Mathematics) 238
sticker price 54, 57, 63, 206; *see also* tuition: discounting
strategic: management 129–32, 156; marketing 204–5, 210, 213, 218; philanthropy 234, planning 92, 96–8, 107, 111, 114, 119, 125, 129–32, 134–5, 153–74, 210, 244; thinking 128, 254
strategy: defined 127; management 116; organizational 129; pricing 63
student affairs 14, 21, 27–32 *31*, 106, 182, 184, 224: strategic planning 156–7, 162–3, 165, 174
student athletes 255
student center 12, 32
student debt *see* financial aid
student fees 30, 32, 256
student learning 7, 141, 166; *see also* assessment; outcomes
student satisfaction 7, 166, 220–1
student Union *31*, 32, 56
students 4–5, 7–14, 201; adult 72; co-producers 13, 15–16, 204–5, 207, 210, 218; as customer 13–15, 205, 207, 218, 220; enrollment **12**, 19, 54, 97, 108; first generation 10, international 13, 40, 48, 63, 203; low-income 50–1, 65; non-traditional 16, 36, 48; as product 13–15, 205–6
supervising 88; employees 150, 193–8; and recruiting 178
supply 40, 43, 47–8, 53; curve 43, *44*, 46–8; and demand 40–1, 43, *44*, 45–9, 57; price elasticity 51–3, *52*; shifts in *47*
SWOT (Strengths, Weaknesses, Opportunities, and Threats) Analysis 160, 167–8; *see also* strategic planning

tactics 127, 130, 155, 158, 160–2, 169–70; difference between strategy and 127
target market 185, 218–19; marketing 214
Taylor, Frederick 125

teaching 5, 15, 17, 42, **91**, 153, 184, 200, 213, 249, 258; *see also* adjunct faculty; faculty
technology 13, 26, 46, 59, 69, 72–3, 90, **91**, 92, 95, 103, 115, 120, 137–9, 209, 258–9; and fees 206; and marketplace 57; transfer and 71
tenure 73; post tenure review 199–200; faculty 54, 178, 258
theory-in-use 142–4
theory of action 142–3
Title IV 5; for-profit institutions and 32; institutions 19, 64, 66; as student financial aid 60, 64–5, 81
Title IX 16, 256
Total Quality Management (TQM) 92, 134–5; *see also* quality management
transfer: budgeting and 104, *104*, 112, 115; credit 48, 72; financial 256; prices 106–7; student 221, 224–5; of wealth 237
trust market 208, 224
tuition 11, 12, 14, 31, 39, 43, 45–54, 60–71, 75–6, 88, 119, 204–9, 256; affordability 7–8; differential 63; discounting 43, 54, 56–7, 63–4, 72, 95, 144, 206, 217; driven 47, 251, 254; endowments and 244; for-profit and 32, 34, 66, 68; increase in 49, 65, 71, 76, 90, 95, 119; model 8; as revenue 60–71, *60*, *61*, *62*, **62**, 90, 99, *101*, *102*, 106, 111–12, 116, 254; subsidy 54, 63; *see also* affordability; cost of attendance; free college; sticker price
tuning project 251
two-year colleges 22, 24, *25*, 40; *see also* community colleges

undergraduate *see* four-year institutions
unions 200; *see also* collective bargaining
universal access 8, 205
universities *see* for-profit higher education; four-year institutions; not-for-profit institutions; research-oriented universities
University at Buffalo 88
University of California System 27
University of Central Florida 164
University of Florida 71
University of Kentucky 87, 244
University of Louisville 244
University of Minnesota 71
University of Missouri 88
University of North Carolina 88, 255
University of Oklahoma 88
University of Oregon 244
University of Phoenix 32, 207
University of Texas 27
University of Wisconsin 188; system 27, 75, *84*, 85
U.S. News & World Report 8

vice-president: accountability 88; in administrative structure 20, 22–3, 27–32; executive 26, *26*; former faculty as 256; as internal president 26; QM 135; *see also* administrators; provost
vision: accountability and 4; administrators and 254, 257; budget and 97; fundraising and 247; drives the theory of action 143; management and 125; marketing and 215; QM and 132, 135; strategic plan and 129–30, 154–8, 162–74; strategy and 127; structure and 73; *see also* mission
value stream map (VSM): defined 139

Weber, Max 20
Western Governor's University 72, 259

Yale University 53, 230
yield rate 30, 54